Uncle John's
~WEIRD,~
WONDERFUL
WORLD

BATHROOM READER

Scanning the Globe for
Strange Stories and Fantastic Facts

The Bathroom Readers' Institute

PORTABLE
PRESS

Portable Press
San Diego, California

Portable Press / The Bathroom Readers' Institute
An imprint of Printers Row Publishing Group
9717 Pacific Heights Blvd, San Diego, CA 92121
www.portablepress.com • mail@portablepress.com

Correspondence regarding the content of this book should be sent to Portable Press / The Bathroom Readers' Institute, Editorial Department, at the above address.

Publisher: Peter Norton • Associate Publisher: Ana Parker
Art Director: Charles McStravick
Senior Developmental Editor: April Graham
Production Team: Beno Chan, Julie Greene

Creator: Javna Brothers LLC

Interior, Illustrations, and Infographics Designer: Eric Watanabe
Cover Illustration and Design: Adam Devaney

In memory of Christopher J. Farley

"What a strange world this would be if we all had the same sense of humor." —Bernard Williams

Library of Congress Control Number: 2023931586

ISBN: 978-1-6672-0306-5

Printed in China

27 26 25 24 23   1 2 3 4 5

OUR "REGULAR READERS" RAVE!

Thank you for your yearly company, Uncle John.
You make the necessary room a much-less-exhausting pleasure.

—Jesse

This is not only a fantastic bathroom reader, it's a fantastic book period!
Thoroughly enjoyed reading it! It amazes me just how much information
and trivia is put into this book. If you're looking
for something interesting to read, look no further!

—Trish D.

Worth every penny.

—Bob P.

From the best by the best.

—David C.

Interesting anecdotes & tidbits of trivia. I laughed until my legs fell asleep.

—Carla K.

I have a ton of their books. All of them are very fun to read
and if you're not careful...you'll learn something.

—Mark J.

I've been a fan of this series since I started using the toilet on my own...
If the Institute keeps popping these bad boys out every year, I'll keep buying them.
Buy this book. Read it. Love it.

—Derek G.

I never get tired of reading these books.
Great if you're stuck somewhere waiting, like the hospital or airport.

—Lorne K.

Best bathroom book ever.

—Camille S.

Love this book, so full of trivia and fascinating facts.

—Cheryl B.

CONTENTS

Because the BRI understands your reading needs, we've
divided the contents by length as well as subject.

Short—a quick read

Medium—2 to 3 pages

Long—for those extended visits, when something a little more involved is required

*   *   *

MAGPIE MOMENTS

In 2022, a female Australian magpie (a black-and-white bird related to crows) noticed that another magpie was wearing a little device on its back. She hopped over and pecked at the strange thing a few times until the tiny harness disconnected and the thing fell to the ground. Over the next few days, she and perhaps other magpies removed five more devices from their feathered friends. At first, this annoyed the researchers who'd placed these GPS devices on the birds to track their social behavior. But observing these altruistic acts—which ornithologists call "cooperation rescue behavior"—turned out to be a huge finding in and of itself.

INTRODUCTION

Holy moly! What a couple of years it's been! As we all tentatively removed our masks in 2022 and ventured back into the outside world, it's evident that things have changed: the Bathroom Readers' Institute staff is washing our hands a lot more and still maintaining a respectful distance from others, and we're also embracing new fashion trends (we wrote most of this year's Bathroom Reader in our comfiest athleisure duds), distracting ourselves with all the streaming services on offer, and taking advantage of relaxed work-from-anywhere policies. (The nice thing about a laptop? It's a lot easier to use in the bathroom than the typewriters we started on 36 years ago.)

Most important about being back on the social scene after doing the socially *distanced* scene for a couple of years: it's reminded me once again that variety is the spice of life, and that unique people, places, and activities are what keep that life interesting. That reminder is what inspired this year's Bathroom Reader:

WEIRD, WONDERFUL WORLD

Luckily for us here at the BRI, "weird and wonderful" is our bread and butter. Since we published our first Reader in the late 1980s, we've been collecting the most interesting, entertaining, astonishing, amusing, and *weird* stories that we can find, and sharing those stories with our *wonderful* readers. This year's absorbing collection is no exception. Speaking of "absorbing," within these pages you'll find instructions for how to create your own toilet paper (so you'll never have to resort to tearing pages out of your beloved Bathroom Reader collection), a story of college students clogging the pipes with TP for a social-media stunt (hope it doesn't cause a shortage—we all remember how that went in 2020!), and innovations in toilet tech that include luxury recycled toilet paper made from bamboo (what's more weird and wonderful than that?).

What else will you find?

WEIRD: Creepy facts about crows, animal-care jobs you have to read about to believe, old radio programs that will make you wonder just how desperate people were for entertainment prior to television, and downright bizarre thrift-store donations.

POP CULTURE: How *Bob's Burgers* came to be, 12 musical artists with real-life Spinal Tap mishaps, a comprehensive look at the life of Betty White, celebrity ghosts, albums by major artists that were recorded but never released, and the biggest flops in video game history.

LAUGHS: Punny racehorse names, random quotes from famous people, accidentally hilarious headlines, and 38 rhyming ways to accuse someone of farting.

LANGUAGE: Tips for writing well, lots of word origins, odd place names, terms invented by Shakespeare, and a guide to the slang you'll hear on the hiking trail.

ARTSY: The origins and mysteries surrounding the Venus de Milo, the 15th-century religious painting that thieves can't keep their hands off, amazing thrift-store finds, and the teenagers who stumbled on the world's best-preserved Paleolithic art.

FOOD: A delicious guide to barbecue styles, an equally delicious guide to tacos, forgotten fad restaurants, food truck names sure to whet your appetite, the origins of macaroni and cheese, and the dark side of licorice.

WONDERFUL: Everyday folks who ended up local heroes, helpful household hacks, long-tenured employees who *really* love their jobs, amazing accidental archaeological finds, and plain ol' nice stories.

And much, much more!

Big thanks to the weird...er, I mean...*wonderful* people at the BRI who have contributed to this year's Bathroom Reader—this book wouldn't be possible without these talented folks.

Gordon Javna	Traci Douglas	Bruce Langley
Jay Newman	Julie Chapa	Nathaniel Hornblower
Brian Boone	Jeanette Rabbit	Samuel Rosenbaum
Angela Garcia	Eric Watanabe	Thomas Crapper

And of course we must thank our readers, who continue to support this annual endeavor. Whether this is your first Bathroom Reader or your 36th, we're so pleased to have you along for the adventure.

Happy reading, and, as ever,
Go with the flow!

—Uncle John and the BRI Staff

YOU'RE MY INSPIRATION

*It's always interesting to find out where the architects of pop
culture get their ideas. Some of these may surprise you.*

Matchbox Cars: In 1952, a little London girl named Anne had the naughty habit of bringing spiders to school in a matchbox. Her dad, an engineer named Jack Odell, wanted to break Anne of that habit, so he made her a tiny brass steamroller that he painted red and green. Anne's friends liked her little "matchbox toy" so much that Odell converted a pub into a factory and started mass-producing them. Since then, more than three billion Matchbox cars have sold.

Forrest Gump: Tom Hanks wasn't sure how he was going to play the slow-witted character—which made it difficult to cast a child actor to play young Forrest. Hanks had a thought: "You'll never get a kid to re-create what I come up with." So they cast the kid first, Tennessee-born Michael Humphreys. Hanks's Forrest is a spot-on impersonation of Humphreys being himself.

Paddington Bear: The hero of the 1958 children's book *A Bear Called Paddington* is first seen by readers at a train station, with the tag, "Please look after this bear. Thank you." While staring at a blank page, British author Michael Bond thought back to 20 years earlier when he was at Reading Station in London and saw child refugees who'd recently been liberated from Nazi Europe. "They all had a label round their neck," he recalled, "with their name and address on and a little case containing all their treasured possessions." Inspired, Bond wrote the first line, "Mr. and Mrs. Brown first met Paddington on a railway platform."

Wonder Woman: Gal Gadot, on how she came up with the persona for her version of Diana Prince: "I remember watching a documentary about Princess Diana and there was a part where they said she was full of compassion and always cared for the people and that was like, 'Ding, ding, ding,' that should be the Wonder Woman we have!"

The Sims: The Oakland-Berkeley Firestorm of 1991 killed 25 people and destroyed more than 3,000 homes—one of which belonged to video game designer Will Wright. Afterward, he had to figure out everything he'd need to rebuild. Wright, who is fascinated by architecture, had already designed the 1985 game *SimCity* and was currently working on *Sim Ant* (which simulates an ant colony). The fire got him thinking about psychologist Abraham Maslow's hierarchy of needs, which posits that you can't seek enlightenment unless your basic needs are taken care of first. "I started to wonder about all the things we have and how we purchased them for a reason," Wright said. From that came *The Sims*, the best-selling personal computer game of all time.

Only major airport in use named after a comedian:
Will Rogers World Airport in Oklahoma City.

36 BITS
OF 36 TRIVIA

*It's our 36th Bathroom Reader, so here are 36 bits of trivia
about subjects closely related to the big 3-6.*

6 FAMOUS PEOPLE BORN IN 1936

- Robert Redford
- Mary Tyler Moore
- Burt Reynolds
- Jim Henson
- John McCain
- Buddy Holly

6 MAJOR EVENTS OF 1836

- The Texas Revolution, with Texas winning its independence weeks after the Battle of the Alamo.
- The U.S. Patent Office is formed and starts numbering patents; no. 1 goes to John Ruggles, who invented a steam locomotive traction wheel.
- Charles Darwin completes his research mission around the world, collecting the research that would become *On the Origin of Species*, the blueprint for the theory of evolution.
- The Arc de Triomphe is completed and dedicated in Paris.
- The first stretch of Canadian railroad opens, stretching from La Prairie to St. John in Quebec.
- Martin Van Buren is elected president of the United States, the first commander in chief for whom English was a second language (after Dutch).

6 HALL OF FAME ATHLETES WHO WORE A NUMBER 36 JERSEY

- Shaquille O'Neal (NBA)
- Dave Cowens (NBA)
- Jim Kaat (MLB)

More than two-thirds of American astronauts, and 11 of 12 moonwalkers, were Boy Scouts.

- Gaylord Perry (MLB)
- Jerome Bettis (NFL)
- Matthew Barnaby (NHL)

6 FAMOUS PEOPLE WHO DIED AT AGE 36

- Princess Diana
- Marilyn Monroe
- Bob Marley
- Lord Byron
- Doc Holliday
- General George Armstrong Custer

6 36TH THINGS

- 36th biggest hit of all time on the *Billboard* Hot 100: "Somebody That I Used to Know" by Gotye featuring Kimbra (2011)
- 36th highest grossing movie of all time: *Pirates of the Caribbean: Dead Man's Chest* (2006)
- 36th pope: Liberius (AD 352–366)
- 36th state to join the U.S.: Nevada (1864)
- 36th largest metropolitan area in the U.S.: San Jose–Santa Clara, California (population 1.95 million)
- 36th play written and staged by William Shakespeare: *The Tempest* (1611)

6 FACTS ABOUT 36

- The atomic number for the element krypton.
- The total number of possible combinations of two thrown dice.
- The total number of inches in a yard.
- Is a perfect score on the ACT college admissions standardized test.
- Is the number of truly righteous people in each generation, according to the Torah, the sacred text of the Jewish faith.
- The number of gods who collaborated to create the first human, according to Maori legend.

Laser tattoo removal procedures can remove birthmarks.

FAST-FOOD FOLLIES

*For better or for worse, fast food is a big part of American life.
With so many of us grabbing a quick burger on the run, the thousands
of fast-food restaurants across the globe are bound to be the setting
of some crimes or weird activity every now and then.*

Taking the Order

In May 2022, Texas school employee Kelsey Golden was working from home; when her two-year-old son, Barrett, started messing around with her phone, she was so busy that she let him have it. "He likes to look at his reflection," Golden said, unaware that her toddler even knew how to use apps or play games on it. A few minutes later, after Barrett returned her phone, Golden received a notification that her DoorDash driver was on the way, even though she hadn't placed an order. She was more confused when a car pulled up to her house, and a driver popped out with a giant bag of the 31 McDonald's cheeseburgers she'd apparently ordered. "Then it dawned on me that Barrett was playing with my phone," she said. "I went back and looked at my phone and an order was placed at that time that he was playing with my phone." Making things all the odder was that Barrett doesn't even like cheeseburgers, and neither does Golden, so she offered them up for free on Facebook. "One woman came by, she was pregnant and wanted six of them," Golden said. "No judgment."

Long Live the King

When Jonathan Pruitt opened a business in the Concord Mall in Wilmington, Delaware, in 2022, he was given a key to a storage room. He opened it up and found not a closet, but a perfectly preserved Burger King. With decor dating to the 1990s, everything in the former fast-food restaurant was intact—booths, bolted-down chairs, kitchen equipment, and the art on the walls. According to mall records, the Burger King opened with the rest of the mall in 1987 but was closed in 2009 and subsequently walled up and made completely invisible from both the inside and outside of the mall; its exterior windows had been boarded up and painted over. It had been used as a storage facility until 2019, at which point new owner Namdar Realty Group purchased the mall and locked it up. Photos and videos of the eerie, totally preserved Burger King went viral in spring 2022. "It's kind of cool. When I first saw it, I was blown away myself," said Tom Dahlke, Concord Mall's general manager.

Oldest unaltered Congressional district:
the one comprising the entire state of Delaware, unchanged since 1789.

Would You Like Drugs with That?

In June 2022, hungover after celebrating her 21st birthday, Emily Somers of Leeds, England, ordered a vegetarian McPlant burger (with ketchup and cheese) from McDonald's, for delivery. When it arrived, the burger box bore a sticker with the handwritten words, "Only Ketamin, Sandwich, Cheese." Fearing that the sandwich was part of some ill-fated drug transaction—ketamine (not ketamin) is a powerful narcotic—Somers and her boyfriend examined the burger for tampering and lacing. "The fact it goes through the kitchen and then someone delivers it, that puts a bit of worry on your mind," Somers told reporters. With nothing amiss, Somers believes that a McDonald's employee added the "-amin" to the "ket" ketchup abbreviation written on the sticker. In response, McDonald's sent Somers a coupon for £7.50 ($9.17) off her next order.

The Footlong Arm of the Law

Businesses that conduct a lot of cash transactions—such as fast-food places and sandwich shops—are a common target for burglars and armed robbers looking to make a quick score. At about 2:00 a.m. one night in August 2019, an unidentified man broke into a Subway near the George Washington University campus in Washington, D.C. But according to surveillance video, the individual had no interest in making off with the outlet's cash on hand. The man walked into the Subway, grabbed a bag of potato chips, then jumped over the counter and made himself a chicken sandwich with all the fixings. Then he walked out with the sandwich and chips. Total amount of stolen goods: $8.49.

Not-So-Secret Sauce

Bel-Fries is a boutique, upscale fast-food restaurant in New York City specializing in French fries, prepared in the traditional Belgian method and served with special sauces, which cost an additional $1.75 apiece. At 4:00 a.m. one night in July 2022, three women put in their orders and asked for some extra dipping sauce. When told they'd be charged accordingly, the trio erupted. "We explained to them that this is a business rule and that it is the same for everyone, but they did not understand," head cook Rafael Nuñez told reporters. The women started grabbing and throwing anything they could get their hands on, including bottles of fry sauce, a computerized cash register terminal, and a plastic barrier bolted to the counter. Then the women climbed up to the counter and started dancing. "Two of my employees were hit in the head with glass bottles," co-owner Annalee Schlossberg said. Chitara Plasencia, Tatiyanna Johnson, and Pearl Ozoria were arrested, with the latter facing additional charges of stealing money out of the register and punching her arresting officer in the face.

Highest-grossing foreign-made film ever in Estonia: *Tenet* ($1.2 million).

OOPS!

*Everyone makes outrageous blunders from time to time. So
go ahead and feel superior for a few minutes.*

EEK EEK! DELETE DELETE!

The 2017 finale of *The Great British Bake Off*—between home bakers Sophie Faldo,
Kate Lyon, and Steven Carter-Bailey—brought in 7.7 million viewers. It's too bad that
a lot of those viewers already knew who the winner was going to be. Blame Dame
Prue Leith for that. The celebrity chef, 81—one of the reality show's two judges—
explained that, six hours before the finale aired, "I was having a siesta in Bhutan
and I picked up my phone and I saw a message from the production company who
said 'don't forget to congratulate the winner after 10 p.m.' I looked at my watch and
quickly tweeted 'bravo Sophie.'" But Leith had forgotten to account for the time
difference. A moment later, "A text came whizzing in which just said 'eek eek it's
tonight delete delete'!" Even though the tweet was barely up for a minute and a half, a
screenshot went viral and caused an uproar on social media. "It was absolutely awful,"
Leith said. But at least one person wasn't mad at her: "What's interesting is the prime
minister of Bhutan rang me up and said, 'You have put Bhutan on the map.'"

A FAILURE TO COMMUNICATE

On April 20, 2022, in Washington, D.C., the United States Congress was in recess,
but there were still scores of people staffing the 20 buildings of the Capitol complex
(including the famous Rotunda). At around 6:30 p.m., an airplane entered the
Capitol's restricted air space. Unaware of any scheduled air traffic, the U.S. Capitol
Police ordered an immediate evacuation of the entire complex. As everyone was
making their way outside, the single-engine airplane flew over...and kept on going
to Nationals Park—home of Major League Baseball's Washington Nationals—where
members of the U.S. Army Golden Knights Parachute Team parachuted onto the field
before a home game.

The team and the fans knew the plane was coming; so did the Federal Aviation
Administration (FAA), which had cleared the flight in advance. How come no one
told the Capitol Police? Because of an "extremely unusual oversight," as the FAA
put it. In other words, they forgot to tell them. It's "outrageous and inexcusable,"
said Rep. Nancy Pelosi (D-CA). "The unnecessary panic caused by this apparent
negligence was particularly harmful for Members, staff and institutional workers still
grappling with the trauma of the attack on their workplace on January 6th." The FAA
apologized, acknowledging that "our actions affect others."

Royal Australian Navy ships are adorned with red kangaroo pictures
to avoid confusion with British Royal Navy vessels.

BASEMENT DWELLERS

"We recommend you have professionals deal with any pest control issue," said Pete Piringer of the Montgomery County (Maryland) Fire & Rescue Service. Because an exterminator would have found a safer way to clear a snake infestation than what this homeowner (unnamed in press reports) attempted in November 2021. Hoping to "smoke" the reptiles out of the basement of his $1.8 million manor, he placed some hot coals near the snakes...and also near some "combustible materials" (also unidentified). Then the homeowner left the house. Hours later, a neighbor saw smoke coming from the building and called 911. It took 75 firefighters all night to extinguish the fire—which cost an estimated $1 million. An investigation concluded that it was an accident. "Firefighters located evidence that some snakes did not survive," said Piringer. "However others likely did."

WAIT, WAS THAT TODAY?

On July 4, 1922, the *New York Times* printed a facsimile of the Declaration of Independence on the final page of its A-section, beginning an Independence Day tradition that went unbroken for 100 years...almost. On July, 4, 2022, readers flipped to that page of the print edition, but there was no Declaration of Independence. The *Times*'s critics quickly took to Twitter, some simply mocking the omission, with others accusing the newspaper of "betraying America"—like former White House Press Secretary Sean Spicer, who tweeted, "As the leftists at the @washingtonpost say, democracy dies in darkness." The *Times* printed the Declaration on July 5, along with an assurance that it was not their intention to break the tradition. The omission was blamed on "human error," thus absolving any nonhumans from blame.

A BRIDGE TOO FAR

A recent population boost to the city of Cuernavaca, located in the Mexican state of Morelos, caused increased pollution in the local waterways. In June 2022, after city leaders announced a cleanup program, they held a ceremonial river walk to inaugurate a new footbridge over a stream. Most of the delegation was on the bridge—made of wooden boards held together by chains—when the chains failed and more than two dozen people plunged 10 feet into the shallow, rocky creek. According to press reports, "Four city council members, two other city officials, and a local reporter were injured and had to be extracted on stretchers from the gully and were taken to local hospitals." Here's the "Oops!" part: Not only did the delegation far exceed the bridge's maximum capacity, but as they were crossing the bridge, several people started jumping up and down to make it sway. "That was reckless," said Mayor José Luis Urióstegui...outside the hospital where he too was treated for minor injuries.

Only person nominated in seven different Oscar categories: Kenneth Branagh.

WORD ORIGINS

This is how we (Rick)roll.

Never: This word goes all the way back to Proto-Indo-European (PIE), the theoretical ancient language that split into dozens of modern languages whose words have similar roots. *Never* entered Old English in the 5th century as *næfre*—from *ne* ("not") and *æfre* (ever).

Gonna: Origin unknown, but linguists believe this contraction of "going to" originated with the Scots' usage of *ganna*. It entered English around the turn of the 20th century.

Give: Another PIE word (*ghabh*, "to give or receive"), *give* entered Old English as *giefan*, and then Middle English as *yiven*. The modern pronunciation comes from the Old Norse word *gefa*. The phrase "give up" dates to the 1570s.

You: This second-person personal pronoun goes back to PIE and entered Old English as *eow*. In early modern English, *you* was the plural form of *thou* (which entered Old English from the Proto-Germanic *thu*). The singular *thou* was used as the subject ("thou singest"); the singular *thee* was the object ("of thee I sing"). Likewise, the plural *you* was the subject (the only modern equivalent is the informal *y'all*) and the plural *ye* was the object ("Hear ye, hear ye!"). So how come only *you* is left? In the 1400s, well-to-do English speakers were influenced by the French plural *vous*, the formal way to address the aristocracy—so they adopted the similar-sounding *you* for formal settings, and it came to be accepted for singular or plural (eventually replacing *ye*). *You* got a big boost in the 15th century thanks to *you*-users Queen Elizabeth I and William Shakespeare substituting it for *thou* and *thee*: "I love you with so much of my heart that none is left to protest" (*Much Ado about Nothing*). By the 1700s, *thou* and *thee* had become so informal that they were considered vulgar. Proper Londoners, afraid of sounding vulgar, dropped the words altogether. Ironic result: English—which has more synonyms than any other language—has only one word for *you*. It can mean one or many, be a subject or an object, and can be formal or informal. Compare that to Spanish's *tú*, *usted*, *ustedes*, *vos*, and *vosotros*. (German has even more.)

Up: One of the oldest unchanged words in English, this adverb entered Old English from PIE with the same basic spelling and pronunciation it has today. The versatile *up* can be a preposition ("up the tree"), a noun ("ups and downs"), an adjective ("the up escalator"), a verb ("up the ante"), or an adverb ("give you up"). So don't worry, *up* will never let you down.

Fan-voted "Best Act Ever" at the 2008 MTV Europe Music Awards: U2, Britney Spears, and Christina Aguilera lost to 1980s English pop singer Rick Astley.

WEIRD ANIMAL NEWS

*This year's installment of Weird Animal News features a "grilled" goose,
a fish out of water, highly aroused sea snakes, and fuzzy widdle baby duckies.*

HOW YOU DOIN'?

A few facts about olive sea snakes: they're highly venomous, they can grow up to six feet long, they have poor eyesight, and the males can get really horny. Added up, that's bad news for snorkelers and scuba divers in Australia's Great Barrier Reef, where these snakes thrive. Tim Lynch learned this all too well when he spent two years in the mid-1990s collecting data about olive sea snakes for his PhD thesis. While diving, he recorded 158 encounters—many of them unprovoked attacks. When Lynch compiled his data (which he didn't publish until 2020), he realized that most of the attacks came during breeding season. Conclusion: "A reproductively active male, highly aroused, mistakes the diver for another snake (a female or a rival male)." That's where the snakes' bad eyesight comes into play. What should you do if a libidinous sea snake swims up and coils around your leg? Absolutely nothing. "Allow for the snake to investigate chemical cues with its tongue," advises Lynch. "A bite is unlikely unless the animal is threatened or injured...Attempting to flee is likely to be futile and may even increase the ardor of the pursuit; and attempting to drive the animal away may induce retaliation." Thankfully, most land snakes are not known to behave so amorously.

FREE RIDE

In June 2019, a Canada goose (or, as Foxnews.com incorrectly spelled it, a "Canadian goose") became lodged in the grille of a pizza delivery car. Behind the wheel was Ryan Harrington of Burlington, Vermont. He said that when he saw the two-foot-tall waterfowl waddling across the road, he slammed on his brakes...but not in time. "I heard a thud, and I thought, 'Oh my god, I just hit a goose.'" Harrington didn't even realize until he got back to work that the goose was stuck in the car's grille. The animal was alive and alert, but Harrington had no idea how to free it, so he notified his manager. They called, well, everyone, and before long, a ragtag team of rescuers—including wildlife officials, firefighters, and Esther Lotz, of a nonprofit called Helping Animals in Crisis—were all working together to get the goose free. Once they did, Lotz took the newly named Roberto (or Roberta, if it's female) to a rehabilitation center, where it was diagnosed with a broken pelvis. At last report, Roberto (or Roberta) was expected to make a full recovery.

Popular snack food in Quebec: communion wafers.

GOOD EGGS

It's a kitchen question: should you store your eggs in the fridge or at room temperature? Adele Phillips tried a third method: an incubator. The 29-year-old British woman performed the experiment in 2020 after learning about it on social media. She went online and bought an incubator (an apparatus used to keep eggs warm when a mother bird can't sit on them), and then she went to a Waitrose grocery store to buy a carton of six free-range duck eggs "delicately hand-collected," according to the packaging. "I was so excited for them to hatch, but I still had in the back of my mind that these are supermarket eggs," Phillips told the BBC. "They have been collected, bashed around on a delivery truck, then rattled around on a trolley onto a shelf, picked up and put down by who knows how many people." A Waitrose spokesperson explained that their eggs are unfertilized...mostly. "As a result of [the] difficulty in sexing, a male white-feathered duck may very occasionally be left with a group of females, although, these instances are extremely rare." The spokesman added that fertilized eggs are as safe to eat as unfertilized, unless they're incubated. After a month, Phillips's persistence paid off: three ducklings hatched! She named the "three little balls of fluff" Beep, Peep, and Meep, and moved them in with her pet chickens.

A FULL TANK

Did you know that goldfish can drive? Not cars, mind you—but a Fish Operated Vehicle (FOV). Developed in 2022 by scientists at Israel's Ben-Gurion University of the Negev, the FOV consists of a small fish tank mounted onto a wheeled platform. It uses a navigation system known as LIDAR (short for Light Detection and Ranging) that, according to the American Geosciences Institute, is a "remote sensing method that uses...a pulsed laser to...generate precise, three-dimensional information about the shape of the Earth and its surface characteristics." This technology allows the fish's movements to steer the FOV. Researchers placed a target outside the tank and then awarded the goldfish a food pellet when it successfully "drove" to the target. After steering aimlessly at first, it took only a few days for the fish to teach themselves how to navigate around obstacles to get to the food, "all while avoiding dead-ends and correcting location inaccuracies," boasted driving instructor Shachar Givon. "It shows that goldfish have the cognitive ability to learn a complex task in an environment completely unlike the one they evolved in." (Watch a video of the experiment online, if you get the chance. It looks very...cartoony.)

HAPPY TRAILS

Here's a riddle: *How can a slug be in two houses at once?* When it's a pet snail. (Think about it.) Never heard of a pet snail? Jessica Noyce wants to change that. In 2020,

It costs $20 million to construct the average Formula 1 race car; 90 percent of the money goes to building the engine.

the British woman launched a mail order website out of her home in England, from which she ships snails to customers throughout the UK and western Europe (using snail mail, no doubt). So the pets are protected during shipping, they're surrounded by moss inside a plastic box that's stamped "Handle with Care." The benefits of having a pet snail? "They're quite easy for kids to handle," Noyce explains. "They don't suddenly jump out at you or jump off you." She also says they require little care and, because they're omnivores, you can feed them anything from strawberries to steak—even their own eggs, if you want. Snails are also "therapeutic to watch" as they "glide around their tank." Noyce also points out that some species are less slimy than others, but she advises that you always wash your hands after handling them. And snails are fine living alone but can also be kept in small groups. One warning: "If you do keep them together they will breed together—so two snails will quite quickly become 1,000." That's when the real fun begins.

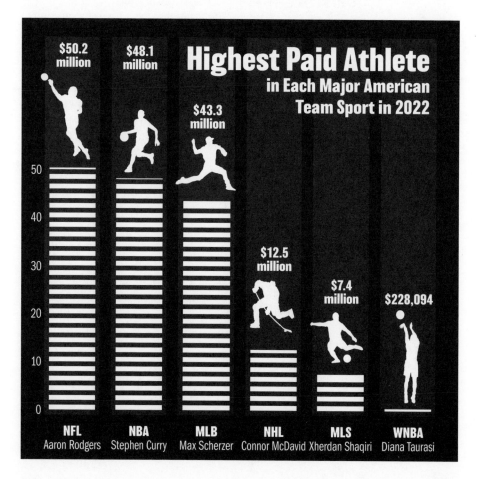

The *Mona Lisa* was painted onto a plank of wood, not a canvas.

ACTORS ON ACTING

People who pretend for a living get real.

"Acting is horrible, painful, and yet also intoxicating and emotionally liberating."
—Jodie Foster

"Acting deals with very delicate emotions. It is not putting up a mask. Each time an actor acts he does not hide; he exposes himself."
—Rodney Dangerfield

"Being the wood that the nail banged into doesn't feel good—that's what acting is."
—Sean Penn

"Your internal dialogue has got to be different from what you say. And you know, in film, hopefully that registers and speaks volumes. It's always the unspoken word and what's happening behind someone's eyes that makes it so rich."
—Viola Davis

"I never took acting classes, but I knew I could do it based on the skill with which I lied to my parents on a regular basis."
—Ryan Reynolds

"Leave me to the thing I love. I love acting. But being called 'the greatest living actress'—a designation not even my mother would sanction—is the opposite of good or valuable or useful. It is a curse for a working actor."
—Meryl Streep

"Almost anyone can give a good representative performance when you're unknown. It's just easier. The real pro game of acting is after you're known—to 'un-Jack' that character, in my case, and get the audience to reinvest in a new and specific, fictional person."
—Jack Nicholson

"You're always after a total suspension of disbelief, but the only people you can really achieve it with is children."
—John Lithgow

"Wanting to be a good actor is not good enough. You must want to be a great actor. You just have to have that."
—Gary Oldman

"Great acting is being able to create a character. Great character is being able to be yourself."
—John Leguizamo

"Great acting is not easy; anyone who says it is, is either shallow or a charlatan. And one of the hardest things about acting is admitting that it is hard."
—Robert Cohen

"Acting provides the fulfillment of never being fulfilled. You're never as good as you'd like to be. So there's always something to hope for."
—Glenda Jackson

THE BETTY WHITE TIMELINE, PART I

In the 2010s, when the U.S. seemed more divided than ever, there was one thing that everyone could agree on: Betty White was a national treasure that must be protected at all costs. Here's a century-long look at one of Hollywood's best lives lived.

AMERICA'S "GOLDEN GIRL"

"Betty White has logged more hours on television, I think, than any other human being," said her old friend Mary Tyler Moore in 2000. It may be true; White was right there at the beginning of TV—actually, she was around before it—and rarely stopped working for more than 80 years. She became a superstar on *The Mary Tyler Moore Show*, and later a national treasure on *The Golden Girls*. And while so many other stars her age either died or faded from the spotlight, White just kept getting more and more famous. She embodied fun, innocence, mischievousness, and compassion, all at once. And she served as one of the last living links to the earliest days of modern entertainment—having befriended everyone from Buster Keaton to Bob Hope to Johnny Carson to Ryan Reynolds. As passionate as White was about entertaining people, she was even more passionate about helping animals. That came from her parents—who, as you'll soon find out, were also responsible for her sense of humor.

1922	Betty Marion White is born on January 17 in Oak Park, Illinois. An only child, her family moves to Alhambra, California, just outside of Los Angeles, when she's a year old. "When I was brought home from the hospital, my mother said we had an orange marmalade cat, Toby. If Toby hadn't approved of the new baby, I would have been sent right back to the hospital."
1920s	Little Betty displays some impressive singing chops, so her parents spring for lessons. But it's on family camping trips to the Sierras where she discovers her love of nature. "As a kid, I didn't want to be a princess or any wonderful movie star or anything like that. I wanted to be a forest ranger with all my heart. I remember on all those wonderful wilderness vacations that we would take, my dad always wore a forest ranger hat. It was his...thing."
1930	Betty's first taste of show business comes at eight years old when she plays a crippled orphan on a radio show called *Empire Builders*. It's obvious in the recording (available online) that the little girl has natural charm and

Roman gladiators didn't eat grains or meat.

perfect comedic timing. When later asked if she was funny as a kid, White answers, "I did a magnificent job of choosing a mother and father. And there wasn't a straight man in the house. I mean that in a nice way."

1930s The Whites spend the Great Depression living in Beverly Hills. Betty's love of animals grows...as her number of pets grows. "My dad made radios to earn extra money because times were bad all over. The problem was nobody else had any money to buy radios, either. So he'd trade them for dogs."

1939 White graduates from Beverly Hills High School. Because women cannot become park rangers (yet), she decides to be an entertainer. Inspired by "America's Singing Sweethearts," Jeanette MacDonald and Nelson Eddy ("I didn't just love Jeanette MacDonald; I *was* Jeanette MacDonald"), White writes and stars in a play she performs at her graduation ceremony. In the audience is an early investor in television, who hires her and another student for a demonstration at the Packard Motor Company. White does a song-and-dance number in front of a camera on the top floor, while people on the first floor watch her on a screen. This marks the first official television broadcast in what would soon be known as "Television City." "I wore my high school graduation dress—and our Beverly Hills High student body president, Harry Bennett, and I danced the Merry Widow Waltz."

1940s Beyond that, however, White has little success finding work in television. "From the start, I knew I had square jawbones and all the things they tell you are not photogenic. I wanted to look like Lana Turner, and I just didn't. But I did do one modeling job: It was for Sears, Roebuck, and I got 50 cents for modeling a dress. My salary went up from then on." Her first official job in show business is a radio commercial for Parkay margarine. The director who hired her, Fran van Hartesveldt, offers her a role on his radio show *The Great Gildersleeve*. White hones her style—for $5 a show—on popular programs such as *Blondie* and *This Is Your FBI*. "Tuesday was casting day. And I would just go in and sit around the office. I figured if they saw me often enough they'd just think they had hired me and then they'd give me a job."

1941 The United States enters World War II. White, 19, signs up for the American Women's Voluntary Services. In addition to working as a truck driver, delivering military supplies to Hollywood Hills, she also entertains the troops before they're shipped overseas. As White recalled in 2010: "It was a strange time and out of balance with everything, which I'm sure the young people are going through now. We'll never learn." Through this work, White gets to meet Bob Hope, and they become friends (and in

According to a recent poll, 6 percent of Americans claim
they could beat a grizzly bear in a fistfight.

1989, she'll convince Hope, 85, to do a guest spot on *The Golden Girls*).

1945 White weds an army pilot named Dick Barker. "I married my first husband because we wanted to sleep together. It lasted six months, and we were in bed for six months." Five of those months are spent on his parents' chicken farm in Ohio, where White is told she'll have to slaughter chickens if she wants to live there. She moves back to Hollywood.

1947 White weds a Hollywood agent named Lane Allen. She later says they were both in love, but, "He didn't want me to be in show business. When you have a calling you have to follow it, so I made the choice, blew the marriage, and I've never regretted it."

1948 White lands her first steady TV job on a show called *Grab Your Phone*. It is "four girls answering phones. They'd ask a question and people would call in with the answers. I got ten dollars a week. They said, 'Don't tell the other girls because they're only getting five dollars, but because you can ad-lib with the host, you get ten.'" It's on this show that White catches the eye of a popular Los Angeles radio disc jockey named Al Jarvis, who has his sights set on television.

1949 Jarvis offers the 27-year-old White a job as cohost of *Hollywood on Television*. White later reveals that the former radio man wanted a woman "so viewers would have something to look at." The show airs all afternoon, every weekday. "There was only one other station on at the time, so it was either us or the test pattern."

1951 White earns her first Emmy nomination for *Hollywood on Television*. She's up against Gertrude Berg, Judith Anderson, Helen Hayes, and Imogene Coca (whom you may remember as crabby Aunt Edna from *National Lampoon's Vacation*). Berg wins. The event "wasn't the lights and fashion it is now," White said in 2014. "You still got dressed up and it was still an honor even that early on, but it wasn't the worldwide schmear it is now." The following year White is nominated for a Los Angeles regional award for "Most Outstanding Female Personality." She's up against sexy socialite Zsa Zsa Gabor. "I was just interested in seeing how it came out, but they announced my name instead of Zsa Zsa's. I was just in shock. I could not believe it. And I don't think Zsa Zsa could, either."

1952 The long hours of *Hollywood on Television* become too much for Jarvis, so White takes over and becomes TV's first female daytime talk show host. (Her pay: $50 per week.) For the next two years, White is on the air with

The Betty White Show for five-and-a-half hours a day, six days a week. She monologues, sings songs, plays funny characters, and interviews "whoever walks through that door." Her highlight: when silent-film comedy legend Buster Keaton appears and they set up a little toy store for an improvisational sketch: "Buster just used everything in the set, and I can't explain to you why it was funny. It was the imagination. If his head was made of glass, you'd be able to see the wheels go around, you know?"

1953 KLAC station manager Don Fedderson (also responsible for Lawrence Welk's and Liberace's big breaks) offers White her own "situation comedy" revolving around one of her sketch characters: a housewife named Elizabeth. "It won't work," White tells Fedderson. "The jokes won't hold up that long, you can't do a half-hour." He persuades her to do the show, and she later says, "How wrong I was." *Life with Elizabeth* lasts two seasons. White also becomes the first American woman to produce a TV show when she cofounds Bandy Productions. Fedderson, on White's appeal: "Women like her because she isn't in competition with them. Men like her because she is the kind of girl they'd like their daughters to grow up to be."

1953 White meets future *Tonight Show* icon Johnny Carson on his first show, *Carson's Cellar*. They hit it off immediately. "We just always kind of cracked each other up," she says. After first making dozens of appearances on *Tonight Starring Jack Paar* (1957–62), White will be one of Carson's most frequent and popular guests. During a 1987 appearance, she quips to Carson, "If you hadn't gotten in such a rush to get married, we could have arranged something."

1954 NBC picks up *The Betty White Show*, and White reaches a national audience for the first time. One of her recurring guests is a Black tap dancer named Arthur Duncan. A flood of complaints come in objecting to the show being integrated. (This takes place against the backdrop of the *Brown v. Board of Education* case that led to desegregation in schools.) White's on-air response: "He stays. Live with it." *The Betty White Show* is canceled not long after (but won't be the last show with that name).

1955 White is named honorary Mayor of Hollywood, a position that holds no actual political power (she emcees events and shows up at ribbon cuttings). But because it's voted on by the viewing public, it shows that Betty White has already amassed a loyal following nearly two decades before she lands her first big sitcom role.

The password is..."game show." Tune in to page 109 for Betty White's rise to TV royalty.

In the early 1800s, tuberculosis caused a quarter of all deaths in Europe.

SHOW OFF THOSE PEARLY GRAYS

Here's a brief history of how people sought to change the shade of their chompers—and "white" wasn't always the desired effect.

GOAT MILK, SAGE, AND SUNFLOWERS

Because of the general wear-and-tear on teeth before the age of modern dentistry, white teeth in ancient Rome were a sign of wealth and prominence. What worked for Caesar and his ilk? A paste made from goats' milk...and urine. By the 12th century in Europe, white teeth remained desirable but the method to get them changed: patients used a rub made from sage and salt, or one made from sunflowers. Did this work? Yes, but it also broke down the teeth's protective enamel.

NOW THE STORY GETS DARK

Ohaguro, or the ingestion of natural ingredients to turn the teeth as black as possible, was practiced in Japan for about 1,000 years. Contrasted with stark white face makeup, black teeth came into fashion during the Heian period and hung around until the end of the Edo period in the 1870s. First the teeth of a fashionable individual were rubbed with pomegranate rinds, which made it easier for the black color to stick. That person then drank a mixture of spices, tea, and *kanemizu*, a liquid made up primarily of iron fillings. As soon as the mixture turned black, it was down the hatch, and the color would adhere to the teeth along the way.

A SWEET CODA

In the 16th century, black teeth were concurrently popular in England. That's when sugar became available, although it was so expensive that only the super rich could afford it. Because sugar rots teeth and turns them black, "naturally" blackened teeth became a status symbol.

THE HEAT OF THE MOMENT

A lot of modern teeth whiteners use hydrogen peroxide. Its ability to turn yellowed teeth to a brighter shade of white was discovered by accident. In the 19th century, early dentists were looking for a way to heal gums broken down from both infection and invasive orthodontics. Hydrogen peroxide worked for that, and dentists noticed that when it was left on the gums for a while, it escaped to the teeth...and made them whiter. In 1918, a dentist discovered that the combination of a heat lamp with a hydrogen peroxide soak made the whitening extremely effective.

Seriously: *Witzelsucht* is a rare mental-health disorder in which a person can't stop telling jokes or making puns.

LIFE IN 1962

Here's a look back at what day-to-day living was like 60 years ago,
during the age of the space race and men wearing hats.

IN THE KITCHEN

- A loaf of bread: **21¢**
- A dozen eggs: **32¢**
- Avocados: **29¢ for three of the then-exotic fruit**
- Potatoes: **79¢ for a 20-pound bag**
- Ground beef: **40¢ per pound**
- Steak: **$1.05 per pound**
- Velveeta: **79¢ for a two-pound brick or loaf**
- Spam: **39¢ for a 12-ounce can**
- Sugar: **89¢ for a 10-pound bag**
- Flour: **55¢ for a five-pound bag**
- Cake mix: A cheaper and faster alternative to baking from scratch, all the rage in the early 1960s, a box of Better Crocker cake mix cost **25¢.**
- Butter: **75¢ a pound**

- Margarine: More commonly called oleo, the butter substitute cost about **20¢ a pound.**
- Milk: **35¢ a gallon**
- Cereal: Kellogg's Corn Flakes and Post Toasties Corn Flakes both cost **27¢ for an 18-ounce box** (but Post's came with a free baseball card).
- Shortening: **A three-pound can cost 49¢.**
- Hershey Bar: **5¢**
- Beer: **$1.70 for a six-pack of Pabst Blue Ribbon**
- Coffee: A two-pound can of Chase & Sanborn ran **97¢.** A six-ounce jar of new and novel just-add-water instant coffee cost **59¢.**

AROUND THE HOUSE

- Blender: A fancy, five-speed model with a chrome base cost **$31.**
- Electric cooker: The popular countertop appliance cost **$20.**
- Automatic dishwasher: The labor-saving device cost **$240** (not counting installation).
- Laundry machines: An average household clothes washer cost **$185**, and an electric dryer ran about **$130.**
- Color TV set: Upgrading from a black-and-white set to a full-color model was expensive. A new one cost around **$500** (down from $700 earlier in the decade).
- Phone call: Need to talk to someone overseas? It cost **$12 for three minutes.**
- Stamps: It cost **4¢ to mail a letter with first-class postage.**
- Newspaper: The price of a weekday

issue of the *New York Times* went up nearly 50 percent...from **5¢ to 7¢.**
- Toys: Some of the top playthings include the Firebird 99 realistic sports car dashboard playset (**$6**), a Fred Flintstone replica pedal car (**$24**), the talking Chatty Cathy doll with movable limbs and realistic hair (**$10**), and the Etch A Sketch drawing tool (**$3**).
- Guitar: An entry-level electric guitar, so you could play that wild and crazy rock 'n' roll all the kids were into, cost **$54.95** at Sears.
- Home: A new single-family home cost, on average, **$12,550.**
- Apartment: Average rent on a one-bedroom apartment in New York City was **$110 a month.**
- Gas: A gallon averaged **27¢.**

"Beauty parlor stroke syndrome" is a rare medical phenomenon
in which people suffer a stroke after having their hair washed in a sink.

WHAT PEOPLE EARNED

- The average household earned $6,000 a year. A factory worker netted an annual average of $5,100, while public school teachers earned $5,500.

IN THE NEWS

- After U.S. espionage missions discovered Soviet Union missiles in communist Cuba just 90 miles from Florida, a monthlong standoff nearly led to nuclear war.
- Movie star and sex symbol Marilyn Monroe died at the age of 36 of an apparently intentional overdose of sleeping pills.
- Albert Sabin's oral polio vaccine was administered to millions of children and helped eradicate the disease.

MUSIC

- Among the most popular records of the year: the instrumental clarinet ballad "Stranger on the Shore" by Mr. Acker Bilk, "I Can't Stop Lovin' You" by Ray Charles, "The Loco-Motion" by Little Eva, and "Monster Mash" by Bobby "Boris" Pickett. Some of the decade's biggest acts were just getting started: Bob Dylan released his first album, the Beatles auditioned for record labels, and the Rolling Stones played their first shows. At the Grammy Awards, in only their fourth year of existence, pianist Peter Nero was named Best New Artist, while Henry Mancini's "Moon River" (from the movie *Breakfast at Tiffany's*) won Song of the Year and Album of the Year.

MOVIES

- On average, a movie ticket cost 85¢ ($6.85 in modern money). The most attended movie of the year was the three-hour, black-and-white World War II epic *The Longest Day*, about the Normandy invasion on D-Day, starring John Wayne, Henry Fonda, and Robert Mitchum. Second-most popular movie of the year: *Lawrence of Arabia*, which won the Academy Award for Best Picture.

TELEVISION

- The biggest thing on TV in 1962 were shows proudly announcing that they were broadcasting in color, urging millions of Americans to replace their old black-and-white models. (ABC's first series broadcast in color: *The Jetsons*.) The top three shows on the air at the time, on the three channels in existence, were all color Westerns: *Wagon Train*, *Bonanza*, and *Gunsmoke*.

Cost of building a mile of railroad track: about $1.5 million.

SPORTS

- Major League Baseball expanded to 20 teams, adding the New York Mets and the Houston Colt .45s (later renamed the Houston Astros) and lengthening the schedule from 154 games to 162. In the NBA, the Boston Celtics beat the Los Angeles Lakers four games to three to win their fifth championship in six years. In hockey, the Toronto Maple Leafs won the 1962 Stanley Cup, and in football, the Green Bay Packers won their eighth NFL championship (and second in a row).

VITALS

- Life expectancy for an American male born in 1962 was estimated at 75.2 years, and for a female, 80.6 years. Population of the United States: 186.5 million. World population: 3.1 billion.

NAMES

- The most popular names for baby boys born in the U.S. in 1962: Michael, David, John, James, and Robert. For girls: Lisa, Mary, Susan, Karen, and Linda.

NOTABLES

- President John F. Kennedy, in the last full calendar year of his life, was named *Time* magazine's Man of the Year for 1962. In a nationwide poll, he was called the Most Admired Man in America, too. Americans won the Nobel Prize in three categories in 1962: *The Grapes of Wrath* author John Steinbeck took the Literature prize, James Watson shared the Physiology award for helping to discover the double-helix structure of DNA, and antiwar activist Linus Pauling won the Peace Prize, having already won for Chemistry in 1954.

INNOVATIONS

- Phil Knight developed the first shoe made specifically for running, which would become the flagship product of his company, Nike. Stan Lee's superhero creation *Spider-Man* made his debut in Marvel Comics. Planters introduced dry-roasted peanuts. Soda and beer manufacturers began distributing their products in cans with pull tabs. The futuristic Space Needle opened in Seattle, as part of the World's Fair.

*   *   *

*"Don't wake me for the end of the world unless it has
very good special effects."*

—Roger Zelazny

**Sherlock Holmes creator Sir Arthur Conan Doyle played professional soccer
and judged the first bodybuilding competition.**

WHAT WAS MARIJUANA?

No matter which side of the legalization debate you fall on, chances are you know a lot more about cannabis (the preferred nomenclature for marijuana) than most people did in 1967–the height of the hippie era, also known as the "Summer of Love." That's the publishing date for a trivia book in our library called More Tell Me Why: Answers to Over Four Hundred Questions Children Ask Most Often, *by Arkady Leokum. It's unclear where Leokum got his information (or his name), but his answer reads just like the 1950s movie* Reefer Madness. *Here's the entire Q and A.*

WHAT IS MARIJUANA?

"Every now and then you read of someone being arrested for using or possessing marijuana. The law prohibits its use in many countries. Marijuana is obtained from the hemp plant. It is a drug but, unlike many other drugs, it is not recognized as a medicine. It acts as a narcotic, which means it can produce a stupor. As a narcotic it is either smoked or eaten, and it has been used by people since ancient times. In India it is known as *bhang, charas,* or *ghanga;* in Egypt it is known as *hashish;* in North Africa it is known as *kif;* in the Western Hemisphere it is called 'marijuana.'

"Marijuana affects the central nervous system. Many people who are emotionally unstable and have been involved in crimes of all sorts have been known to be marijuana users.

"When a person takes marijuana it can produce all kinds of strange results. A person may feel thirsty, hungry, and crave sweet foods. It may make him nauseous, dizzy, or sleepy. It may make him very irritable, give him delusions of grandeur, or the feeling that he is being persecuted. Sometimes it makes people very talkative and unable to control their laughter, or it may cause fear, depression, mental confusion, and even delirium.

"Some people who have smoked just one marijuana cigarette have suffered very disagreeable effects a short time afterward. Young people who make the mistake of wanting to 'try it' are often led into the terrible practice of using heroin or morphine afterward, and they become addicts.

"Marijuana itself is a complex kind of drug and much study remains to be done about it by scientists. But there is no question that it should be avoided by everyone who wants to lead a healthy, happy life."

* * *

"Normal is an illusion. What is normal for the spider is chaos for the fly."
—Charles Addams

According to Guinness World Records, the most children delivered in a single birth is nine, to a mother from Mali in 1999.

ACCIDENTAL ARCHAEOLOGISTS

*History isn't just something you find in a book. These folks
are proof that it can also be found by accident.*

THE FIND: THE DEAD SEA SCROLLS

Found in 1947 by: Muhammed edh-Dhib and his cousin Jum'a Muhammed, two
young bedouin shepherds working near the area of Qumran on the northwestern edge
of the Dead Sea, a salt lake in the Judean Desert (now part of the West Bank in Israel)

The Story: As Jum'a's long workday was nearing an end, he scuttled up a sandstone
cliff to retrieve a wayward goat when he came across a small cave, one of several that
dotted the cliff side. It was too dark inside to see anything, so Jum'a tossed in a stone
and heard the sound of pottery breaking. Excited, he ran down to tell Muhammed.
The two went back the next morning, and Muhammed crawled into the cave first.
The young bedouin was hoping to find a treasure, but found only jars. He removed
the stopper from one and pulled out a bundle of cloth wrapped around a very old
scroll written in a language he didn't recognize.

The cousins had no clue how significant their find was, but they knew enough
not to damage the scrolls. They brought three of them to a cobbler in Bethlehem
named Kando, who dealt in antiquities. Kando couldn't read the text, either. He told
the teens to go back and retrieve the rest. They brought back four more scrolls, for
which they were paid the equivalent of about $35.

As word spread throughout the Middle East about the discovery of ancient
biblical texts, many dismissed them as a hoax, but that didn't stop theologians
and archaeologists from traveling to the region to see the "Dead Sea Scrolls" for
themselves. The first academic to view them was Eliezer Lipa Sukenik, a professor at
the Hebrew University of Jerusalem: "My hands shook as I started to unwrap one of
them," he wrote in his diary. "It was written in beautiful biblical Hebrew...I suddenly
had the feeling that I was privileged by destiny to gaze upon a Hebrew Scroll which
had not been read for more than 2,000 years." Over the next decade, archaeologists
excavated ten more Qumran Caves and found intact scrolls and fragments of more
than 900 texts written in Greek, Hebrew, and Aramaic.

The History: Widely regarded as the greatest biblical archaeological find of all time,
the Dead Sea Scrolls "have provided Old Testament manuscripts approximately 1,000

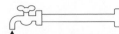

Bees won't fly in the dark unless they absolutely have to.

years older than our previous oldest manuscript," explains archaeologist Dr. Bryant Wood of the Associates for Biblical Research, demonstrating that "the Old Testament was accurately transmitted during this interval. In addition, they provide a wealth of information on the times leading up to, and during, the life of Christ."

THE FIND: THE EDINBURGH VAULTS

Found in the 1980s by: Norman "Norrie" Rowan, a pub owner and former rugby player for the Scottish national team

The Story: Rowan was renovating a room in his pub in downtown Edinburgh when he hammered through a wall and discovered a passageway. He got a flashlight and followed the passageway into a large room with an arched stone ceiling. The air was stale, and the floor was littered with piles of rubble and discarded junk—including antique toys, medicine bottles, broken dishes, and oyster shells.

Rowan soon discovered that this was just the beginning of a network of passageways and vaults that had been abandoned for who knows how long. Over the next few years, he and his sons removed tons of debris from the vaults—one of which he converted into a living space for traveling rugby players. In 1989, Rowan became a national hero after he hid a defecting rugby player named Cristian Raducanu in the vaults, helping him elude the Romanian secret police.

Today, the Edinburgh Vaults are privately owned. A few are rented out for events, including for the Edinburgh Fringe Festival. The vaults also boast a reputation as one of the most haunted places in Europe. You can take a ghost tour, or watch one of the numerous paranormal TV shows that attempt to make contact with such Edinburgh Vaults spirits as the Cobbler, the Aristocrat, Jack the Child, and Mr. Boots.

The History: The vaults are located beneath the surface of Edinburgh's elevated South Bridge. Constructed between 1785 and 1788 to connect two sections of hilly city, the bridge is 30 feet high and 1,000 feet long. After the sides were enclosed with basalt, shops and taverns opened on top, and the city steadily rose up on either side. Though not originally intended to be occupied, the arched vaults and tunnels below were soon converted into wine cellars, storage areas, and workshops. But not for long—the porous basalt let in too little air and too much moisture, resulting in a mold infestation. The vaults were abandoned after a few years.

Then came 1845, when Ireland's potato famine led to a major influx of Irish immigrants, and Edinburgh's population rose rapidly. The vaults took on a second life as the city's seedy underbelly—rife with shady taverns, illegal brothels, and organized-crime hideouts (not to mention—according to rumors—a convenient place to store the bodies of murder victims). The U.K.'s infamous Hellfire Club, where

Twelve percent of all world languages are used in Papua New Guinea (population: 8 million).

the well-to-do went to get up to no good, used the Edinburgh Vaults as a secret meeting place.

But the vaults truly were hell to the hundreds of impoverished and ostracized people who lived in them. "The inhabitants are morally and geographically of the lower orders and seldom come up to the light of day," wrote Scottish poet Alexander Smith in 1865. "Their condition is as little known to respectable Edinburgh as are the habits of moles, earthworms, and the mining population." Whenever fires broke out in the city, the vaults filled with smoke, turning them into death traps. (No wonder there are so many purported ghosts down there.)

In 1875, the Edinburgh Vaults were abandoned, filled with rubble, sealed shut, and forgotten about for more than a century, until Rowan came along with his hammer. Then came the archaeologists and historians, who are still sorting through the artifacts. One of the more ironic finds: thousands of oyster shells. Considered a delicacy today, oysters were a staple food of the poor in the 19th century.

THE FIND: WARRATYI, A PREHISTORIC SETTLEMENT

Found in 2011 by: Clifford Coulthard, an Aboriginal elder of the Adnyamathanha people, who inhabit the Flinders Ranges—a remote, rugged mountain chain in South Australia's Outback

The Story: This accidental archaeologist was working with actual archaeologist Giles Hamm, a doctoral student from Melbourne's La Trobe University. Hamm was surveying the Adnyamathanha ancestral lands, with the Aborigine as his guide. But they hadn't had much luck finding places to search for artifacts until the moment Coulthard asked to pull the car over for a pit stop. Then, as Hamm later recounted, "Nature called and Cliff walked up this creek bed into this gorge and found this amazing spring surrounded by rock art."

Intrigued by the petroglyphs he saw, Coulthard ventured higher up the steep terrain—to about 65 feet above the dry creek bed—and found himself on a ledge, at the base of which was a shallow cave. Technically a rock shelter, it's 30 feet wide by 12 feet deep, but barely tall enough to stand in. Peering inside, Coulthard saw piles of tiny bone fragments and stone tools. The ceiling was blackened from soot, meaning people once lived inside. Coulthard rushed back down to retrieve Hamm, who agreed that this could be a significant find. His preliminary estimate for the age of the settlement, dubbed Warratyi: around 5,000 years old. During the next five years, archaeologists carefully catalogued the site, finding 4,300 artifacts and 200 animal bone fragments. Further study has revealed that the site is much older than Hamm's estimate.

The New Yorker founding editor Harold Ross quit school at 13.

The History: Radiocarbon dating puts Warratyi's age between 46,000 and 49,000 years old. That means early modern humans were in the continent's harsh, arid interior a full 10,000 years earlier than researchers previously thought. "There is a Eurocentric view that material culture in Australia is quite simplistic and backward," said Michael Westaway, an Australian paleoanthropologist, "but this helps rewrite that story." Among the oldest artifacts found at the site were stone axe heads, sharpened bone points, ochre pigments, and feather shafts. These show a much more complex culture than that of mere "cavemen"—the residents were expert tool makers and artists who wore ceremonial feathers and face paints.

The bone fragments also reveal a lot about prehistoric Australia. They come from more than a dozen mammals and at least one reptile—along with a 5,000-pound marsupial called a *Diprotodon*. This odd-looking creature was the size of a hippo, with a bearlike head and a squished nose. Prior to this find, there was no evidence that humans and *Diprotodon* ever interacted. It was theorized that the animals went extinct 46,000 years ago due to climate change. But now it appears—as Australia's climate became hotter and drier—the early modern humans who'd made it that far south were forced to adapt, so they ate all the megafauna.

Warratyi would have been the perfect spot to take refuge: After the creek dried up, the spring still provided fresh water (as it continues to today). The shelter offered protection from the elements and a wide view of the valley. And it might still be unknown today, if not for, as Hamm tells it, "A man getting out of the car to go to the toilet led to the discovery of one of the most important sites in Australian pre-history." Coulthard said the find only helps to reaffirm his people's knowledge that they've lived there for a very long time. And he doesn't believe his discovery was by chance: "The spirits showed me the way" (via his bladder).

* * *

NOW BATTING...TODD BONZALES

In the 1990s, a Japanese video game designer attempted to come up with American-sounding names for baseball players. Here are the results.

- Sleve McDichael
- Onson Sweemey
- Darryl Archideld
- Anatoli Smorin
- Glenallen Mixon
- Mario McRlwain
- Raul Chamgerlain
- Kevin Nogilny
- Tony Smehrik
- Bobson Dugnutt
- Willie Dustice
- Jeromy Gride
- Scott Dourque
- Shown Furcotte
- Dean Wesrey
- Mike Truk
- Dwigt Rortugal
- Tim Sandaele
- Karl Dandleton
- Todd Bonzales

Two most-used substances on Earth: 1) water; 2) concrete.

MORE "FLORIDA MAN" STORIES

Oh, those Florida Men, always getting themselves in the news.

FLORIDA MAN WRITES SOME NOTES

The COVID-19 pandemic was especially difficult for high school seniors in 2021. Knowing their final year was mired in "negativity and turmoil in the world," Jeff Reaves, a principal from Palm Coast, Florida, decided to write a personal note to each of his graduates. In order to make sure every note was personal and positive, he recalled all the interactions he'd had with the students and looked at their transcripts—whatever it took to make sure he really knew them. Then Principal Reaves left the notes on all the students' seats at the graduation ceremony. The kicker: there were 459 graduates at Matanzas High School that year. Every one of them received a note. The project took Reaves several months to complete, and his good deed made international headlines. (But it went over best with the graduates.)

FLORIDA MAN FINDS SOME MONEY

One night in 2015, a homeless 62-year-old Florida man with a beard and disheveled gray hair walked into Tampa's newly opened Community Housing Solutions Center, which required identification. He said his name was John Helinski, but his personal identification had been stolen, and he'd been living in a cardboard box under a bench in downtown Tampa for three years. Helinski was assigned a case manager named Charles Inman, who also enlisted the help of a police officer named Daniel McDonald. McDonald has made it his mission to use his position in law enforcement to help people living on the streets. But this case wasn't easy. In order to get an ID, Helinski needed a birth certificate, but he'd been born as a U.S. citizen in Poland. "There was no other option than to succeed," said Inman. After two weeks of red tape, they were able to procure a birth certificate from the U.S. State Department's Bureau of Consular Affairs and get Helinski a new Social Security card. With the proper documents in hand, Helinski went to his old bank (which had changed names) and discovered that his long-forgotten-about account had been collecting Social Security benefits for years. The full amount wasn't disclosed, but the "small fortune" was enough to get Helinski back on his feet and into an apartment. "I haven't felt this peaceful in years," he said.

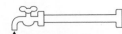

The 1930 Philadelphia Phillies set a record for most hits by a team in a season (1,783)...

FLORIDA MAN LOSES SOME MONEY

"The last year and a half hasn't been easy on this industry," said Shawn Shepherd, who owns Wahoo Seafood Grill in Gainesville, Florida, in August 2021. He was talking about COVID-19. "We're hurting and we're exhausted, but this incredible act of kindness has restored our faith in humanity." That act came in the form of a $10,000 tip left by an unidentified customer, who thanked all 10 of Wahoo's workers—each of whom received $1,000—for "showing up and working hard." The restaurant said the employees would all do something to "pay the kindness forward."

FLORIDA MAN PAYS SOME BILLS

In December 1983, a young Florida dad named Mike Esmond couldn't pay his electric bill, so he and his three daughters spent that Christmas shivering through one of the coldest spells that Pensacola has ever had—with temps dropping to 9 degrees and icicles hanging from the eaves. Esmond never forgot that time. By December 2019, he'd done well enough as a small business owner that he was able to pay the past-due utility bills of everyone in Gulf Breeze who was in danger of losing gas and water services. So, instead of a cancellation notice, 36 people—who owed a collective $4,600—were all informed that their December bills had been paid. Merry Christmas from Mike.

FLORIDA MAN GETS ON THE LAWN

While walking to work in a Palm Beach neighborhood in 2021, a Florida lawn-care worker named Tony (no last name was given) saw a car driving erratically. In the driver's seat was one of his neighbors—and the man was convulsing! Tony sprang into action and tried to stop the car, but it ran over his foot (with no injuries, thanks to his steel-toe boots) and came to a halt in a nearby front yard. The driver was unresponsive, and the doors were locked. Tony yelled for help and called 911; first responders were able to extract the driver and get him to a hospital, and Tony was credited with saving the man's life. Of course, this being Florida, this story made national headlines because of the Florida man that lived in the house where this all took place: he was heard shouting from his window, "Get off our lawn! Get the man out of here, have him die somewhere else!"

*   *   *

LABOR OF LOVE

The Huichol Indians have lived in Central Mexico for up to 15,000 years. One of their ancient traditions revolves around Dad feeling what Mom feels...during childbirth. The soon-to-be-father attempted this by straddling two poles suspended above his wife. A rope was then tied around his scrotum, and she held onto the other end. Whenever Mom felt pain during the birthing process, she'd yank on the rope just so Dad could feel it, too. *Aww.*

UNCLE JOHN'S STALL OF SHAME

*We're always amazed by the creative ways people get into trouble with
bathrooms, toilets, toilet paper, and other bathroom accoutrements.
To "honor" them, we've created the Stall of Shame.*

Dubious Achiever: Kyle Maitai, 33, an employee of Whakatane Brownfreight Tank
Service in New Zealand

Claim to Shame: Losing his load where it should never have flowed

True Story: In May 2021, Maitai was arrested for dumping a truckload of raw
sewage into the Orini canal, a protected waterway that serves as an important habitat
for indigenous birds and fish, and as a significant cultural location for local Maori.
He initially told police that a clamp had come loose while he was driving, creating a
leak, so he pulled over on a bridge and tried to fix it but the pressure was too high
to keep the tank from bursting. There were two problems with that story: the valve
opening wasn't damaged, so it couldn't have leaked, and two eyewitnesses saw Maitai
standing beside the truck as the waste flowed from it with no hose attached. The only
way the waste could flow was by someone manually opening the release valve with a
lever. Maitai opened the valve, then stood by as nearly 1,600 gallons of brown goo
gushed out of the tank and into the canal. So why did he do it? According to police,
he simply wanted to go home, and the wastewater facility where he was supposed to
dump it was too "out of the way."

Outcome: Maitai was found guilty and, at last report, was awaiting sentencing. The
habitual offender was fired from his job (he later got a new one as a bus driver). The
prosecutor, Adam Hopkinson, pressed for jail time in lieu of a fine that Maitai couldn't
afford or community service that he'd just skip out on (as he had before). "Normally
your Honor would be dealing with carelessness, negligence, and systemic failures," said
Hopkinson. "It's unusual to have a deliberate case of pollution like this."

Dubious Achiever: Phil Ateto, 39, of Annapolis, Maryland

Claim to Shame: Dressing up like a poo and then making a stink

True Story: If Ateto had left the stink bomb at home and just worn the Pile of Poo
emoji costume, he might have landed himself a place in "Uncle John's Stall of Fame,"
or at least in "Bathroom News." But instead, he really did stink the place up. Ateto
showed up to the Anne Arundel County Council meeting in May 2022 wearing street
clothes. But after a vote about police accountability didn't go the way he hoped it

would—he wanted more accountability—he ducked out and put on a full-body poop emoji costume, emblazoned with the words "Police Accountability Board." Then the man in brown walked up to the podium to speak his mind. Afterward, back at his seat, Ateto brandished a vial labeled "Stink Bomb" and poured foul-smelling liquid onto himself.

The meeting took a 20-minute recess while Ateto was escorted out of the building. By this point, the stench was overtaking him and he could barely breathe. He declined medical assistance.

Outcome: In an ironic twist, police held Ateto accountable for his actions and charged him with disorderly conduct and disturbing the peace.

Dubious Achiever: Timothy Sled, 38, of Kingsland, Arkansas

Claim to Shame: Shooting the Man in Black...just to watch him pee

True Story: Kingsland (population 514) is the birthplace of country music legend Johnny Cash. That's why there's a silhouette of Cash holding his guitar painted on the water tower—about 150 feet off the ground. In May 2022, Timothy Sled aimed his rifle toward the "Ring of Fire" singer's midsection and fired one shot. If his desire was to make it look like Cash was peeing, he was successful, as a steady stream of water started leaking out in just the right location. As amusing as it may have looked, it wasn't funny for the townsfolk, considering the tank holds most of their water and the leak caused a loss of 30,000 gallons per day. Because Johnny's leak couldn't be plugged from the outside, workers had to wait for him to finish up before they could go inside the tank and fix it. The leak continued for more than a week; in the meantime, residents had to deal with reduced water pressure and, in some cases, brown water. The water loss cost $200 per day and the repairs another $5,000. "That might seem small in bigger places," said Mayor Luke Neal, "but for somewhere like here it's a pretty large number."

Outcome: Sled was still awaiting sentencing at press time, but was facing two felony charges that carried fines of up to $20,000 and 16 years in jail. (Uncle John believes the shooter should have to pay...in cash.)

Dubious Achievers: Students attending Gettysburg College in Pennsylvania

Claim to Shame: Clogging pipes for shallow pursuits

True Story: "It kind of ruins the things at the school," said student David Parella, "and we need to use those bathrooms and stuff, so it's not funny at the end of the day." Nor is it funny at the beginning of the day—or any other time—to walk into your college dorm's shared bathroom only to discover that the toilets have been stuffed full of toilet paper. Parella and other students blame the string of pranks—which occurred in December 2021—on social media: "People want the reaction, like, attention from

The moon is constantly leaking sodium into space.

that." There doesn't seem to be much more to it. The pranksters place the end of a TP roll into the toilet, flush it, and watch it unroll down the drain until the toilet clogs. Then they post photos and videos of the TP-riddled bathrooms on TikTok.

Facilities administrator Jim Biesecker sent a school-wide email warning that if the vandals aren't caught, then the rest of the students will have to pay for the damages—which were extensive. Restrooms in at least six buildings were targeted, and the ensuing backups caused major plumbing problems all over campus. For a few days, the three-story school library had to make do with just two small bathrooms. But no one had it worse than the school's already overworked plumbers.

Outcome: Despite posting their pranks online, the vandals weren't caught: there were rumors, but no solid proof. Will they strike again? For now, Gettysburg's toilets are flowing just fine.

* * *

PATRON SAINTS

The Roman Catholic Church has more than 10,000 saints,
many of whom are "patron saints"–protectors of certain professions,
people suffering from various ailments, and even certain hobbies. Here are a few of note.

Saint Matthew:
Patron saint of accountants.

Saint Fiacre:
Patron saint of gardeners, taxi drivers, and hemorrhoid sufferers.

Saint Adrian of Nicomedia:
Patron saint of arms dealers and butchers.

Saint Anne:
Patron saint of women in labor. (Not to be confused with
Saint John Thwing, patron saint of women in *difficult* labor.)

Saint Nicholas of Myra:
Patron saint of children and pawnbrokers.

Saint Joseph:
Patron saint of opposition to atheistic communism.

Saint Joseph of Arimathea:
Patron saint of funeral directors.

Saint Martin de Porres:
Patron saint of race relations, social justice, and barbers.

Saint Martha:
Patron saint of dieticians.

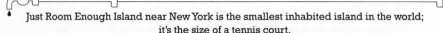

Just Room Enough Island near New York is the smallest inhabited island in the world;
it's the size of a tennis court.

FLUBBED HEADLINES

*Here are some honest-to-goodness headlines, proving that even
the most careful editors sometimes make mistooks.*

Man Arrested for Everything

VOLCANO IN HAWAII MAY SPEW FRIDGE-SIZED REFRIGERATORS

Bear Attacks Woman while Walking Dogs

Greenland Meteorite May Be from Space

Quebec Man, Mangled by Boat Propeller, Pieces His Life Back Together

Sex Education Delayed, Teachers Request Training

Close Look at Dating Finds Men Choose Attractive Women

Body Search Reveals $4,000 in Crack

Body in Duffel Bag May Be Homicide

VOLUNTEERS SEARCH FOR OLD CIVIL WAR PLANES

Lawyers Give Poor Free Legal Advice

Woman Missing Since She Got Lost

Was Bank Robber a He or a She? Breasts Might Be a Clue

Feral Cats Cover More of Australia Than Internet Does

Prisoner Serving 2,000-Year Sentence Could Face More Time

Tuna Biting off Washington Coast

Survey Finds Fewer Deer after Hunt

Rooms with Broken Air Conditioners Are Hot

Police Help Woman in Heat

Police Found Drunk in Street

TO AVOID SNAKEBITES, AVOID BOTHERING SNAKES

Infant Pulled from Wrecked Car Involved in Short Police Pursuit

It takes around three million presses to wear out an Xbox controller button.

MYTH-CONCEPTIONS

*"Common knowledge" is frequently wrong. Here are some examples of things
that many people believe...but, according to our sources, just aren't true.*

Myth: Cows sleep standing up.
Fact: They might doze off while standing around a pasture, but for an intense period
of sleep—which doesn't usually last much more than two hours—they'll lie down.

Myth: Toilet paper manufacturers bleach the product to make it white, so as to make
it seem clean and pristine.
Fact: Toilet paper, which finishes up as a pale brownish gray, is bleached to make the
final product softer. The fact that it turns white is a happy accident.

Myth: The Indianapolis 500, the most famous car race in the United States, is held
in Indianapolis, Indiana.
Fact: The Indianapolis Motor Speedway is so large that it actually occupies its
own geographic enclave of Indianapolis called Speedway, established around the
racetrack in 1912.

Myth: Hawaii is a part, albeit a distant one, of North America.
Fact: It's part of the United States of America, but otherwise Hawaii doesn't have
anything to do with America. It's not part of the continent of North America, but is
situated inside of the geographic grouping called Oceania.

Myth: Warthogs are aptly named—they're covered in warts.
Fact: Warts are lumps caused by a virus, and warthogs just have bumpy, thick, roughly
textured skin. It protects them from sustaining damage during fights with other animals.

Myth: Muscles get sore the day after exercising hard because of a buildup of lactic acid.
Fact: That pain is actually a phenomenon called DOMS, or delayed-onset muscle
soreness. It's caused by inflammation and tiny, temporary muscle tears.

Myth: White and green asparagus are different varieties of the same vegetable.
Fact: They're the exact same plant and species. To make asparagus white, farmers
cover the shoots with dirt; they'll still grow, but without access to the sun to trigger
photosynthesis, they don't turn green.

Myth: Some buildings, such as skyscrapers and office complexes, are so big they have
their own zip codes.

Number of people born on Antarctica: 11.

Fact: A handful of individual edifices do have zip codes all their own—but it's not because they're large, rather because they send and receive such a high volume of mail.

Myth: In 1947, Jackie Robinson became the first African American man to play Major League Baseball.
Fact: In 1879, the Providence Grays of the National League signed African American athlete William Edward White. He played in one game.

Myth: On the popular 1970s TV detective show *Columbo*, the rarely used first name of the titular detective, played by Peter Falk, was Phillip.
Fact: A couple of times, Columbo flashed his badge and his police ID showed that his name was Frank. "Phillip" came from *The Trivia Encyclopedia* author Fred L. Worth, who planted the item in his book as a copyright trap—if he saw it in other trivia publications, he could sue for infringement. The "fact" spread and appeared in *Trivial Pursuit*, and Worth unsuccessfully sued the publishers.

Myth: The sun is a ball of incandescent gas.
Fact: It's really a miasma, or self-attracted, mass of plasma—meaning it's simultaneously in gas, solid, and liquid states.

Myth: Possums pretend to be dead in order to trick predators into leaving them alone.
Fact: "Playing possum" isn't voluntary. When a predator comes near, the animals go into shock and then faint. They'll wake up and come out of their comatose state some unpredictable amount of time later on.

Myth: Olive oil is oil.
Fact: Olive oil is olive juice. Vegetable-derived oils are fatty liquids obtained by extraction through squeezing and pressing a particular part of the plant, usually the seeds. Olives are the fruit of the drupe tree, and to get olive "oil," they're juiced like apples or oranges. It's called olive oil, not olive juice, because oils are made of fat—as is what comes out of an olive.

Myth: Polaris, the North Star, is a star.
Fact: The famous navigational reference point looks like a single source of light to the naked human eye, 432 light years away. But Polaris is a triple star system, comprised of three gravitationally bonded celestial bodies.

Myth: Foxes are solitary creatures.
Fact: Fully grown foxes live in social groups of two to six animals. They do prefer to hunt and forage alone, however.

The last time the U.S. officially declared war: against Germany in World War II.

BOBBING FOR LAUGHS

This just in: Bobs are funny.

"A guy walks into a psychologist's convention with a banana in his pocket. When asked about the significance of this, he says, 'Well, they were all out of grapes.'"
—**Bob Newhart**

"My wife is a saint. She's Gandhi. She walks around in diapers and won't eat."
—**Bob Saget**

"I got a horse for my wife. I thought it was a fair swap."
—**Bob Monkhouse**

"You can lead a horse to water, but you can't climb a ladder with a rabbit in each hand."
—**Bob Mortimer**

"People ask me, 'What do you miss most about *Price Is Right?*' And I say, 'The money.' But that is not altogether true. I miss the people, too."
—**Bob Barker**

"Sporting goods companies pay me not to endorse their products."
—**Bob Uecker**

"Whenever someone says, 'I love writing,' I always think, 'You probably suck at writing.'"
—**Bob Odenkirk**

"I'm really small, so I think if I shrink, I'd turn into a puddle."
—**Millie Bobby Brown**

"Most dictators were short, fat, middle-aged, and hairless. Besides Danny DeVito, there's only me to play them."
—**Bob Hoskins**

"Getting the nomination is like gravy. Winning would be like whatever is better than gravy."
—**Billy Bob Thornton**

"Kurt Vonnegut said, 'The best of *Bob and Ray* is virtually indistinguishable from the worst.' I'm sure he meant that as a compliment."
—**Bob Elliott**

"If you can't laugh at yourself, make fun of other people."
—**Bobby Slayton**

"People go, 'Oh, Trump must be good for comedy,' and I go, 'Ehhh.'"
—**Bobcat Goldthwait**

"Instead of eating, I do Botox. I have about 1,100 pounds of Botox all over my body. If it ever cracks, I'm in trouble."
—**Bob "Super Dave Osborne" Einstein**

"I don't feel old. I don't feel anything till noon. That's when it's time for my nap."
—**Bob Hope**

"The sun's not yellow. It's chicken."
—**Bob Dylan, "Tombstone Blues"**

Nintendo games are coated in a foul-tasting substance to prevent babies from trying to eat them.

HISTORY'S MOST PILFERED PAINTING, PART I

Some of the most famous, valuable, and important pieces of art have been
the subject of heists over the years—some successful, some not so much.
Most stolen masterworks are eventually located and returned to their places of origin,
securely guarded to prevent theft and to guarantee enjoyment by the public.
But then there's this 15th-century religious painting made by a Belgian painter
for a cathedral. For hundreds of years, bad guys haven't been able to leave it alone.

HELLO, FLANDERS

Jan van Eyck was one of the most important painters working in the 15th century in Flanders (now part of Belgium). After a work period of about eight years, and with assistance from his brother, Hubert, he completed *Adoration of the Mystic Lamb* in 1432. Regarded as Van Eyck's masterpiece and a definitive work of the early Renaissance period, the painting is absolutely massive, measuring 17 feet wide by 12 feet tall. It weighs more than 4,000 pounds, and that's because of the heavy medium in which Van Eyck worked—*Adoration of the Mystic Lamb* is regarded by art historians as the first major oil painting, composed in a lush, velvety, realistic but also dreamlike way that would afterward come to define fine art for centuries.

Adoration of the Mystic Lamb isn't really *one* painting—it's 12. The piece is comprised of 12 individual panels of various sizes, arranged in two rows and winged out on the ends, each depicting a different biblical figure, biblical event, or moment in Christian history. When the 12 individual paintings are combined, the work tells the story of Christianity, and among the figures represented are the Virgin Mary, Saint John the Baptist, angels, Adam and Eve, and Cain and Abel. The panel placed front and center, and the largest of all, shows a crowd of religious figures deep in prayer, worshipping a lamb on a sacrificial altar while a dove flies overhead—the lamb represents Jesus Christ at the moment of crucifixion, and the bird is meant to be the Holy Spirit.

Such large, multifaceted works of art were commonly commissioned by Roman Catholic Church officials in this era, and were meant to be prominently displayed and used as a worship aid in cathedrals. And that's what *Adoration of the Mystic Lamb* was intended for: Van Eyck painted it at the behest of the Church, which placed it in Saint John the Baptist's Church (now Saint Bavo Cathedral), located in the Flemish city of Ghent. That's what gives the painting its alternate name, the *Ghent Altarpiece*.

And yet, despite its massiveness, prominence, and display in a public place watched over by powerful authorities, the *Adoration of the Mystic Lamb* didn't remain safe and sound for long.

CLEANING AND CALVINISTS

Adoration of the Mystic Lamb remained untouched, unmoved, and appreciated for 200 years, up until the tumultuous mid-1500s. The piece was originally even bigger, as Van Eyck painted a *predella*, a step or shelf at the bottom of the piece, which depicted limbo, or purgatory, in Catholic doctrine. Around 1550, painter Jan van Scorel was hired to clean the altarpiece, and he messed up the predella so badly that it was taken off the rest of the painting, placed in storage, and then irretrievably lost.

The Roman Catholic Church elevated Ghent's Saint John the Baptist Church to Saint Bavo's Cathedral by 1559, an assertion of its power in the area during a time of extreme tension between the city's Catholics and residents following the rise of various Protestant sects, particularly the austere and aggressive Calvinists. Calvinists deeply opposed what they saw as greed and corruption in Catholic leadership, along with a perceived obsession with iconography; they argued that adherents of the Catholic faith prayed to those objects and graven images, thus violating God's law. And sitting right there in the big church in their hometown was the *Adoration of the Mystic Lamb*, one of the greatest examples of iconography ever created.

UP AND DOWN

In 1566, things boiled over, and, after violent riots, Calvinists took over Ghent. On April 19 of that year, the inevitable happened: they tried to break into Saint Bavo's, torches in hand, aiming to remove the *Adoration of the Mystic Lamb* and then ritualistically burn it. Ghent Catholics were ready, stationing guards inside the cathedral, but the rioters couldn't break down the heavy, locked wooden doors. Two nights later, the mob came prepared, busting down the doors with a tree trunk used like a battering ram. And they discovered that the *Adoration of the Mystic Lamb* was... gone. After the close call on April 19, the Catholics disassembled the artwork into its 12 individual panels and hid them in a cathedral tower, then stationed a single-file line of guards inside the narrow spiral staircase leading to it.

After the coast was clear, the guards secretly moved the painting to Ghent's guarded town hall. It remained there until 1567, when Catholics regained control of the city and the *Adoration* went back to Saint Bavo's. When Calvinists took over again from 1577 to 1584, the *Adoration* once again went into storage; leaders considered sending it to Queen Elizabeth I in England to thank her for funding their Protestant uprising, but ultimately decided against it. When Catholic Spanish invaders occupied

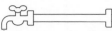

Ghent from 1584 on, the 12-panel piece returned to the cathedral, where it would stay, unperturbed, for nearly two centuries.

ADAM AND EVE AND JOSEPH

Emperor Joseph II took over the Holy Roman Empire in 1769 and passionately embraced the rationalism and intellectualism of the Age of Enlightenment, but didn't act on his philosophies until after the death of his Catholic mother in 1781. At that point, he ordered all masterworks of religious art across the European empire removed from churches and placed into museums, thus divorcing them from their spiritual associations and allowing them to be appreciated purely on their artistic merits.

Adoration of the Mystic Lamb was allowed to stay in Saint Bavo's Cathedral, since it was already universally perceived as art detached from religious meaning—thousands of artists made pilgrimages to Ghent to see it each year. Joseph II traveled to the city to see it himself, and while he appreciated it overall, he was appalled by the nude and naturalistic panels depicting Adam and Eve. While the couple's private parts are obscured by leaves, the figures are painted to look like regular people—a little lumpy, with skin imperfections—not the idealized specimens of humanity favored by classical artists. Depicting humans as imperfect went against Joseph II's rational, humanity-boosting philosophy, and, seeing his disgust and rage, the mayor of Ghent ordered that the Adam and Eve panels be detached from Adoration of the Mystic Lamb and placed into storage in the cathedral.

OFF TO FRANCE

Launched in 1789, the French Revolution was declared a success by 1792. By that point, antimonarchist rebels had abolished royal rule (and guillotined the king and queen) and established the democratic French Republic. Reinforcements called in by the French royals before their deaths—in the form of the armies of their allies Austria and Prussia—were the Republicans' next target, and they expelled the invaders, pushing them into what is now Belgium, specifically the region of Flanders, including the city of Ghent.

The new French leaders loathed grand, classical art, finding it a symbol of aristocratic privilege and obscene wealth reflecting a corrupt, money-driven Catholic Church. Art, Republicans believed, should be for the people—all the people—and after they executed more than 15,000 elites and monarchial allies, the Republicans seized their victims' artworks and brought them all back to Paris. Among the spoils of this social war: Adoration of the Mystic Lamb, which resided in the Cathedral in Ghent, now under French control. General Charles Pichegru's army carefully removed the central panels of Adoration—leaving behind the wings, and the Adam and Eve panels that were hidden in storage—and brought them to the Louvre, Paris's central and

Blind musician Stevie Wonder temporarily lost his senses of smell and taste after a 1973 car accident.

most prominent art museum. Now a symbol of the power of the French Revolution, *Adoration* became one of the top draws at a museum filled with priceless masterworks.

FINALLY FACING THEIR WATERLOO

A revolution upending the status quo in France gave way to Napoleon's French armies attempting to conquer most of Europe in the early 1800s. In 1815, those efforts definitively ended at the Battle of Waterloo. A group of allied armies, led by Prussian and British forces, defeated Napoleon in the city of Waterloo, in the United Kingdom of the Netherlands (now Belgium). Following the signing of the Treaty of Paris in 1815, Napoleon abdicated power, royal heir King Louis XVIII restored the monarchy, and France was ordered to pay reparations, in the form of hundreds of millions in francs and the return of treasures looted during the war.

This official decree signed by representatives of multiple governments meant that *Adoration of the Mystic Lamb* would once again come home to Saint Bavo's Cathedral in Ghent, reuniting the central panels that had been a primary attraction at the Louvre with the wings and removed panels that had stayed behind. *Adoration of the Mystic Lamb* continued to enjoy the same popularity and renown it had received at the Louvre, with art aficionados traveling to Ghent to see it; the publicity boost that came with the order to return it to its point of origin made it the most famous painting in the world at the time. In the 1810s, other works by Van Eyck sold for more money than those by any other artist, including Michelangelo, while a thriving cottage industry of faked Van Eyck works emerged to meet demand.

STEALING AND DEALING

In 1816, just over a year after *Adoration of the Mystic Lamb* returned to its ancestral home in Ghent and was put back together again, it was once more broken down into its various panels. Some of them were stolen, but not brazenly and openly by an army or agents of a foreign government—this time it was an inside job, by a Saint Bavo Cathedral official working in concert with a seedy, international conspiracy of art dealers.

While the bishop of Ghent was out of town on business, Jacques-Joseph Le Surre, the vicar general of Saint Bavo's Cathedral, clipped off the wings of the altarpiece, six panels in all. A French-born priest and Napoleon-supporting imperialist, Le Surre deeply resented how France had been forced to return *Adoration of the Mystic Lamb*, believing it should have stayed in France. Maurice Jean de Broglie, the bishop of Ghent, was similarly French and nationalistic, and together they worked in secret to get the painting back to Paris—or, at the very least, out of Ghent, which at that time was under Dutch control.

PRUSSIAN GALL

Le Surre and de Broglie's prearranged buyer for the painting was a prolific French-speaking art dealer based in Brussels named Lambert-Jean Nieuwenhuys, who loved *Adoration of the*

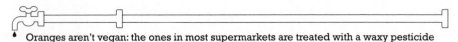

Mystic Lamb so much and knew its value because he'd made a fortune selling forgeries of the hidden and stored panels of the original to wealthy clients, claiming them to be the genuine article. Nieuwenhuys paid the men from Ghent 3,000 guilders (equivalent to about $3,600) for the six wing panels of *Adoration of the Mystic Lamb.*

After that, with Nieuwenhuys in control, the panels didn't wind up anywhere near the Louvre. In 1818, he sold them to Edward Solly, a British, Berlin-based art dealer, for 100,000 guilders, or $120,000 in today's money—turning an enormous profit for himself. Solly got an even better deal. In 1821, he sold his entire art collection, including *Adoration of the Mystic Lamb,* to King Frederick William III of Prussia (now part of Germany) for the tidy sum of what works out to $1.3 million. Frederick wanted to create a Prussian National Gallery, a great art museum of Europe that would rival the Louvre. With the *Adoration of the Mystic Lamb* panels in his possession, that dream could become a reality.

Already decimated by theft, what remained of *Adoration* in Ghent suffered further. In 1822, a fire broke out inside Saint Bavo's Cathedral. Many old and valuable artworks were completely destroyed, but staff and firefighters, knowing that everything was relatively expendable in relation to *Adoration of the Mystic Lamb,* worked quickly and specifically to save those central panels. In the end, the piece sustained only minor smoke damage.

This is nowhere near the end of drama and trauma for Adoration of the Mystic Lamb. *Turn to page 329 for the further harrowing adventures of the gigantic, famous, and widely adored painting.*

*   *   *

ALMOST CAST

Howard the Duck, starring Robin Williams? In 1986, Williams was cast in this odd George Lucas comic-book movie as the voice of the titular space duck. But the comedian, who'd never done voice-over work, got frustrated because he couldn't utilize his improvisational skills. "I can't do this," he said. "It's insane. I can't get the rhythm of this. I am being handcuffed in order to match the flapping duck's bill." So Williams dropped out, and the role went to a professional voice actor named Chip Zien.

That's why Williams initially balked at the Genie role in 1993's *Aladdin.* In fact, he didn't agree to it until he watched a short reel of the Genie animated to go along with Williams's stand-up comedy. With that, and the assurance that he could improvise as much as he wanted, Williams let loose as the Genie and paved the way for other big-name actors to take voice-over parts.

Only about half of all people experience smelly asparagus urine.

WHEN WORLDS COLLIDE

Humans and animals occupying the same space at the same time...
with memorable results.

A TALE OF TWO PIGS

November 21, 2021, was a Sunday like any other at Lightcliffe Golf Club in West Yorkshire, England. That is, until two very large black pigs—described by witnesses as "boar-like"—galloped onto the course at full speed, chased after the golfers, and knocked over their golf bags. One golfer who wasn't fast enough to run away got a tusk to the leg (which broke the skin and required a hospital visit for a tetanus shot). Then the pigs ran off. A few days later, they returned and started digging up the 18th green. A course worker attempted to "shoo one of them off," only to receive a tusk to the leg (and a tetanus shot at the hospital). The course was closed until police were able to wrangle the animals and take them to a more suitable pasture. According to news reports, where the pigs came from—and exactly what they were trying to achieve—remains a mystery.

FILLING UP FOR UNDER A BUCK

In September 2019, the Associated Press reported that a Brunswick, Georgia, woman named Lynda Tennent "went to fill up her gas tank...when a deer leaped over her head, kicking her in the process." No word on how the deer fared, but thankfully, Tennent's head was merely grazed by the animal's hoof—which is lucky considering how fast the deer was running. The station's surveillance video caught the action: Tennent is seen casually walking toward the store when a brown blur speeds past, leaving Tennent scratching her head. At first, she thought she was being mugged; then she saw the animal dart off and realized she'd been kicked by a leaping deer. "I don't know what I did [to deserve this]," said Tennent, "but I promise you I won't do it again."

A BITTER PILL

In 2021, a juvenile humpback whale was swimming in the shallow waters off the Massachusetts coast, feeding on tiny crustaceans called krill, when it accidentally captured something else in its gaping mouth: 56-year-old Michael Packard. Finding the lobster diver (and his scuba suit) unpalatable, the whale attempted to spit him out, but it took about 40 seconds of head shaking and tongue churning, during which Packard "could feel the whale squeezing with the muscles in his mouth" before he came tumbling back out. Packard was scratched and bruised but was able to make it back to his boat. "I thought to myself: There's no way I'm getting out of here," he recounted at Cape Cod Hospital. Added the whale: "Naaaaaraaaaawaaahooooo."

The tiny vertical lines following height measurements aren't quotation marks, but "primes."

THE BROOD ABIDES

Vincent Bingham never thought too much about cicadas. "I would pick them up and I would throw them in my sister's hair," explained the 20-year-old to a Cincinnati news station. Every 13 or 17 years, biblical swarms of these large, flying insects emerge from underground to feed and mate. The June 2021 "Brood X" swarm (as the press called it) saw trillions of cicadas wreaking havoc throughout eastern North America. "Remember to keep your windows rolled up until our little red eyed friends are gone," warned the Cincinnati Police Department on its Facebook page...after Bingham totaled his car. How? He was driving to work when a "red eyed friend" flew in through the open window and smacked Bingham's face so hard that it left him stunned. The next thing Bingham knew, his Toyota Camry was wrapped around a utility pole. (Karma for his sister, perhaps?) The cicada was last seen crawling around on the back seat before the totaled car was towed away. "It sucks so much," said Bingham.

DREAD AND SHOULDERS

Leonard Shoulders, 33, was waiting for a bus in the Bronx, New York, in October 2020, when a small section of the concrete sidewalk gave way and he plunged into a sinkhole. After a 15-foot freefall into what the *New York Daily News* described as a "dilapidated vault," Shoulders hit the cement hard, breaking an arm and a leg and injuring his spine. Then came the rats—*hundreds* of them—crawling around and all over the injured man. Shoulders was trapped in the dark rat den for 30 minutes until firefighters rescued him. Left partially paralyzed from the incident, at last report Shoulders had filed a negligence suit against the city and the building owner. Yet as bad as his injuries were, the psychological trauma he endured is the stuff of nightmares. As his attorney explained, "[Shoulders] was fearful of screaming out because he didn't want [the rats] to go in his mouth."

OUT OF THE FRYING PAN

On a Sunday afternoon in rural Brazil in November 2021, firefighters arrived at a small lake on a farm to find two distraught men yelling that their friend was still in the water. The three friends (not named in press reports) had been fishing when a swarm of bees chased them into the lake. Only two of the men made it out. As a firefighter was preparing to jump into the water, the men yelled for him to stop. Why? "Piranha!" These carnivorous fish—known for their razor-sharp teeth that can easily tear through flesh—are native to the region, but they live only in rivers and streams. It's unclear why they'd been released in a lake—or by whom (or if the fishermen even knew they were in there)—but that bit of information turned the rescue mission into a recovery mission. A few hours later, a little more than ten feet from the shore, firefighters discovered what was left of the third fisherman. (He might've been better off trying his luck with the bees.)

A papaya contains liquid latex.

RIGHT PLACE, WRONG NAME

Sometimes the names we use to refer to cities, states, and countries aren't technically accurate, but are instead abbreviations, informalizations, outdated, or just plain wrong. Here are the real titles of some places that we commonly reference incorrectly.

RHODE ISLAND

One of the first states (formerly one of the original 13 British colonies) and the smallest of all 50 states by area, Rhode Island has a doubly inaccurate name. Not only is not an island, geographically speaking, but its full name was the State of Rhode Island and Providence Plantations, reflecting a 17th-century merger of two settlements, Rhode Island and Providence Plantations. Because of the slavery connotations suggested by the word *plantations*, Rhode Island voters approved a referendum to drop "Providence Plantations" from the state's official name, so it's now just the State of Rhode Island.

VIRGINIA, MASSACHUSETTS, PENNSYLVANIA, CONNECTICUT

Myth: the United States comprises 50 states. Truth: the U.S. is made up of 46 states, and four *commonwealths*. The official, legal names of those four East Coast non-states are the Commonwealth of Virginia, the Commonwealth of Massachusetts, the Commonwealth of Pennsylvania, and the Commonwealth of Connecticut. How is a state different from a commonwealth? Usually, a commonwealth is defined as a loose alliance of politically or culturally connected countries, but in this context, it means exactly the same thing as *state*.

BANGKOK

Thailand's capital and largest city is called Bangkok, at least to non-Thai speakers and for the sake of brevity. In Thailand, and in the Thai language, the city's name is Krung Thep Maha Nakhon, which itself is an abbreviation of one of the longest place names in the world. The full, flowery, and official Hinduism-referencing name is Krung Thep Maha Nakhon Amon Rattanakosin Mahinthara Ayuthaya Mahadilok Phop Noppharat Ratchathani Burirom Udomratchaniwet Mahasathan Amon Piman Awatan Sathit Sakkathattiya Witsanukam Prasit. Translated into English, that means, roughly, "The city of angels, the great city, the residence of the Emerald Buddha, the impregnable city of Ayutthaya of the God Intra, the grand capital of the world endowed with nine precious gems, the happy city, abounding in an enormous royal palace that resembles the heavenly abode where reigns the reincarnated god, a city given by Indra and built by Vishnukarma."

Marx brother Zeppo Marx patented a heart-rate monitor in 1969.

LOS ANGELES

Los Angeles's nickname is the "City of Angels," a fairly direct translation of the real name, which means "the angels" in Spanish. But that's just a part of it. When Spanish settlers established what would eventually become the second-largest city in the U.S. along what at the time was called the Porciuncula River (now the Los Angeles River), they gave it the full and descriptive name of El Pueblo de Nuestra Señora la Reina de Los Angeles del Rio de Porciuncula, or "The Town of Our Lady the Queen of Angels of the Porcincula River." (Ironically *and* fittingly for the abbreviation that would occur, *porciuncula* means "little section.")

UNITED KINGDOM

Britain, *Great Britain*, and *United Kingdom* are widely used interchangeably to refer to a collection of nations off the coast of western Europe, anchored by England and ruled by the British crown. They don't all mean the same thing. *Britain* casually refers to the area, and *British* to the people who live there, usually those who, technically, are English, being from England. *Great Britain* isn't a political designation but a geographic one, referring to the landmass occupied by England, Scotland, and Wales. Therefore the full name of the entity is the United Kingdom of Great Britain and Northern Ireland. The last part reflects the non–Great Britain status of Northern Ireland, a member of the U.K. politically but geographically located on the island of Ireland, which it shares with the country commonly called Ireland but properly known as the Republic of Ireland, in part to differentiate itself from Northern Ireland.

NEWFOUNDLAND

Newfoundland is known as the easternmost province of Canada and the second smallest by population. That's not completely true. The island of Newfoundland is one of two landmasses that make up the bulk of the province of Newfoundland and Labrador. Labrador is a part of mainland Canada, sharing a border with Quebec. It's separated from the other main section of the province, the island of Newfoundland, by a narrow waterway, the Strait of Belle Isle. Another 7,000 small islands are also part of the province of Newfoundland and Labrador, but most Canadians almost always refer to the place as just Newfoundland.

OTHER COUNTRIES THAT RECENTLY CHANGED NAMES

- In 2014, the African nation of Cape Verde became the Republic of Cabo Verde.
- In 2016, 23 years after Czechoslovakia split into the Czech Republic and Slovakia, the former rebranded itself Czechia.
- African country Swaziland changed its name to Eswatini in 2018.
- In 2022, tired of confusion with the bird of the same name, the Republic of Turkey rebranded itself as the Republic of Türkiye.

On average, the Tooth Fairy pays the highest in Delaware ($8.91 per tooth) and the lowest in Iowa ($2.30).

ACCORDING TO THE LATEST RESEARCH

It seems like every day there's a report on some scientific study with dramatic new info on what we should eat, or how we should act, or who we really are. Did you know, for example, that science says...

YOU DON'T NEED THAT MANY FRIENDS

Researchers: Suzanne Degges-White of the Counseling and Higher Education department at Northern Illinois University, and Jeffrey Hall of the University of Kansas

Methodology: In 2020, Degges-White polled 297 middle-aged women about their friendships and their overall levels of happiness. Meanwhile, Hall, in two separate studies, examined how people actually make friends by tracking "the correlation of time spent together to personal closeness." First, he polled 350 adults who'd recently moved house, and then 100 college freshmen who were acclimating to life on campus.

Findings: According to Degges-White, if you want to be happy, you really need only three to five close friends in your life (55 percent of the respondents said two or three is ideal; 31 percent said four to six). And according to Hall, if you want to make a new friend, it'll take a little over eight days of quality time spent together. Only by then will you know if your platonic pal is a keeper.

These studies and others like them owe heavily to Robin Dunbar, of "Dunbar's Number" fame, who in the 1990s determined that a well-adjusted adult can have up to 150 "meaningful social relationships" (that number has increased since then), but that the ideal number of close friends is five. That's consistent with Degges-White's three-to-five findings.

However, the rise of social media has muddied up the distinction between friends and acquaintances—can you call someone you've never met "irl" (in real life) a friend? Hall's findings say no. In order to form a true friendship with someone who shares many of your interests and makes you comfortable enough to be yourself, you'll need about 200 hours together to make a "best friend," 90 hours for just a "friend," and 50 hours for a "casual friend." As the saying goes, choose your friends wisely.

But when it really comes down to it, says Hall, the most important thing is to have at least one close person in your life—be it a spouse, family member, or BFF (best friend forever). Numerous studies have found that loneliness can shorten your life, whereas meaningful relationships help you live longer. "Going from zero to one is where we get the most bang for your buck, so to speak," Hall says. And if you're

Remains of about 3 million shipwrecks rest in the world's bodies of water, and only 1 percent have been explored.

unable to make friends, remember that a book is the next best thing. (You wouldn't really want a friend in here with your right now, would you?)

SOAP IS BAD FOR YOUR SKIN

Researcher: Dr. James Hamblin of the Yale School of Public Health, and author of the 2020 book *Clean: The New Science of Skin and the Beauty of Doing Less*

Methodology: He didn't use soap for five years.

Findings: "As I gradually used less and less, I started to need less and less. My skin slowly became less oily, and I got fewer patches of eczema. I didn't smell like pine trees or lavender, but I also didn't smell like the oniony body odor that I used to get when my armpits, used to being plastered with deodorant, suddenly went a day without it."

At first, Hamblin didn't ditch the soap for the sake of science. He was trying to save money after an expensive move. He'd already been diminishing his soap use when he read about the emerging field of microbiome science and decided to "try going all out for a bit."

If you're unfamiliar with your microbiome, allow us to introduce you to the millions of microscopic germs that colonize your skin. They help fine-tune your immune system and protect you from pathogens and unsightly autoimmune conditions such as acne, eczema, and psoriasis. Everyone's individual microbiome is as unique as their fingerprint.

But ever since the 1920s—when the Lifebuoy soap company launched a successful ad campaign to "Wipe Out B.O. Forever"—Americans have been at war with their microbiomes. Antibacterial soaps wash the helpful germs away and scented soaps and perfumes hinder their return. Soap also washes away the oils that they feed on. Hamblin points out that the global soap market in 2019 was worth $34 billion. Despite that, cases of acne, eczema, and psoriasis are on the rise. And as human contact diminished during the COVID-19 pandemic, social distancing stopped people from sharing their microbiomes—but that sharing, in the long run, makes the entire population stronger and healthier.

Hamblin acknowledges that it won't be easy for most people to give up their skin regimens and get back to a more natural state—because people do naturally smell. And if someone else doesn't like that smell? "It's one of the few remaining things for which we feel fine telling someone that they're gross." Hamblin claims that his regimen has worked so well with his own skin that, at age 37, people often compare him to Doogie Howser, MD (the 1990s TV character who is a teenage doctor).

One final note: Hamblin isn't telling you to throw away all your hygiene products. You should still wash your hands with soap before eating and after using the bathroom. Also, during the five years he stopped showering with soap, he didn't completely give up on underarm deodorant.

Only person to top the U.K. pop chart solo, and as part of a duo, trio, quarter, quintet, and ensemble: Paul McCartney.

WALKING AND TEXTING CAN MAKE YOU SMARTER

Researchers: Edward G. Freedman, PhD, of the Cognitive Neurophysiology Lab at the University of Rochester, New York

Methodology: Incorporating a "Mobile Brain/Body Imaging system"—which consists of a backpack wired to a skullcap that measures electroencephalography (EEG) in the brain—the researchers tasked 26 volunteers between 18 and 30 with performing a mental task while sitting at a desk, and then repeating that task while walking on a treadmill. The task: looking at a series of photos and then clicking a button whenever the photo changed to a new one, but not clicking if the photo is a repeat of the previous one. It wasn't difficult, but it required paying attention to the screen.

Findings: Fourteen of the participants showed an improved performance when they took the test while walking on the treadmill, which researcher Eleni Patelaki called surprising: "Most studies in the field show that the more tasks that we have to do concurrently, the lower our performance gets." In the subjects who performed better while multitasking, the EEG data showed higher activity in the frontal lobe, "suggesting increased efficiency."

The scientists are planning to expand on this research in the hopes of finding out why some people's brains age differently than others, and to identify the "super agers," people who show no decline in mental performance throughout their lives. That being said, if you try texting while walking on a busy sidewalk, you might not get a chance to find out how your brain ages.

THE INTERNET MAKES YOU THINK YOU'RE SMARTER THAN YOU REALLY ARE

Researcher: Adrian Ward, assistant professor of marketing at the University of Texas at Austin

Methodology: In 2021, Ward conducted a series of experiments that asked the participants general-knowledge questions. Some of them could search for the answers on Google; others had to rely on their memory. In subsequent tests, participants used a version of Google that took 25 seconds to yield a result, and another test let some people use Google, while others could use Wikipedia. Between the tests, the participants filled out questionnaires that asked them to rate their past performance, predict how they'd do on future tests, and give an overall impression of their own intelligence.

Findings: "We mistake the internet's knowledge for our own," reported Ward. The test subjects confirmed it over and over. Those who enlisted online help had an inflated sense of not just their current memory but their future ability to get the

French power plants recycle 96 percent of their nuclear waste.

correct answers—even when they were informed they wouldn't have external help. They even thought they'd performed better than they had on previous tests. "We're seeing that people even forget that they Googled a question," he said.

The reality is that an overreliance on instant knowledge is causing people to forget how to remember things—to actually tap into that recall mode we all have and work out an answer. One reason Google is so successful is that its simplicity of listing one possible answer after another mimics how our brains try to recall information, so it's comfortable to us. However, the test subjects that used Wikipedia had to sort through more information to get the answer, and as such they absorbed more knowledge about the subject and performed better on recall quizzes than the Google users. And the subjects who used "slow Google" didn't have the same inflated sense of intelligence, suggesting that it's the speed with which you obtain the answer on the internet that affects your perception of how smart you are.

"When we're constantly connected to knowledge, the boundaries between internal and external knowledge begin to blur and fade," said Ward. That can lead to making bad financial and medical decisions, and make some people have more entrenched views about science, culture, and politics—which can be dangerous when that "knowledge" is gained from misinformation. Ward and others who are studying "the intersection of the internet and human memory" recommend that you give the Googling a break every so often and try on your own to remember how many ounces are in a gallon or what year *The Matrix* was released.

READING MAKES YOU LIVE LONGER

Researchers: Researchers at Yale University

Methodology: This 12-year study followed 3,635 people over 50 who were periodically questioned about their reading habits. Participants were divided into three categories: nonreaders, people who read less than three and a half hours per week, and people who read more than three and a half hours per week.

Findings: In 2022, the journal *Social Science and Medicine* reported that those who read more than three and a half hours per week lived nearly two years longer than people who didn't read at all. Even more impressive, the results did not discriminate based on someone's age, sex, bank account, or how well they were educated. (For the record, the group that read the most were "college-educated women in a higher-income bracket.")

That makes reading one of the few sedentary activities you can undertake to keep you from the undertaker. Even better news: it doesn't matter what kind of books the readers were into—all they had to do was read. (The lesson: go buy yourself and everyone you know—especially your elders—a big healthy stack of Uncle John's Bathroom Readers.)

The heritage of 70 percent of all macadamia nuts produced today can be traced back to one tree in Australia.

BEASTLY BATHROOM HABITS

Does a bear...you know what in the woods? Yes, it does.
Here are some other things that happen in the woods..

Sloths. A sloth spends its few waking hours eating leaves, twigs, and flower buds. Once a week, it slowly climbs out of its tree, and then slowly crawls to a good spot to poop. First, it does a little dance (a slow dance, no doubt) to get things moving, and also to make a hole in the dirt big enough to contain a very long, two-pound poop shaped like a banana. According to biologists, this process is so difficult that the sloth's pain is similar to a human woman giving birth.

Binturongs. Also known as bear cats, these stocky raccoon-like animals (with prehensile tales) live in Southeast Asia and will eat just about anything, including smaller mammals, birds, fish, worms, bugs, and figs. They *really* like figs, and are crucial to spreading the fruit's fertilized seeds through their scat. But the weird thing about the binturong is its urine: it contains a chemical compound known as 2-AP. You know what else has a lot of 2-AP? Freshly popped popcorn... which is exactly what the binturong's pee smells like.

King Penguins. Wanna get high? Head south to the sub-Antarctic island of South Georgia, home to king penguins. Their diet of fish, krill, and squid produces a lot of nitrogen in their guano. When that guano hits the bacteria that live in the island's soil, the nitrogen is converted into nitrous oxide—also known as laughing gas. According to the study that discovered this, one of the researchers, surrounded by a colony of pooping penguins, "went completely cuckoo."

C. ginnaga Spiders. Predatory wasps prey on these orb-web spiders, but they don't prey on bird poop. (Who would?) So these spiders have taken to building silvery-white clumps of silk into their webs that have the same shape, size, and pattern of bird poop. Then the silvery-white spiders hide in plain sight right on top of the "bird poop" as the wasps fly right past them none the wiser.

Giant Pandas. These prolific poopers go between 40 and 60 times per day. Why so much? Because their diet is 99 percent bamboo, but their digestive systems never evolved from when the animals were meat eaters two million years ago. Result: pandas can digest only about 17 percent of the 30 pounds of bamboo they eat per day. The rest literally goes to waste. Also bizarre: when a panda pees, it stands on its hands with its legs resting on a tree, allowing it to shoot a clean stream on the bark, letting fellow pandas know, "Hey, I peed here."

Early 20th-century asthma treatment:
Asthmador cigarettes, which replaced the tobacco with a hallucinogenic medicine.

NOT COMING TO A THEATER NEAR YOU

You'd be surprised how many films in Hollywood are started...
without ever being finished. Here's a look at a few that will
probably never make it onto the big screen.

OIL AND VINEGAR

Great Idea: John Hughes was prolific, influential, and beloved in the 1980s, making big-screen comedies and sensitive teen films. He wrote (and sometimes directed) a string of hits between 1983 and 1986 including *National Lampoon's Vacation, Mr. Mom, Sixteen Candles, The Breakfast Club, Weird Science, National Lampoon's European Vacation, Pretty in Pink,* and *Ferris Bueller's Day Off*. He almost had one more entry in that historic run. In 1986, Hughes was set to team up the stars of the latter two movies, Molly Ringwald and Matthew Broderick, respectively, for *Oil and Vinegar*. Hughes's script concerned a twenty-something man (Broderick) driving cross-country to his own wedding but picking up a hitchhiker (Ringwald) along the way, only to get stranded in a motel and spend hours on an intimate conversation about life and maybe start to fall in love.

Why It Was Doomed: *Back to School* director Alan Metter was asked to direct, but he said no, prompting Hughes to helm it himself (despite frequent collaborator Howard Deutch asking if he could have the job). Hughes then lost interest in *Oil and Vinegar* and hired Deutch to direct the next script he whipped up, *Some Kind of Wonderful*, and everybody moved on.

GET IT WHILE YOU CAN

Great Idea: Canadian filmmaker Jean-Marc Vallée had a history of making movies about real people (*The Young Victoria, Dallas Buyers Club*), many of them dealing with substance abuse issues (*Wild*). Vallée started his career as a music video director, too, making him an ideal candidate to helm *Get It While You Can*, a biographical movie about the life of Janis Joplin, the iconic 1960s rock star who died of a drug overdose in 1971. Vallée signed up in 2014, around the same time that Amy Adams agreed to star as Joplin and do all the singing the part required.

Why It Was Doomed: But while producers had a script, they hadn't secured the rights either to tell the story of Joplin or use her music. That prevented filming from starting,

Oldest surviving Christmas movie: *Santa Claus* (1898).

as did producers running out of money. Vallée and Adams departed *Get It While You Can* around the same time that two other Joplin biopics were announced, *Joplin* and *Piece of My Heart*. As of 2022, none of these movies have shot a frame of film.

MONSTERPOCALYPSE

Great Idea: By 2010, formerly quirky cult filmmaker Tim Burton was the toast of Hollywood, having directed several big hits in a row: *Big Fish*, *Charlie and the Chocolate Factory*, *Corpse Bride*, *Sweeney Todd: The Demon Barber of Fleet Street*, and *Alice in Wonderland*. In 2010, Warner Bros. announced that Burton (and screenwriter John August, who wrote all those movies except *Alice in Wonderland*) would team up for *Monsterpocalypse*. Based on a popular board game released in 2008, the film would be about giant monsters from outer space invading and attacking Earth, then plunging themselves deep into the center of the planet after humanity fights back. Should they ever return (and they most definitely will), humans have built gigantic war robots to permanently vanquish the invaders.

Why It Was Doomed: Just a few months after Warner Bros. announced the development of *Monsterpocalypse*, Legendary Studios broke the news that they'd fast-tracked production on a new movie with famed horror director Guillermo del Toro. That film: *Pacific Rim*, about a battalion of human-controlled giant robots who square off against massive alien monsters. In other words, it was the same movie, prompting Warner Bros. to back off and cancel *Monsterpocalypse*.

DUFUS

Great Idea: *The Catcher in the Rye* is one of the most important (and popular) novels of the 20th century. Published by American author J. D. Salinger in 1951, it tells the tale of angry, angst-riddled teen Holden Caulfield as he wanders around New York City. A shockingly honest and progressive take on the teenage mindset, the book influenced the entire genre of young-adult fiction and ultimately sold more than 65 million copies. Salinger, however, entered a self-imposed seclusion for the rest of his life, and by the time he died in 2010, he'd never published another novel. He also hated the Hollywood movie-making system, rejecting the many offers he received over the years to turn *The Catcher in the Rye* into a film. In the late 1980s, Disney boss Michael Eisner tried to get around Salinger's refusal by changing the nature of the story just enough so that it wouldn't be a rights-requiring adaptation.

Why It Was Doomed: Disney wooed Broadway lyricist Howard Ashman to the studio with a list of in-development projects he could work on. Selecting the movie that would become *The Little Mermaid*, Ashman passed on *Dufus*—a coming-of-age story similar to *The Catcher in the Rye* but not a direct adaptation of *The Catcher in the Rye*, but also

animated, a musical, and in which all the characters would be German shepherds. *Dufus* never got past the idea stage.

THE NICKTOONS MOVIE

Great Idea: Inspired by Disney's mega-blockbuster *The Avengers*, in which dozens of well-known Marvel Comics characters (Captain America, Iron Man, Thor, the Incredible Hulk, and more) get together to save the world from intergalactic bad guys, rival studio Paramount wanted its own team-up movie showcasing its own valuable in-house intellectual properties. In 2015, executives started planning a big-budget animated film featuring characters from more than 20 years' worth of Nicktoons, cartoons that originated on the Paramount-owned Nickelodeon kids network. Among the very popular shows that aired under the Nicktoons banner: *SpongeBob SquarePants* (already the subject of two hit spin-off movies), *Rugrats, Doug, The Ren & Stimpy Show, Hey Arnold!, The Angry Beavers,* and *CatDog.*

Why It Was Doomed: Obtaining and securing the film rights to each and every character from each and every show proved costly, time-consuming, and impossible. Paramount's lawyers couldn't get every show's creator to sign off, so even though *Napoleon Dynamite* director Jared Hess had agreed to direct and write *Nicktoons,* the film never really entered production.

CITY THAT SAILED

Great Idea: In 2010, A-list movie star Will Smith was lining up what film to shoot after *Men in Black 3*, and he circled *City That Sailed*. A potentially mega-budgeted, special-effects-heavy fantasy adventure family drama, the movie is about a young girl in New York City who misses her father, traveling in Europe, so much that she magically causes Manhattan to break free of North America and sail across the ocean to create a reunion. Smith didn't officially sign on for *City That Sailed* until 2013, at which time he also agreed to produce, and Shawn Levy (*Real Steel*) agreed to direct and oversee the project. It look a long time for filming on such an ambitious movie to begin, and various delays and scheduling conflicts on Smith's part pushed things back even more.

Why It Was Doomed: When Disney's multibillion-dollar acquisition of Fox was finalized in 2019, the company inherited the old studio's massive debts and operating losses, prompting it to cancel almost every project that had been in various states of production. More than 250 movies were immediately axed, including *City That Sailed*, which had been in development at the now-nonexistent Fox for almost a decade.

* * *

"Laugh and the world laughs with you, snore and you sleep alone."

—Anthony Burgess

First Disney character to fart on screen: Pumbaa the warthog in *The Lion King* (1994).

HOW TO SPEAK POLARI

Here's a look at how the marginalized members of a subculture communicated for decades, so as not to arouse suspicion...or risk arrest.

BACKGROUND

Combining circus-worker slang, Italian, Romani, French, and Yiddish words, along with theatrical terms, Polari is the name for the performative, extra-enunciated jargon and vernacular used among members of the British navy, the London theater scene, and European circuses—particularly and mostly by gay men, as something of a secret code, until homosexuality was legalized in the U.K. in the late 1960s. Some words—*shade* ("resentment"), *tea* ("gossip"), and *butch* ("masculine")—have made their way into common usage, but most Polari terms, such as these, are lost to history.

Chicken: a handsome young man

Bijou: little

Dona: a woman

Bungery: a bar

Buvare: a beverage

Strillers: a piano

Vera: gin

Vogue: a cigarette

Batts: shoes

Strides: pants

Stimps: legs

Martinis: hands

Oven: mouth

Pots: teeth

Yews: eyes

Onk: nose.

Aunt Nells: ears

Aunt Nell danglers: earrings

Riah: hair

Riah zhoosher: a hairdresser

Switch: a wig

Cackle: gossip

Latty: a home

Metzas: money

Barney: a fight

Bonaroo: wonderful

Fantabulos: wonderful

Ecaf: a face

Dolly ecaf: a pretty face

Mince: to walk

Screech: to speak

Carsey: toilet

Cod: bad

Cove: taxi

Dorcas: term of endearment for a friend or a loved one

Sharpy: police officer

Shush: to steal

Slap: makeup

Naff: heterosexual

So: homosexual

Only NFL team to never record a tie: the Jacksonville Jaguars.

A MYSTERY OF HISTORY: THE VENUS DE MILO, PART I

Every list of the Louvre Museum's most famous artworks begins with the Mona Lisa, painted by Leonardo da Vinci, immediately followed by the Venus de Milo, sculpted by... who again? (Alexandros of Antioch.) Why isn't the artist better known? And how did a broken Greek statue become so popular? And what is the deal with those missing arms? Here's the little-known story of a flawed masterpiece that people once fought for, lied for, and died for.

CLASSICAL BEAUTY

Exquisitely sculpted more than two-thousand years ago from Parian marble (a smooth, white stone once quarried from the Greek island of Paros), the Venus de Milo has long been associated with the perfect female form. Said to depict Aphrodite, the Greek goddess of love and fertility (or Venus, as the Romans later called her), she stands with the Classical Greek S-curve posture; she is half nude with a pensive look on her face as drapery is slipping from her hips. And somehow, not detracting from her allure, is the Louvre's "Condition of the Work":

> Incomplete: the left arm is missing, a large part of the right arm, the left foot. The nose has chips. The back has many scars. The plinth was recut in antiquity. The bun has been glued back and the end of the nose has been redone in plaster.

Despite these flaws—but also *because* of them—the Venus de Milo is as steeped in popular culture today as when she was introduced to the modern world over 200 years ago, having shown up everywhere from *The Simpsons* (in the form of a priceless gummy bear) to the logo of the American Society of Plastic Surgeons.

The statue even has an entire room to herself in the Louvre's *Galerie des Antiques*. "Her name comes from the Greek island of Melos (now called Mílos), where she was found in 1820 and acquired almost immediately by the Marquis de Rivière, the French ambassador to Greece at that time," reads the Paris museum's description. "He then presented her to King Louis XVIII, who donated her to the Louvre in March 1821. In barely two years, the Venus had moved from the shadows to the light."

As it turns out, there's a lot more to Venus's story (especially that "acquired almost immediately" part) that the Louvre's curators would rather leave forgotten to history.

THE FARMER AND THE SOLDIER

Milos is part of the Cyclades, a picturesque island group in the Aegean Sea off the southern coast of Greece. Today, the island's volcanic terrain and white cubist villages—rising above the blue Mediterranean waters—make Milos a hotspot for tourism. Two millennia ago, when the Romans ruled Greece, then-Melos was a major exporter of obsidian (volcanic glass used for blades), and there was a thriving city there. Two-hundred years ago, when Greece was ruled by the Ottoman Empire (present-day Turkey), the city was in ruins and Melos was inhabited by peasants, farmers, and fishermen.

On the morning of April 8, 1820, in the village of Trypiti, two searches were taking place at the ruins of a civic gymnasium. One search consisted of a small band of French soldiers—led by an ensign named Olivier Voutier, who had a background in archaeology—looking for ancient Greek artworks to take to Paris. About 20 steps away from Voutier, a young farmer named Yorgos Kentrotas was in his field excavating a crumbled wall, searching for stone blocks for a barn he was building. As he was clearing out a niche (an arched, cave-like indentation in the wall, several feet off the ground, several feet deep, and about five yards wide), he found the top half of a marble statue—of a woman—lying on its side, halfway buried in the rubble.

The farmer stopped digging to get a closer look...until he noticed that the soldier was walking over, and he hastily started covering up his find. Voutier, who spoke Greek, saw the statue and insisted that Kentrotas keep digging. Reluctantly, Kentrotas unearthed the top half and, sensing the Frenchman's eagerness, offered to excavate the rest of the niche for a price. Voutier (who had only a few small shovels) paid up. Working together, they dug out the lower portion along with a chunk of broken marble that, when inserted between the statue's upper and lower halves, allowed the Venus de Milo to stand up for the first time since antiquity. "It has no arms," Voutier wrote in his notebook, adding, "the nose and the knot of the hair are broken, it's horribly dirtied. Nevertheless, at first glance, one recognizes a remarkable piece."

Kentrotas and Voutier also found a *plinth* (base) along with two *herms* (three-foot-tall pillars with carved heads on top, possibly used as boundary markers). According to various reports—and do they ever vary!—they also unearthed a sculpted hand holding an apple and a deteriorated left arm. Had the soldier not been there to witness the discovery, it's likely that the farmer would have cooked all the marble in his kiln to make lime, which was used for cement.

NEGOTIATORS OF THE LOST ARTWORK

Because Kentrotas discovered the statue on his land, he claimed ownership and offered

Longest narrative movie ever made: the Argentinian production *La Flor* (2018), at 14 hours.

to sell it to the French. As Gregory Curtis describes in his book *Disarmed: The Story of the Venus de Milo*, "Yorgos had decided he wanted four hundred piasters for it, about the price of a good donkey." That was more than Voutier was carrying, so he ran to the village to fetch vice-consul Louis Brest, the only representative of the French government on Melos. Brest was equally impressed with the statue, but he didn't want to risk using his own money, should the armless artwork turn out to be worthless. The Frenchmen needed to procure the funds from the Marquis de Rivière, the French ambassador to Greece, who was stationed in Constantinople (in modern-day Turkey). After agreeing to not sell it to anyone else, Kentrotas erected the statue in his sheep barn for French soldiers to admire. That was the Venus de Milo's first modern public exhibition.

By the time Voutier and Brest returned a few days later with the ambassador, Kentrotas had been pressured into selling the statue to the ruling Ottoman empire; it was about to be loaded onto a ship bound for Turkey. Thanks to some crafty negotiating—and, rumor has it, bribes to Turkish officials—the French took possession of the statue for, writes *Smithsonian* magazine, "a price of 1,000 francs, roughly the cost, in those days, of a nice herd of goats."

AT ANY COST

By this point, word of the find had spread throughout the Cyclades. What happened next has been glossed over by most historical accounts—at least those written in French and English. But according to a translated *Greek City Times* article from 2021, exactly 200 years earlier, when the locals tried to stop the Venus de Milo from being loaded onto a ship:

> French soldiers, said [Greek historian Dimitris A.] Fotiadis, fired at the angry islanders, killing several, and the invaluable statue was put on the ship and taken away as hundreds of islanders followed on small boats in a desperate, failed rush to stop it. When the French ship docked in [the Athens port of] Piraeus, the Mílos islanders and some 1,000 other Greeks tried to stop the ship from leaving...but in a clash with the crew more than 200 were killed, the historian said.

In 1821, after sailing a "victory lap" around Europe, the statue arrived in Paris, where it was presented to King Louis XVIII. (His Majesty was so debilitated by gout that he could get around only in a wheelchair, so they set up a special viewing room just for him.) Then the statue was delivered to the Louvre Museum, which at the time was less than 30 years old and in desperate need of a new treasure from antiquity.

Largest pyramid on the planet, by volume: the Great Pyramid of Cholula, Mexico.

MUSÉE NAPOLÉON

That brings us to how this severely damaged piece of art became so famous—which is odd considering there are numerous other ancient Greek statues in much better condition on display that are less famous. Compare the Venus de Milo to the Venus de' Medici, sculpted in Athens around the same time. Another nude depiction of the goddess of love, Medici Venus (as she's also called) is intact. And until 1815, she was on display at the Louvre, along with thousands of other artworks that Napoleon Bonaparte's armies had looted during his European conquests. (The French emperor even renamed the museum after himself.) But after he was forced to abdicate his throne, more than 5,000 works of art—most of the museum's collection—were returned to their rightful owners. The Medici Venus went back to Italy, where it's still on display in the Uffizi Gallery in Florence. In 1816, the Louvre suffered another setback in the war for cultural supremacy when the British Museum took possession of the Elgin Marbles, now known as the Parthenon Sculptures, that date back to ancient Greece's Classical Age.

This need for new treasures was why Voutier was so interested in searching the ruins on Melos. When he saw that the farmer's find was made of the same Parian marble as the Medici Venus, he knew the French had to have it. Not long after the discovery, Voutier fought as a colonel in the Greek army in Greece's War for Independence (1821–28). As for the "remarkable" statue he rescued from a possible kilning, it wasn't quite as remarkable as the French were hoping it would be.

THAT DARN PLINTH

The Louvre's curators really, really wanted their new acquisition to come from Greece's Classical Age (500–336 BC). Why? Most "ancient Greek" statues displayed in museums are merely Roman-commissioned copies of the originals—still expertly crafted, just not the original designs. The plinth found with the Venus de Milo (which was connected to her still-missing left foot) bore the inscription "Alexandros, son of Menides, citizen of Antioch of Meander made the statue." Known as Alexandros of Antioch, the artist traveled throughout the Mediterranean creating commissioned works. (His second-most famous sculpture, Alexander the Great, was also sculpted on Melos.)

Antioch (in present-day Turkey) wasn't founded until *after* the Classical Age, which places the statue's creation between 150 and 125 BC, making it a prime example of Hellenistic art. Today, the Hellenistic Age (323–33 BC) is just as revered as the Classical Age, but it wasn't until the mid-20th century that Hellenistic artworks came to be viewed as anything but lesser copies of original Greek masterpieces. "Had her true author been known, she likely would've been

What are *gastroliths*? The small rocks animals
swallow (and later pass) that help them digest food.

locked away in the museum's archive, if not sold off," explains art historian Jane Ursula Harris in *The Believer* magazine. "Hellenistic art had by then been denigrated by Renaissance scholars who re-conceived it in anti-classical terms, finding in its expressive, experimental form and emotional content a provocative realism that defied everything their era stood for: modesty, intellect, and equanimity." Not only was the statue from the wrong period, there's strong evidence that it was inspired by or blatantly copied from two earlier Greek works. So, while Alexandros was no doubt a master of his craft, the design wasn't his.

BURYING THE TRUTH

Louvre officials kept all of this under wraps—even from the king himself—and then "lost" the plinth with Alexandros's name on it. (To this day, it's uncertain whether it was destroyed or is tucked away in storage.) Then, starting in the 1820s, the Louvre launched an international branding campaign, claiming that its newly christened "Venus de Milo" was sculpted during ancient Greece's Classical Age by one of the great masters, Praxiteles of Athens. The discovery was credited to the Marquis de Rivière. And all that inconvenient "killing the islanders" stuff was left out. Result: the Venus de Milo became instantly famous and has long since surpassed the Venus de' Medici and Elgin Marbles in popularity. And the Louvre is the largest, most visited art museum in the world.

To find out what happened to the Venus de Milo's missing arms,
and if she really is who we think she is, turn to page 181.

* * *

THE FIRST 13 MUSIC VIDEOS PLAYED ON VH1 (JANUARY 1, 1985)

1. "The Star-Spangled Banner" by Marvin Gaye
2. "Missing You" by Diana Ross
3. "You've Lost That Lovin' Feelin'" by Daryl Hall & John Oates
4. "Nobody Told Me" by John Lennon
5. "Shaking You" by Olivia Newton-John
6. "After All" by Al Jarreau
7. "Steppin' Out" by Joe Jackson
8. "I Just Called to Say I Love You" by Stevie Wonder
9. "I Knew You When" by Linda Ronstadt
10. "Always Something There to Remind Me" by Naked Eyes
11. "Centipede" by Rebbie Jackson
12. "I'm Alright" by Kenny Loggins
13. "Joanna" by Kool & the Gang

On the cover of the Beatles album *Sgt. Pepper's Lonely Hearts Club Band*, John Lennon wears medals that belonged to the grandfather of fired drummer Pete Best.

LUCKY FINDS

Ever stumble upon something valuable? It's an incredible feeling. Here's the latest installment of one of the Bathroom Readers' Institute's regular features.

A SPOIL OF WAR

The Find: An ancient Roman statue

Where It Was Found: At a thrift store in Austin, Texas

The Story: In 2018, Laura Young, 43, was perusing the aisles at her local Goodwill store when she looked under a table and spotted a bust of a man with short, curly hair. It looked a lot like a Roman statue, so she expected it to be a kitschy yard ornament made of plastic or resin. But when she inspected it, the 19-inch-tall bust looked and felt like marble. It weighed more than 50 pounds and was obviously very old. And it was only $34.99! Young, who deals in antiques herself, took the bust home. She and her husband named the stern-faced statue Dennis Reynolds, after a character on the irreverent sitcom *It's Always Sunny in Philadelphia*. "He's aloof," she told the *Washington Post*. "No emotion, possibly a little sociopathic."

Young started contacting auction houses, and it took her only a couple of weeks to confirm that Dennis is indeed a genuine Roman bust that was sculpted from marble more than 2,000 years ago. There's no name chiseled into it, but experts think that Dennis is a Roman commander named Nero Claudius Drusus Germanicus, also known as Drusus the Elder. A photograph from the 1930s confirms that this very same bust had spent 80 years on display at the Pompejanum museum in Aschaffenburg, Germany.

How did Dennis get to Texas? In the final days of World War II, American forces defeated the Nazis in the battle of Aschaffenburg. What remained of the museum was looted, and the bust was taken to the United States by a returning soldier. That's the going theory, anyway. It then spent 75 years in anonymity until Young came across it at the Goodwill. Unfortunately for her, because the statue had been stolen, it was the property of Germany, so she couldn't keep it or sell it. All the while, Dennis was "on display" on a credenza in her house; "Every time you walk into the kitchen, you pass the head," she told NPR. In 2022, after nearly four years of bureaucratic red tape and legal wrangling, an agreement was reached: the German government would pay Young a "finder's fee" (undisclosed), and Dennis would spend a year at the San Antonio Museum of Art before going home to Europe. Young was glad to get Dennis out of her house, but she does kind of miss him: "He's probably the coolest thing I'm ever going to find."

KEEP THE CHANGE

The Find: A rare penny

Where It Was Found: In a high school cafeteria

The Story: In 1947, a Massachusetts teenager named Don Lutes was looking at his lunch change, when he noticed a 1943 penny that was made of copper. That didn't make any sense because everyone knew (back then) that the U.S. Mint didn't make pennies out of copper in 1943 as part of the war effort: copper was needed for shell casings and telephone wire, so that year, every U.S. penny was made of zinc-plated steel. There was a rumor, however, that due to a production error, 20 of that year's pennies were made from copper.

Lutes became a coin collector and held on to his most prized possession—despite rumors that Henry Ford himself would trade anyone a brand-new car for one of the "copper '43s" (a rumor that turned out to be false). Lutes told the U.S Treasury about his find, but the agency flatly denied the existence of any 1943 copper pennies. But then a few more copper pennies turned up, and as the years passed, these rare coins became known as the "holy grail of mint errors." According to Heritage Auctions, "Stories appeared in newspapers, comic books, and magazines and a number of fake copper-plated steel cents were passed off as fabulous rarities to unsuspecting purchasers." In 1958, Lutes had an expert confirm that his penny was indeed the real deal—one of the only 1943 copper pennies in existence. Despite receiving some offers from collectors over the years, he hung onto the penny for the rest of his life.

In 2022, Lutes's family decided to sell the coin. "This is the most famous error coin in American numismatics and that's what makes this so exciting," said Sarah Miller of Heritage Auctions. "No one really knows what it's going to sell for." Winning bid: $204,000—or 20,400,000 pennies.

LEROY WAS HERE

The Find: A 362-year-old oil painting

Where It Was Found: At a thrift store in Anderson, South Carolina

The Story: An 81-year-old man who identified himself only as Leroy was thrifting in 2012 when he came across an oil painting. He figured it was a steal for $3; he sells antiques and knows a good frame when he sees one. The painting—a still life of turkey, shellfish, caviar, and bread—looked nice, too, but Leroy bought it mainly for that frame. He thought it might bring in a few hundred bucks. But his daughter-in-law took the painting to a taping of PBS's *Antiques Road Show*. Good move: it was a prized work from a Flemish art school in Amsterdam, painted circa 1650. The initial appraisal was $20,000 to $30,000. It ended up selling at auction for an astounding $190,000. "It's the biggest find I've ever had," Leroy boasted. "It's that one thing one you're always looking for."

Classical music record label Vivendi Universal began as a water company created by decree by Napoleon.

UNHEARD ALBUMS

The music industry is notoriously difficult for artists to thrive in. And as these examples show, not even being a platinum-selling artist ensures that your music will be heard.

● JIMI HENDRIX

In 1970, the celebrated guitarist home-recorded himself singing and playing acoustic guitar on 16 demo versions of songs he'd written for *Black Gold*, an intended concept album about the story of his life. Hendrix had just one copy of the tape, and he gave it to his Jimi Hendrix Experience drummer, Mitch Mitchell, to see what he thought. Before Mitchell could weigh in, or Hendrix could develop the project further, the guitarist died at age 27. And then Mitchell just forgot he even had the tape of a lost Hendrix album. After Mitchell died in 2008, the tape came into the possession of Hendrix's sister and musical-estate executor Janie Hendrix, and she promised to release *Black Gold* in some way, someday.

● GEORGE MICHAEL

In 1990, George Michael—formerly of Wham! and a newly minted solo superstar with his blockbuster *Faith* album—released the moody, soulful *Listen Without Prejudice Vol. 1*, which spawned four hit singles. By 1992, Michael had almost finished two new albums, the dance-pop collection *Listen Without Prejudice Vol. 2*, and *Trojan Souls*, which would feature the singer dueting with a different performer on each of its 10 tracks, including Sade, Stevie Wonder, Anita Baker, and Elton John. But 1992 was also the year that Michael sued his label, Sony Records, to get out of what he believed to be an exploitative and unfair contract. He donated three songs intended for *Listen Without Prejudice Vol. 2* for use on the 1992 AIDS awareness benefit compilation *Red Hot + Dance*, while all work on *Trojan Souls* abruptly ended, even though it was about half finished. Michael died in 2016; that album has never been issued.

● BEASTIE BOYS

In the late 2000s, venerable rap-rock trio the Beastie Boys began recording *Hot Sauce Committee*, a proposed two-album saga. In 2009, member Adam Yauch was diagnosed with cancer and took some time off from the group, prompting the other Beastie Boys to delay the release of *Hot Sauce Committee Part 1*. Yauch died in 2012, just a few months after *Hot Sauce Committee Part 2* hit stores. So what happened to *Part 1*? The Beastie Boys literally lost it. "We can't find it. If we find it, we're gonna try to work on it and put it out," Beastie Boy Adam Horovitz said in a 2020 video. It was all recorded to a computer hard drive, which the group misplaced.

Pioneering nurse Florence Nightingale was also a statistician who wrote more than 150 reports.

MY BLOODY VALENTINE

In 1991, the Irish alternative rock band released its second album, *Loveless*, heralded at the time and for years after by music magazines as one of the best albums of the decade—an intricately produced, layered soundscape. It took band leader Kevin Shields 22 years to record the follow-up album *mbv*, and five years after *that*, he told *Sound on Sound* that My Bloody Valentine had lots of music in the works and was planning to release two mini-albums in 2018 and 2019. But then 2018 came and went, with Shields telling reporters that the first record was actually going to be a full-length album instead. Then he changed his mind and said the band would issue two completely new albums in 2019. Those never surfaced either, and in 2021, Shields again said he'd have new records out by the end of the year. As of press time for this book...*mbv* remains the last My Bloody Valentine album released to the public.

THE WEEKND

In March 2018, Canadian pop star the Weeknd released a six-track miniature album called *My Dear Melancholy*. Because it contains a bunch of sad songs about a romance gone wrong, music writers and fans speculated that it was a breakup record, as the Weeknd had written and recorded it quickly, in the weeks after his highly publicized breakup with actress Selena Gomez. He was so upset by the split that he scrapped another album, an up-tempo pop record, that he'd completely finished just before Gomez broke up with him. "Prior to *Melancholy*, I had a whole album written, done, which wasn't melancholy at all because it was a different time in my life," he told *Time*. "It was very upbeat, it was beautiful. I don't want to perform something that I don't feel." He also told the magazine when fans might get to hear it: "Never."

THE DOORS

The Doors were probably the biggest new band of 1967, releasing two albums of radio-friendly psychedelic rock propelled by the vocals of mysterious, charismatic, deep-voiced frontman Jim Morrison. The singer also fancied himself a poet, and when the band was about to head into the studio to record its third album, with no songs composed, the group decided to go with Morrison's idea to account for one whole side of an LP with *A Celebration of the Lizard*, a seven-part odyssey through Morrison's mind in poetic free verse. Producer Paul A. Rothchild fully rejected the poem idea and wouldn't allow the Doors to record it. The band reconvened and recorded a pop album called *Waiting for the Sun* instead, which included one song, "Not to Touch the Earth," based on a part of Morrison's multisectioned poem. (Morrison's books of poetry, published posthumously in 1988 and 1990, became instant best-sellers.)

By law, no building in Canada's Yukon Territory can be taller than 65 feet.

⊙ MC HAMMER

In the early 1990s, MC Hammer was the most famous and successful rapper on earth, responsible for friendly, curse-free hits like "U Can't Touch This" and "2 Legit 2 Quit." As soon as gritty gangsta rap, which aimed to depict the brutal life of gangs and street violence in Los Angeles, came around, MC Hammer was instantly passe. In 1996, Hammer attempted to get with the times and signed with Death Row Records, home of the biggest names in gangsta rap, including Dr. Dre, Snoop Dogg, and 2Pac. MC Hammer recorded an album for Death Row called *Too Tight*, and 2Pac rapped on a few of the songs. But Death Row decided it wasn't good enough to release and kept it in a vault. 2Pac died later that year, and it wasn't until 2016 that one of the songs featuring 2Pac would leave the vault.

⊙ SUDDEN IMPACT

The popular 1980s boy band New Edition split up at the end of the decade as some members (including Bobby Brown and Johnny Gill) embarked on solo careers, leaving the three remaining guys, Ricky Bell, Michael Bivins, and Ronnie DeVoe, to form a new R&B group called Bell Biv DeVoe. Their debut album, *Poison*, and its hit singles, "Poison" and "Do Me," sold so well in 1990 that Capitol Records gave Bivins his own imprint, Biv 10 Records, with a contract to sign three acts. The first two: mega-successful group Boyz II Men and briefly popular kiddie singing group Another Bad Creation. The third: Sudden Impact, a vocal group of five White teenage boys that Bivins thought could compete with New Kids on the Block (a group created by New Edition's estranged manager, Maurice Starr). All of the Biv 10 acts featured prominently in Boyz II Men's first music video, for "Motownphilly," but Sudden Impact never released an album, even after changing their name to Whytgize and singing on the collaborative song "1-4-All-4-1" with a bunch of other acts Bivins was mentoring. But then Biv 10 moved to Motown Records from Capitol Records, taking Whytgize with him, but leaving the music they'd recorded behind—and in limbo for more than 30 years.

* * *

14 CEREALS SEEN ON THE SIMPSONS

- Alfalfa-Bits
- Belfast Charms
- Count Fudge-ula
- Count Branula
- Chocolate Frosted Frosty Krusty Flakes
- Penicill-Os
- Jackie O's
- Stabby-Oh's
- Aerosmith Sweet Emotions
- Toasted Bran Logs
- Bran Cheks
- Branny Charms
- Celtic Charms
- Krusty Charms

Colt 45 malt liquor wasn't named after the gun, but after 1960s Baltimore Colts running back Jerry Hill (who wore #45).

UNCLE JOHN'S PAGE OF LISTS

Top tidbits from our bottomless files.

10 "Thingamajigs" in Other Languages

1. *Watsenaam* (Afrikaans)
2. *Dimsedut* (Danish)
3. *Grunkimojs* (Swedish)
4. *Hilavitkutin* (Finnish)
5. *Bidouillou* (French)
6. *Shtukovina* (Russian)
7. *Mäsmäsak* (Norwegian)
8. *Chisme* (Spanish, Spain)
9. *Chingadera* (Spanish, Mexico)
10. *Veeblefetzer* (Yiddish)

7 Brits Who Played American Superheroes

1. Christian Bale (Batman, *Batman Begins*)
2. Robert Pattinson (Batman, *The Batman*)
3. Andrew Garfield (Spider-Man, *The Amazing Spider-Man*)
4. Tom Holland (Spider-Man, *Captain America: Civil War*)
5. Henry Cavill (Superman, *Man of Steel*)
6. Benedict Cumberbatch (Doctor Strange, *Doctor Strange*)
7. Tom Hardy (Eddie Brock, *Venom*)

10 Smartest Dog Breeds

1. Border collie
2. Poodle
3. German shepherd
4. Golden retriever
5. Doberman pinscher
6. Shetland sheepdog
7. Labrador retriever
8. Papillon
9. Rottweiler
10. Australian cattle dog

Top 10 Polluters (CO_2 released, 2019)

1. China
2. United States
3. India
4. Russia
5. Japan
6. Germany
7. Iran
8. South Korea
9. Saudi Arabia
10. Indonesia

10 Food Phobias

1. Cibophobia: fear of food
2. Acerophobia: fear of sour food
3. Fructophobia: fear of fruit
4. Lachanophobia: fear of vegetables
5. Xocolatophobia: fear of chocolate
6. Dipsophobia: fear of alcohol
7. Mageirocophobia: fear of cooking
8. Phagophobia: fear of swallowing
9. Brumotactillophobia: fear of foods touching each other
10. Consecotaleophobia: fear of chopsticks

8 Movies Written by Women

1. *Halloween* (1978): Debra Hill
2. *E.T. the Extra-Terrestrial* (1982): Melissa Mathison
3. *When Harry Met Sally...* (1989): Nora Ephron
4. *Thelma & Louise* (1991): Callie Khouri
5. *The Piano* (1993): Jane Campion
6. *Lost in Translation* (2003): Sofia Coppola
7. *Juno* (2007): Diablo Cody
8. *Nomadland* (2020): Chloé Zhao

Lawrence Levine's novel *Dr. Awkward & Olson in Oslo* is a 31,594-word palindrome.

LET'S TIME TRAVEL!

All the latest news about traveling into the future or back into the past, delivered to you right now, in the present.

NOAH'S LARK

In 2018, a man identifying himself only as Noah posted a video to YouTube of himself passing a lie detector test when answering questions about who and what he purported to be: a time traveler visiting from the year 2030. With his face and voice digitally obscured over fears of "assassination," he continued to outline life in the not-too-distant future and got passing, "not lying" results from the polygraph. Among his revelations: renewable energy will gain widespread popularity, most Americans will wear virtual-reality goggles all day long, Donald Trump will win a second presidential term in 2020, a woman named Ilana Remikee will succeed Trump in the presidency, and that in 2028, humans will both set foot on Mars and reveal that time travel is real and has secretly been used by the world's governments since 2003. Age-reversing drugs are also widely available in 10 years' time, it would seem, because Noah is really 50 years old but took supplements to appear to be 25.

DESTINATION FUNERAL

Stephen Hawking was among the most important scientists of our time, demystifying heady concepts in books such as *A Brief History of Time* and speaking and writing often on subjects such as black holes and the time-space continuum. When he died at age 76, a public memorial service was scheduled for Westminster Abbey in London on June 15, 2018, at noon. Mourners had to book a seat in advance online, and in providing their personal information were asked to select a birth date from a drop-down menu, which gave options all the way up to 2038. That wasn't an error— Hawking believed that time travel was theoretically possible, and, in 2009, once threw a party for time travelers. Nobody showed up, but just in case time travel had been invented on some other timeline after, he invited such voyagers to his funeral. (None showed up there, either.)

GOTTA SAVE SOMEBODY

In September 2021, Thomas W. Lee stole a Nissan Altima parked outside a pizza parlor in Hempfield, Pennsylvania. Police located the man and vehicle two hours later in the town of Cheswick and gave chase. Lee then led the police on a 100-mile-per-hour chase that spanned 40 miles of the Pennsylvania Turnpike and several more miles of a rural highway before Lee drove over a spike strip and flew over an embankment. Then he

Rule of thumb: if an actor appears in fewer than half of the episodes in a season of a TV show, they're a "guest star."

ran out of the car with police pursuing on foot and finally subduing Lee with a Taser. The suspect ultimately entered a guilty plea to all 24 charges levied against him, but he also offered a Westmoreland County judge a reason for his behavior. At the time of the accident, Lee believed that he was a time traveler on a high-stakes mission. "I stole a car because I was tired of walking," Lee said in court. "I thought I was a time traveler because I was on drugs. I wasn't trying to hurt anyone. I was just trying to save my son." That son, Lee said, had been in the clutches of a corrupt government agency.

TINY TIME TRAVEL

In 2019, researchers from the Laboratory of the Physics of Quantum Information at the Moscow Institute of Physics and Technology reversed the direction of time, at least at a subatomic level. Using a "quantum computer," researchers created a program to agitate quibits, information units made from arranged electrons. When launched, the quibits constantly and consistently changed their pattern of positive and negative charges. All order and the usual laws of physics that would determine how the electrons would move went out the window, and the particles reset themselves to their original positions, essentially going backward in time. "We have artificially created a state that evolves in a direction opposite to that of the thermodynamic arrow of time," lead researcher Dr. Gordey Lesovik told reporters.

FATHER TIME

Dr. Ron Mallett is an accomplished scientist, a physics professor at the University of Connecticut specializing in research into black holes and Albert Einstein's general and special theories of relativity. Those subjects inform his passion project, something he's been working on for decades but didn't speak out about until the 2010s when he attained the rank of tenured professor, insulating himself from termination: Mallett has been trying to prove that time travel is possible, and he's driven by the desire to go back to his childhood in 1950s New York City and see his father again, who died when the future scientist was 10 years old. According to Mallett, it's theoretically possible. "Einstein said that time can be affected by speed," like how when astronauts travel at close to the speed of light, time passes differently for them in the spaceship than it does for people on Earth; they'd return home to a planet where decades had gone by but be only a few years older themselves. Additionally, the stronger a gravitational force, the more it slows down time. Mallett (and Einstein) argue that gravity is really the bending of space. "If you can bend space, there's a possibility of you twisting space," Mallett said, and because space and time are linked, anything that happens to space happens to time. Mallett theorizes the creation of a time tunnel with lasers, with two openings, traveling from the present to the past and then forward to the future again.

Commemorative, non-postage stamps are called "Cinderella stamps" by collectors.

THE NATURAL GAS REPORT

*"Breaking wind," as the British so politely call it, is a natural and inevitable
part of life. So it's not surprising that farts occasionally make the news.*

THE POWER OF A SHOWER

Most people can tolerate the smell of their own farts, except for in one particular
situation: in the shower. One's own farts are seemingly much more intolerable in
there, meaning they just smell way worse. And there's some actual science behind
the phenomenon. Hussein Abda, clinical director of Medicine Direct online, told
reporters that three factors make shower farts smell worse than regular farts. "The first
reason is that you're naked. When you fart while dressed, some of the smell and gas
are absorbed in your clothes," he said, pointing out that nudity offers no obstruction
between farts and nostrils. Secondly, a shower is a small, enclosed area, making the
smell of the fart more intensified. Finally, the steam that's naturally generated from a
shower's hot water opens up the nostrils and makes them more sensitive—particularly
to foul odors.

AFTER ALL, CARS ARE GAS POWERED

In October 2021, Karly Sindy of Asheville, North Carolina, received approval from
the state's Department of Motor Vehicles for her request of personalized license plates
reading "FART." The plates arrived a few weeks later, and she happily affixed them to
her pickup. Then in February 2022, Sindy received a letter from the DMV, informing
her that the office had received numerous complaints about the "FART" plates. If she
wanted to keep them on her truck, the DMV explained, Sindy would have to explain,
in writing, the important personal significance of the word fart. Sensing the need to
make something up, Sindy and some friends fudged an explanation: that FART was
an acronym for the name of their hiking group, Friends of Asheville Recreational
Trails. Then they went ahead and formed the group for real, and created a mailing list
and "FART" T-shirts. The North Carolina DMV let Sindy keep the "FART" plates.

FIRED FOR FARTING

French professional soccer team Olympique Lyonnais, or Lyon, dropped star defender
Marcelo from its top squad in August 2021. At the time, the organization claimed
the sacking came after management was offended by Marcelo laughing during team
captain Léo Dubois's inspirational speech to try to rally players during a losing
game. But nine months later, in May 2022, anonymous sources within the Lyon
organization told ESPN that Marcelo's laughing fit was merely the last straw after a

What are *atomgrad*? "Atomic cities," or company towns in
Cold War–era Eastern Europe set up to run nuclear power plants.

string of incidents. In the months leading up to his dismissal, he'd been cited and punished multiple times for farting on or near his teammates in their locker room.

DON'T FART SO HARD...

Dr. Anthony Youn is a plastic surgeon who made himself a star on the social network TikTok with videos responding to viewers' strange medical questions. After a follower posted a clip claiming to have once farted with such intensity that they "went blind for three minutes," Dr. Youn explained that it is actually possible for a human being to fart so hard that they're rendered permanently without sight. "Although this is very unlikely, if the gas you pass is extremely pungent, it could contain large amounts of hydrogen sulfide," Dr. Youn said. "Studies show that hydrogen sulfide is very effective in reducing blood pressure. And if it reduces blood pressure to the central retinal artery, your silent but deadly toot could theoretically make you go blind."

...BUT DON'T HOLD THEM IN, EITHER

According to a TikTok video she posted, a 19-year-old from County Louth, Ireland, named Cara Clarke experienced stomach pain so severe while working her barista job that she visited her doctor, who immediately referred her to a hospital. "I was limping when I was walking all hunched over," Clarke told reporters. Blood tests indicated that Clarke's appendix had burst, and she underwent corrective surgery. However, after speaking with Clarke for a while, doctors realized what had caused the great disturbance in the patient's insides that triggered the appendicitis: she refuses to fart while in the presence of her boyfriend of two years. "I do hold in my farts but I didn't think I would be in hospital over it," Clarke said.

PUT A LID ON IT

Stephanie Matto first found fame as a cast member on the reality TV show *90 Day Fiancé*. When the show ended, Matto parlayed her fame into a business selling jars containing her farts via her social media channels. She uses those platforms, such as Instagram and TikTok, to post videos about her fart-selling business, and what she eats to make sure she can fart enough to meet demand (beans, protein-loaded muffins, yogurt, and hard-boiled eggs). In just a few weeks, Matto sold $200,000 worth of fart jars (200 at $1,000 each). "I think my main motivation was money, but I also thought it'd be a hilarious publicity move that would get a lot of people's attention," Matto told reporters. Within weeks, however, all that income was largely eaten up by medical bills. Doctors say she ate so much protein to up her farting potential that she triggered heart palpitations, which landed her in the emergency room. Matto stopped selling the fart jars at that point.

Highest civilian honorific given out in Nebraska, a landlocked state: Admiral in the Great Navy of the State of Nebraska.

CELEBRITY UTTERANCES

Random thoughts from famous folks.

"I think I'm a tiny bit like Harry 'cos I'd like to have an owl. Yeah. that's the tiny bit actually."
—Daniel Radcliffe

"I wish I could trade my heart for another liver so I could drink more and care less."
—Tina Fey

"One of my goals in life is to have the biggest residential pool on the planet."
—Drake

"If my life wasn't funny, it would just be true, and that's unacceptable."
—Carrie Fisher

"MY THING IS THIS; IF I'M SICK ENOUGH TO THINK IT, THEN I'M SICK ENOUGH TO SAY IT."
—Eminem

"I try not to be but I'm super neurotic about diet. I'm neurotic about trying not to be neurotic!"
—Gwen Stefani

"Now I usually try not to give advice. Information, yes, advice, no. But what has worked for me may not work for you. Well, take for instance what has worked for me. Wigs. Tight clothes. Push-up bras."
—Dolly Parton

"In every circle of friends there's always that one person everyone secretly hates. Don't have one? Then it's probably you."
—Will Ferrell

"I really don't think I need buns of steel. I'd be happy with buns of cinnamon."
—Ellen DeGeneres

"I like changing diapers. There's a beginning, middle, and an end, so I feel accomplished."
—Seth Meyers

THESE ARE SPINAL TAP

Every other list about This Is Spinal Tap *goes to 11.*
That's why ours is the best: it goes to 12!

BACKGROUND

This Is Spinal Tap, released in 1984, wasn't the first rock 'n' roll "mockumentary." But it has since become the movie that defines the entire genre. Directed and cowritten by comedy legend Rob Reiner (*The Princess Bride*, *When Harry Met Sally...*), Reiner also stars as the director of a documentary about a British heavy metal band attempting a comeback tour. Americans Christopher Guest, Michael McKean, and Harry Shearer (all comedy legends in their own right) star as the band and also cowrote the movie, which still lands on virtually every "Funniest Movies of All-time" list. The original idea for *Spinal Tap* was Guest's, and it launched his mockumentary career (*Waiting for Guffman*, *Best in Show*). But the movie wasn't a hit right out of the gate. How come? At first, people didn't really get it: as absurd as some of the movie's scenes are, they're similar enough to mishaps experienced by real-life rock stars that viewers didn't know the movie was a spoof.

"Everybody thought it was a real band," recalled Reiner. The movie *really* confused actual rock stars. When guitar god Eddie Van Halen saw *Spinal Tap* in the theater, he didn't laugh once, nor did he understand why other people were laughing (or why someone would make a documentary about a band no one's ever heard of). When U2's guitarist, the Edge, saw it, not only did he not laugh, "I wept. I wept because I recognized so much and so many of those scenes"—scenes such as the band members getting lost on their way to the concert stage, embarrassing prop malfunctions, and ludicrous arguments between bandmates. The scene that really struck a pop-culture chord: lead guitarist Nigel Tufnel (Guest) bragging about how all the control knobs on his custom-made amplifier "go to eleven." Why? So the sound will be "one louder" than ten.

Here are 12 real-life rock-star stories that sound like they could easily be straight out of *Spinal Tap*.

1. YES AND THE GIANT SEASHELL

In 1974, the British progressive rock band Yes was touring for the album *Tales from Topographic Oceans*. The elaborate stage set was a re-creation of the fantasy album cover created by longtime Yes collaborator Roger Dean. As keyboardist Rick Wakeman recounted in his book, *Grumpy Old Rock Star*, these shows were so elaborate that, "Sometimes I needed directions just to get to my keyboards. 'Take a left here, Rick,

Algae, moths, insects, and fungi all grow in sloth hair.

climb over that giant mushroom, past the spaceship and just behind, beyond that cloud, are your keyboards.'" At least he didn't have to play from inside a giant seashell. That task went to drummer Alan White. At the start of every show, the clam would open to dramatically reveal White playing the drums. Well...not *every* show. One night, the shell jammed. And it was airtight. Wakeman continues:

> As this was live on stage in front of thousands of people, Alan, the consummate professional, continued playing. Meanwhile the roadies began trying to smash the pod open, staying out of the line of sight of the crowd... Before long, they had to start pumping oxygen in until eventually, somehow, they prised the wretched thing open with pickaxes. By now the audience must have noticed the rescue effort because as the pod sprang open a huge cheer went up, and Alan stumbled out gasping for breath.

It's suspected (but not confirmed) that this incident inspired the *Spinal Tap* scene where bass player Derek Smalls (Shearer) is supposed to emerge from a translucent "alien pod" after his bandmates emerge from theirs, but his gets stuck closed and he has to play—awkwardly—from inside it.

2. U2 AND THE GIANT LEMON

You can't help but wonder if U2 was intentionally trying to create its own Spinal Tap moment(s) on the 1997 PopMart tour—which included the largest video screen ever built for a concert (170 feet by 50 feet); a giant, golden arch that made the stage look like a sci-fi McDonald's; and the hokey costumes donned by the once-gritty Irish band, especially Bono's infamous "muscleman" T-shirt. The grandest spectacle of all came before the encore song, "Lemon," when the band descended to the stage inside a 40-foot-tall lemon-shaped mirror ball. After "landing" like an alien ship (cue the dry ice), the top half of the lemon lifted to reveal the band members...except when it didn't. One night, in front of 40,000 fans in Oslo, Norway, the lemon got jammed and the band just stood there inside it while the backing track played and the roadies spent the entire song struggling to get the pod open. In Las Vegas, the roadies couldn't open the lemon at all and had to wheel U2 off the stage. At a few other shows, it opened only partway. Toward the end of the tour, drummer Larry Mullen Jr. refused to get in the lemon and instead went straight to his kit.

3. BELLE AND SEBASTIAN AND THE SYDNEY OPERA HOUSE

Another reason a lot of rock stars initially thought *This Is Spinal Tap* was a true story: they all had their own tales of getting lost on the way to the stage. Lead singer Stuart Murdoch of the Scottish indie-pop band Belle and Sebastian told his tale to the music magazine *NME*:

First and only rock band to play *The Lawrence Welk Show*: the Chantays (1963).

I have a cordless microphone and during the song "If You Find Yourself Caught in Love"...there was an instrumental passage and I would disappear off the stage with my microphone. The idea was that I would pop back somewhere in the auditorium. Like we were playing Sydney Opera House, I would run in the back steps and suddenly at the end of the instrumental they would put a spotlight on me and I would be on the third balcony, or something, and fans would be like, "Oh you're standing right there." But I went the wrong way and I ended up in a shopping center.

4. MUSE AND THE DRONES

Muse lead singer Matthew Bellamy is a big fan of unmanned aerial vehicles—aka drones—just not for their use in warfare. As he complained in his British band's 2015 hit song "Drones," "You can kill from the safety of your home with drones." Bellamy prefers to race them (he's invested money in the Drone Racing League). In 2016, he brought some along for the band's Drones World Tour...

The first mishap occurred in Detroit. Twelve spherical drones—each taller than a person, made of clear plastic, and filled with helium—were gracefully flying in formation around the arena...until three of the drones inexplicably lost their lift and gently fell onto the crowd. No one was injured, but a video of the slow-motion accident went viral. At a concert in London, Muse flew a massive, blimp-shaped drone during the song "The Globalist." The blimp was supposed to fly a full circle around the arena but barely made it halfway around before lazily falling onto several rows of concertgoers. Again, no one was injured. At three other shows, the tech crew couldn't even fly the drones for various bureaucratic and logistical reasons. Muse's next tour was drone free.

5. GENESIS AND THE SPEAKER CABINETS

"This happened to me at an open-air gig in Sardinia," reminisced Genesis guitarist Steve Hackett, referring to the scene in *This Is Spinal Tap* when Nigel leans so far back while playing a guitar solo that he falls onto his back, and continues to "shred" while roadies awkwardly pick him up. Just like Nigel, Hackett said, "I moved backwards, fell over and got wedged between two speaker cabinets with my legs in the air like a dead fly, pinned down by a very heavy Les Paul. I was aided to my feet by the road crew, who of course loved it. It was immediately dubbed a *Tap* Moment."

6. THE FIGHTING STONES

Life in a band often leads to short tempers, as depicted in the *Spinal Tap* scene where a botched recording session becomes a profanity-laced shouting match. When the

Four chemical elements are named after Ytterby, Sweden (population: 3,000): yttrium, terbium, erbium, and ytterbium.

Rolling Stones were on tour in Amsterdam in 1984, tensions were that high. As Keith Richards recounted in his 2010 autobiography, *Life*, lead singer Mick Jagger had let superstardom go to his head. At around 5:00 one morning, after drinking in a bar all night, Richards and Jagger returned to their hotel room and Jagger slurred that he wanted to speak to Stones drummer Charlie Watts, who was sleeping in an adjacent room. After a few rings, the phone picked up and Jagger blurted out, "Where's my drummer?" No reply. Jagger hung up.

A few minutes later, Watts (who Richards explained was usually an even-tempered man) knocked on the door. Dressed to the nines in a tailored suit, Watts walked past Richards and right up to Jagger and said, "Never call me your drummer again." Then Watts planted a right hook on Jagger's mouth. "Mick fell back onto a silver platter of smoked salmon on the table and began to slide towards the open window and the canal below it," wrote Richards. Fortunately, he was able to catch the Rolling Stone before he slid through the window.

7. THE BEATLE AND WHITESNAKE

The 1979 36th birthday party for George Harrison, the "quiet Beatle," got a bit awkward—mainly because it was hosted by his next-door neighbor Jon Lord, keyboardist for the British heavy metal band Whitesnake. There was also rock's first female roadie, Tana Douglas, who loaded instruments for everyone from AC/DC to the Go-Go's. She wrote about the party in her 2021 memoir, *Loud*.

The festivities grew more raucous, then a naked woman jumped out of a cake and started dancing erotically to the Beatles' early hit song "She Loves You." Harrison (who preferred gardening to partying) had had enough: he retreated to the kitchen and struck up a conversation with Douglas, the only woman at the party who *wasn't* a stripper. As she lit another cigarette, he said to her: "I would marry you tomorrow if you gave up smoking." But Douglas didn't want to quit, and Harrison was already married.

8. SUZI QUATRO AND THE PAPARAZZI

In Spinal Tap's (fictional) heyday, they were one of rock's most successful touring acts. But at the time of the movie's events, the band is in a hotel lobby when a throng of female fans ignore them and run over to a younger heavy metal band. Suzi Quatro can relate. The Michigan-born singer ("Can the Can," "Your Mama Won't Like Me") has sold 50 million albums over her 40-year career. Even though Quatro gained a much larger following in the U.K. and Australia than in North America, she also gained lifetime pop-culture cred thanks to her recurring role as Leather Tuscadero on the 1970s sitcom *Happy Days*. Recalling her own *Spinal Tap* moment, Quatro said, "I went out for dinner one night in L.A., and there were lots of photographers there. I

On two occasions, the Nasdaq stock exchange was shut down
when squirrels chewed through power lines.

assumed they were going to take my picture, but they didn't. I had a bit to drink and got rather annoyed. On the way out I shouted, 'Do you know who you just missed?' A photographer shouted, 'Yes, Suzi, we do.' I nearly died."

9. BLACK SABBATH AND STONEHENGE

"And oh how they danced, the little children of Stonehenge," narrates Nigel into his microphone as a comically small replica of the ancient monument is lowered to the stage. It's one of *This Is Spinal Tap*'s most enduring gags: the band wanted an 18-*foot*-long replica, but their crude drawing said 18" (inches), not 18' (feet). So instead of a life-size ancient monument, the crew built them a prop that was "in danger of being crushed by a dwarf." The blunder is reminiscent of British heavy metal band Black Sabbath and their mistaken instructions with the opposite effect. In 1983, the year before *This Is Spinal Tap* was released, Sabbath—by coincidence—wanted a Stonehenge replica for their stage's set. Bass player Geezer Butler "thought it was really corny." And he later recalled,

> We had Sharon Osbourne's dad, Don Arden, managing us. He came up with having the stage set be Stonehenge. He wrote the dimensions down and gave it to our tour manager. He wrote it down in meters, but meant to write it down in feet. The people who made it saw 15m instead of 15ft. It was 45-feet high and it wouldn't fit on any stage anywhere so we just had to leave it in the storage area. It cost a fortune to make, but there was not a building on earth that you could fit it into.

(It should come as no surprise that Black Sabbath's antics heavily inspired *Spinal Tap*.)

10. KEITH MOON AND MAE WEST

We could have easily found a dozen *Tap*-esque Keith Moon stories to fill this article. The Who's unpredictable drummer once drove a Lincoln Continental into a hotel swimming pool. He played disturbing jokes like spending almost a week in uniform (and in character) as a Nazi. And he passed out on stage more than once. Moon was also quite the ladies' man. In 2021, heavy-metal/glam pioneer Alice Cooper dished out this gossip about Moon and one of Hollywood's original starlets. It was 1977:

> Mae West and I did this movie called *Sextet*. She did this play in 1925 and was put in jail for it. It was too racy…So now she wants to redo it and the cast is Ringo [Starr], Keith Moon…and I played an Italian waiter who does a song with her. We are all having lunch one day and I said, "Guys, this is weird. I got done with the song and she whispered in my ear, 'Why don't you come on back to my trailer?'" And I'm going, "Well, because you're 86 and I'm not sure if you're a woman." She said, "Oh, I'm all woman." Everybody said, "She came onto me, too." We all went

New Zealand's official languages are te reo Maori and New Zealand Sign Language, though 90 percent of residents speak English.

around the table and it got to Keith Moon and we all looked at him and went, "No." And he says, "Well, how many chances do you get to be with Mae West?"

A year later, Moon died from an overdose of a drug prescribed to treat alcoholism. Perhaps he would have preferred to go out like any of Spinal Tap's ill-fated drummers—including John "Stumpy" Pepys, who died in a "bizarre gardening accident"; Eric "Stumpy Joe" Childs, who "choked on vomit of unknown origin"; Peter "James" Bond, who spontaneously combusted on stage; and Mick Shrimpton, who also exploded on stage.

11. BILLY IDOL AND THE THAI MILITARY

Did Spinal Tap ever smash up a hotel room? Not in the movie, but considering their heyday was the early 1970s—when rock stars turned trashing hotel rooms into an art—it's safe to assume that, at the very least, Spinal Tap upset some hotel maids. In 1989, Billy Idol upset an entire country. The snarling British punk rocker ("White Wedding," "Dancing with Myself") threw a three-week-long party in a luxury penthouse in Bangkok, Thailand. After he refused to vacate the room, the situation went full Spinal Tap when the Thai military arrived and shot Idol with a tranquilizer dart. He was removed from the hotel on a stretcher and put on a plane out of Thailand. When Idol sobered up, he was presented with a bill for $250,000 for room fees and damages. "I was very lucky," he said. "I expect they could've put me in prison."

12. WHERE'S YOUR BASS?

In 1974, a British rock 'n' roll band (identity lost to history) was checking into a Los Angeles hotel with their manager, who said to the bass player, "Where's your bass?" The bass player looked around, stammered, and said (in a dopey British accent), "What?" The manager asked again: "Where's your bass?" "I dunno. I fink I left it at de airport." "You *what!?*" "I dunno." "You left your bass at the airport?" "I dunno. Where is it?" "I don't know! I'm asking you!" "I dunno." This went on for about 15 minutes.

Across the hotel lobby was 26-year-old Christopher Guest, who was waiting for a friend. The up-and-coming comedian watched the entire scene unfold with glee. That was the moment Spinal Tap was born. "I don't think I've ever been happier," said Guest, "except for the night I met my wife." (Fun fact: Guest has been married to Jamie Lee Curtis since 1984, the year *This Is Spinal Tap* was released.)

* * *

"There was a knock on our dressing-room door. Our manager shouted, 'Keith! Ron! The Police are here!' Oh, man, we panicked, flushed everything down the john. Then the door opened and it was Stewart Copeland and Sting."

—**Keith Richards**

More champagne is consumed in France each year than in the rest of the world combined.

ROBOTS IN THE NEWS

Get up to speed now on the exciting developments in the world of robots...before they rise up and take over the planet.

ROBOT GOATS

Real goats aren't really riding animals, but Kawasaki has created the world's first robotic goat designed with a human passenger in mind. Debuting at the 2022 International Robot Exhibition in Tokyo, Bex (named after the Middle Eastern goat known as the ibex) resembles a goat—if a goat had skin that was gleaming white, an emergency shut-off switch, robotic legs with wheels on the bottom, and useless metal horns. Bex is covered in flashing lights and can fold its legs in half to make itself shorter for easier mounting and dismounting, and foot-pegs also help keep the rider in place. The rider controls Bex's actions through a button-covered handlebar near the goat's neck.

JUMPING ROBOT PENGUINS

Penguins can't fly, and neither can penguin robots, which were developed by Japanese electronics giant Ricoh just to set an obscure and specific Guinness World Record. Real penguins can't really jump, either, but Ricoh's Penta-X can: the robot is made from five modified penguin stuffed animals that work in tandem as a single unit and can hop a few inches into the air. In 2022, Penta-X set the record for most times jumping rope in one minute—an impressive 170 hops.

ROBOT HOUSEKEEPER NO MORE

A Travelodge in Orchard Park, Cambridge, England, makes use of an automatic robotic vacuum cleaner to keep its public areas tidy. The robot vacuum apparently tired of the tedious job in January 2022, because it took off. Programmed to stop at the hotel's front door and return to its base and charging unit, the robot instead just kept going, down the street, to parts unknown. Staff didn't notice it was gone for at least 15 minutes, and after searching the surrounding area, put up a "missing" notice on the hotel's social media accounts. A passerby found the vacuum under a bush.

ROBOT PRIEST

A 6'4" tall, 132-pound Buddhist priest named Mindar presides over the mountainside Kodai-ji Temple in Kyoto, Japan. Adherents believe Mindar to be the earthly embodiment of Kannon, the Buddhist mercy goddess, as well as the Buddha himself. Also, Mindar is a robot, a humanoid with smooth silicone skin, bones made of aluminum, and cameras for eyes. He makes hand gestures to emphasize points in his sermons on Buddhist scripture and teachings. The Kodai-ji Temple and the Department of Systems Innovation at Osaka University teamed up in 2019 to create Mindar, with

World record for fastest 100-meter run in high heels: 13.557 seconds.

the goal of reversing decreasing numbers of Buddhists in Japan by engaging the interest of younger people. Mindar cost $1 million to develop. "I often experience mood swings, taking care of my elderly mother. Mindar's sermons on the Heart Sutra help me control my emotions and bring salvation," temple-goer Miyuki Tanaka told reporters.

ROBOT DEFENSE BASS

In 2018, scientists at the University of Western Australia built robot fish programmed specifically to scare away the *gambusia*, or mosquitofish, one of the most insidious invasive species in the world, and one that's threatening fish, frogs, and tadpoles native to Australian waters. Researchers conducted field research on the robot—built to resemble the mosquitofish's chief natural predator, the largemouth bass, in both appearance and behavior—by placing it in freshwater bodies around western Australia; four years later, they published their results. In short, the robot fish were very effective. "We made their worst nightmare become real: a robot that scares the mosquitofish but not the other animals around it," Dr. Giovanni Polverino told reporters, citing how the robot's presence affected the behavior and fertility levels of the gambusia, more or less "scaring it to death." The researchers believe such fake predatorial robots could repel invasive species of all kinds in various habitats around the world.

ROBOT FLOSSERS

Two programs at the University of Pennsylvania—the School of Dental Medicine and School of Engineering and Applied Science—developed sophisticated shapeshifting miniature-robot technology that researchers think could one day completely eradicate the bacteria that cause mouth plaque and tooth decay. Iron oxide nanoparticles activated by a magnetic field can form into bristles that comb away plaque from surfaces or collect as strings that go between teeth like floss. A catalytic reaction then makes the particles push out antimicrobial substances that kill bacteria. "You have to brush your teeth, then floss your teeth, then rinse your mouth; it's a manual, multistep process," said Hyun Koo, professor at the School of Dental Medicine. "The big innovation here is that the robotics system can do all three in a single, hands-free, automated way."

ROBOT RESCUE FIREFLIES

In 2022, roboticists at the Massachusetts Institute of Technology built soft-tissue robots made to resemble fireflies. That tissue is used to make muscles that control the tiny robots' wings, allowing them to fly and emit multicolored lights. Mimicking the size and activity of fireflies, the robotics similarly use luminescence as a communication tool. MIT scientists think their robotic fireflies could be used to communicate with one another quickly and wirelessly using coded light signals, a useful tool in search-and-rescue missions inaccessible by other, larger, robots.

In recorded history, 600 polar bears have surfaced on the beaches of Iceland.

HELP WANTED: WOMBAT CUDDLER

*Ever seen those videos of biologists wearing (unconvincing) panda costumes
to interact with real pandas? (Had Uncle John known this was a viable
profession, he might never have gone into book publishing.) Perhaps you'd
like to try your hand at one of these weird—but real—animal jobs.*

BABY ELEPHANT BUNKMATE

The David Sheldrick Wildlife Trust Elephant Nursery is located in Nairobi National Park, Kenya, and their work is crucial to the survival of critically endangered African elephants. "Being orphaned is a profoundly traumatic event, both physically and psychologically," reads the Trust's website. "Our rescue teams are equipped with milk, stretchers to carry the orphan, and vital medicines." Once these 250-pound babies arrive at the nursery, they get personalized care. That includes staffers playing with the elephants, massaging their trunks (to clear their noses), and bottle-feeding. And this is a 24-hour job: "Keepers give each orphan the tailored care they need throughout the night. In fact, each stable has a bunk for a keeper to sleep in, ensuring the orphans don't ever lack for company or comfort."

LION FOOT MASSEUSE

For more than 20 years, Alex Larenty has worked at the Lion Park, located just outside of Johannesburg, South Africa. Having raised many of the safari park's big cats from kittenhood, Larenty enjoys a special bond with them. Here, he explains how he gained the trust of a lion cub named Jamu by applying insect repellant to the lion's feet. "He eventually realized he liked being scratched and tickled." Now weighing 550 pounds, Jamu's "favorite game is This Little Piggy. He loves it." The game goes like this: Whenever Larenty approaches the pride, Jamu and the other lions flop onto their backs and stick their paws up in the air. One by one, Larenty gives them foot massages.

COW STRIPES PAINTER

Zebras' stripes have long baffled biologists. Some theories about the stripes' purpose: to deter predators by making it difficult to distinguish between members of a running

Each ring of Saturn has its own atmosphere, and each is made up mostly of oxygen.

herd, to regulate body temperature, or to provide camouflage in dappled sunlight. In 2019, Japanese researchers released the results of a study that could finally solve this mystery...and it's none of the above. They painted white vertical lines onto Japanese Black cows and observed them against a control group of unpainted cows. Results: the striped cows received 50 percent fewer bites from biting flies. Why? "Flies are less likely to land on black and white surfaces due to the polarization of light, which impairs their perception." The ramifications could be huge, as these voracious insects wreak havoc by causing emotional and physical distress to livestock, and financial distress for farmers— biting flies cost the beef and dairy industry $2 billion per year. More research is needed, but if it's proven that stripes do indeed repel insects, that could lead to fewer pesticides and happier cows...and a new job market for cow stripe painters.

FALCON SEX HAT WEARER

"The imprinted males were extremely easy to work with," explains falconer Les Boyd, inventor of the falcon sex hat. Boyd has been involved in bird conservation since the 1970s, back when the peregrine falcon was in danger of going extinct due to heavy use of the pesticide DDT. Captive breeding wasn't working because the captive-born males wouldn't copulate with females. Why not? When a baby bird is born, it imprints upon the first thing it sees and instinctively knows it will be raised by that thing. Then it will instinctively mate with that same species. But Boyd's birds imprinted on *him*...and some later tried to "do it" with him, sometimes on his arm, sometimes on his head (which was both painful and gross). Solution: Boyd fashioned a porous rubber hat—with a tight chin strap to keep it in place—that serves as both a sperm collector and cranial protector. But the hat alone isn't enough. "Learning to mimic the falcon's vocalizations is the most direct approach in accomplishing cooperative artificial insemination," he says. In addition to screeching like a female falcon, he arches his back and lowers his neck, imitating the falcon mating dance until the male raptor flies onto his head and does the deed. Then Boyd collects the sperm and inseminates a female. His invention has helped save the no-longer-endangered peregrine falcon. Today, there are safer collecting methods, but insemination hats, as they're technically called, have been crucial in keeping several raptor species from going the way of the dodo.

SNAKEBITE RECEIVER

Tim Friede has been collecting deadly snakes since he was a teenager in his native Wisconsin. Now in his 50s, Friede has been bitten more than 200 times by rattlesnakes, cobras, mambas, and other highly venomous snakes...on purpose.

"The Good Ship Lollipop" Shirley Temple sang about was a plane, not a boat.

He says he's not trying to be a "tough guy." His mission is to create a universal antivenin—an antitoxin used to counteract the effects of venom—and the antibodies in his blood could be the key to success. At first, he started experimenting purely for self-preservation. Then he nearly died in 2001 after he was bitten by two cobras in the space of an hour. "I had enough immunity for one bite, but not for two. I completely screwed up," Friede told *National Geographic UK* in 2022. After emerging from a four-day coma, he had a choice to make: quit tempting fate, or do this the right way. He chose the latter and pressed on.

While making ends meet as a truck mechanic, Friede posted videos of his self-inflicted snakebites on his popular (and controversial) YouTube channel. One video shows him getting bitten by a taipan after he was bitten by a mamba. How much does that hurt? "Like a bee sting times a hundred." In 2017, an immunologist named Jacob Glanville found Friede online and invited him to work at Centivax, a California vaccination company. Friede, whose title is Director of Herpetology, receives venom via injection after it's been milked and diluted. He's done this over 700 times and vows not to quit until they crack the code for a universal antivenin—crucial because snakes are responsible for up to 138,000 deaths annually. At last report, Friede and Glanville had successfully tested a universal antivenin on mice, and human trials were just a few years away. "I want to take the worst snakes on the planet and beat them," said Friede.

CHIEF WOMBAT CUDDLER

In what ABC News said "may be the best job opening in the world," a contest was held by Tourism Tasmania in 2016. The winner (who had to be over 21 and live in Australia) would receive the title Chief Wombat Cuddler and then have to "work" for three days cuddling with Derek the wombat at Kate Mooney's wildlife rehabilitation center. Known as the "Wombat Lady of Flinders Island," Mooney has rehabilitated more than 100 of these four-legged marsupials that can weigh up to 70 pounds. Derek was an especially sad case that caught the attention of Australians after his mother was hit by a car while he was in her pouch. He survived but was left orphaned and needed constant care that required someone to, as the contest rules said, "smother our little friend with affection." Applicants had to write in 25 words or less why they would be the best person for the job. The winner: Justin Johnstone of Melbourne. He said afterward that he and the wombat hit it off, but that Derek is "a bit of a tear-away and he likes to chew things."

* * *

"With all the classes they offer at school, how come they don't have one for common sense?"
—Gabriel Iglesias

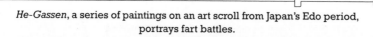

He-Gassen, a series of paintings on an art scroll from Japan's Edo period, portrays fart battles.

AUDIO TREASURES

How many times have you found yourself in a music store, or staring at Spotify or Apple Music, and wondering what's worth checking out? It happens to us all the time—so we decided to offer a few recommendations. They're not necessarily weird or obscure...just good.

Album: Elizabeth Cotten, *Folksongs and Instrumentals with Guitar* (1958)

Genre: Blues/Folk

Review: "Elizabeth Cotten has created beautiful, timeless music, been profoundly influential [on] countless artists, and even created her own guitar style...Much like the better-known guitar virtuoso, Jimi Hendrix, Cotten was [a] left-handed guitarist who played a righty guitar. She would pluck the melody with her thumb while picking the rhythm with her fingers, a style which became known as 'Cotten Picking.' This music is unbelievably raw and soulful." (Sputnik Music)

Album: The Turtles, *The Turtles Present the Battle of the Bands* (1968)

Genre: Pop/Rock

Review: "The Turtles pretend to be a different band on each track, mocking soul combos, psych groups, corny C&W pickers, surf bands, jazz fusionists, Booker T. & the M.G.'s, errr 'world music'? and themselves." (*33 1/3 Revolutions Per Minute: A Critical Trip Through the Rock LP Era 1955–1999*)

Album: The Flying Burrito Brothers, *The Gilded Palace of Sin* (1969)

Genre: Country

Review: "Gram Parsons invented 'country rock,' a utopia where the working folks back on his daddy's Florida orange plantation split a beer with the hippie aristocracy. Featuring an Aretha Franklin cover, an anti-Vietnam ditty, and a mess of Buck Owens twang, *Gilded Palace* was *Easy Rider* in reverse, a vision of America where rednecks and Deadheads sing the same song." (Spin Alternative Record Guide)

Album: Mort Garson, *Mother Earth's Plantasia* (1976)

Genre: Electronic

Review: "If you purchased a snake plant, asparagus fern, peace lily, or what have you from Mother Earth on Melrose Avenue in Los Angeles (or bought a Simmons mattress from Sears), you also took home *Plantasia*, an album recorded especially for plants...It was full of bucolic, charming, stoner-friendly, decidedly unscientific tunes enacted on the new-fangled device called the Moog. Plants date back to the dawn of

The last surviving American Revolution soldier, Nicholas Veeder, died in 1862, during the Civil War.

time, but apparently, they loved the Moog, never mind that the synthesizer had been on the market for just a few years." (Sacred Bones Records)

Album: Dennis Wilson, *Pacific Ocean Blue* (1977)
Genre: Rock
Review: "[Wilson]'s increasingly emotional and epic contributions to the Beach Boys' albums in the late '60s and '70s showed that perhaps big brother Brian wasn't the only genius in the group. *Pacific Ocean Blue* allowed Dennis to bare his soul magnificently. The songs were given expansive, dreamy settings in delicately complex arrangements, taking in orchestral and choral passages. The spirit that Dennis brought to the Beach Boys comes shining through, especially on some of the vocal codas, which recall the band at their best." (*Mojo*)

Album: Sparks, *No. 1 in Heaven* (1979)
Genre: Synth-pop
Review: "This record is an amazing blend of frantic rock and Germanic disco that pushes beyond both idioms and into a state of pop-flash and fantasy that leaves one breathless. Every cut sizzles your head and your feet at once." (*Hit Parader*)

Album: Cocteau Twins, *Heaven or Las Vegas* (1990)
Genre: Alternative rock
Review: "Behind its icy exterior lies the album's beating heart—a core of ungodly gorgeous songs...Elizabeth Fraser's vocal performance...is strikingly nuanced, imbuing the record's haunting melodies with an entirely unique and entrancing character. The songs themselves are remarkably complex, weaving crisp electronic beats, monolithic synthesizers, effects-laden guitar, and Fraser's stately and angelic voice into a seamless sonic velour." (*Pitchfork*)

Album: That Dog, *Retreat from the Sun* (1997)
Genre: Alternative rock
Review: "Driven by Tony Maxwell's power drumming and Anna Waronker's own guitar, *Retreat from the Sun* leaps from big-hair solos to arty noodling in a single bound. Throw in Petra Haden's mournful violin and Waronker's lush piano, and *Retreat*'s jauntily soul-searching sound reflects the emotional content of Waronker's musings entirely." (*Rolling Stone*)

* * *

"My plumbing is all screwed up. Because it turns out, I do not own a garbage disposal."

—Demetri Martin

Tiniest chameleon ever found: 21.66 millimeters.

IT'S KIND OF OUR TRADEMARK

Sometimes a product becomes so ubiquitous that we wind up referring to all similar products by that brand name—how any tissue is a "Kleenex," or all gelatin can be "Jell-O." That use is called a generalized trademark. Here are some other commonly used words that started off as specific, branded product names.

Item: Escalator
Story: Invented, patented, and introduced in 1897 by the Otis Elevator Company.
Generic non-branded name: Moving staircase

Item: Highlighter
Story: A yellow-ink felt-tip pen created by Carter's Ink Company in 1963 as a study aide and a way to "highlight" pertinent parts of books or documents.
Generic non-branded name: Felt-tip writing device

Item: Kitty Litter
Story: A mixture of fine-grain sand used to absorb cat waste, Ed Lowe coined the term in 1947 and used it to start the company that makes Tidy Cat.
Generic non-branded name: Cat litter

Item: Scotch tape
Story: That's the product name of transparent, lightly sticky tape with all kinds of home and office uses, introduced by 3M in 1930.
Generic non-branded name: Transparent adhesive tape

Item: Granola
Story: The trademark lapsed decades ago and so other manufacturers can use it, but the word was invented by the Kellogg's company to sell its toasted, sweetened cereal made from a mixture of whole grains ("grains" being the root of *granola*).
Generic non-branded name: Whole grain cereal

Item: Mace
Story: In 1965, Allan Lee Litman registered the trademark Chemical Mace for his product, which offered self-defense in a spray can. Popularly marketed to women who lived in unsafe areas, *mace* is now used as an umbrella term to encompass a variety of similar products.
Generic non-branded name: Aerosol self-defense spray

Item: Ping-Pong
Story: Based on the sound the lightweight ball makes when hit by a paddle and onto the playing surface, Ping-Pong was the trademarked name of a version marketed by the J. Jacques & Son company of the U.K. in 1901. It later sold the trademark to game maker Parker Brothers, who aggressively enforced the trademark, forcing other companies to use a broader name for the game and its equipment.
Generic non-branded name: Table tennis

Item: Seeing Eye dogs
Story: Only dogs that train to be

Vincent Price was paid $20,000 for his spoken-word performance on Michael Jackson's "Thriller," turning down a portion of album profits.

assistance animals to blind humans at the Seeing Eye, Inc. facility in Morristown, New Jersey, can officially be called "Seeing Eye dogs."
Generic non-branded name: Guide dogs

Item: Dry ice
Story: The Dry Ice Corporation received a trademark for its signature product, an alternative, portable chemical refrigerant for food and medicine, in 1925, and it expired in 1989.
Generic non-branded name: Solid carbon dioxide

Item: Tater Tots
Story: Frozen potato product processor and distributor Ore-Ida invented the Tater Tot—a bite-sized cylinder of formed-and-fried potato shreds.
Generic non-branded name: Potato puffs

Item: Laundromat
Story: The trademark expired decades ago, but in the 1940s and 1950s, appliance maker Westinghouse secured the word *Laundromat* to refer to places full of coin-operated washing machines and dryers.
Generic non-branded name: Coin laundry

Item: Baggies
Story: Small plastic sandwich bags are made by many companies, including Reynolds Group Holdings, a subsidiary of the Pactiv Corporation. Only Reynolds can legally put *Baggies* on their packaging.
Generic non-branded name: Plastic sandwich bags

Item: Muzak
Story: The word used for smooth instrumental music heard in lobbies, in elevators, on hold during phone calls, and in stores implies a grotesque mutation of music, turning familiar songs into sleepy, toothless concoctions. It's actually the name of the company that records and distributes that piped-in music.
Generic non-branded name: Background music

Item: Botox
Story: The injectable, wrinkle-eliminating cosmetic treatment derives its name from its active ingredient, botulinum toxin, but *Botox* is a registered trademark of Allergan PLC.
Generic non-branded name: Intramuscular botulinum toxin

Item: Zeppelin
Story: In the early 20th century, flying via airship or Zeppelin was a very popular mode of transportation among Europe's wealthy, thanks to German inventor Ferdinand von Zeppelin's creation. It pretty much died out after the *Hindenburg* disaster in 1937, but Zeppelin's company, Liftschiffbau Zeppelin, is still around today, making various kinds of aircraft and maintaining the trademark on its foundational production.
Generic non-branded name: Rigid airship

Item: Tarmac
Story: *Tarmac* isn't just a word that refers to an airport's runways and areas where planes board. It's the name of the actual material used to make that surface, and it's the trademark of Lafarge Tarmac, a British company.
Generic non-branded name: Asphalt road surface

Abraham Lincoln's vice president, Andrew Johnson, married his wife in a ceremony presided over by Lincoln's cousin.

BUN INTENDED

The biggest trend in restaurants in the past decade hasn't been restaurants at all, but food trucks, mobile quick-service eateries serving all kinds of cuisine. More often than not, it seems like every food truck has a clever or pun-based name. Here are some of the funniest ones we've found.

Basic Kneads (Denver)

Fried Egg I'm in Love (Portland)

I Dream of Weenie (Nashville)

Nacho Bizness (Miami)

Any O'Cajun (New Orleans)

Serial Grillers (Tucson)

Bun Intended (Asheville)

Deli LlaMMMa (Asheville)

Planet of the Crepes (Tucson)

Be More Pacific (Austin)

Electric Sliders (Phoenix)

NaanSense (Seattle)

Grillenium Falcon (Fayetteville, AR)

Patty Wagon (Los Angeles)

India Jones (Los Angeles)

Sticks and Cones (Charlotte)

Kangaroostaurant (Madison, WI)

Great Balls on Tires (Los Angeles)

The Dump Truck (Portland)

Cheesy Does It (Saratoga, NY)

Holy Mole (Portland)

Lettuce B. Frank (Rochester, NY)

The Codfather (Reno)

Getting Baked (Las Vegas)

Dirty Dishes (New Orleans)

Baguettaboutit (Durham, NC)

Queso Good (Phoenix)

Dine-1-1 (Minneapolis)

Thyme Machine (Pittsburgh)

The Dining Car (Boston)

Jamaica Mi Hungry (Boston)

OhMyGogi (Houston)

Eatsie Boys (Houston)

Pasta La Vista, Baby! (Baltimore)

Dough Boy Pizza (Denver)

God Save the Cuisine (San Diego)

Curry Up Now (San Francisco)

Kim Jong Grillin (Portland)

Just Fork It (Philadelphia)

Bad Mother Shuckers (Philadelphia)

Vincent Van Doughnut (St. Louis)

Devilicious (San Diego)

There's more fresh water in the atmosphere than in all of the planet's rivers combined.

TO THE ROYAL ACADEMY OF FARTING

Warning: this article contains old-timey writing, graphic descriptions of flatulence, the French language, and a few too many fart puns. Reader discretion is advised.

A CALL FOR HELP

In the late 18th century, the Royal Academy of Brussels—perhaps because their students were eating too many Brussels sprouts—emitted a call to the world's scientists to come up with a way to make farts smell better, or, as they put it: "To discover some Drug wholesome & not disagreeable, to be mix'd with our common Food, or Sauces, that shall render the natural Discharges of Wind from our Bodies, not only inoffensive, but agreeable as Perfumes." It should be noted that this wasn't the Academy's only request to the world's greatest thinkers, but it's the one that Benjamin Franklin chose to respond to.

The American Founding Father—who signed the Declaration of Independence, invented the public library (and lots of other things), and famously flew a kite during a thunderstorm—penned a letter to "The Royal Society of Farting," titled "Fart Proudly." Franklin was living in Paris at the time and growing weary of pretentious scientists at stuffy institutions. Armed with a quill and his infamous wit, Franklin really let one fly. (To get the joke at the end, it's important to know that a farthing was a British coin worth one-quarter of a penny.)

Benjamin Franklin, to The Royal Academy of Farting, May 19, 1780

GENTLEMEN,

I have perused your late mathematical Prize Question, proposed in lieu of one in Natural Philosophy, for the ensuing year, viz. *"Une figure quelconque donnee, on demande d'y inscrire le plus grand nombre de fois possible une autre figure plus-petite quelconque, qui est aussi donnee."* I was glad to find by these following Words, *"l'Acadeemie a jugee que cette deecouverte, en eetendant les bornes de nos connoissances, ne seroit pas sans UTILITE,"* that you esteem Utility an essential Point in your Enquiries, which has not always been the case with all Academies; and I conclude therefore that you have given this Question instead of a philosophical, or as the Learned express it, a physical one, because you could not at the time think of a physical one that promis'd greater Utility.

Not a cliché: 5,400 mail carriers get bitten by dogs each year.

Permit me then humbly to propose one of that sort for your consideration, and through you, if you approve it, for the serious Enquiry of learned Physicians, Chemists, &c. of this enlightened Age.

It is universally well known, That in digesting our common Food, there is created or produced in the Bowels of human Creatures, a great Quantity of Wind.

That the permitting this Air to escape and mix with the Atmosphere, is usually offensive to the Company, from the fetid Smell that accompanies it.

That all well-bred People therefore, to avoid giving such Offence, forcibly restrain the Efforts of Nature to discharge that Wind.

That so retain'd contrary to Nature, it not only gives frequently great present Pain, but occasions future Diseases, such as habitual Cholics, Ruptures, Tympanies, &c. often destructive of the Constitution, & sometimes of Life itself.

Were it not for the odiously offensive Smell accompanying such Escapes, polite People would probably be under no more Restraint in discharging such Wind in Company, than they are in spitting, or in blowing their Noses.

My Prize Question therefore should be, *To discover some Drug wholesome & not disagreeable, to be mix'd with our common Food, or Sauces, that shall render the natural Discharges of Wind from our Bodies, not only inoffensive, but agreeable as Perfumes.*

That this is not a chimerical Project, and altogether impossible, may appear from these Considerations. That we already have some Knowledge of Means capable of *Varying* that Smell. He that dines on stale Flesh, especially with much Addition of Onions, shall be able to afford a Stink that no Company can tolerate; while he that has lived for some Time on Vegetables only, shall have that Breath so pure as to be insensible to the most delicate Noses; and if he can manage so as to avoid the Report, he may any where give Vent to his Griefs, unnoticed. But as there are many to whom an entire Vegetable Diet would be inconvenient, and as a little Quick-Lime thrown into a Jakes will correct the amazing Quantity of fetid Air arising from the vast Mass of putrid Matter contain'd in such Places, and render it rather pleasing to the Smell, who knows but that a little Powder of Lime (or some other thing equivalent) taken in our Food, or perhaps a Glass of Limewater drank at Dinner, may have the same Effect on the Air produc'd in and issuing from our Bowels? This is worth the Experiment. Certain it is also that we have the Power of changing by slight Means the Smell of

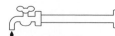

Adjusted for inflation, the top-grossing R-rated movie of all time is 1973's *The Exorcist*.

another Discharge, that of our Water. A few Stems of Asparagus eaten, shall give our Urine a disagreeable Odour; and a Pill of Turpentine no bigger than a Pea, shall bestow on it the pleasing Smell of Violets. And why should it be thought more impossible in Nature, to find Means of making a Perfume of our *Wind* than of our *Water*?

For the Encouragement of this Enquiry, (from the immortal Honour to be reasonably expected by the Inventor) let it be considered of how small Importance to Mankind, or to how small a Part of Mankind have been useful those Discoveries in Science that have heretofore made Philosophers famous. Are there twenty Men in Europe at this Day, the happier, or even the easier, for any Knowledge they have pick'd out of Aristotle? What Comfort can the Vortices of Descartes give to a Man who has Whirlwinds in his Bowels! The Knowledge of Newton's mutual *Attraction* of the Particles of Matter, can it afford Ease to him who is rack'd by their mutual *Repulsion*, and the cruel Distensions it occasions? The Pleasure arising to a few Philosophers, from seeing, a few Times in their Life, the Threads of Light untwisted, and separated by the Newtonian Prism into seven Colours, can it be compared with the Ease and Comfort every Man living might feel seven times a Day, by discharging freely the Wind from his Bowels? Especially if it be converted into a Perfume: For the Pleasures of one Sense being little inferior to those of another, instead of pleasing the *Sight* he might delight the *Smell* of those about him, & make Numbers happy, which to a benevolent Mind must afford infinite Satisfaction. The generous Soul, who now endeavours to find out whether the Friends he entertains like best Claret or Burgundy, Champagne or Madeira, would then enquire also whether they chose Musk or Lilly, Rose or Bergamot, and provide accordingly. And surely such a Liberty of *Expressing one's Scent-iments, and pleasing one another*, is of infinitely more Importance to human Happiness than that Liberty of the *Press, or of abusing one another*, which the English are so ready to fight & die for. — In short, this Invention, if compleated, would be, as *Bacon* expresses it, *bringing Philosophy home to Mens Business and Bosoms*. And I cannot but conclude, that in Comparison therewith, for *universal and continual UTILITY*, the Science of the Philosophers above-mentioned, even with the Addition, Gentlemen, of your *"Figure quelconque"* and the Figures inscrib'd in it, are, all together, scarcely worth a FART-HING.

David Bowie's first choices for stage names were Davy Jones and Tom Jones (he had to change them when guys by those names got popular).

THE REPLY...240 YEARS LATER

Franklin shared his letter with some friends, who thankfully saved it for poster(ior)ity—but he never submitted it to the Royal Academy of Brussels (now called the Royal Flemish Academy of Belgium for Science and the Arts). In 2020, Brian VanHooker, who writes for the men's magazine *MEL*, wrote to the academy to see if they had an answer. The academy took the request seriously and enlisted the world's foremost "fartologists"—including microbiome experts Sarah Lebeer of the University of Antwerp, Belgium, and Glenn Gibson of the University of Reading, U.K. "Your suggested topic on improving flatulence odour is amusing, but indeed also very relevant," they wrote in their reply to Franklin. "An outstanding answer to the contest as you formulate it would be ground-breaking." The good news is that microbiome researchers like Lebeer and Gibson are experimenting with probiotic and prebiotic sciences that have the potential to actually solve this problem. "In other words, Mr. Franklin, they're working on it," the response concludes, "and, perhaps sometime within the next 240 years, your dream of non-smelly farts might just come true." (Mrs. Uncle John would like them to hurry up.)

* * *

SANTA CLAUS, THE TRIPPING SHAMAN

Have you ever wondered why Santa Claus lives at the North Pole, wears a red-and-white suit, and flies around with reindeer to deliver presents through chimneys in late December? One theory goes that hundreds of years ago, every winter solstice, Arctic and Siberian shamans delivered *Amanita muscaria*, better known as "magic mushrooms," through an opening near the top of villagers' snow-covered tepees. Adding credence to this theory: the mushrooms are red and white and grow near the trunks of pine trees—which might explain where "presents under the tree" comes from. The shamans were also known to dress up in costume like the red-and-white mushrooms, and they even told hallucinogenic-inspired tales about flying reindeer.

In 1823, when Clement Clarke Moore wrote "'Twas the Night before Christmas," he combined the legend of Saint Nicholas—who lived in the fourth century and was known for his generosity—with Nordic folk tales that could have stemmed from these shamanic practices. "At first glance, one thinks it's ridiculous, but it's not," Boston University historian Carl A. P. Ruck told *Live Science*. "Whoever heard of reindeer flying? I think it's becoming general knowledge that Santa is taking a 'trip' with his reindeer."

Only three states where it's legal to ride a motorcycle without a helmet: Iowa, Illinois, and New Hampshire.

HOW SWEET IT ISN'T

Almost everybody loves candy, and those that do have a handful of favorites.
It's hard for even well-established sweets manufacturers to penetrate the
lucrative candy market with a new product, but they keep on trying...
and failing. Here are some candy bars that totally flopped.

HERSHEY'S GOLD

The Hershey Company has sold dozens of chocolate bars and candies, but it's reserved its official "Hershey Bar" moniker for just four products: the standard Hershey's Milk Chocolate Candy Bar, Hershey's Milk Chocolate with Almonds, Hershey's Cookies 'n' Creme, and Hershey's Gold, which hit stores in late 2017. The Gold candy bar wasn't even chocolate, but rather "caramelized creme" dotted with chunks of peanuts and salted pretzels. Hershey was a sponsor of the 2018 Winter Olympics and used the opportunity to heavily promote Gold, giving away bars every time an American athlete won a gold medal—a stunt that unleashed 150,000 bars unto the public. Despite the Hershey pedigree and big promotional push, people just weren't interested in the new candy bar. By early 2020, Hershey had quietly ended production on Hershey's Gold.

LIFE SAVERS HOLES

Probably the two most popular and famous ring-shaped sweet treats in the world are doughnuts and Life Savers, bite-sized hard candies resembling life preservers and named after a colloquial term for the item. Sold in many different flavors in foiled-wrapped rolls since 1912, the Mars candy company attempted a brand extension in mid-1990 with Life Savers Holes—after all, doughnut holes (the supposed middle "cut out" of doughnuts) were commonplace. Sold in pocket-size plastic tubes, a Life Savers Hole looked like it could've come out of the inside of a Life Saver. It was about the size of a tooth and presented a major choking hazard, and that's precisely why Mars recalled all Life Savers Holes in January 1991, just six months after the product launch. Four months later, Life Savers Holes returned to stores in a slightly less throat-clogging permutation, but they didn't sell well and disappeared for good by the end of 1991.

PB MAX

In 1989, Mars created the PB Max, a thick square brick consisting of a cookie topped with oats and peanut butter, and then drenched in milk chocolate. The peanut butter–centric product was designed to compete with Hershey's best-selling Reese's Peanut Butter Cups, but also as a protein-rich snack, akin to a granola or energy bar (as opposed to a candy bar). However Mars positioned the product, it worked, because they sold about $10 million

The town of Wheeler, Virginia, is closer to nine other states' capitals
than it is to Virginia's capital of Richmond.

worth of PB Max bars every year for five years—yet still discontinued the treat in 1994. The reason: executives at Mars, a family-owned company, personally didn't care for peanut butter–flavored candy, and didn't want to mess with the PB Max any longer.

BAR NONE

When Bar None arrived in American stores in 1987 (and in Canadian stores the same year with the name Temptation), it was one of the most complex, chocolate-centric bars available. Made by Hershey, Bar None consisted of chocolate-flavored wafers sandwiched with chocolate creme and peanuts, then covered in chocolate. A marketing campaign touted that the Bar None could "tame the chocolate beasty within" even the most voracious of chocoholics. Bar None sold well, but it was too expensive to produce in its original form, so in 1992, Hershey added caramel (a cheap filler) to the recipe and started selling Bar None as two smaller candy sticks instead of one larger bar. That drove customers away, and dwindling sales led Hershey to end production on Bar None in 1997.

SUMMIT

The early 1980s Summit bar was simple and appetizing: chocolate-covered wafers and peanuts enrobed in a thick layer of chocolate, presented to the public as a combination of candy and cookies. The problem with Summit was that the chocolate that manufacturer Mars used had a low melting point—the bars routinely melted in shipping, or on store shelves, or when consumers brought them home. The company received so many letters of complaint (particularly from customers who said they had to keep their Summits in the freezer) that they reformulated the chocolate and relaunched the bar in 1983, accompanied by a massive marketing campaign designed to attract the attention of teenagers by offering a free cassette single from rock bands REO Speedwagon, .38 Special, or Jefferson Starship in exchange for 10 wrappers. The reboot failed, and Summit disappeared by 1984.

SPACE DUST

General Foods scored a major hit in 1976 with Pop Rocks, tiny fruit-flavored candy rocks that sizzled on the tongue. As a follow-up in 1978, General Foods unveiled Space Dust, essentially Pop Rocks in powder form. Parents groups instantly issued letters of protest to General Foods, arguing that Space Dust encouraged kids to try illicit drugs, as the name of the candy was so similar to that of the powerful hallucinogenic "angel dust," or PCP. Concerned moms and dads also worried that Space Dust could make kids' heads or throats explode—the end result of a widely disseminated urban legend that the actor who played Mikey in a series of Life cereal commercials in the early 1970s died after eating Pop Rocks. The controversies cast such a shadow over Space Dust that General Foods stopped making the candy altogether by the end of the 1970s.

A quarter of the U.S. population (10 million) attended the
1876 Centennial Exposition in Philadelphia.

SUCH SWEET WORDS

You can have this page of quotes about candy, as a treat.

"As a child, the only clear thought
I had was 'get candy.'"
—Jerry Seinfeld

"Candy is childhood,
the best and bright
moments you wish could
have lasted forever."
—Dylan Lauren

"Chocolate is cheaper than therapy
and you don't need an appointment."
—Catherine Aitken

"A lollipop is
hard candy plus
garbage. I don't
need a handle.
Just give me
the candy."
—Demetri Martin

"ONE OF THE
SECRETS OF A
HAPPY LIFE IS
CONTINUOUS
SMALL TREATS."
—Iris Murdoch

"It's not that
chocolates are a
substitute for love.
Love is a substitute
for chocolate."
—Miranda Ingram

"Candy is my religion."
—Sarah Addison Allen

"CANDY IS NATURE'S WAY OF
MAKING UP FOR MONDAYS."
—Rebecca Gober

"You know someone is your
friend when they give you more
than half of their candy bar."
—Liam Holland

"You're never too old
for free candy."
—Kathy Debiec

"Where there is
chocolate there
is hope."
—Marge Howe Wagner

"CHOCOLATE: THE POOR
MAN'S CHAMPAGNE."
—Daniel Worona

"ALL I REALLY NEED IS LOVE, BUT A LITTLE CANDY NOW
AND THEN DOESN'T HURT."
—Charles M. Schulz

COINED BY THE BARD

Sure, William Shakespeare is considered one of the finest writers in the history of the English language. But did you know that he also helped create it? Here are some common phrases that originated in his plays in the 16th and 17th centuries.

Phrase: Vanish into thin air

Meaning: To disappear, either literally or metaphorically, instantly and without warning.

Origin: To make a band of musicians go away in *Othello*, the Clown admonishes them to "put up your pipes in your bag, for I'll away; go, vanish into air; away!"

Phrase: A method to the madness

Meaning: Strange or cruel behavior that's carefully calculated.

Origin: When Polonius wonders whether Hamlet in *Hamlet* is actually insane or just acting that way to trap his stepfather into confessing that he murdered the king, Polonius proclaims, "Though this be madness, yet there is a method in't."

Phrase: A wild goose chase

Meaning: A complex pursuit that's ultimately fruitless because the sought-after prize doesn't really exist.

Origin: "Nay, if thy wits run the wild-goose chase, I have done; for thou hast more of the wild-goose in one of thy wits than, I am sure, I have in my whole five: was I with you there for the goose?" In *Romeo and Juliet*, Mercutio says all this to Romeo when he's frustrated that he doesn't understand the latter's many jokes and uses of wordplay—it's pointless trying to follow, he says, an utter wild-goose chase. Shakespeare made the first literary, comparative use of a wild-goose chase, a real game played in 16th-century England: a form of Simon Says in which players had to precisely imitate a series of maneuvers on horseback.

Phrase: Break the ice

Meaning: Begin the possibly awkward or uncomfortable task of initiating a conversation.

Origin: In the romantic comedy *The Taming of the Shrew*, Tranio tells Petruchio that he'll be able to charm Katherina after he just gets a conversation started: "And if you break the ice, and do this feat..."

Phrase: Wear one's heart on one's sleeve

Meaning: To openly express powerful emotions, particularly sadness and grief—displaying vulnerability.

Origin: Iago, the duplicitous villain of *Othello*, delivers a soliloquy (an interior monologue said aloud for the audience) in which he explains that if his appearance matched that of his mood and thoughts, he would "wear my heart upon my sleeve for daws to peck at: I am not what I am." In other words, birds would attack and peck at his wounded heart...which wouldn't be ideal.

Phrase: Have a heart of gold

Meaning: Used to describe a person of kindness, sweetness, and innocence.

Origin: In *King Henry V*, the titular character goes incognito as a commoner and asks a soldier named Pistol if King Henry is a good ruler. "The king's a bawcock, and a heart of gold, a lad of life, an imp of fame." A *bawcock* is a good man, someone whose heart is so precious and treasured that it could be made from gold.

Phrase: Love is blind

Meaning: When you're in love with someone, you're incapable of noticing their negative qualities.

Origin: The phrase first appeared in Geoffrey Chaucer's *The Canterbury Tales* in the year 1400 ("for loue is blynd alday, and may nat see"), but it didn't enter common usage until after Shakespeare dropped it into *The Merchant of Venice*: "But love is blind and lovers cannot see the pretty follies that themselves commit." Jessica, dressed up as a man to sneak out and see her paramour, Lorenzo, delivers the line while reflecting on the powerful nature of love.

Phrase: The world is your oyster

Meaning: You can do anything you want; opportunities that await you are virtually unlimited.

Origin: Perhaps alluding to the treasure of a pearl found inside of an oyster, the contemporary meaning of the phrase has changed since Shakespeare created it for an exchange between two recurring characters, Falstaff and Pistol, in *The Merry Wives of Windsor*. Falstaff refuses to loan Pistol any money, not even a penny. "Why then, the world's mine oyster," Pistol replies, "which I with sword will open." Pistol means to say that the world is his oyster because it's his to shuck—he'll take what he wants with violence and force.

UNSEEN TV

Ever wondered what the television network geniuses do behind closed doors?
Here are some TV shows that they approved and produced...but never broadcast.

SHOW: *NEXT CALLER*

STORY: Lots of hit sitcoms started off as vehicles for popular stand-up comedians: *Home Improvement* with Tim Allen, *Roseanne* with Roseanne Barr, and *Everybody Loves Raymond* with Ray Romano, for example. Dane Cook could have been added to that list. In the 2000s, his observational comedy was so popular that he was selling out arenas and hitting the top 10 of the album charts with his recordings—two feats not accomplished by the same person since Steve Martin in the late 1970s. In 2012, NBC ordered a series starring Cook called *Next Caller*, set in the world of talk radio. Created by *Weeds* staff writer Stephen Falk, Cook starred as a brash, sexist, top-rated radio show host forced by his bosses to bring in a cohost, a feminist National Public Radio personality (Collette Wolfe). NBC announced that the show would air sometime in the 2012-13 season, and two episodes were filmed...only for the network to decide it didn't want to air the show at all. On his blog, Falk thinks NBC pulled out because they had too many shows and didn't have room for *Next Caller* on its schedule. (That, or as Falk said, the network simply "didn't like" the show.)

SHOW: *THE ROBERT TAYLOR SHOW*

STORY: Robert Taylor—one of Hollywood's most popular leading men in the 1930s and 1940s with films like *A Yank at Oxford*, *Bataan*, and *Waterloo Bridge*—became one of the first movie stars to give television a try. In the late 1950s, he starred in *The Detectives* and a decade later, performed the introductions for the Western anthology *Death Valley Days*. In between, in 1963, NBC developed a starring vehicle for the actor called *The Robert Taylor Show*. Taylor played a case worker for the U.S. Department of Health, Education, and Welfare (now the Department of Health and Human Services), but failed to get permission from the actual agency. The HEW wouldn't sign off on the show, so the four already-filmed episodes of *The Robert Taylor Show* never aired.

SHOW: *GOOD GRIEF*

STORY: This reality TV series for the Lifetime network was supposed to give viewers a behind-the-scenes look at the day-to-day operation of the Johnson Family Mortuary—a

There are six distinct communities in Tennessee named Shiloh.

Fort Worth, Texas, funeral home. But then actual reality stepped in to prevent this reality show from hitting the air. Just a few weeks before the August 2014 debut of *Good Grief*, the funeral home was shut down amid an extensive investigation by authorities. While serving eviction papers to the Johnsons for months of unpaid rent, the owner of the building where the funeral home operated discovered a house of horrors: bodies that hadn't been embalmed, others left on tables, and some leaking bodily fluids onto the floor. When all of those legal violations hit the news, Lifetime killed *Good Grief*.

SHOW: *THE GRUBBS*

STORY: This 2002 Fox sitcom boasted a stellar cast—Randy Quaid, Carol Kane, and Michael Cera—as a dysfunctional and idiotic family. And after it was screened for critics before it hit the air, it also boasted some of the worst reviews of a TV show ever. One critic called it "the worst new show" of the season, another called it "painfully unfunny," and yet another said it was "incredibly awful." A remake of an obscure British sitcom called *The Grimleys*, *The Grubbs* was the rare show that critics actually hated so loudly that it got taken off the air. Fox pulled it from the schedule (it was supposed to air on Sunday nights after *The Simpsons*) because it "failed to live up to its creative potential."

SHOW: *12 MILES OF BAD ROAD*

STORY: Linda Bloodworth-Thomason has worked in TV for decades, creating popular, Emmy-winning comedies based in the South, such as *Designing Women* and *Evening Shade*. In 2007, she sold a show to HBO called *12 Miles of Bad Road*. The cable channel agreed to make 10 episodes of the series about a shrewd Texas real estate developer (Lily Tomlin) and her dimwitted family and employees. HBO spent around $25 million on the rights and on production of six episodes until *12 Miles*, like every other TV show, was shut down due to the 2007–2008 Writers Guild of America strike. When the strike was over, HBO executives reviewed the six episodes it had paid for, didn't like what they saw, and decided not to make the last four episodes. Not only that, but it didn't want to air the six completed episodes. Bloodworth-Thomason then sent tapes of the finished episodes to TV critics in an attempt to get critical support for the show as she shopped it around to other networks. But critical response was lackluster, and no other TV network picked up *12 Miles of Bad Road*.

SHOW: *HIEROGLYPH*

STORY: HBO's *Game of Thrones* is so popular that other networks have tried to find their own epic action dramas. Fox thought it may have had a contender in 2013 with

Species of SpongeBob SquarePants: *Aplysina fistularis*.

Hieroglyph. Created by Travis Beacham, who wrote the blockbuster *Pacific Rim,* the show was about a thief in ancient Egypt released from prison in order to serve as a right-hand man to the Pharaoh. There was also plenty of *Game of Thrones*–like intrigue, politics, sex, and magic thrown in for good measure. Fox ordered a 13-episode season—and forked out millions—for the show, sight unseen. About a year later, after numerous production delays that meant the show wouldn't even premiere until 2015, there was a change of leadership in the Fox head office and the new executives didn't like *Hieroglyph,* which had been approved by their predecessors. The network cut their losses and canceled the show after the production of just one (ultimately unaired) episode.

SHOW: *ANGELS '88*

STORY: The 1970s action-drama *Charlie's Angels* was a massive hit, starring Farrah Fawcett, Kate Jackson, Jaclyn Smith, and others as jet-set agents working for a private detective agency. The show went off the air in 1981, but just seven years later, producer Aaron Spelling attempted to revive it with a comic, self-referential premise: after their *Charlie's Angels*–esque detective show is canceled (crushed in the ratings by *The Cosby Show*), four young actresses start up a detective agency and use what they learned as fictional PIs to work real cases. Spelling held a widely publicized national talent search, selecting four unknown actresses (including future TV star Téa Leoni). All were introduced at a big press conference, but a TV writers' strike in the fall of 1988 delayed the premiere of *Angels '88,* necessitating a name change to *Angels '89,* before ABC decided not to air the rebooted *Charlie's Angels* at all.

SHOW: *HEATHERS*

STORY: The 1988 teen-oriented black comedy *Heathers* developed into a cult classic: the movie follows a troubled teen who teams up with a jaded member of a high school's dominant social clique to systematically kill off the other popular kids. Fox ordered a TV series adaptation in 2009, but it never entered production, prompting Bravo to give it a try in 2012—but they passed after reading a pilot script. In 2017, Paramount-owned TV Land ordered a new *Heathers,* set in contemporary times, but then handed it off to Paramount-affiliated Spike TV, which was soon renamed the Paramount Network. An entire first season was produced and a second season was written, but after a school shooting in Parkland, Florida, in February 2018 made the *Heathers* content look tasteless and tacky, the Paramount Network delayed the debut of the show from June 2018 to October of that year, with one particularly violent episode not slated to air at all. Before that date arrived, however, Paramount canceled the show entirely, and producers attempted to get Netflix or the cable channel Freeform to pick up *Heathers.* Both outlets declined.

First *American Idol* contestant to win an EGOT:
Jennifer Hudson (she came in 7th place in 2004).

SHOW: *HEAVENS TO BETSY*

STORY: About the only thing that singer, songwriter, actress, author, advocate, and theme-park entrepreneur Dolly Parton hasn't been successful at is television. In 1976 and 1987, two separate variety shows called *Dolly* flopped, and in 1994, Parton gave the small screen one more shot with a sitcom called *Heavens to Betsy*. The country music superstar played sleazy Las Vegas lounge singer Betsy Baxter, who dies and, in order to earn her angel wings and a place in Heaven, has to return home to Tennessee and do good deeds for her family and friends. Six episodes were filmed and completed, and CBS placed the show on its schedule as a midseason replacement with a tentative debut for some time in early 1995. But those six episodes were fraught with production difficulties, and shooting shut down indefinitely to fix them, which gave CBS cold feet about airing what was already in the can.

* * *

CHANGE MY MIND

One of our favorite memes was born out of a 2018 photo tweeted by conservative commentator Steven Crowder, who set up a table on the Texas Christian University campus with a sign that read, "Male privilege is a myth. Change my mind." Internet users quickly co-opted the pic with other topics of discussion, some of which are quite funny.

- Milk is cereal sauce. Change my mind.

- Pineapple goes on pizza. Change my mind.

- Brushing your teeth before breakfast is like wiping before pooping. Change my mind.

- The brain is the only thing that named itself. Change my mind.

- The youngest picture of you is also the oldest picture of you. Change my mind.

- Dave Grohl is the Tom Hanks of rock 'n' roll. Change my mind.

- Carly was the worst character of *iCarly*. Change my mind.

- Romantic movies should be considered sci-fi because none of that sh*t happens in real life. Change my mind.

- A Russian wedding should be called a Soviet union. Change my mind.

- Facts don't always change people's minds. Change my mind.

- This meme is dead. Change my mind.

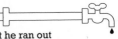

Jeopardy! champ Ken Jennings won so many games that he ran out of personal anecdotes to tell on the show, so he made up some.

THERE'S SOMETHING IN THERE!

The Mütter Museum in Philadelphia houses a macabre collection of curiosities involving human biology, including more than 2,000 items removed from the throats, lungs, tonsils, tracheae, and stomachs of woefully curious children, and then kept by Dr. Chevalier Jackson (1865–1958). Here are just a few of the strangest items Dr. Jackson recovered.

Tooth roots

Toy wristwatch

Real wristwatch

Crucifix on a chain attached to rosary beads

Metal letter Z that came off a toy airplane

Tin steering wheel from a toy car

Audubon Society member pin

"Perfect Attendance" pin

U.S. dime depicting the Roman god Mercury

Buffalo nickel

1892 half-dollar

Goat figurine

A single tiddledywink

Jacks

Toy donkey

Teddy-bear eye

Metal tip of an umbrella

Bundle of string

A glob of hardened and congealed pus

Ball of copper wire

Double-pointed staples

An alarm clock's brass foot

Rivets

Wood screws

Two-inch-long nail

Owl pellets

Radiator key

Tiny opera glasses

Toy horse made of lead alloy

Ear from a toy horse

Two-inch-long nail

Padlock

Metal paperweight shaped like a greyhound

Shawl pin

Brooch

Pin with a head made of white glass

Carpet tack

Campaign button

Cambric needle

Toothbrush bristles

Toothpaste cap

Poker chip

Christmas tree ornament

A mass of burrs

Mutton bone

Prune seed

Lily seeds

Cockleburs

Job's tears plant

Ball of orange pulp

Unroasted coffee berry

Oyster shells

Eggshell

Raw beans

Stove bolt

Rubber-band ball

Crayon nib

Bird shot

Bullet

First Olympic disqualification for a banned substance: Swedish pentathlete Hans-Gunnar Liljenwall drank two beers before his event at the 1968 Summer Games.

THE MATILDA EFFECT

Have you ever worked really hard on something only to watch as someone else gets the credit? It happens to women more than to men—so much so that there's a term for it: the Matilda effect.

BACKGROUND

The Matilda effect comes from the world of science, but it applies to the arts, business, and politics as well. It refers to a systemic bias against women, whose contributions are often credited to men. The phrase was coined in 1993 by science historian Margaret W. Rossiter, who was inspired by suffragette Matilda Joslyn Gage's 1883 essay in which Gage points out that...

> No reference to woman is more common than that she possesses no inventive or mechanical genius . . . But, while such statements are carelessly or ignorantly made, tradition, history, and experience alike prove her possession of these faculties in the highest degree. Although woman's scientific education has been grossly neglected, yet some of the most important inventions of the world are due to her.

Here are three women whose contributions were overshadowed by the Matilda effect.

SALLY MUMBLE-GRUNTER

Accomplishments: Her name probably wasn't Sally Mumble-Grunter, but anthropologists do believe that Paleolithic people communicated orally through mumbles and grunts. Anyway, about 15,000 years ago, Sally was an artist. She toiled away in the flicking firelight of a cave using pigments, oils, and furry dabbers to paint a running bison with vivid colors and nuanced shading. When her picture was complete, she placed her open hand against the rocky wall and blew paint through a hollow bone, creating a hand stencil, thus "signing" her work.

Matilda Effect: If the image of a female cave painter is surprising, that's because, for centuries, science and academia have been depicting cave painters as men, despite having no evidence to support that notion. Because men did most of the hunting, it was assumed that they came home and painted pictures of their conquests.

In the 2010s, Dean Snow, a professor of anthropology at Pennsylvania State University, analyzed the stenciled handprints left next to 32 of the world's most famous cave paintings in France and Spain. Using an algorithm that compares the length of the ring and index fingers to determine sex, he discovered that adult men were responsible for only 10 percent of the paintings: 15 percent were painted

According to a 2015 study, vinegar attracts more flies than honey.

by adolescent males, and the other 75 percent of the cave paintings were done by women. "There has been a male bias in the literature for a long time," Snow told *National Geographic*, which supported the study. "In most hunter-gatherer societies, it's men that do the killing. But it's often the women who haul the meat back to camp, and women are as concerned with the productivity of the hunt as the men are. It wasn't just a bunch of guys out there chasing bison around."

ALICE BALL

Accomplishment: You don't hear much about leprosy today, but this chronic infectious disease has killed untold millions of people since ancient times. "Leper colonies" were common all over the world, especially in tropical regions where the culprit, *Mycobacterium leprae*, thrives. Patients who were sent to these colonies almost never made it out, and faced an excruciating, disfiguring, and lonely death. There wasn't an effective treatment for the disease until the 14th century when the chaulmoogra root (native to India) was shown to decrease the symptoms of skin lesions and rashes. But it wasn't *that* effective.

The chaulmoogra root was only partially effective for three reasons: it doesn't absorb well when used topically (and it leaves a sticky mess); it causes nausea and vomiting when taken orally; and the oils clump when injected under the skin. In 1915, Dr. Harry Hollmann, a surgeon at Kalihi Hospital in Honolulu (nicknamed "the land of the living dead" because of all the leprosy patients) knew that the problem could be solved by a chemist, so he hired Alice Ball to make the root soluble in water.

Born in Seattle in 1892, Ball had made a name for herself as not just the only woman to receive a master's degree from Hawaii College (now the University of Hawaii), she was also the first African American to do so. She stayed on after graduation to continue her research, while also teaching chemistry alongside Harvard graduate Arthur Dean, president of the college.

"After a great deal of experimental work," Hollman wrote years later, "Miss Ball solved the problem for me by making ethyl esters of the fatty acids found in chaulmoogra oil." He called it the Ball Method, and even though it didn't cure leprosy, the resulting treatment finally allowed some sufferers to live with the illness and not be shunned for it.

However, before Ball had a chance to publish her findings, she died suddenly at 24 years old. It's unclear what killed her—the most likely scenario is that she accidentally inhaled chlorine while showing her class how to wear a gas mask (World War I was raging and Hawaii was in danger of an attack). She became very sick and died soon after.

The asteroid that led to the end of the dinosaurs set 70 percent of the world's forests on fire.

The Matilda Effect: After Ball died, the Ball Method was renamed the Dean Method...by Dr. Dean himself. He published several articles that never even mentioned Ball's work. He later defended that decision by saying that he "finished" her research. In recent years, researchers have taken a closer look at Ball's notes and compared them to Dean's papers, and he didn't actually expand anything—he just took credit for what she'd done.

Ball had her defenders, none bigger than Hollman, who wrote an article in 1921 that tried to set the record straight. But it went largely unnoticed at the time, and the Dean Method became the go-to treatment for leprosy until the 1940s, when an antibiotic cure was finally discovered. In the meantime, Dean mass-produced the serum and sold it all over the world.

Thanks to some dedicated sleuths at the University of Hawaii who learned the truth in the 1970s, Ball's contribution is finally known to the world. In 2022, Hawaii governor David Ige signed a proclamation making February 28 Alice Augusta Ball Day.

M.I.A.

Accomplishments: This British rapper (real name: Mathangi "Maya" Arulpragasam) is known today for her activism and her music. When she was a teenager, her family became refugees after escaping the Sri Lankan civil war. Starting out as an underground artist, M.I.A.'s first two singles in 2005, "Sun Showers" and "Galang," made her a star. Her debut 2005 album, *Arular*, further cemented her status as a producer, vocalist, and socially conscious lyricist. For her 2007 follow-up, *Kala*, her famous boyfriend, an American music producer known as Diplo (real name: Thomas Wesley Pentz), contributed samples and produced a few of the songs. That's it.

Matilda Effect: After the release of *Kala*, M.I.A. told *Pitchfork*, "I read like five magazines in the airplane...and three out of five...said, 'Diplo: the mastermind behind M.I.A.'s politics!'" She reiterated that even though her politics and her lyrics are her own, she felt the media consistently described her as the protégé of a more accomplished White man. She even accused *Pitchfork*'s interviewer of spreading that false narrative, to which he replied, "We certainly have made reference to Diplo playing a part on your records, but it seems like everyone plays that up."

M.I.A.'s response: "I just find it a bit upsetting and kind of insulting that I can't have any ideas on my own because I'm a female or that people from undeveloped countries can't have ideas of their own unless it's backed up by someone who's blond-haired and blue-eyed."

To read about how Matilda affected the discovery of DNA, go to page 286.

Pollen isn't just yellow; it can be blue, red, gray, or green.

BATHROOM NEWS

*Here are a few fascinating bits of bathroom trivia
that we've flushed out from around the world.*

IN THE HOT SEAT

Are you afraid of going number two during a thunderstorm? You will be after reading
this. In May 2022, a bolt of lightning struck an apartment complex in Okmulgee,
Oklahoma. The bolt traveled through a vent in the roof and blew a toilet to
smithereens. It's a good thing that particular apartment was vacant at the time, or it
could have been a disgusting end.

BEWARE THE WILDKAKKERS!

The strict COVID-19 lockdowns in the pre-vaccine days of 2020 had many unfortunate
byproducts. One of the worst—at least in the Belgian city of Ghent—was crap. Literal
crap. In an attempt to keep the deadly virus from spreading, officials closed most of
Ghent's public buildings and restrooms. That smelled bad news for this picturesque
medieval town. Ombudswoman Helena Nachtergaele called it the "phenomenon of
wildkakkers," which translates to "wild poopers." It started almost immediately: walkers
were dropping their leavings between buildings, beneath bushes, and in other not-so-
conspicuous spots. Nachtergaele explained that, even before the pandemic, there weren't
enough toilets in Ghent; the lockdown then made the dam burst (so to speak). She said
Ghent would be adding €790,000 to the budget to clean existing bathrooms while the
city investigated the public's needs for additional offerings.

MISSION: IMPOSSIBLE

A California woman in her 40s (unnamed in press reports) was hiking in
Washington's Olympic National Forest in April 2022 when she stopped to use an
outhouse toilet. It's always a risk to check your phone in such a place, but she checked
hers anyway...and dropped it into the vault. The phone was out of reach, so the hiker
decided to go in after it: She secured one end of her dog's leash to the outhouse door,
and held the other end as she lowered herself down—head first—into the deep pit full
of composting waste matter. Then she lost her grip and fell. After righting herself, she
yelled for help, but there was no one else around. She then spent the next 20 minutes
trying in vain to climb out. Then she called 911, because her phone still worked

Oldest commercial plane still in use: Nolinor Aviation of Canada
flies a Boeing 737-200 built in 1974.

and there was cell service. When firefighters arrived (it took a while), they lowered a platform and lifted the woman to safety, then rinsed her off with a hose and gave her a hazmat suit. The woman refused medical attention, saying she just wanted to get home. According to the fire department, "The patient was extremely fortunate not to be overcome by toxic gases or sustain injury."

FARTS IN SPACE

On a 1984 NASA mission, Marc Garneau became the first Canadian to travel to space. Shortly after achieving orbit, the space shuttle crew held a live press conference. It was Garneau's big moment to say something profound—his entire country would be watching. What happened next (though not verified) might be explained by bathroom humor. As the seven astronauts—all wearing shorts—floated next to one another in the cabin, a reporter asked Garneau, "Can you tell us what it is about this entire experience that has perhaps most moved you?"

"Well..." said Garneau. He was visibly trying to suppress a laugh. "I won't tell you what we've just been talking about." Then his fellow astronauts started cracking up. As hard as they all tried, none of them could keep a straight face as Garneau struggled through his "profound" answer:

Umm, I think probably the most moving thing for me uh, has to be the view of the Earth. When you look at, down at your own planet, and see the, uh, absolutely out-of-this-world, incredible pictures, views, of entire subcontinents and, uh, seas, and uh, absolutely, uh, incredible sights, you, uh... [The astronauts were laughing so hard by this point that the video feed switched to an external view.] You begin to appreciate what the world is really like.

That must have been one whopper of a fart.

BROWN OUT

On a cold day in 2019, an unidentified Russian man was driving a BMW X6 in the city of Samara when the car's engine caught on fire! He pulled over, jumped out, and begged for help from a nearby tanker driver—who was driving a *septic* truck. The stranger pulled up next to the BMW, jumped out, aimed the hose, and started dumping sewage onto the hood of the $66,000 sports car. That wasn't working, so after about 30 seconds, the BMW driver managed to get the hood open, and the truck driver doused the flaming engine compartment in raw sewage until the fire was extinguished. This was all caught on a video that, not surprisingly, went viral. Most of the commenters said they would have just let the car burn. (Uncle John agrees.)

Abraham Lincoln was shot during *Our American Cousin* at Ford's Theatre in Washington, D.C., in 1865; the venue still hasn't staged a revival.

STRANGE LAWSUITS

These days, it seems like people will sue each other over practically anything. Here are some real-life examples of unusual legal battles.

THE PLAINTIFF: Kevin Berling, a former employee of Gravity Diagnostics

THE DEFENDANT: Gravity Diagnostics, a medical company in Covington, Kentucky

THE LAWSUIT: Berling's birthday was coming up in 2019 and, being prone to panic attacks, he made a request to his manager to cancel the obligatory office birthday party that would be held in the break room during lunch hour. Berling explained that a party could trigger "bad memories" and make him hyperventilate. But the manager reportedly forgot to inform whoever was in charge of birthday parties. Berling didn't know that, though, so when his birthday arrived, he was taken off guard when he arrived in the break room and saw that his party was indeed happening. Result: he had a panic attack and spent the rest of the lunch hour in his car.

The next day, Berling was called into a meeting with management to discuss his behavior at the birthday party...which triggered another panic attack. He tried some coping exercises (undescribed in news reports), but they weren't working. He was given a few days off...and then fired. Why? The coping exercise had his bosses concerned that Berling might become violent—which he flatly denied.

Berling sued the company for wrongful termination. According to his lawyer, "They started giving him a pretty hard time for his response to the birthday celebration, actually accusing him of stealing his coworkers' joy." Berling said it was Gravity Diagnostics that stole from him what would have been a huge raise. Not long after he was fired, the COVID-19 pandemic created a never-before-seen need for his former company's testing kits.

The case went before a jury...which triggered another set of panic attacks and put Berling back in therapy. Some of his former coworkers testified that they got significant raises while Berling was out of work.

THE VERDICT: The jury ruled in favor of the plaintiff. Berling was awarded $450,000 in damages, and $300,000 more for mental anguish.

THE PLAINTIFF: James Romine, an independent game developer who co-owns Arizona-based Digital Homicide Studios with his brother, Robert

THE DEFENDANT: Jim Sterling (they/their pronouns) of Mississippi, described in their official bio as "an English American freelance video game journalist, critic, pundit, YouTuber, and professional wrestler"

When animals sleep through winter, it's *hibernation*.
If they sleep through summer, it's *estivation*.

THE LAWSUIT: Sterling reviews video games while playing them, and then posts the videos to their popular YouTube channel. There's a lot of snark and hyperbole to be expected, but Romine felt that Sterling was being way too critical of the Digital Homicide game *The Slaughtering Grounds*. Calling it a contender for "the worst game of 2014," at one point Sterling compared the Bromine brothers to the "wet bandits from *Home Alone*." This wasn't the first time that Sterling had criticized Digital Homicide for releasing what they consider to be low-quality copycats of better games.

In 2016, Romine sued Sterling—for upwards of $11 million—citing "assault, libel, and slander." From the suit: "The Defendant...falsely accused...Plaintiff... and caused damage to reputation, damage to product, loss of product, and causing severe emotional distress to The Plaintiff." Bromine was also suing over the harassment he said he received from Sterling's online fan base. "We hope this case and documentation will show others they don't have to take it, what to do when it happens, and that those who do it will be punished."

The case was nearly dismissed early on because of some clerical goofs: Romine named only himself as Plaintiff, and not his actual company. And he should have filed the case in Mississippi, where Sterling does business, but he filed it in his home state of Arizona. In an attempt to cover the goof, Bromine reportedly bought a T-shirt from Sterling and had it sent to his home address to prove that "Sterling does business in Arizona."

THE VERDICT: Case dismissed, with prejudice. Sterling commented on their website that "the whole thing was an instant waste of time and money that could never be recuperated. Even if this went to court and we counterclaimed, what would we get out of it? A dismissal with prejudice is even better than the simple dismissal I'd originally aimed for—this effectively means these ludicrous charges aren't coming back."

THE PLAINTIFF: Cilla Carden, a massage therapist from the Perth suburb of Girrawheen, Western Australia

THE DEFENDANTS: Carden's neighbors on either side of her house

THE LAWSUIT: Carden is a vegan, and her neighbors are not. In 2017, she filed a lawsuit accusing them of moving their outdoor grills closer to her property, and then barbecuing smelly fish in order to "irritate" her. She told a local news channel that her beef with the neighbors goes back a few years. "They just bang the wall at any time when I've been sleeping. The kids with their basketballs—it vibrates this part of the house." But the smell is what led her to sue them. "All you can smell is fish. I can't enjoy my backyard."

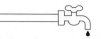

First grain ever cultivated and consumed by humans: barley.

When reporters showed up at the neighbors' homes, they declined interviews but did say that they have as much of a right to enjoy their backyards as she does. One of the neighbors said he moved his grill away from the fence and no longer lets the kids play basketball.

But after the news story aired, area carnivores were concerned that Carden was trying to destroy "a good old Aussie tradition," so they organized a "Revenge Barbecue" on Facebook to "help Cilla Carden GET SOME PORK ON HER FORK." After more than 3,000 people clicked that they were "going" to the event—to be held in front of Carden's house—her lawyer warned "any person who seeks to attend Ms. Carden's property on Saturday October 19, 2019, or at any other time in relation to this event or matter will be referred to the WA police on the ground of trespass." The organizers decided to cancel the event.

THE VERDICT: The case went all the way to Western Australia's supreme court, which dismissed it on the grounds that the neighbors are simply "living in their backyard… as a family." Carden appealed the ruling and lost a second time, but she says she won't give up. "All I want to do is live my life in peace."

THE PLAINTIFF: Mark and Maxine Beasley of Sacramento, California

THE DEFENDANT: Tootsie Roll Industries (TRI)

THE LAWSUIT: In 2018, the Beasleys filed a class action suit against the Chicago-based candy maker on the grounds that Tootsie Rolls are "immoral." Not only that, they're also "unethical, unscrupulous, or substantially injurious to consumers." Why? Because they taste too good. And the reason is that, in addition to a lot of sugar, Tootsie Rolls contain trans fats—substances known to be unhealthy (though yummy). The suit points out that partially hydrogenated oils (PHOs), the most common type of artificial trans fats, have been banned in many places, and that Tootsie Roll's competitors—including Hershey, Mars, and Reese's—use healthier (less yummy) alternatives to trans fats. The lawsuit claimed that TRI made this decision solely to "increase its profits at the expense of consumers' health," which violates California's Unfair Competition Law.

THE VERDICT: The case was dismissed in 2020 but refiled in 2021—so as of this writing, it's pending. That didn't stop it from taking the top spot on the Institute for Legal Reform's "Most Ridiculous Lawsuits of 2021." "At last count, the U.S. spends over $3,000 per household on its tort system," said ILR President Harold Kim, "while small businesses are paying more than half—$182 billion—of the commercial liability costs. The only winners are the plaintiffs' lawyers and litigation funders. The more frivolous lawsuits they file, the more they get paid."

More people of Lebanese descent live in Brazil than there are people living in Lebanon.

THE BETTY WHITE TIMELINE, PART II

Betty White was on this planet before sliced bread, Scotch tape,
canned beer, and helicopters. When we left off in Part I (page 15), the
33-year-old was already a talk show veteran, but she was just getting going.

1956   It's the "Golden Age of Television" when all the shows are live. White
finds work wherever she can and gets a starring role as Virginia Lennart on
an episode of the anthology drama *The Millionaire*, wherein regular people
get an unexpected inheritance. From the promo: "When Virginia Lennart
receives her million dollars, she closes the hamburger diner she owns in
Keokuk, Iowa, and travels with her friend, Emmy, through Europe where
she finds romance in Rome with an Italian count."

1956   White and Bonanza star Lorne Greene cohost the Tournament of
Roses Parade on NBC. The popular pair will preside over the annual
parade until they're both replaced in 1971, which really hurts White's
feelings: "On New Year's Day, I just sat home feeling wretched, watching
someone else do my parade." White and Greene will also host the Macy's
Thanksgiving Day Parade for CBS from 1963 to 1972...which also marks
the Donald Duck balloon's final appearance. White: "Bye-bye, Donald.
We won't see you in our parade again, but it sure has been nice knowing
you." Greene: "It is a time of mixed emotions."

1957   Before *Bewitched* and *I Dream of Jeannie*, and way before *Sabrina the Teenage
Witch* and *The Good Place*, White stars in the first "fantasy sitcom"–ABC's
Date with the Angels–as newlywed Vicki Angel. Nearly half of each episode
consists of a dream sequence, which the sponsor, Chrysler, soon tires of...
and nixes. "Without our dream sequences, our show flattened out and
became just one more run-of-the-mill domestic comedy. I can honestly say
that was the only time I have ever wanted to get out of a show."

1958   After *Date with the Angels* is canceled, the cast still has three months left on
their contract, and White has control of the studio. Result: "We changed
the format completely. The title had to go, so for the next thirteen weeks
we were known as *The Betty White Show*. We would do sketches, we would
have guest stars: Boris Karloff and Buster Keaton and Charles Coburn,

First coin-operated arcade game in the U.S.: Sega's *Periscope* (1966).

great and good fun, Basil Rathbone." However, *The Betty White Show* doesn't garner great reviews and lasts only a season.

1959   White stars in her first play, *Third Best Sport*, at Legion Star Playhouse in Ephrata, Pennsylvania. Years later, she sends a framed headshot to the playhouse with a handwritten note: "To my Ephrata friends: You were my first time 'on stage,' and aren't we both thrilled to see how we can grow? So many congratulations, Love, Betty White." It still hangs in the lobby.

1961   The 1960s mark White's tenure as the "First Lady of Game Shows." Over the next few decades, she makes her mark as the "funny celebrity guest" on *Match Game*, *Tattletales*, *To Tell the Truth*, *Hollywood Squares*, *Pyramid*, and more. The show that changes her life is *Password*. That's where the 39-year-old White meets the love of her life, Allen Ludden. She and the *Password* host fall for each other right away, but she's in no hurry to remarry (which doesn't stop him from asking her...repeatedly).

1962   White is beginning to be ubiquitous: she's all over TV and even stars in a stage production of *The King and I*. She shows off her dramatic acting chops in her first feature film, *Advise & Consent*, starring Henry Fonda. In her only scene, during a hearing, she plays a young U.S. senator named Bessie Adams who takes the stand against a sexist senior senator named Fred van Ackerman (George Grizzard). Sen. Van Ackerman: "Mr. President, is the senator calling me a liar?" Sen. Adams: "The record must stand as it is, Mr. President. How the senator interprets that record is his own problem, not mine." (Laughter in the chamber.)

1963   Betty White becomes Betty White Ludden (though she keeps Betty White as her stage name). After their honeymoon, the newlyweds return to *Password*. At the end of the first post-marriage episode, Ludden turns to her and says, "And the password is..." White responds, "Home. Will you take me home, Mr. Ludden?" "I certainly will, Mrs. Ludden." (*Awwws* in the audience.) White becomes stepmom to Ludden's three children. When asked if she regretted not having kids, White answered, "I'm so compulsive about stuff, I know if I had ever gotten pregnant, of course, that would have been my whole focus. But I didn't choose to have children because I'm focused on my career. And I just don't think as compulsive as I am, that I could manage both."

1971   Not having kids also lets White focus on her second career as an animal welfare advocate. She produces and hosts *Betty White's Pet Set*, where she interviews celebrities and their pets. She also begins her tenure as a trustee for the Morris Animal Foundation, and later becomes president emeritus until 2009. She'll also serve on the board of directors at the Los Angeles Zoo (where she befriends Jane Goodall). But White will always have a special place for *Pet Set*, when she met stars like Carol Burnett and James Brolin (and their pets). "What a time! It remains one of my favorite shows even 50 years later."

1973 Before season 3 of *The Mary Tyler Moore Show*—already considered among the best sitcoms of all-time—Moore and the writers add a character to the fictional newsroom who is wholesome in front of the camera but a vicious vixen in real life. Regarding casting, Moore says, "We need somebody who can play sickeningly sweet, like Betty White." White, now 51, lands her biggest role to date as Sue Ann Nivens, host of the fictional *Happy Homemaker Show*. Originally intended to appear in just one episode, series creator James L. Brooks afterward tells White, "Don't make too many plans." Here's Sue Ann coyly revealing her nocturnal activities to her coworkers: "I was lying in bed last night and I couldn't sleep, and I came up with an idea. So I went right home and wrote it down."

1976 White's portrayal of Sue Ann yields her back-to-back Primetime Emmy Awards for Outstanding Performance by an Actress in a Supporting Role in Comedy. The accolades keep piling up as she receives the Pacific Pioneer Broadcasters Golden Ike Award and the Genii Award from the Alliance for Women in Media. She also makes her first appearance on the sketch-comedy classic *The Carol Burnett Show*. "Betty would come on," recalled Burnett, "and if there was a tinge of risqué humor in one of our sketches, she'd roll with it and make it even funnier and add a little wink to show that she was thinking of something sexy. She's not a stand-up. She's not a jokester. It's the way she can twist a line to get a laugh."

1977 A new sitcom, *The Betty White Show*, premieres on CBS. White plays an actress who is cast on a cop show (hilariously called *Undercover Woman*) that happens to be directed by her pompous ex-husband, played by John Hillerman (*Magnum, P.I.*). Unfortunately, *The Betty White Show* is scheduled against ratings juggernaut *Monday Night Football*. White learns of its first-season cancellation right before she does a guest spot on *The Tonight Show*. She tells Carson from the couch: "You were mentioning at the beginning of the show that CBS canceled four shows. Make that five." Carson and the audience groan their disappointment. "Yes, Betty's bitten the dust." Carson:

"You didn't have to mention that." White: "Well, I can't be out here under false pretenses—wait, can I still stay on this show?" Carson: "Well, sure, no, you don't have to...[then he jokingly stands up and says] Too bad! Next guest! Bring me out somebody who has their own show!" The audience erupts in laughter. (Speaking of talk shows, White's husband, Allen Ludden, will give David Letterman his big break. White also befriends Carson's replacement on *The Tonight Show with Jay Leno*—who likes to play "Let's Make Betty Blink"—and becomes close friends with the irreverent host of *The Late Late Show with Craig Ferguson*, with whom she likes conducting "silly fake interviews.")

1981 Allen Ludden dies of cancer. "What got us together was his enthusiasm," White remembers. "Allen was interested in everything. There wasn't anything that he didn't want to know more about and hear about. That's fun to live with." White will live for another 40 years but never remarry. "Once you've had the best, who needs the rest?"

1983 In a field dominated by men, White becomes the first and only woman to win the Daytime Emmy Award for Outstanding Game Show Host for the ironically titled *Just Men!* The show's premise: two female contestants have to guess the lifestyles of seven male celebrity guests. White, once again, proves she's a natural: "I'm your hostess, Betty White [applause, applause] and this is a good group [points to celebrities]. Now, once again... [she pauses and turns to the camera] Can I talk to you just for a second? This key starts this beautiful Ford Mustang convertible. And I'm going to put it in with six sets of keys that don't start the Ford Mustang convertible, and [gesturing at the contestants] I'm not rooting against you girls, but I gotta tell you, we're all keeping our fingers crossed, because this is the only show where we're now saying, 'Let's try not to give away a car.' We've been giving away cars like popcorn!" (Laughter)

1983 White, now 61, gets a recurring role on the ABC sitcom *Mama's Family* as Ellen, the snobby daughter of Mama (played by 34-year-old Vicky Lawrence in a gray wig). Also on the show: Rue McClanahan. *Mama's Family* is canceled after the 1984 season but is reborn at CBS two years later. McClanahan and White aren't available to reprise their roles because they've been hired for a new NBC show.

1985 White auditions for a sitcom called *The Golden Girls*, about four senior women sharing a Miami home. She is originally cast as the proudly promiscuous Blanche Devereaux; Rue McClanahan will play Rose

By U.K. law, 5 percent of all TV shows must include a sign language interpreter.

Nylund, the airhead who knows more than she lets on. But because Blanche is similar to the character of Sue Ann Nivens from *The Mary Tyler Moore Show*, and Rose is similar to a character McClanahan played on *Maude*, White and McClanahan trade parts. *The Golden Girls* is a hit, and Rose becomes the breakout character thanks to White's delivery of lines like this: "You know what they say: You can lead a herring to water, but you have to walk really fast or he'll die."

1986 Rumors fly that there are tensions on the *Golden Girls* set. Formally trained actress Bea Arthur doesn't appreciate White's less-than-serious approach to the craft, nor the way she likes to joke with the studio audience. It gets even more awkward at the Emmys—in which White, Arthur, and McClanahan are all nominated...and White wins. In her acceptance speech, White clutches her Emmy and diplomatically says, "I am the lucky one who gets to come and pick up this beautiful 'Golden Girl,' but Estelle [Getty], and Rue, and Bea, and I all thank you. We're a matched set—you can't split us up. And we want to thank the network for taking a chance on four old broads—er, ladies." (Laughter.) White was later asked about her lack of formal training: "I just want to bring as much natural as I can. I'm not saying that people who take acting lessons are false. They're much better than I am, but it doesn't work for me."

1987 White receives the Humane Award for her charitable work with the American Veterinary Association. She also receives the American Comedy Award for Funniest Female, for saying stuff like this: "I have no idea what color my hair really is, and I never intend to find out."

1992 After seven seasons, Bea Arthur announces that she's leaving *The Golden Girls*, and the show ends...only to be reborn two years later as *The Golden Palace* with White, McClanahan, and Getty reprising their roles. *Palace* fails to make the same impact as the original. Despite the off-screen tensions during *Golden Girls*, White cherishes the stars' working relationship: "We showed up for the read through, and it was like batting a tennis ball over the net. It was so exciting to be with four people with that chemistry. I'll never forget that first read. It was like we had been working together forever! I still get goosebumps thinking about it."

Even if White had retired after The Golden Girls, *her place as one of America's most beloved entertainers would be solidified. But in a way, she was just getting going.*
Part III is on page 249.

First dashboard-mounted coffee maker: the Hertella Auto Kaffeesmachine, made for the Volkswagen Beetle in 1959.

BASS ON BASS!

The term "aptronym" was coined by early 20th-century humorist Franklin P. Adams to describe the funny situation that occurs when a person's name perfectly suits, or is "apt," for his or her passion or profession—such as toilet manufacturer Thomas Crapper, for example. Here are some others.

Dr. Henry Head: Editor of the neurology journal *Brain*

Heather Carb: Philadelphia-area bakery manager

Scott Speed: Formula 1 race-car driver

Paddy Driver: Professional motorcycle racer

John Laws: Appellate court judge in England

Marc Webb: Director of two Spider-Man movies

Dana Strum: Bassist for Slaughter and Ozzy Osbourne

Colin Bass: Bassist for the progressive rock band Camel

Dr. David Bird: President of the Society of Canadian Ornithologists

Amy Freeze: Fox Weather meteorologist

Brittany Rainey: Dallas–Fort Worth meteorologist

Sue Law: Law school professor

Dan Eaton: TV chef

Dr. Paul A. Babey: Arizona pediatrician

Dr. Walter Bohne: New York orthopedic surgeon

Gerald LaFlamme: Massachusetts fire chief

Rosemary Trout: Food scientist and writer

Sue Yoo: Lawyer in California

Gary Player: Professional golfer

Alec Steele: Blacksmith

Dr. Graeme Hart: Australian cardiothoracic surgeon

Mark De Man: Belgian professional soccer defender

Lonzo and LaMelo Ball: Professional basketball players

Philander Rodman: Father of NBA star Dennis Rodman, and of 29 total children by 16 women

Solo act: 75 percent of bees live and work alone, not in hives.

FOUNDING FATHERS

You know their names. Now here's a look at the real people behind them.

ELY REEVES CALLAWAY

By 1973, Ely Reeves Callaway was the second most powerful executive at Burlington Mills, one of the world's biggest fabric companies, with most of its 8,000 employees working out of manufacturing facilities in North Carolina. But when the board of directors passed him over for CEO, Callaway quit and decided to focus on another business venture: his recently purchased 150-acre vineyard in Temecula, California, an hour north of San Diego. Scientists and climate consultants told Callaway that it would be difficult for high-quality grapes to grow there, but he figured that the first grapes grown in Southern California would taste different from other wines, and that was something he could market. By 1977, Callaway Wines—sold via an all-female sales team—had made their way into fine restaurants and hotels on both coasts. In 1981, Callaway sold the business to big wine company Hiram Walker and Sons for $9 million, and retired into a life of traveling through California and golfing.

Around the same time, a golf supply company called Hickory Sticks USA launched, selling clubs with wooden shafts made of hickory and cores made of steel, an early lightweight hybrid club that could deliver power and distance. In trying to introduce a new style of club to the traditional game of golf, Hickory Sticks wasn't successful and was nearly out of business by 1982, which is when the company's four founders (and its only employees) approached Callaway about investing. In 1982, he bought a 50 percent interest in Hickory Stick. Within two years he'd bought the rest and installed himself as president, and, in 1988, the company was permanently renamed Callaway Golf Company.

WALLY AMOS

After earning his GED while serving in the air force, Wally Amos joined the William Morris Agency in 1957, working his way up from an entry-level mail room job to become the first African American talent agent in the American entertainment industry. WMA put him in charge of pop and rock acts, and he worked with Simon & Garfunkel, the Supremes, Sam Cooke, and Dionne Warwick. By the early 1970s, and after moving to Los Angeles, the long hours and stress of being a top agent left Amos burned out; to relieve stress, he turned to baking crispy chocolate chip cookies. He'd bring along a batch (made from a recipe of his own creation) to meetings with talent or record companies, and soon his reputation would precede him as the agent who brought wonderful cookies—often overshadowing the business at hand.

Ulysses S. Grant's 1885 funeral procession included 1.5 million people.

In 1975, Amos quit his agency job and opened a Famous Amos cookie store on a dilapidated section of Sunset Boulevard, across the street from a strip club and where prostitutes waited for clients, but also just a few blocks away from an A&M Records facility. Word spread among musicians, who became regular customers of Famous Amos, then investors. Marvin Gaye and Helen Reddy were among the high-profile celebrities who gave Amos the seed money to launch the Famous Amos Cookie Company, a line of cookies in eye-catching yellow packaging with the founder's picture. In year one, Famous Amos sold $300,000 of gourmet cookies—a grocery industry first—and in 1982, the company moved $12 million worth of chocolate-chip treats.

ANNE BEILER

Anne Beiler was born into a traditional fundamental Amish family in Pennsylvania, but when she was a young child, her parents switched to the Amish Mennonite faith and lifestyle, which allows the use of electric appliances. Beiler quit school after eighth grade per Amish tradition, got married at 19, and moved to Texas. After spending Christmas in her hometown, Beiler, her husband, and their two children decided to move back to Pennsylvania; they arrived in 1987 with just $25 in their bank account. After settling in and looking for ways she could earn a living without a completed education, Beiler bought a stall in a Downingtown, Pennsylvania, farmers market that had previously been used to bake and sell soft pretzels. All the equipment was there, and all Beiler had to do was concoct a pretzel recipe, which she perfected after several bad batches and trial and error. The pretzels at Auntie Anne's—named on account of Beiler having 30 nephews and nieces at the time—were such a hit that she opened a second location at another Pennsylvania farmers market within a year. By 1992, there were 100 Auntie Anne's Pretzels outlets, mostly in malls. Beiler sold the company to a cousin in 2005, by which point there were 1,200 stores.

CARL ZEISS

Look closely on a camera, microscope, or the tools at an optometrist's office, and you'll probably see the name Carl Zeiss stamped or etched on the equipment. That's the name of one of the world's leading producers of precision, professional-grade optical glass, and it started as an engineer's workshop and machine shop in Jena, Germany, in 1846. Thirty years old and educated in natural sciences and math at the University of Jena, Carl Zeiss opened for business and within a year had a long list of clients, mostly researchers and professors from his alma mater. He repaired, serviced, and custom built scientific instruments and tools, including chemical scales, glass containers, telescopes, and microscopes, which Zeiss (and his growing Zeiss Workshops) would focus on throughout the 1850s and 1860s as he obtained more clients at European colleges and scientific guilds.

New York state is named after New York City, which was named after the Duke of York, namesake of the English city of York.

CHICK IT OUT!

Chick Hearn provided colorful commentary for the Los Angeles Lakers for more than 40 years, with his rapid-fire, play-by-play work flavoring both radio and TV broadcasts. He served for so long, and in such a prominent position in a crucial development period for the sport of basketball, that many of the terms he coined became common and familiar. Here are but a few of those "Chickisms."

Slam dunk: When a player powerfully forces the ball into the basket at close range

Airball: When a player takes a shot and misses the hoop and net completely

"No harm, no foul": If it appeared someone was flagrantly fouled but the referees didn't call it as such, Hearn said this, indicating that since the player didn't seem to be in any physical pain, it wasn't much of a rules violation after all

Brick: A missed shot that loudly and forcefully bounces off the rim of the basket

Finger roll: Hearn's term for a successful layup made by a player releasing the ball from his hand and letting it glide off his fingertips, a shot popularized by Wilt Chamberlain

No-look pass: Hearn coined this in response to the Lakers' Magic Johnson's skill of throwing passes to teammates without having to glance at where they were on the court

Charity stripe: The free-throw line

Boo birds: Angry fans

Ticky-tack: A foul so minor the refs shouldn't have even called it

Picked his pocket: When a defender deftly executes a steal

Pup: A very young player

Frozen rope: A direct, straight shot to the hoop with little to no arc

Yo-yoing up and down: When a player stands in one spot, just dribbling the ball to waste time

In civilians: When an injured player who is ineligible to play sits on the bench, dressed in street clothes instead of a uniform

"Can't throw a pea in the ocean": What Hearn would say of a team that's shooting poorly and not scoring much

"Throws up a prayer": A player hoists up a wild but potentially game-winning, buzzer-beater shot from half-court or from across the court

"Caught with his hand in the cookie jar": A defender reached in, hit the shooter's hand, and got called for the foul

"This game is in the refrigerator": One team harbors an insurmountable lead

Garbage time: When the game is in the refrigerator and the rest of the fourth quarter plays out with the stars benched and the reserves on the court going through the motions of finishing the game as the clock winds down

The flames generated by methanol—used in race cars—are invisible and produce no smoke.

LOCAL HEROES

*Now for some harrowing true stories that will restore your faith in humanity,
brought to you by the kindness of strangers (and coworkers).*

FASTING IN THE SLOW LANE

Laurie Rabyor has no memory of what happened. The 63-year-old Boynton Beach,
Florida, woman had left work early because she wasn't feeling well. (She'd been fasting
for a colonoscopy and was having a bad reaction to her blood pressure meds.) While
stopped at a traffic light at a busy four-way intersection, she passed out behind the
wheel of her Mazda. It just so happened that one of her coworkers, Jannette Rivera,
was in the next car over. Rivera watched in horror as Rabyor's car slowly started
rolling into the intersection. Luckily, the cross traffic had already cleared, but the light
was about to change, and there were four lanes of cars waiting to go. The Mazda was
slowly veering toward them as it rolled across the wide intersection.

Rivera jumped out and started banging on the car while yelling and waving for
others to help. The doors were locked, so she couldn't get in. And then the light
changed. A postal worker named DaVida Peele, who was on her way home from work,
started directing traffic while five other people—Juan Chavez, Jr., Michael Edelstein,
David Formica, Marko Bartolone, and Muriel Vaughns—tried to stop the car. Things
got really tense when the drivers at the front of the line started steering out of the
way to avoid the oncoming car while the drivers behind them, who couldn't see what
was happening, started going forward. After a lot of pushing and yelling and a few
near misses, the five strangers finally stopped the Mazda. It had traveled all the way
through the intersection and was parked next to the curb in the oncoming lanes.

Nothing or no one was hit, but Rabyor was still unresponsive, and they were
still on a very busy road. After a frantic search of their vehicles, one of the bystanders
arrived with a dumb-bell and smashed the Mazda's back window. Then they drove
the car to a nearby gas station, where they all waited with Rabyor until an ambulance
arrived. She made a full recovery.

A few days later, she was reunited with the heroes when they were honored by
the Boynton Beach Police Department. "I wish I was a millionaire," said Rabyor, "so I
could buy y'all a boat." The city did the next best thing and awarded all six life savers—
as well as the woman they saved—$2,000 gift cards and a Caribbean cruise.

THE FIRE MAN

Late one night in July 2022, Nick Bostic, 25, was driving home when he saw flames
billowing out of a two-story house in Lafayette, Indiana. He pulled over and ran

Smallest celestial body with rings: 10199 Chariklo, an asteroid with a diameter of 155 miles.

inside through the back door. "Anybody home!?" No answer. The flames were spreading fast. He looked upstairs and saw two little kids and their 18-year-old babysitter, who was holding a baby. (Mom and Dad were still out for the evening.) Bostic helped the four of them down the stairs and made sure they got out safely, but the babysitter was panicking—a six-year-old girl was still inside! Bostic darted back in and called for the little girl through the thick smoke. No answer. Unable to see and barely able to breathe, he made his way upstairs and searched every room, but he still couldn't find her. Then he heard a faint cry coming from downstairs, so put his shirt over his face and made his way back down, where he crawled around on the floor, following the sound of her voice until he found her. But their way out was blocked by the fire, so Bostic carried the girl upstairs, knocked out a bedroom window, jumped out shoulder first—with her clinging to the front of him—and landed on his back. Despite intense pain and shortness of breath, Bostic got up and carried the girl to the front yard, just as the arriving firefighters were about to go in after them.

The little girl had a cut foot but was otherwise fine. Bostic had a broken arm and a bad case of smoke inhalation, not to mention ember burns dotting his entire body. After only two days in the hospital, he was expected to make a full recovery. The young man's heroics made international news, and he was honored by the town of Lafayette. But the best thing that came of it was a new friendship with the family he saved from tragedy. "It was all worth it," Bostic said.

LIFEGUARD ON DUTY

It was a little after midnight on a Saturday night in July 2022 at a popular hangout for teens in Moss Point, Mississippi. Three teenage girls (unidentified in press reports) were parked at the top of a boat ramp directly underneath Interstate 10. When the driver of the car entered the directions for home into her GPS unit, which tracks cars via satellite, the device assumed they were *on* Interstate 10. So the voice told her to drive in the direction she was facing. The girl did as she was instructed, and before she even turned on the headlights, she had driven the car right into the Pascagoula River. By the time it came to a stop, only the roof was above the water.

Sixteen-year-old Corion Evans, a high school football player and experienced swimmer (described in news reports as a "rising star"), couldn't believe what he was seeing. "I thought, 'There is no way that they drove into that water.'" Evans, who was in his car getting ready to leave (so he'd be home before curfew), sprinted over as the girls were calling for help and trying to get on top of the car. They were too scared to swim in the rushing river, so Evans left his shoes, shirt, and phone on the riverbank and swam over to them.

He got the first two girls to safety, one by one. By then, a police officer named Gary Mercer had arrived on the scene. He left his gun belt, vest, and body cam

Late "Crocodile Hunter" Steve Irwin named his daughter Bindi after his favorite crocodile.

in his squad car and swam over to rescue the third victim. But the struggling girl pulled the cop under and he swallowed a lot of water. Neither of them came up. Evans jumped back in and rescued both Mercer and the teen girl. "We're always proud when our young men do the right thing," said Moss Point Mayor Billy Knight at a ceremony to honor Evans, "because so many times our young people are not doing the right thing."

REMOTE LEARNING

Darren Harrison and his friend were the only two passengers onboard a Cessna that was taking them back to Florida after a fishing trip in the Bahamas in May 2022. Toward the end of the flight, the pilot, 64-year-old Kenneth Allen, said he had a headache and then started acting confused and lethargic. At around 11:20 a.m., the plane went into a nosedive over the Atlantic Ocean. Harrison, wearing flip-flops and shorts, attempted to revive the pilot, without success. So Harrison took the yoke (the plane's "steering wheel") and managed to get the single-engine aircraft level again. He put on the pilot's headset and said to anyone who was listening, "I've got a serious situation here. My pilot has gone incoherent. And I have no idea how to fly an airplane."

Air traffic controller Chip Fuller took the call and calmly told Harrison how to keep the plane in the sky until he could get a flight instructor on the radio. They reached Bobby Morgan, an air traffic controller and flight instructor at Palm Beach International Airport.

The first order of business: figuring out where the plane was. Harrison didn't know, but he could see the Florida coast on the horizon. After the controllers determined the plane was near Boca Raton, Morgan told Harrison he was going to guide him to Palm Beach. Despite reminding them many times of his complete lack of flying knowledge, Harrison remained relatively calm for someone in his predicament.

It wasn't just about landing the plane safely, but doing so as quickly as possible to get Allen to a hospital. As the plane was fast approaching the airport, Morgan gave Harrison a crash course (so to speak) in how to land a plane. "I felt like I was in a movie," Morgan recalled.

An hour and sixteen minutes after the initial distress call, Harrison landed the Cessna successfully. Allen was rushed to a hospital; he'd suffered a tear in his aorta and underwent nine hours of life-saving surgery. Doctors said he'll recover, but his flying days are over. A commercial pilot named Justin Dalmolin, whose own landing was delayed while the Cessna was guided in to Palm Beach, later explained the magnitude of Harrison's feat: "The level of difficulty that this person had to deal with in terms of having zero flight time to fly and land a single-engine turbine aircraft is absolutely incredible. I remember when I first started flight training I was white-knuckled and sweating."

Ninety-nine percent of a human body's mass comes from six elements: oxygen, carbon, hydrogen, nitrogen, calcium, and phosphorus.

CROCODILE DONNIE

That's what the press called him: Crocodile Donnie. With good reason. In August 2021, during a five-year-old's birthday party at the Scales and Tails Zoo in West Valley City, Utah, the kids and their parents were watching from behind glass as a handler named Lindsay Bull was hand-feeding Darth Gator, an eight-and-a-half-foot-long American alligator. Bull was standing outside the enclosure...until the gator clamped down on her hand and pulled her into the two-foot deep water. "Hey! We've got trouble in here!" shouted one of the dads, Donnie Wiseman. There were no other zookeepers around, so as the scared kids were being taken away, Wiseman tried to pull Bull out, but the gator was thrashing around, attempting to get her in a "death roll"—which is how these prehistoric reptiles kill large prey. Wiseman jumped in to the water and got on the alligator's back, which calmed it a little, but it still didn't let go of the keeper's hand. "What do I do next?" he asked Bull.

"Talk to him," she answered. So he did, for nearly a minute until Bull was able to remove her mangled hand from the gator's mouth. Another dad at the party then pulled her to safety. But Wiseman was still in there, wrapped around Darth Gator's back, and he knew if he let go that he could easily be taken under. He held on tight while Bull instructed him to sit upright. After a few more tense moments, Bull could tell that Darth Gator was calm. She told Wiseman to let go and get out—fast. He was out in two big steps.

Wiseman received some cuts and scratches, but Bull had to undergo hand surgery. They both credit the other with saving their lives. Wiseman's wife, who witnessed the whole thing, told reporters, "I'm not surprised that Donnie did that, that's the kind of person he is, but I asked him if he please wouldn't do it again anytime soon."

* * *

THE OTHER MOVIES THAT OPENED IN MOVIE THEATERS THE SAME DAYS THAT THE *STAR WARS* MOVIES DEBUTED

1977: *Smokey and the Bandit* vs. *Star Wars*

1980: *Carny, The Gong Show Movie,* and *The Shining* vs. *The Empire Strikes Back*

1983: *Chained Heat* vs. *Return of the Jedi*

1999: *The Love Letter* vs. *The Phantom Menace*

2002: *About a Boy* vs. *Attack of the Clones*

2005: *Dominion: Prequel to The Exorcist* vs. *Revenge of the Sith*

2015: *Sisters* and *Alvin and the Chipmunks: The Road Chip* vs. *The Force Awakens*

2017: *Ferdinand* vs. *The Last Jedi*

2019: *Cats* vs. *The Rise of Skywalker*

President Andrew Johnson was illiterate until age 17.

COURT TRANS-QUIPS

The verdict is in! Amusing court transcripts make for some of the best bathroom reading there is. These lines were actually spoken, word for word, in a court of law.

Lawyer: Now, sir, I'm sure you are an intelligent and honest man...
Witness: Thank you. If I weren't under oath, I'd return the compliment.

Lawyer: Doctor, how many of your autopsies have you performed on dead people?
Witness: All of them. The live ones put up too much of a fight.

Lawyer: Do you recall the time that you examined the body?
Witness: The autopsy started around 8:30 p.m.
Lawyer: And Mr. Denton was dead at the time?
Witness: If not, he was by the time I finished.

Lawyer: What happened then?
Witness: He told me, he says, "I have to kill you because you can identify me."
Lawyer: Did he kill you?
Witness: No.

Lawyer: Was that the same nose you broke as a child?
Witness: I only have one, you know.

Lawyer: Are you married?
Witness: No, I'm divorced.
Lawyer: And what did your husband do before you divorced him?
Witness: A lot of things I didn't know about.

Lawyer: Were you acquainted with the deceased?
Witness: Yes, sir.
Lawyer: Before or after he died?

Judge: Why were you going so fast in a residential zone?
Defendant: Well, it's not my fault. The truck behind me was tailgating me and making such a racket. I was just trying to get away.
Judge: What kind of truck was it?
Defendant: A fire truck.

Judge: And next time, don't show up to court looking like you're going to the beach!
Defendant: But I am going to the beach!

Judge: Do you have any other questions before you're taken into custody?
Defendant: Yeah, can I call my wife and have her come get my girlfriend's truck? I didn't think I'd be going to prison today.

Judge: I'm going to hold you in contempt.
Defendant: You can come down here and hold me in your arms.

Lawyer: Did you ever make that comment?
Witness: I don't remember.
Lawyer: But it is possible that you made it?
Defense Attorney: Objection. Anything is possible.
Lawyer: It is not possible that I can jump out of this window and fly.
Witness: You could try.

Judge: How many in your home that you are financially responsible for?
Defendant: I'm going to say three. I have a dog, a lizard, and a female.

Judge: What's your relationship status?
Juror: Single. Well, I'm engaged, but legally I'm single. I'm glad my fiancé didn't hear that.

There are exactly 412 doors in the White House.

GAME OVER!

Ready, reader one, for this article about the worst and most spectacularly failed video games ever made.

GAME: *E.T. the Extra-Terrestrial*
YEAR: 1982
GAME ON: The biggest thing in pop culture in 1982: the movie *E.T. the Extra-Terrestrial*, a phenomenon directed by Steven Spielberg that became the highest-grossing movie of all time, despite competition from video games, particularly Atari's 2600 Console that brought the bleeps and bloops from the arcades and into millions of homes. After programmer Howard Scott Warshaw designed the hit games *Yar's Revenge* and *Raiders of the Lost Ark*, Atari assigned him the plum project of a 2600 title based on *E.T.* The problem: Atari didn't close the deal with Spielberg until late July 1982. They wanted a game designed, programmed, and ready for manufacture by September 1, so it could be in stores in time for the holiday shopping season—an alarmingly short period of about five weeks. (Conversely, it took Warshaw 10 months to make *Raiders of the Lost Ark*.) Warshaw had just 36 hours to come up with a concept to pitch to Atari brass, and he devised an idea loosely based on the movie's plot, where E.T. collects pieces of a communications device to "phone home." There's little more to the game than E.T. (and human friend Elliott) navigating a field full of holes (which, if fallen into, end the game) and finding little objects to assemble into a communicator.
GAME OVER: The nascent video game press savaged the game, citing its poor graphics and confusing gameplay. However, Atari was so confident that the popularity of *E.T.* the movie would drive sales of *E.T.* the game that it manufactured more than 4 million cartridges. About 2.6 million copies sold, but nearly 700,000 were returned, leaving millions unsold. The company buried its unsold stock in a New Mexico desert and called the whole thing a write-off.

GAME: *Superman 64*
YEAR: 1999
GAME ON: Superman, beloved all-American superhero institution, has starred in almost every type of media there is, including comic books, radio shows, television, movies, and video games. In 1999, Nintendo aggressively promoted *Superman 64*, a title for its popular N64 home gaming console, playing up the game's three-dimensional-style graphics to bring the somewhat old and tired Superman character into a new age. The game itself was immediately criticized as one of the worst ever

---

Three states are named for women: Virginia and West Virginia
(after Queen Elizabeth I, the "Virgin Queen"), and Maryland (for England's Queen Maria).

for failing to meet the bare minimum requirements of a video game, in that it had characters that were nearly impossible to control, bad graphics, and repetitive gameplay.

GAME OVER: The plot: Lex Luthor has trapped Superman's friends in a strange virtual computer world, so the Man of Steel goes into the digital world to save them. That pretty much entails flying, very slowly—as the game inches along from a poorly rendered Superman's point of view—through blurry rings gathering pixelated coins under a certain time limit. And then he does this several more times. Nintendo estimated it would sell at least a million copies of *Superman 64*, but it sold fewer than half that many. Sony was so dismayed by the reaction that it canceled plans to bring the *Superman* game to its brand-new PlayStation console.

GAME: *Cyberpunk 2077*
YEAR: 2020
GAME ON: An open world title, meaning players can explore the game's vast and detailed world of the futuristic town of Night City in the distant 21st century, *Cyberpunk 2077* allows gamers to step into the shoes of a mercenary called V, cursed with a computer chip in his brain that he hurries to remove before it, and the consciousness of a dead movie star, take over his mind and body forever. It wasn't just the concept that was ambitious; developer CD Projekt Red hired 500 programmers to make *Cyberpunk 2077*, and hired Keanu Reeves to provide voice and motion capture movements for the V character.

GAME OVER: After announcing in 2012 that the game was in development, CD Projekt Red released the game for the PlayStation 4, Xbox One, and home computers in late 2020, and even after all that time it was glitchy and full of bugs. Despite offering refunds to the millions of people who returned their copy of the game, CD Projekt's stock value fell by 10 percent and was the subject of a class-action lawsuit that was settled for nearly $2 million. That's a fraction of the cost of making *Cyberpunk 2077*, however. With a price tag of $174 million, it was the most expensive video game in history to that point.

GAME: *APB: All Points Bulletin*
YEAR: 2010
GAME ON: Scottish video game designer David Jones created two games that spawned long-running franchises—*Lemmings* and *Grand Theft Auto*—and in 2002, he took his talents and started his own video game publisher, Realtime Worlds. In 2008, Jones announced that his company's biggest title yet would hit stores that same year: a multiplayer online game called *APB: All Points Bulletin*. Similar to the *Grand Theft Auto*

games in that players could drive around a crime-ridden city and explore and commit acts of mayhem, it would also be like the popular *World of Warcraft* in that gamers would interact in real time in the world of the game with other players. Production issues forced a delay of the game's release to 2009, and then to 2010, by which time Realtime Worlds had already spent $124 million, making *APB* one of the costliest video games ever.

GAME OVER: *APB* finally hit stores in the U.S. and the U.K. in the summer of 2010, but with a caveat: video game magazines and websites weren't allowed to publish their reviews until more than a week after release. In all kinds of media, that kind of embargo is usually enacted on lackluster products—no prerelease reviews mean no bad word of mouth to cut into initial sales. Instead, news of the review ban spread around gamer circles, and *APB* sold so poorly that just two months after it hit stores, publisher Realtime Worlds filed for bankruptcy and sold the rights to the game to competitor Reloaded Productions, who redeveloped the game and rereleased it in 2015.

GAME: *Pac-Man*
YEAR: 1982
GAME ON: The first big video game craze in the 1980s was driven in large part by *Pac-Man*, a game where players control a yellow, pie-shaped creature as it navigates a maze, eats pellets, and avoids villainous ghosts. Millions of *Pac-Man* stand-up machines wound up in arcades, pizza parlors, lobbies, and convenience stores, generating billions in revenue for publisher Namco as people in the U.S., Europe, and Japan got virtually addicted to the game. The leading home video-game company at the time, Atari, paid millions to Namco to license *Pac-Man* for its popular Atari 2600 system. Working with technology of a home console that was much more limited than that of an arcade machine, Atari programmers turned out an at-home *Pac-Man* that doesn't much resemble the wildly popular and familiar game. For example, the maze dimensions are off, the ghosts are the wrong color, and Pac-Man eats brown lines instead of white pellets.

GAME OVER: Seven million people bought a copy of *Pac-Man* for the Atari 2600, which still ranks among the best-selling video games of all-time. However, Atari was so confident that the possibility of quarter-free *Pac-Man* in the comfort of one's TV room would be such a powerful lure, that it manufactured and distributed 12 million cartridges. To make money on the deal, Atari would've had to sell a *Pac-Man* game to every single person who already owned an Atari 2600 and then to five million people who hadn't bought one yet. Atari couldn't absorb the cost of five million unsold games; the financial loss led directly to the company filing for bankruptcy a year later.

Avid golfer Dwight Eisenhower was inducted into the World Golf Hall of Fame in 2009.

HE WHO SMELT IT . . .

Sometimes, a light shines upon the Bathroom Readers' Institute—just like it did the day we discovered a Wikipedia page called "Flatulence Humour," which concludes with a list of farting rhymes (the best known being "He who smelt it dealt it"). Here are our favorites, along with some we made up ourselves. (We are the experts, of course.)

- Whoever started it farted it.

- They who introduced it produced it.

- She who declared it blared it.

- He who denied it supplied it.

- He who detected it ejected it.

- They who observed it served it.

- He who claimed it aimed it.

- He who blew it knew it.

- She who yelled at us produced the flatus.

- Whoever made a frown laid the brown.

- Whoever made the fuss cleared the bus.

- He who did complain did not restrain.

- She who is guilty made the flowers wilty.

- He that did the teasing did the squeezing.

- She who sensed it dispensed it.

- He who blamed the dog made the smog.

- Whoever made the quip let it rip.

- The one poking fun is the smoking gun.

- She who is squealing is also concealing.

- He who called me rude spoiled the mood.

- They who policed it released it.

- She who tattled rattled.

- He who theorized terrorized.

- They who grumbled rumbled.

- The smeller's the feller.

- He who articulated it particulated it.

- He who caused the stress made the mess.

- She who's full of sass passed the gas.

- She who made the rhyme did the crime.

- He who did accuse blew the fuse.

- He who deduced it produced it.

- He who's in dispute committed the toot.

- She who faked the sneeze cut the cheese.

- He who faked the cough let one off.

- He who remarked on it embarked on it.

- Whoever gave the call gassed us all.

- The one who disapproved was the one whose butt cheeks moved.

- The reciter of this verse has made the air so much worse.

Biggest single thing ever sold: the 530-million-acre area acquired by the U.S. through the Louisiana Purchase in 1803.

WARD TOUR

Cleveland newspaper columnist Charles Farrar Browne (1834–1867) took his act on the road in the mid-19th century, reciting his works under the persona of a fictional orator named Artemus Ward (who also happened to write a few books, too). Historians regard this as the first stand-up comedy act. Here are some of the best jokes, bits, and witty observations of Artemus Ward.

"Let us all be happy, and live within our means,
even if we have to borrow money to do it with."

"A writer who can't write in a grammerly manner better shut up shop."

"One of the principal features of my Entertainment is that it
contains so many things that don't have anything to do with it."

"I prefer temperance hotels. Although they sell worse
liquor than any other kind of hotels."

"We have a passion for oratory in America—political oratory chiefly.
Our political orators never lose a chance to 'express their views.'
They will do it. You cannot stop them."

"Have you ever had the measles, and if so, how many?"

"I'm not a politician and my other habits are good."

"Let's have the Union restored as it was, if we can; but if we can't,
I'm in favor of the Union as it wasn't."

"We wish genius and morality were affectionate companions,
but it is a fact that they are often bitter enemies.
They don't necessarily coalesce any more than oil and water do."

"It is true, that all married men have their own way, but the trouble is
they don't all have their own way of having it!"

"Trouble will come soon enough, and when he does come, receive him
as pleasantly as possible...the more amiably you greet
him the sooner he will go away."

"Why is this thus? What is the reason of this thusness?"

"They drink with impunity, or anybody who invites them."

"Why don't you show us a statesman who can rise up to the Emergency,
and cave in the Emergency's head?"

ALMOST CAST: SUPERVILLAINS

If you ask most actors, they'll tell you that it's more fun to play the villain than the hero, but there was a time when most serious thespians scoffed at the idea of appearing in a comic book movie. Here's how that changed.

RAY LIOTTA AS THE JOKER (*BATMAN*, 1989)

When you think of Batman today, you picture a gruff-talking "Dark Knight" patrolling the mean streets of Gotham. But in 1988, when word got around that director Tim Burton, fresh off the success of *Beetlejuice*, was going to make a Batman feature film, what came to mind for most people was the campy 1960s *Batman* TV show ("Holy hamstrings, Batman!" and *Pow! Biff! Bam!*). That's all that Ray Liotta could picture when Burton asked him to audition for either Bruce Wayne or the Joker.

At 33, Liotta's film career was picking up steam after his menacing turn as a violent ex-husband in 1986's *Something Wild*. Burton told Liotta he wanted a more menacing Joker, Liotta (even though he loved *Beetlejuice*) thought to himself, "That's a stupid idea." He didn't even audition, smugly telling Burton, "I'm an actor." Later on, Liotta called it one of the biggest mistakes of his career: "I've always regretted not going to meet him. Just to meet him, just to talk—whether I agreed with playing it— because I couldn't wrap my head around it."

Burton's Joker search also included David Bowie, Tim Curry (who was the original cartoon voice of the Joker before he was replaced by Mark Hamill), and John Lithgow (who tried to talk Burton out of hiring him during his audition). Lithgow also regretted his decision: "I didn't think the movie would be such a big deal." Other Joker considerations: Mel Gibson, Kevin Costner, Charlie Sheen, Tom Selleck, Bill Murray, Harrison Ford, Dennis Quaid, John Glover, Brad Dourif, James Woods, and Willem Dafoe. Robin Williams really wanted the part, but in the end, the Joker role went to Jack Nicholson, whom Warner Bros. execs had had their eye on ever since he scared the hell out of moviegoers in 1980's *The Shining*. Nicholson ended up starring opposite the controversial choice of Michael Keaton, who was cast more for his portrayal of Bruce Wayne than for his Batman. Keaton won the role over the studio's first choice, Pierce Brosnan. (The future James Bond wasn't interested.)

Not long after not auditioning for *Batman*, Liotta landed the part of Shoeless Joe Jackson in the baseball fantasy drama *Field of Dreams*. Then came his career-defining

George Washington wanted to name Washington, D.C., "Federal City."

role as mobster Henry Hill in 1990's *Goodfellas*. Who knows if he would have gotten either of those parts if he'd played the Joker?

BILLY CRUDUP AS NORMAN OSBORN/THE GREEN GOBLIN (*SPIDER-MAN*, 2002)

What Tim Burton did for Batman, Sam Raimi did 13 years later for Spider-Man: turned him from a niche character reserved for comic book nerds into a hero for the masses. *Spider-Man* also gave a big boost to superhero movies in general, after the 1990s Batman sequels grew progressively campier until Joel Shumacher's infamous "bat nipples" in *Batman & Robin* put an end to the Burton era. Superhero movies started to make a rebound with *Blade* (1997) and *X-Men* (2000), but those were modest hits. Sony Pictures execs wanted more, and they knew that the right combination of casting and storyline could put them on top.

Raimi, a Spider-Man fan since childhood, landed the directing job after deals fell through with James Cameron, David Fincher, Roland Emmerich, Tony Scott, Chris Columbus, Barry Sonnenfeld, Michael Bay, Ang Lee, M. Night Shyamalan, and even Tim Burton (who said he was a "DC guy").

Before Raimi could cast the villain, he had to choose which one to include. He landed on the Green Goblin because the father-son dynamic of the dad of Peter Parker's troubled best friend (played by James Franco) becoming the bad guy would add real drama to the story. So, like Burton before him, Raimi went looking for seasoned actors. His first choice was Billy Crudup (*Almost Famous*), who quit his other projects to play the Green Goblin—but he was ultimately deemed too young to be believable as Franco's father. The role was offered to Robert De Niro, Mel Gibson, John Malkovich, and John Travolta—who all turned it down. Also considered were Bill Paxton, Brad Dourif, and Nicolas Cage.

So how did Willem Dafoe get the role of Green Goblin? He fought for it. In the same way Raimi had gotten himself hired as director by persuading Sony of his love for the source material, Dafoe had to do the same thing: "I met with Sam and the studio and I said, 'I want to do this.' And the studio said, 'Well, we've got a long list of people in mind.' And I said, 'Put me on tape.'" Dafoe did his screen test in a hotel room in Spain, and he got the part. Sony's gamble paid off big time. Not only did *Spider-Man* take home the top domestic box office in 2002, with a haul of over $400 million, it outperformed *Star Wars: Episode II–Attack of the Clones* and *Harry Potter and the Chamber of Secrets*. The age of the superhero movie had begun.

ADRIEN BRODY AS THE JOKER (*THE DARK KNIGHT*, 2008)

Christopher Nolan's The Dark Knight Trilogy, which started with 2005's *Batman Begins*, made the Caped Crusader darker, more foreboding, and more grounded in

Makes sense: the original name for a computer mouse was "pointing device."

realism. Nolan wanted his villains to be less campy than Jack Nicholson's Joker. In fact, he didn't even want to bring in the "Crown Prince of Crime" until the second installment.

When Nolan was originally casting Bruce Wayne for *Batman Begins* (a part that eventually went to Christian Bale), one of the first people he approached was Australian actor Heath Ledger, best known at the time for *A Knight's Tale*. Ledger told Nolan he didn't want to do a sequel to the 1990s "bat nipples" movies. Nolan assured Ledger the film would be a total reboot. Ledger was intrigued, but they both agreed he wasn't right for Bruce Wayne.

Two years later, when Nolan was casting *The Dark Knight*, Ledger had recently delivered his Oscar-winning performance in *Brokeback Mountain*. Having loved *Batman Begins*, Ledger agreed to play the Joker before the script was even completed. "I'd seen what world it was that I would be playing in. So I knew it was open for a fresh interpretation. I also instantly kind of had something up my sleeve, which happened to be exactly what Chris was kind of looking for."

But Warner Bros. wanted to look at other actors. Adrien Brody lobbied hard to get the Joker part. He'd proven he could do action in 2005's *King Kong* and drama in 2002's *The Pianist* (for which he won an Oscar), and with his angular face and expressive eyebrows, he certainly had the right look. Nolan still wanted Ledger. Other possible Jokers: Sam Rockwell, who played the unhinged Zaphod Beeblebrox in *The Hitchhiker's Guide to the Galaxy* (2005), and Crispin Glover, who may be the only actor considered for the Joker in 1989 *and* 2008 (thanks to his odd, star-making role as George McFly in *Back to the Future*). Paul Bettany, who costarred with Ledger in *A Knight's Tale*, was also considered. (He'd later be cast as Vision in the Marvel Cinematic Universe's Avengers franchise.) Nolan still wanted Ledger. His persistence more than paid off: Ledger's sadistic take on the Joker, even though it consumes only 32 minutes of the movie's 2.5-hour run time, propelled *The Dark Knight* to become the highest-grossing movie ever (at the time), and earned Ledger an Academy Award, albeit posthumously. (He died at 28 shortly after the movie finished filming).

RYAN GOSLING AS THE JOKER (*SUICIDE SQUAD*, 2016)

The Suicide Squad first appeared in DC Comics in 1959, and over the years there have been various lineups in the team comprised of imprisoned supervillains recruited by the government to go on suicide missions. The highly anticipated 2016 movie would introduce a new Joker. Adrien Brody was still interested, but he struck out again, saying, "To me, the villains are way fun! But studios don't offer me those roles."

Smallest number with an "a" in its spelling: one thousand.

In 2015, it was announced that Ryan Gosling was in talks to take over the Joker role. Gosling, a former child actor who became an A-lister in dramas such as *The Notebook* and *Drive*, had never done a comic book movie before; he didn't want to commit to a multi-picture deal, so he bowed out.

Jared Leto, who'd recently won an Oscar for *Dallas Buyers Club*, landed the role as the Joker. He said he purposely didn't watch Ledger's performance in *The Dark Knight* so he could give the character a fresh take. He took the role so seriously that he stayed in character for the entire shoot—to the point of giving Joker-like gifts to the other actors, including a live rat he gave to Margot Robbie. "I did give some really nice, sweet gifts as well," he said on press junkets. "I gave cupcakes."

But unlike Nicholson and Ledger before him, Leto's David Bowie–inspired Joker didn't leave a lasting mark. Not that it was all his fault—most of the Joker's scenes were cut, and the movie received only a 26 percent rating on Rotten Tomatoes. Screenwriter David Ayer was given just six weeks to write the screenplay; as he admitted in an open letter to disgruntled fans, the story suffered for it: "Would I do a lot of things different? Yep, for sure. Wish I had a time machine. I'd make Joker the main villain and engineer a more grounded story."

As of this writing, Gosling still hasn't done a comic book movie. Neither has Brody.

DAMION POITIER AS THANOS (*GUARDIANS OF THE GALAXY*, 2014)

Who's Damion Poitier? His Internet Movie Database biography begins like this: "Damion Poitier is an African American actor who is known for his cameo as Thanos at the very end of the first Avengers film before he got replaced by Josh Brolin in *Guardians of the Galaxy*." This brief bio isn't quite fair to Poitier, because he played memorable characters on shows such as *True Blood* and *The Flash*. But his role as Thanos was a last-minute addition to *The Avengers* (2012) post-credits scene. Director Jon Favreau didn't have time to properly cast the role—nor was it even certain that Thanos would appear in the next Avengers movie (he didn't)—so Poitier, who's played a lot of bit parts in Marvel movies, including "Man #1" in *Avengers*, ended up with the job.

But when it came to creating what would become one of the most iconic (and brutal) movie villains since Darth Vader, *Guardians of the Galaxy* director James Gunn decided to recast the role with a heavyweight. So Poitier was out. Fan speculation ran rampant. One comic book site's top picks for Marvel's "Mad Titan" (as Thanos is called) included Tom Waits, Ron Perlman, Arnold Schwarzenegger, and Vin Diesel.

Tallest iceberg on record: the Melville Bay iceberg,
spotted near Greenland in 1958, at 550 feet.

Other rumored names were Hugh Laurie, Alan Rickman, and Ken Watanabe. Gunn had another idea: stone-faced Josh Brolin. From playing the big brother in *The Goonies* (1985) to portraying George W. Bush in *W.* (2008), Brolin certainly had range. And even though the character's look was going to be CGI, the voice acting and facial expressions required a top-tier actor. Brolin was offered the part in 2015 and didn't hesitate to say yes. He drew inspiration from Marlon Brando's Colonel Walter E. Kurtz in *Apocalypse Now* (1979). But Thanos's appearance in *Guardians* was brief—just a scene to show that he's looking for the Infinity Stones—and Gunn almost cut it, but he liked the way it tied in with the Avengers movies.

When it came time to cast Thanos for *Avengers: Infinity War* (2018), directors Joe and Anthony Russo didn't even consider anyone else: "[Brolin] is so uniquely suited to Thanos," said Anthony. "He is perhaps the best example that you can find where you have somebody who has a physical presence and brings that level of intensity and threat, while at the same time having another layer always at work underneath that, which is a very complex inner life and a lot of emotional depth and texture." Like we said, it's more fun to play the villain.

* * *

BILLY WILDER'S 10 SCREENWRITING TIPS

Billy Wilder (1906–2002) is widely considered to be the best screenwriter in movie history. The evidence: *Double Indemnity* (1944), *Stalag 17* (1953), *Sabrina* (1954), *Some Like It Hot* (1959), *Casino Royale* (1967), and a couple dozen more. In the 1999 book *Conversations with Wilder* by Cameron Crowe, Wilder divulged the secrets to his success:

1. The audience is fickle.

2. Grab 'em by the throat and never let 'em go.

3. Develop a clean line of action for your leading character.

4. Know where you're going.

5. The more subtle and elegant you are in hiding your plot points, the better you are as a writer.

6. If you have a problem with the third act, the real problem is the first act.

7. A tip from [Ernst] Lubitsch: "Let the audience add up two plus two. They'll love you forever."

8. In doing voice-overs, be careful not to describe what the audience already sees. Add to what they're seeing.

9. The event that occurs at the second act curtain triggers the end of the movie.

10. The third act must build, build, build in tempo and action until the last event, and then—that's it. Don't hang around.

Only time a state changed its postal code: Nebraska went from NB to NE...

KILLER OR BROADWAY STAR?

It seems as if only two classifications of people are commonly and publicly referred to by three names: deadly criminals—murderers, assassins, and serial killers—and prominent stage actors. Can you determine which of the following people are notorious killers and which are Tony Award–nominated or Tony Award–winning actors? Answers are on page 405.

1.	Simon Russell Beale	**21.**	John Douglas Thompson
2.	Paul John Knowles	**22.**	William Biff McGuire
3.	Brian Stokes Mitchell	**23.**	Mark David Chapman
4.	Michael Robert Ryan	**24.**	Jon Michael Hill
5.	John Benjamin Hickey	**25.**	Alfred Leonard Cline
6.	Billy Edwin Reid	**26.**	Ruben Santiago-Hudson
7.	Robert Sean Leonard	**27.**	Gary Leon Ridgway
8.	David Marshall Grant	**28.**	Brenda Ann Spencer
9.	Gordon Stewart Northcott	**29.**	John-Andrew Morrison
10.	Steven Brian Pennell	**30.**	Gordon Joseph Weiss
11.	Dick Anthony Williams	**31.**	David Malcolm Gray
12.	Allan Patterson Newman	**32.**	Brandon Victor Dixon
13.	Charles Nelson Reilly	**33.**	Bruno Richard Hauptmann
14.	Wilson Jermaine Heredia	**34.**	Sean Allan Krill
15.	Christopher Wayne Hudson	**35.**	Edward James Adams
16.	Robert William Pickton	**36.**	John Lloyd Young
17.	Johnny Paul Penry	**37.**	Orville Lynn Majors
18.	Norbert Leo Butz	**38.**	Harry Hadden-Paton
19.	David Alan Grier	**39.**	Tony Ray Amati
20.	James Edward Pough	**40.**	William Dale Archerd

…to avoid confusion with Canadian province New Brunswick.

STRANGE MEDICAL NEWS

The human body is a complicated organic machine, and modern medicine hasn't unlocked all its secrets yet. Here are some of the oddest happenings to befall patients and baffle doctors in recent years.

JUST A LITTLE BIT

Sixty-year-old Illinois resident Tom Jozsi went to his dentist in March 2022 to be fitted for a filling. Jozsi's body accidentally received far more metal than anyone had intended. While the dentist drilled into a tooth, the inch-long bit came loose. Just as Jozsi was taking a breath, and before a cough, he managed to inhale the tool part. "I didn't really even feel it going down. All I felt was a cough," Jozsi told reporters. "When they did the CT scan they realized, 'You didn't swallow it. You inhaled it.'" Dr. Abdul Alraiyes at Aurora Medical Center in Kenosha, Wisconsin, warned Jozsi that if they couldn't retrieve the bit from his lung, the organ itself would have to be partially removed. Fortunately, with a cancer-detection tool—not normally used for removing foreign objects—Dr. Alraiyes successfully retrieved the bit, which Jozsi now proudly displays on a shelf.

HOLD IT

In 2018, *BMJ Case Reports* shared the novel story of an 80-year-old patient complaining of a distended abdomen. It wasn't causing him pain, but it had been slowly growing for the last 10 years, and he thought he should get it checked out in light of the leg swelling he'd experienced for the last four months. The man also reported occasional trouble with incontinence, constipation, and urinary tract infections, among other symptoms. Doctors investigated and found the source of the patient's issues: a condition rightfully called giant urinary bladder, so rare that it affects less than 1 percent of only elderly populations. The man's bladder had ballooned and contained 11 liters of urine—more than 20 times the organ's healthy average. It took doctors four hours to drain, and several days for the patient's abdomen to return to normal size.

A WORM FEELING

An April 2022 edition of *The New England Journal of Medicine* carried the story of a 53-year-old man in France who was more than a little bugged when sheep bot fly larvae hatched in his eyeball. In other words, maggots had incubated in his eye, and then started squirming around. He'd gone to the emergency room because his eye had been overly red and itchy, and an exam found about a dozen tiny worms infesting the patient's eyeball and nearby tissue. With a pair of forceps, doctors individually removed each of the larvae, which normally eat the blood of sheep and goats (living in their nostrils) for sustenance. The patient also got a prescription for antibiotics to kill off any unhatched larvae that may have remained.

When fax machines were invented in 1924, it took six minutes to send one page. Today, it takes two seconds.

BLOOD PACT

Per Scottish law, anyone who gives birth in the country has to wait six months after delivery to donate blood. As part of its donor questionnaire, the Scottish National Blood Transfusion Service asks potential suppliers if they're currently with child. But the SNBTS asks *everybody* that question, regardless of gender, something that greatly confused 66-year-old Leslie Sinclair, a regular donor over the last almost 50 years. He quietly demurred from answering the question, but a staff member at the Albert Halls clinic in Stirling said that he had to answer the question—that he wouldn't be allowed to donate blood unless he answered the intake questionnaire in full. "I told them that was stupid and that if I had to leave, I wouldn't be back," Sinclair said. "And that was it, I got on my bike and cycled away." "Whilst pregnancy is only a relevant question to those whose biological sex or assigned sex at birth is female, sex assigned at birth is not always visually clear to staff," SNBTS director Marc Turner explained.

OH, BABY

A British woman named Jess Davis went viral on the video site TikTok after sharing her story of medical surprise. She explained that a few hours earlier, she'd thought she needed to go to the bathroom really badly, as she felt extra full in her abdomen and required the familiar release one gets from evacuating their bowels. So, she went into a restroom, sat on the toilet, and pushed...and pushed...and pushed some more. Davis didn't need to defecate—it was time to give birth. She'd had no idea she was pregnant, and hadn't experienced or noticed any of the common symptoms of pregnancy, such as morning sickness or food cravings—and oddly, she'd still menstruated throughout her baby's gestation. That's a medical phenomenon known as a "cryptic pregnancy."

FISH OUT OF WATER

A spear fisher (name withheld in news reports) was plying his trade in the Phatthalung province of Thailand in May 2022, attempting to catch a spiked freshwater fish called an anabas. He caught one alright—when the fish jumped out of water, into the man's open mouth, and straight down his throat. With the man's breathing impaired, other fishermen rushed him to a hospital, where X-rays show the five-inch fish stuck between the throat and nasal cavity; it looked like it had tried to swim out the nose but got lodged in there. After a one-hour operation, doctors removed the fish, and the patient made a full recovery.

INITIALLY STRANGE

After several years of suspensions, criminal charges, fines, and pleading for reinstatement, British surgeon Simon Bramhall finally lost his medical license for good in 2022. That marked the (likely) final chapter in a saga that began in 2013, when Bramhall used a surgical device to carve his initials into a liver he'd just finished transplanting into a patient. The initials were discovered a week later when another doctor had to remove the new liver after it had failed.

The first patented glue was invented in England in 1750 and was made from fish oil.

THERE, THEIR, THEY'RE

Now for some jokes about our bizarre language.

A misplaced modifier walks into a bar owned by a man with a glass eye named Ralph.

I before *e*...except when you run a feisty heist on a weird beige foreign neighbor.

The word *queue* is ironic. It's just a *q* with a bunch of silent letters waiting in line.

Q: Why should you never date an apostrophe?
A: They're too possessive.

The past, the present, and the future walk into a bar. It was tense.

Teacher: Sandy, name two pronouns.
Sandy: Who? Me?

Did you hear the one about the pregnant woman who went into labor and started shouting "Don't! Won't! Can't!"? She was having contractions.

Q: What do you call Santa's helpers?
A: Subordinate clauses.

A writer dies and finds himself at the pearly gates. Saint Peter says, "I will let you choose between Heaven or Hell."
"Can I see both first?" asks the writer.
Saint Peter takes him down to Hell where rows of writers are chained to their desks and being whipped by demons. "Ugh," says the writer. "Can I see Heaven now?" To his astonishment, Heaven is the same: rows of chained writers getting whipped by demons. "I don't get it," says the writer. "What's the difference?"
"Up here," replies Saint Peter, "you get published."

I enjoy subtle humor, the serial comma and irony.

Teacher: Can you think of a word that has all the vowels, including *y*?
Ramon: Unquestionably.

It's important to have a good vocabulary. If I had known the difference between the words *antidote* and *anecdote*, my friend would still be alive. At least I got a little story out of it.

Knock knock!
Who's there?
To.
To who?
It's "to *whom*"!

If you can't think of a word, say, "I forgot the English word for it." That way people will think you're bilingual instead of an idiot.

Don't you hate people who use big words just to make themselves look perspicacious?

Reader: Your book left a bad taste in my mouth.
Flannery O'Connor: You weren't supposed to eat it.

Albert Einstein had a patent for an ammonia-powered refrigerator.

MUSICAL CHOPS

The most popular and enduring stage musicals usually get their start on Broadway and then find a new life for years as productions of high school theater departments. That necessitates some edits to the shows, including changing or eliminating the more sensitive and adult-oriented material.

Musical: *Rent* (1996)

Plot: Loosely based on the 1896 opera *La Bohème*, a group of artists and drag queens—most of them members of the LGBTQ community—try to do good work and fall in and out of love while living in squalor in the Alphabet City neighborhood of New York and facing the horrors of AIDS.

School Version: In the original show, Maureen has left boyfriend Mark and falls in love with a woman named Joanne. In the adaptation, Maureen and Joanne are just friends. And instead of living with AIDS, the illness-stricken characters have diabetes.

Musical: *Les Misérables* (1987)

Plot: A stark and serious stage version of Victor Hugo's 19th-century novel, *Les Misérables* details the various miseries and indignities—starvation, disease, police intimidation, prostitution, abandonment—faced by a group of interconnected people living in early 1800s France. Once memorable number: "Lovely Ladies," which takes place on a dock, with pimps and prostitutes offering their services to passing sailors.

School Version: "Lovely Ladies" evolved into "Lovely People," and the desperate women were forced to sell fruit, not themselves, in an open-air market.

Musical: *Avenue Q* (2003)

Plot: *Avenue Q* is like *Sesame Street* if the latter took place in the real New York City. Puppets and humans alike struggle with dissatisfaction, loneliness, addiction, humiliation, and their sexual identity.

School Version: The *Sesame*-esque instructional spoof song "The Internet Is for Porn" became "My Social Life Is Online."

Musical: *Hairspray* (2002)

Plot: Based on John Waters's 1988 movie of the same name, *Hairspray* is about the 1960s civil rights movement, focusing on a group of teenagers—some Black and some White—working to integrate a Baltimore TV dance show.

School Version: Schools and camps that don't have enough variety in their student bodies have substituted race with other forms of differentiation, such as height.

Musical: *Fame* (1988)

Plot: An adaptation of the hit 1980 movie and subsequent TV series, *Fame* tracks the aspirations of a talented and diverse group of teenagers at a performing arts magnet school in New York City.

School Version: While one character suffers a lot of anguish in the original show when he tells his friends he's a homosexual, the equivalent character in the school version of *Fame* announces he's impotent.

Musical: *Rock of Ages* (2009)

Plot: A jukebox musical set amidst the "hair metal" scene of bars and clubs on the Los Angeles Sunset Strip in the 1980s, *Rock of Ages* is as vividly obsessed with sex and drugs as the 1980s rock songs that fill its soundtrack.

School Version: A character with the highly suggestive name of Regina (pronounced ruh-JINE-uh) Kuntz is renamed Anita Bath. Lead character Stacee Jaxx is blackmailed into performing by a promoter who threatens to tell the world about the singer's hair plugs (in the original play, the blackmail centers on a disgusting act Stacee committed with a llama). Gay couple Dennis and Lonny are said to have a "bromance" in the school adaptation, while the central location of the Venus Gentlemen's Club, a sleazy strip joint, becomes a Hooters-like restaurant.

Musical: *Hair* (1967)

Plot: A series of edgy, musical vignettes and sketches about the late 1960s hippie, anti-war countercultural generation, it famously ends with the cast dancing naked to the psychedelic "Let the Sunshine In."

School Version: Nobody gets naked, but teen actors are encouraged to disrobe to reveal full flesh-colored bodysuits beneath their costumes.

Musical: *Grease* (1972)

Plot: The romantic and sassy exploits of two teenage gangs—the male T-Birds and female Pink Ladies—over a year at Rydell High School, circa 1959.

School Version: The 1978 movie version of *Grease* was a blockbuster hit, particularly with younger audiences, prompting the writers of the stage musical to create an officially sanctioned school version. All mentions and depictions of cigarettes and alcohol were cut, along with off-color language, the overtly explicit sexual lyrics in the song "Greased Lightning," and the entire B-plot about teenager Rizzo's pregnancy scare.

Musical: *The Sound of Music* (1959)

Plot: Widower Captain Georg von Trapp hires plucky Maria out of a convent to be the governess for his seven children, and she turns them into a family singing act. The Captain and Maria fall in love and escape Austria as the Nazis take it over in the early days of World War II.

School Version: There's no Nazi backdrop at all. It's just a musical about the Captain and Maria falling in love while a bunch of little kids sing a lot.

Color of the Crayola crayon prototype: black. (It was made of charcoal and oil.)

BOB'S BURGERS, PART I

The first animated primetime sitcom was The Flintstones *(1960–66),*
which begat The Simpsons, *which begat* South Park, King of the
Hill, Family Guy, *and loads more. In 2011 came a low-key show about*
a family-owned burger joint with an exasperated dad who says "Oh, my
God" a lot, an over-exuberant mom prone to breaking out in song, and
three weird kids. More than a decade later, Bob's Burgers *has become*
a beloved Sunday-night stalwart thanks to its perfectly topped blend
of humor and heart (and at least one bathroom joke per episode).

EVERY WRITER'S DREAM

In 2009, Suzanna Makkos, executive vice president in charge of comedy at the
Fox TV network, was looking for an animation house (for another show she was
developing) when she stumbled upon a 30-second clip of an Adult Swim cartoon.
Called *Lucy: The Daughter of the Devil*, the deadpan-voiced Devil reluctantly agrees to
buy Lucy a dress and asks, "What size are you?"

She answers, "I'm a 4."

"Are you *really* a 4? I don't want to have to return it."

It might not sound that funny reading it here, but the timing and the voice acting
struck a chord with Makkos. She no longer cared about finding an animation house;
she wanted to know who wrote *Lucy*. Not long after, Loren Bouchard, an animator
living in San Francisco, received a call from Makkos inviting him to Los Angeles to
pitch a show for Fox's Sunday night "Animation Domination," home of *The Simpsons*,
King of the Hill, and *Family Guy*. This is not a common occurrence—usually, writers
approach a network, not the other way around.

BLUE-COLLAR CREATIVES

Born in New York City in 1969 and raised in Medford, Massachusetts, Bouchard
grew up in a close-knit family. After his mother died when he was a teenager,
he quit high school and was working as a bartender in the early 1990s when he
had a chance encounter with a family friend and former teacher named Tom
Snyder. While they were catching up, Snyder asked Bouchard if he still liked to
draw. Bouchard did. So Snyder offered him a job on a project that featured a new
animation style called "Squigglevision." That project ended up being the critically
acclaimed cult-classic animated sitcom *Dr. Katz: Professional Therapist*, which aired

on Comedy Central from 1995 to 2002. From there, Bouchard created two Adult Swim cartoons, *Home Movies* and the aforementioned *Lucy*.

When Bouchard got the call from Makkos, he got right to work on a concept. He liked the idea of a family that owned a restaurant and lived above it, so the show could be both a workplace comedy and family comedy at the same time. After trying out some different restaurant ideas, he came up with a burger joint run by a dad named Bob Belcher and his overenthusiastic wife, Linda, with their three children, Daniel, Gene, and Louise. The family lives in an unnamed northeastern U.S. tourist beach town, across the street from a mediocre Italian restaurant that pulls in more customers than Bob and his ambitious attempts at elaborate burger specials. Oh, and the family members are all cannibals. "I really appreciate what I've come to think of as blue-collar creatives," explained Bouchard, "people who are struggling to make a living, but also struggling to express themselves creatively. I think Bob is a perfect example of that, but so is Linda and so are the kids. It's a kind of life that I grew up around, but that I don't think is represented on TV that much."

Bouchard put together a 12-minute presentation for the network that looks remarkably close to how the show ended up, right down to the ukulele theme song, the punny store names in the opening credits, and all the voice actors in place. Fox execs loved it...mostly. They didn't think the oldest boy, Daniel, was as fresh or dynamic as the nerdy Gene or the scheming Louise. And they also didn't like the fact that the Belchers were cannibals. Makkos asked Bouchard, "Do you really want to do 100 episodes' worth of cannibal jokes?"

A DIFFERENT APPROACH

Bouchard developed *Bob's Burgers* with veteran *King of the Hill* writer and executive producer, Jim Dauterive. They went about it a bit differently than most other animated sitcoms, starting with casting all the voice actors first and then forming the characters to the actors' talents and personalities. (To keep the dialogue fresh, Bouchard has his actors record their lines together—either in the same room or remotely. That includes special guest stars. Most other cartoons record the actors one at a time. Bouchard explains the advantage: "It's not eye contact so much as it's timing. Ear contact, you might say.")

Then Bouchard made the tweaks Fox requested. He wasn't really keen on the cannibal idea in the first place and did it only because of his Adult Swim background: he'd assumed that Fox wanted something dark like that. Then he changed the oldest sibling from male to female and made the pilot. Plot: Louise spreads a rumor that the Belchers are cannibals.

What does the name of image-scanning software TWAIN stand for?
"Technology without an interesting name."

IT'S A MODEST HIT!

Bob's Burgers premiered mid-season on January 9, 2011, and its prospects weren't great. For one, the humor was more quirky than edgy, and it took audiences and critics a while to get on board. "Pointlessly vulgar and derivatively dull," wrote *The Washington Post*. "Not very tasty," said *USA Today*. With so-so ratings, *Bob's Burgers* was perpetually "on the bubble." Fox is notorious for axing underperforming shows before they've found their audience. "You come to work feeling like any joke, any bad drawing, anything might be the nail in your coffin," said Bouchard. "The ratings were fine, but they were never so great that we felt like we had job security." Had *Bob's Burgers* come out a few years earlier, it most likely would have suffered the same fates as the all-but-forgotten animated Fox sitcoms *Life with Louie* (1994), *The PJs* (1999), *Sit Down, Shut Up* (2009), and *Allen Gregory* (2011).

Then came the rise of social media, giving regular viewers—not critics—a louder voice than before. And viewers really had an appetite for *Bob's Burgers*. Word of mouth by way of memes and fan art helped keep the Bob's bubble from popping. In fact, the viewers have become such a powerful voice that Bouchard has become more worried about them. "We now fear disappointing the fans the way that we used to fear being canceled. In other words, if there comes a day when a fan says, 'This season isn't as good as last season,' then we've all agreed to kill ourselves."

As of this writing, they haven't killed themselves. In fact, the creators, writers, and cast of *Bob's Burgers* have all said that they want to keep doing it for the rest of their lives. The show is now an institution—with a comic book, a pinball game, soundtrack albums, and even a feature film that came out in 2022.

To learn more about this quirky family, turn to page 214.

*   *   *

A MAN OF MANY TALENTS

Harrison Ford didn't grow up wanting to be an actor. He took a drama class in college only because he was struggling academically and hoped an "easy" class would raise his GPA. Instead, he caught the acting bug. But it turned out to be harder than it looked, and for most of the 1970s, the struggling young actor got only bit parts and had to support himself in Los Angeles as a carpenter and...with other gigs.

As the Mamas & Papas singer Michelle Phillips recalled years later, when she saw *Star Wars* in 1977, she didn't even know Ford was an actor. "I was sitting there, watching the screen, and all of a sudden Harrison comes on and I gasped and said, 'That's my pot dealer!'"

The average cremains of a human being weigh about nine pounds.

MAY THE HORSE BE WITH YOU

Thoroughbred horse racing offers thrilling speed,
impressive animal and human athletic feats...and ridiculous names.
These are all the names of real racehorses.

Long Face	First Dude
Zippy Chippy	Flat Fleet Feet
Passing Wind	Wool Sandals
Potoooooooo	Sahara Toga Party
Ghostzapper	Brangelina
Hoof Hearted	Turducken
Nope	Shakalakaboomboom
Dit	Thunder Down Under
Sinister Minister	Maythehorsebewithu
Doremifasollatido	Fiftyshadesofhay
ARRRRR	Horsey McHorseface
Soup and Sandwich	Pepper Roani
Mywifenosevrything	My Daddy's Vacation
Ha Ha	Shimmy Shack
Onoitsmymothernlaw	The Slug
Notacatbutallama	Burnt Toast
Panty Raid	Four Left Feet

WEIRD OLD RADIO

*TV can be pretty weird, but it's only carrying on a tradition set forth by its
entertainment predecessor. Here are some of the weirdest shows to ever grace
the airwaves of the "old-time radio" era, the 1920s through the 1950s.*

THE FAT MAN (ABC, 1946). Created by well-known mystery writer Dashiell
Hammett, *The Fat Man* was a fairly standard detective show, but the writers were
seemingly obsessed with the weight of the title character, Brad Runyon. Each
episode begins with Runyon weighing himself on a pharmacy scale, which tells
him and listeners that he comes in at 239 pounds. In the first series of episodes,
Brad Runyon doesn't even have a name: he is known simply as "the fat man,"
which was an attempt by programmers to cash in on creator Hammett's popular
novel *The Thin Man*.

THE HALL OF FANTASY (Mutual, 1952). Each weekly episode of this anthology
series tells a different, self-contained story of horror and the supernatural. The
twist, and what set it apart from similar shows of the era: evil forces almost always
win on *The Hall of Fantasy*. The innocent woman gets captured by the vampire
and bitten, or the monster everyone believes is dead jumps up out of his grave
and attacks. Frightening, indeed.

THE BICKERSONS (NBC, 1946). This sitcom is comprised of vignettes and short
sketches about the lives of John and Blanche Bickerson, a long-married (and
aptly named) couple who can't stand each other and spend all their time fighting
and screaming at each other about longstanding feuds. Most episodes take place
in bed, with the perpetually exhausted John trying to sleep and the insomniac
Blanche prodding him awake.

AUCTION GALLERY (Mutual, 1945). Auctions are probably fun and exciting
because buyers can see and examine the items they're looking to bid on, before
the fast-paced highest-price-wins action begins. *Auction Gallery* had no visuals, of
course, and also no drama. Host Dave Elman would describe antiques and curios
on the air, and a studio audience could place their bids. Then, listeners at home
could bid on the items, too—by mail.

ETHEL AND ALBERT (NBC, 1944). The titular characters are a happily married
couple who live in the fictional, bustling small town of Sandy Harbor. Many
residents, and friends of Ethel and Albert, keep getting themselves into sticky
situations. But listeners never hear any of that dramatized. *Ethel and Albert* was
so low-budget that nearly every episode consists entirely of the two characters
just talking about the local goings-on.

BABY ROSE MARIE (NBC, 1932). Actress Rose Marie—probably best known
to modern audiences for her role as sassy TV writer Sally Rogers on the 1960s
sitcom *The Dick Van Dyke Show*—got her start as a child star. First appearing on

various NBC radio shows at the age of three singing popular songs of the day, tiny Rose Marie got her own show, a 15-minute program airing on Sunday afternoons.

AMERICAN AGENT (ABC, 1950). In this thriller series, Bob Barclay lives three lives. He travels the world as a foreign correspondent for Amalgamated News, but he's also a soldier of fortune and mercenary who joins rogue organizations and militias so he can spy on them on behalf of the U.S. government. Hundreds of real-life reporters were so offended by the portrayal of a fictional reporter with such poor ethical standards and a lack of journalistic integrity that they wrote letters of protest to network ABC, which canceled *American Agent* after just one season.

HOBBY LOBBY (CBS, 1937). In this primetime series that aired on Wednesday nights, Dave Elman (from *Auction Gallery*), the self-proclaimed "dean of American hobbyists," discusses his many collections. Then he has on a guest to discuss a hobby, be it beekeeping, hypnotism, baking, or teaching kangaroos to box. *Hobby Lobby* ran for 12 years.

THE LIGHT OF THE WORLD (NBC, 1940). This melodramatic soap opera—with all of its clichés such as swelling organ music and hammy, emotional line readings— used some unprecedented source material: the Old Testament of the Bible. Writers took these well-known Bible stories, updated the language to make them modern, and had people act them out like they were soaps. The 15-minute daily series ran for 10 years.

MEET THE MEEKS (NBC, 1947). This sitcom aired on Saturday mornings and concerns a shy dweeb named Mortimer Meeks. The comedy derives from him suffering through the whims of his flaky wife, Agatha, who screams at him and goes on long tirades against the rest of the family pretty much constantly.

THAT'S A GOOD IDEA (CBS, 1945). It's a presumptuous title for a show so bizarre. Producers of *That's a Good Idea* paid listeners $5 for quirky invention ideas. Then, they wouldn't produce those inventions, but would pass the ideas off to writers who would write short playlets about them.

THE OPEN ROAD (NBC, 1935). In 1934, budding writer Red Quinlan dropped out of high school and successfully persuaded sponsors to give him enough money to hitchhike around America for a year. In the meantime, the sponsors sold the show to NBC, which debuted *The Open Road* in 1935. The show is little more than Quinlan just telling repetitive stories about getting into fistfights with hobos and getting arrested for vagrancy.

RFD AMERICA (Mutual, 1947). The topics on this weekly quiz show were of a general knowledge variety, but the contestants were all farmers. The winner was crowned "Master Farmer of the Week."

What is *hexadactyly*? Six digits on a hand or foot.

ARE CRAYONS FATTENING?

Technically anything with mass has calories, a unit of energy, even things that aren't technically food. You definitely shouldn't eat most if not all of these things (see page 194 for better ways to satisfy your hunger), but it's still interesting to know just how many calories they're packing.

A GALLON OF GASOLINE: 31,000 calories.

COAL: 200,000 calories per ounce.

URANIUM: 20 billion calories per gram.

DIRT: You'd have to eat about 15 pounds of it to acquire just 6 calories.

COTTON BALLS: 4 calories each.

GRASS CLIPPINGS: 4 calories per ounce.

HUMAN BREAST MILK: 170 calories in one cup.

A PENNY: 10 calories.

HAIR: On average, a full head of hair would provide about 140 calories.

STAINLESS STEEL FORK: 15 calories.

A 9MM BULLET: Slightly less than one calorie.

MODELING CLAY: A standard-size plastic can of Play-Doh packs 127 calories.

EGGSHELLS: About 2 per egg.

A CRAYON: 50 calories.

A DOLPHIN: The average adult bottlenose dolphin weighs 4,400 pounds—
and contains around 1.7 million calories.

YOU: An average adult's flesh equals about 32,375 calories. Add in the skin and
organs, and the calorie total goes up to 125,000.

SANTA'S CHRISTMAS EVE SNACKS: If you ate the milk and cookies
that Santa Claus eats at millions of homes each December 24,
you'd consume about 115 billion calories.

THIS COPY OF *UNCLE JOHN'S BATHROOM READER*: About one-half calorie.

* * *

"My friends tell me I have an intimacy problem. But they don't really know me."
—Garry Shandling

Ketchup flows at a rate of 25 miles per year.

CUNNING CROWS, PART I

Crows are smarter than the average bird. Heck, some are even smarter than the average kid.

 ## "ONCE UPON A MIDNIGHT DREARY"

You're taking a walk in the park, minding your own business, when all of a sudden a murder of crows starts making a huge ruckus as the birds flit and hop from tree limb to tree limb. What are they all cawing about? You? Or are they cawing...*at* you? The latter is more likely than you think. In fact, crows and ravens have more interactions with people than most any other wild animal, even if we don't notice it.

Modern science is only just beginning to realize how humanlike corvids—the family of birds that includes crows and ravens, along with jays and magpies—really are. We've known since time immemorial that crows and ravens have an awareness that other birds lack. The 6th-century BC Aesop fable "The Crow and the Pitcher" tells of an inventive bird that drops stones into a pitcher of water until the level is high enough to drink. It's for this kind of unmatched ingenuity that crows and ravens have been both feared and revered.

- The Druids, Norse, and Celtics believed that crows were wise messengers sent by the gods.

- In ancient Greece, a raven served as the familiar to Apollo, the god of prophecy, and was said to bring bad luck.

- Ravens are all over the Bible. Noah sent one out from the ark to test the waters after the Great Flood.

- In the Middle Ages, the carrion crow was seen as a harbinger of the Black Death.

Our modern fascination with these big black corvids as a sign of the macabre began with Edgar Allen Poe's 1845 poem "The Raven." The titular bird "comes tapping" at the narrator's chamber door, and won't let him forget his lost love, Lenore: "Quoth the raven, 'Nevermore.'"

 ## SIGNS OF INTELLIGENCE

At first, Poe's narrator thinks the raven is only repeating "Nevermore" because its master has taught it that word, but then he sees that the raven's "eyes have all the seeming of a demon's that is dreaming." Poe was right: there's a lot more going on behind these birds' eyes than you might think. Today, biologists rank their intelligence right up there with great apes, elephants, octopuses, whales, and dolphins.

If heated to 1400°F, a diamond will disintegrate and leave nothing behind.

But how can this be, when crows have literal bird brains inside their tiny cranial cavities? Because those brains pack a lot of neurons. Neurons are cells that transmit information to one another throughout the nervous system. The more neurons you have, the smarter you are. The human cerebral cortex, with 14 to 16 billion neurons, has the most in the animal kingdom. The cerebral cortex is the part of the human brain that remembers facts and faces, uses language, solves complex problems, makes tools, creates art and culture, frets about death, and forms long-lasting bonds. In short, it's why you're self-aware. Birds, however, do not have cerebral cortices. Instead, their neurons are contained in the pallium, which is much smaller. Birds in the genus *Corvus*—which includes more than 40 species of crows, ravens, and rooks—make up for this with more compact neurons that fit closer together inside their thumb-sized brains. The palliums of crows contain more than 1.5 billion neurons. (Dogs have 500 million, twice as many as cats.) And boy, do these corvids put those neurons to use. Here are some of the remarkable things that crows and ravens can do.

 CROWS CAN TALK

And they have a lot more to say than "caw." Crows can also screech, honk, click, and rattle. They can even mimic sounds from their environment...including the human voice. But they don't simply "parrot" what they hear. One morning in December 2021, an actual talking crow named Cosmo showed up at an elementary school in Grants Pass, Oregon. After pecking at the window, he flew into a classroom, landed on a table, and said, "What's up?" (Then he helped himself to some snacks.) The amiable avian had *a lot* to say...including language not suitable for fifth graders. The headlines all read "Foul-mouthed crow befriends elementary school." But there's more to the story.

A few years earlier, Cosmo had befriended a woman named JaNeal Shattuck, who lives on a farm about 20 miles to the south of the elementary school. The wild bird grew up with humans and has especially strong bonds with children. (He shows up every morning at a nearby day care as soon as the kids arrive.) Over time, Cosmo learned about 40 words and knows how to put them together to communicate. For example, he'll say to the family dog, "Tonka, you come outside." "You have no idea how smart this bird is," Shattuck said. "It's beyond imagination."

According to Shattuck's daughter, Daphnie Colpron, Cosmo got lost when a neighbor trapped him and took him to a wildlife sanctuary near Grants Pass. After Cosmo was released (because he's a wild bird that wasn't injured), the brainy bird followed a truck—one that he recognized because it belongs to a Shattuck family friend—to the elementary school. As soon as Cosmo found the kid he knows, he jumped around while repeating, "I'm okay. I'm fine." At last report, Cosmo was back

If a pack-a-day smoker consumed the nicotine in the pack all at once, it would be deadly.

on Shattuck's farm. "His vocabulary has expanded quite a bit in the last few weeks," said Colpron. Maybe the kids taught the bird some new swear words.

CROWS HAVE EXCELLENT MEMORIES

Crows have been observed memorizing weekly sanitation pick-up schedules so they'll know exactly where to be when the garbage cans are rolled out to the street. They can even recognize a person's face (by one account, for nearly ten years)—that's why you should never cross a crow.

This was the focus of a two-year University of Washington study in the late 2010s. PhD student Kaeli Swift gave 25 volunteers the unenviable task of holding a taxidermied dead crow while standing near a spot where food had been left out for wild crows. But not all the volunteers held a dead crow; some held dead pigeons, and, in some cases, a dead hawk (the crow's natural predator) was placed on the ground nearby. Other volunteers—the control group—held nothing. And sometimes volunteers wore latex masks to hide their identities. (Because it was such a creepy sight, they all wore a sign with the UW logo and the words "Crow Study.")

As you might expect, the local population of crows became most upset with the volunteers holding a deceased member of their own species (especially if the dead hawk was nearby). The angry birds made loud warning calls and refused to eat the food that was offered to them. And for the next two years, whenever that particular volunteer returned to that spot—with or without a dead bird—the crows refused to take the food...that is, unless the volunteer wore a mask to hide their identity. In addition to demonstrating that crows can remember faces and hold grudges, the study also showed that they react to potential danger, and not just imminent danger. That's another sign of intelligence: understanding the concept of *caws* and effect. (We'd have to eat crow if we didn't use that pun at least once.)

CROWS SOLVE CRIMES

The "holding a grudge" behavior documented in the University of Washington study helps explain another weird *Corvus* quirk: crow funerals. At least, these gatherings look like what we might call a funeral. A murder of crows—sometimes more than 50—surrounds a fallen comrade; they caw and screech to one another as some hop in for a closer look. It might appear as if they're sharing stories, but Swift and other ornithologists posit that the crows are working together in order to find out what led to the deceased's demise, and whether that danger is still imminent. If the crows somehow determine that the danger is *you*, then it's best to keep your distance. "It has become accepted and really exciting within the wildlife scientific community to really

Huh? Banana oil comes from petroleum, not bananas.

break down what have been rigorous barriers between ourselves and animals," said Swift. "One of the ways we're seeing that manifest is paying more and more attention to how non-human animals attend to their dead."

As John Marzluff puts it (he heads UW's Avian Conservation Lab, and coauthored Swift's study), crows divide us into broad categories: "Some people will kill you, other people will feed you."

CROWS DISPLAY ALTRUISM

Another sign of intelligence is aiding another member of your species—or another species—when there's no direct benefit to yourself. An eyewitness account posted to Reddit in 2017 told of a crow that landed on a windowsill and stole a piece of bread that a smaller songbird had been enjoying. As the crow was eating, it tore off a few bits of bread and tossed them to the songbird. It's impossible to know why the crow did this, but what's important is that it didn't have to. In some cases, crows have also been known to give presents to people.

- For about four years, Stuart Dahlquist of Seattle, Washington, placed food on his back porch for the neighborhood crows. One morning in 2019, he found in the food's place a pine sprig (the needled end of a branch) with a shiny pull tab looped around the middle of it. A nearly identical gift came the following day. Photos of the trinkets caught the attention of ornithologists around the world, including Swift, who commented, "It's definitely not a behavior that I've ever seen before, but it wouldn't necessarily surprise me if a crow did it." Crows have long been known to bring humans shiny rocks or keys, but this is the first known instance of a wild crow actually making someone a present.

- That being said, ornithologists don't know what motivates the birds to commit these altruistic acts. Is it gratitude? Or does it happen by accident? Perhaps the crow dropped something by chance and came back for it, only to find food, so it brought a second one to get more food. Could that mean that the crows are training us?

- In 2021, a woman in Portland, Oregon, inspired by stories of gifting crows, started putting food outside. "It worked a little too well," she reported on Reddit. The crows started "defending her" by ambushing anyone who came to visit. The woman was actually looking for legal advice, specifically if she could be held liable if "her" crows hurt a neighbor. The local chapter of the National Audubon Society didn't weigh in on that question, but conservation director Bob Sallinger warned that aggressive behavior can occur when you feed any wild animal, and that crows are perfectly capable of finding food on their own.

Fly on over to page 346 to learn about more ways that crows are like people.

Just like Uncle John: gassy giants (such as Saturn) are planets
that radiate more heat than they absorb.

ALL ABOUT ANTARCTICA

It's time to head south—extremely south—for some cold,
hard facts about cold, hard Antarctica.

On average, no landmass on Earth has a higher elevation, receives less rain, or endures more wind than does Antarctica.

A full 98 percent of Antarctica is covered in ice. And of all the world's ice, 90 percent of it is in Antarctica.

Climate change is affecting Antarctica more than any other place. In the past 50 years, temperatures on the continent have increased by 5.4°F—five times the global average.

Antarctica is the largest land area on Earth not controlled by any one country. The U.S., U.K., Russia, and Chile, among 30 nations total, have scientific research stations there.

Because there's no single time zone in Antarctica—and because it's constantly light out in the summer, and perpetually dark in the winter—each scientist at the outposts abides by a prominent time zone in their home country.

Population of Antarctica: 1,000 scientists in the winter, and 4,000 in the summer.

There are two active volcanoes in Antarctica. Weird things happen on Mount Erebus, including fumaroles venting ice.

A natural phenomenon specific to Antarctica: "diamond dust." Near-microscopic ice crystals hang in the air and sunlight catches them, making them shine and sparkle like clouds of diamonds.

Antarctica isn't *entirely* ice. It's home to the aptly named Dry Valleys, the driest location on the planet. It has such low moisture and humidity levels that, despite the cold, snow and ice instantly dissipate, making for just a large area of dirt.

Antarctica's Deep Lake is one of the coldest bodies of water on Earth, with temperatures sitting around 5°F. That's below freezing level—but Deep Lake doesn't freeze because it's also one of the saltiest bodies of water on Earth.

The Gamburtsev Mountains stretch more than 700 miles across Antarctica, with peaks reaching nearly 10,000 feet. But you probably won't see any of them—the mountains are completely hidden under ice sheets.

Polynyas, or massively giant holes of water surrounded by ice, open up every so often in Antarctica. The one that emerged in the Weddell Sea in 2017 was the first to form in 40 years, and it measures about 50,000 square miles, roughly the size of Ireland.

There are species of fungus native to Antarctica. Found nowhere else on Earth, one kind feeds on the rotting wood of huts left by explorers hundreds of years ago. Another evolved to live off of the slow trickle of gasoline leaking out of abandoned exploration boats.

More meteorites have struck Antarctica than any other place on Earth.

Most densely caloric fruit: the avocado, with 167 calories per 100 grams.

TOILET TECH

Better living through bathroom technology.

KEEN TO BE CLEAN

Product: Toto Neorest NX2 Dual-Flush Toilet

How It Works: With the lid down and when it's not occupied, the NX2 looks like an unassuming toilet, although stylishly curved where the bowl meets the lid to maximize comfort. But don't be deceived by the minimalist appearance, because there's some state-of-the-art germ-killing technology quietly doing its thing beneath the surface. The toilet is outfitted with Toto's patented Actilight system, which involves an ultraviolet light constantly working to kill any bacteria it detects. There won't be much hanging around, however, because the bowl is lined with germ-averse titanium dioxide. And to make sure that you stay as clean as the toilet, the NX2 houses a front and rear washer with pressure control and a dryer.

Cost: $15,000

GET YOUR FILL

Product: PerfectFill Bath Filler and Drain

How It Works: Plumbing fixtures company Kohler touts its new product as "smart bath technology," letting users draw a bath to the precise predetermined temperature and depth of their choice. Consisting of a digital valve and drain, the system makes the perfect bath, programmed for up to 10 household users, including pets. It can be controlled through Kohler's app for voice commands via Amazon's Alexa—simply say "draw a bath for Uncle John" and it does the rest, preventing the tub from flooding and preventing you from scalding or freezing when you're ready to get in.

Cost: $2,700, plus the cost of professional installation by an authorized Kohler plumber.

WIPE RIGHT

Product: Who Gives a Crap

How It Works: The manufacture of toilet paper is a massive drain on natural resources—about 27,000 trees are felled each day, on average, to meet the huge demand for TP. Recycled toilet paper (made from all kinds of repurposed paper products, not from used TP) exists, but it's almost categorically too thin to be effective, prone to ripping and forcing the captive consumer to use more...which kind of defeats the purpose of buying paper-saving TP in the first place. Enter Who Gives a Crap, maker of the first premium, luxury recycled toilet paper. So who exactly gives a crap? Who Gives a Crap does. The secret: they use sustainable, re-plantable, fast-growing bamboo in the recipe along with recycled paper, resulting in an ultra-soft

What are *arêtes*? Sharp, jagged rocks at the top of a mountain.

tissue that purportedly feels like expensive, thick, plumbing-clogging all-paper stuff.
Cost: $48 for 62 rolls

BIDET, MATE!

Product: Discovery DLS Bidet Seat

How It Works: In the early days of the COVID-19 pandemic, when store runs led to toilet-paper shortages, many Americans purchased an alternative post-bathroom clean-up system: a bidet, a device popular in Europe and Japan that shoots water up at one's undercarriage, negating the need for TP (or for as much). Instead of a standalone bidet (because who has the room for a second plumbing hookup?), Bio Bidet offers high-tech seats that fit onto toilets, with all of the bidet machinery—and then some—enclosed within. The Discovery DLS Bidet Seat is the top-of-the-line model, boasting an ultraviolet light–powered sterilizer that cleanses the water nozzle after each use. It also features adjustable temperature controls and a warm air vent, meaning it washes and dries the user's downstairs. It even has a sensor that can tell when a human is approaching, and it lifts its lid and gets itself ready for you.

Cost: $899

A PURR-FECT SOLUTION

Product: Kitten Proof Toilet Paper Guard

How It Works: A lot of cats (particularly kittens) like to wreak a little havoc around the house, and to get some use out of their claws, they'll run their paws over a roll of toilet paper until the whole thing is unwound and lying on the bathroom floor in a useless pile. The Kitten Proof Toilet Paper Guard stops felines from unspooling the TP before they can even get started. It's a plastic sheath that fits over a wall-mounted toilet-paper holder and extends down over the top of the roll and then some, preventing the cat from going for a spin.

Cost: GE Aviation engineer Johnny Lawrence invented the device, and he made the plans to 3-D print it at home downloadable on the internet at no cost.

WRITE ON

Product: Aqua Notes Water Proof Note Pad

How It Works: How many times have you been in the shower and had a great idea for an article (if you're Uncle John), or needed to jot down something to remember? By the time you get out, you've forgotten it, or, if you can get to a pad or phone you may have in the bathroom, you get it all wet. Aqua Notes looks like a regular notepad of 40 perforated pages, except the pages are completely waterproof. They won't crumble in the water, and they work with a special vegetable-ink pen that won't run if wet. And with suction cups on the back, they're perfect for hanging in the shower, too.

Cost: $12

Parrots eat clay.

ODD FINDS

What's the strangest thing you've ever found? Was it stranger than the strange things these folks stumbled upon?

A CACHE OF BOWLING BALLS

In 2021, David Olson, a machinist from Norton Shores, Michigan, took a sledgehammer to the four crumbling cement steps leading up to his back porch. He knew something was odd when there wasn't dirt beneath the steps, but sand. Then he saw a half-buried bowling ball. That in itself isn't too surprising, considering that Olson lives in Muskegon County, home of the Brunswick Bowling and Billiards Company. When he removed the ball, there were two more, so he removed them, too...and then found even more. It started getting ridiculous: Every excavated ball exposed even more balls. Before long, Olson's five-year-old son, Zeke, joined him, and they kept finding bowling balls—or as Zeke called them, "alien eggs." Then it became an obsession. "I couldn't stop," Olson told ESPN. "I had to get to the bottom." After four hours—and numerous Facebook posts documenting his progress that quickly went viral—the final tally was...158 bowling balls. (Another four found later brought the total to 162.)

Most of them were unfinished, but some were painted and even embossed with the Brunswick logo. Only a handful had finger holes. Kirk Bunke at the Muskegon Heritage Museum confirmed that, back in the mid- to late 20th century, rejected bowling balls were available to employees to take home and reuse. So, sometime in 1959, when Olson's house was under construction, workers filled the porch cavity with reject bowling bowls and sand. (It proved to be quite structurally sound.) Olson—whose own grandfather worked at Brunswick for 50 years—donated some of the oldest relics to the company. (He used the rest as lawn ornaments.) In return, Brunswick gave the Olsons two brand new bowling balls. The couple entered a tournament and—despite neither having bowled in years—they won! "I feel like the universe is telling me that our family should be bowling," he said.

A CANNONBALL INSIDE A TREE

The walnut tree was already several decades old when the now-historic Overfelt-Johnston Home was built next to it in Independence, Missouri, in 1850. By 2022, the tree was 100 feet tall and riddled with disease. It had to come down. That job went to Jeff's Tree Service owner Jeff Eastham. While removing the tree's upper limbs, Eastham found six very old, handmade chains embedded in the wood, so he knew right away that this tree had history. Later, when he was chain-sawing the limbs into timber, Eastham saw something fall out of the wood onto the lawn. It was a small

Pill bugs (or roly-polies) are crustaceans, not insects.

iron ball—a bit larger than a golf ball—much heavier than Eastham expected it to be. "I had no idea it was in there," he said. "You couldn't see a hole in the log."

This wasn't the first cannonball discovered at the Overfelt-Johnston Home. Forty-two years earlier during a renovation, one was removed from a brick wall. It makes sense: During a Civil War battle in 1863, the home served as a field hospital. The Union troops guarding it were overtaken by the Confederates, so they fired off a few cannon shots before retreating. One cannonball entered through a second-story window and became lodged in the bricks. The one that Eastham found landed in the tree and—as the decades passed—the wood swallowed it whole. "It was a part of the tree for at least 157 years," said Randall Pratt, current owner of the Overfelt-Johnston house. "And it will stay with the house as a reminder of its history."

A "MYTHICAL" AXE

It was a dark and stormy afternoon in May 2022. Matthew Decker and his wife had just returned home from the store and were preparing to rush inside to avoid the rain. That's when Decker noticed what looked like an axe head sticking up out of his front lawn. He ran over to grab it, but it was connected to a...handle? It felt more like a tree root, especially after Decker kicked it. As he later told NPR, "I grabbed it and gave it a strong bend—and snap, there it was." He took the thing inside and washed off all the mud, then "held it up to the light with wide eyes." (Decker happens to be a *Lord of the Rings* fan and knows a mythical axe when he sees one.)

Apparently, a tree root had grown through the hole in the axe head where the handle goes. As the root expanded, it secured the iron to the wood perfectly. Decker doesn't know how long the old axe head had been buried in his yard—or what happened to the original handle. But the axe was in just the right spot for Mother Nature to give it a new one. "From the very first moment I picked it up," Decker said, "it had a very special weight to it." Photos of the odd find went viral, and at last report, Decker planned to sell his mythical axe to pay for some non-mythical car repairs.

A 100-YEAR-OLD MURDER CONFESSION

In 1986, a homeowner (unnamed in press reports) was renovating his century-old mansion in Fountain, Colorado, when his daughter noticed writing on the backside of a piece of decorative window molding he'd removed from a bedroom wall. Written in cursive with pencil, the 170-word message begins:

> To whoever may happen to find the confession, I, John W. Spicer of the City of Fountain, State of Colorado, being about to shuffle off this mortal act to make this my full confession in the hope that when I am gone it may be found and at last clear up the darkest mystery that ever embraced one in human murder.

Longest non-ocean-draining river in North America:
the 350-mile Bear River ends at the Great Salt Lake.

The murder, he wrote, took place in 1893, six years before Spicer drafted his secret confession while working as a builder on the now historic home. He provided specific details of how he "did kill and wilfuly murder with a club one John J. Sebastian for his money and jewelry to the value of $5,000.00 and did drag the mutilated body to a deep ravine some 500 yds."

The homeowner gave the murder confession to a journalist, who turned it over to the Colorado Bureau of Investigation. The agency took the case but was unable to find any record of the murder, nor could they locate the ravine where the body was stashed. But they did confirm that the confession is authentic. As for Spicer, he later moved to Florida and lived for 44 more years, never having been charged with the crime. Today, his confession is on display in the Fountain Valley Historical Society Museum.

A WITCH BOTTLE

Chris Langston didn't consider himself superstitious. That was before his macabre discovery in the summer of 2021. The 48-year-old metal detectorist was searching a secluded forest near his home in the English countryside, where, a few months earlier, he'd found some broken pottery. This time, Langston dug deeper and unearthed a blue poison bottle—as in, a bottle that once contained poison—along with a severed doll's head. Next he found an apothecary bottle; inside was a clear liquid, some hair, and a tooth. Langston brought the bottle home and, after some online research, was surprised to learn that he'd found a Victorian-era "witch bottle." People used to bury these so-called countermagical vessels full of various ingredients believed to protect the land from evil spirits. Urine, hair, and teeth—usually from the same person—were very common.

What would you do if you found a witch bottle? Langston asked his 30,000 Instagram followers, most of whom responded, "Put it back!" He still wasn't sure, so, "I did take it to my mum's and she said to me, 'Get that thing outside!'" The next day, he brought the bottle back to where he found it and returned it to the earth. Langston said he didn't think he was cursed but did reveal this juicy tidbit: "Because a bit of the wax and cork had broken, I got 150-year-old wee all over my hands."

* * *

THE SIX MAIN TYPES OF CORN

- Dent (most field corn grown in the U.S. used for a variety of products and uses)

- Flint (found in many different colors, commonly known as Indian corn)

- Pod (wild corn from which cultivated corn originated)

- Sweet (sold and consumed "on the cob")

- Flour (starchy and grindable)

- Popcorn

Quarterback Gale Gilbert played on five straight Super Bowl–losing squads (1991–95), an NFL record.

FAMOUS GHOSTS

Celebrities spend the better part of their lives being adored and worshipped by millions of people. It's no wonder that when it's time to say farewell, they don't want to go–and so they don't. Here are some stories of famous movie stars and musicians whose ghosts may still be hanging around their favorite haunts.

CLIFTON WEBB

Broadway and Golden Age of Hollywood star Clifton Webb so loved his mansion on Rexford Drive in Beverly Hills, where he spent the last five years of his life due to debilitating health problems, that he told friends he planned to never leave–promising to haunt it. Webb died in 1966, and the home sold to gossip columnist Joyce Haber and TV producer Douglas Cramer, who claimed to have felt the presence of the previous resident on several occasions: While sitting out by the swimming pool, they'd see through the window of the master bedroom a figure that matched Webb's shape. They'd also hear a ghostly voice chant Webb's catchphrase, "Well, well."

KAREN CARPENTER

The Jim Henson Company's studio complex on La Brea Avenue in Hollywood used to be the home of A&M Records. One of the label's most successful acts, Karen Carpenter–singer and drummer for the band the Carpenters–kept an office there. Carpenter died of heart failure caused by anorexia at age 32 in 1983, but her ghost is said to haunt the Henson lot. In the mid-1980s, Tom Petty and the Heartbreakers settled into Studio 2, the Carpenters' favorite recording spot at A&M. A lot of takes were ruined by buzzing noises and funky equipment, and the bandmembers were told by staff that Karen Carpenter's ghost was displeased and taking it out on them. (Petty was told to place a crystal inside a studio wall to appease Carpenter into ending her interference–and it worked.) The Henson complex also houses a soundstage with some adjacent dressing rooms, which is where Henson employees say they've seen a woman bearing a strong resemblance to Carpenter appear...and then disappear.

JOHN BELUSHI

Dan Aykroyd and John Belushi were best friends and *Saturday Night Live* castmates, and Aykroyd wrote the part of Peter Venkman in *Ghostbusters* for Belushi. After Belushi died of a drug overdose in 1982 at age 33, Bill Murray stepped into the role, but as a tribute to his deceased friend, Aykroyd asked *Ghostbusters* special effects artist Steve Johnson to design and build Slimer–the chaotic, slovenly, voraciously hungry green ghost–in Belushi's image. While the cocaine Johnson snorted off a headshot of Belushi at the time he started work may have played a factor in what came next, Johnson says he was visited by the actor's spirit. "John Belushi's ghost came to me

By the time you're 70, you'll have shed a total of 105 pounds of skin.

to help me out," Johnson said. Belushi reportedly offered his opinions, posed for sketches, and then told the artist to stop doing cocaine because, "It'll kill you."

MARILYN MONROE

Marilyn Monroe, the quintessential "blonde bombshell," died at 32 in 1962 in her home in the Brentwood neighborhood of Los Angeles of an overdose of sleeping pills. Looming large over Hollywood in death as in life, reports have been made ever since of her ghost popping up around town. She's been seen walking around the house where she died, sitting on a bench near the Santa Monica pier, and at the Roosevelt Hotel, both on the dance floor and in the mirror of her favorite suite, room 246.

AMY WINEHOUSE

The English neo-soul singer Amy Winehouse died of acute alcohol poisoning at age 27 in July 2011. Reportedly, Winehouse's ghost almost immediately started haunting the apartment in London occupied by her close friend Pete Doherty, lead singer of the rock band the Libertines. Doherty repeatedly saw Winehouse's spirit around the house, and it so spooked him that in November 2011, he moved out of the apartment and resettled in Paris.

JIM MORRISON

Jim Morrison, front man of 1960s psychedelic rock band the Doors, died of drug-related heart failure in his Paris apartment in 1971. Morrison's body was interred at the local Père Lachaise Cemetery, which became a tourist attraction and hangout spot for hardcore Morrison fans, one of whom claims to have photographed the singer's ghost standing on his own grave in 1997. Morrison spent most of his life in Los Angeles, and that's evidently where his ghost went, too: there were numerous reports of his long-haired spirit hanging out in the bathroom of the now-defunct Mexico Restaurante Y Barra, a restaurant built on the spot where the Doors' recording studio once stood.

GEORGE REEVES

Just over a year after completing a six-year stint playing the Man of Steel on the TV series *Adventures of Superman*, actor George Reeves was found dead of a self-inflicted gunshot wound to the head in the bedroom of his home in Benedict Canyon, a neighborhood in west Los Angeles, in June 1959. The house still stands, with several tenants and visitors claiming that Reeves never quite left. One couple who rented the home said they heard odd sounds coming from the upstairs bedroom where Reeves died, and when they went to investigate, the room had been torn apart; when they returned downstairs, their drinks had been moved from the living room to the kitchen. Those same renters claim to have seen Reeves's ghost in his room in the middle of the night on one occasion, dressed in his Superman costume; a film crew making a documentary about Reeves witnessed the same sight.

World's strongest insect: the horned dung beetle can lift 1,100 times its own body weight.

ANTI-JOKES

*If a joke isn't funny and you still laugh at it, does that mean
it really is funny...or that you're just a weirdo?*

Q: What's red and bad for your teeth?
A: A brick.

Q: What do you call a boomerang that doesn't come back?
A: A stick.

I remember when the candle store burned down. Everyone stood around singing "Happy Birthday."

Q: What's worse than finding a worm in your apple?
A: Getting diagnosed with cancer.

Dark humor is like food. Not everyone gets it.

Q: What did one stranger say to the other?
A: Nothing. They didn't even make eye contact. That's what's wrong with the world today.

Q: Why can't men get mad cow disease?
A: Because they're all pigs.

Interviewer: "Describe yourself in three words."
Me: "Lazy."

Q: How do you confuse a blonde?
A: Dress up like a pirate and perform a river dance while throwing napkins at her.

Q: What did the cowboy say at his second rodeo?
A: "This ain't my first rodeo."

Q: What's green and has wheels?
A: Grass. I lied about the wheels.

Q: Why did the monkey fall out of the tree?
A: Because it was clumsy. Sadly, it died on impact.

Q: What do you call someone who points out the obvious?
A: Someone who points out the obvious.

Q: What do you call a broken can opener?
A: A can't opener.

Dads are like boomerangs. I hope.

Q: Which joke isn't really that funny?
A: This one.

A horse walks into a bar and the bartender says, "Why the long face?"
   The horse replies, "Mostly due to evolution via natural selection, but also due to some selective breeding."

Q: What's the best way to bring a smile to your face?
A: Adjust the mimetic zygomaticus major muscles located beneath each of your cheek bones to pull the angle of your mouth superolaterally.

Q: Why did the chicken cross the road?
A: Can we just stop asking this silly question and all agree that if we don't know by now, we'll never know?

Q: How many nihilists does it take to change a light bulb?
A: It doesn't matter.

Most pyramids have four sides, but the Great Pyramid of Giza has eight.

FAILED CALENDARS

*Most of the world operates under a calendar, or time organization system,
in which a year consists of 365 days arranged into 12 months. Though not
totally perfect, this Gregorian calendar is a pretty good system, and history is
full of tales of ill-fated plans from people who spent days, months, and years
trying to figure out a better way to track the days, months, and years.*

GEORGIAN CALENDAR

In 1745, Reverend Hugh Jones, an English loyalist living in colonial Maryland writing
under the pseudonym Hirossa Ap-Iccim, published a proposal for the Georgian
calendar, named for then-ruling monarch King George II. It consisted of 13 months of
28 days each, with the 365th day—Christmas—toward the end of the year, untethered
to any month. A new year would begin right after that. When there was little interest
in a widespread adoption of the calendar, Jones slightly revised the system in 1753,
naming each of the 13 months after notable saints.

HOLOCENE CALENDAR

Italian-born geologist Cesar Emiliani put forth an idea in 1993 to alter the nearly
universal Gregorian calendar with one small fix, which would better reflect the
geological epoch in which modern society found itself. The Holocene calendar would
add exactly 10,000 years to the date, reflecting the Earth's historical period in the
Holocene geological epoch, dating back to the birth of agriculture and humanity's
move away from nomadism. Therefore, the year in which Emiliani proposed his
calendar, 1993, would've been reset and notated as 11993 HE.

POSITIVIST CALENDAR

French philosopher Auguste Comte proposed the Positivist calendar in 1849. Also
broken down into 13 months that each consisted of 28 days, Comte was mainly
concerned with renaming measures of time after European thinkers, writers, and other
important figures to get away from the Roman mythological influence on the Gregorian
calendar. The namesakes of the months included the biblical Moses, chronicler
Homer, philosopher Aristotle, mathematician Archimedes, William Shakespeare, René
Descartes, Charlemagne, St. Paul, and Julius Caesar. Furthermore, each week began
with Monday rather than Sunday, and the yearly tally would've been reset so that 1789
(the year of the French Revolution) would become year 1, so 1849 would've been 61.

FRENCH REPUBLICAN CALENDAR

While Comte paid tribute to the French Revolution and the creation of the
French Republic with his Positivist calendar, the first leaders of post-royal-overthrow France

Spanish name for yellow fever: *vomito negro*, or "black vomit," after a telltale symptom.

invented their own calendar at the time. In 1793, the newly installed government created the French Republican calendar. It was broken down into 12 months, but eliminated the concept of weeks, with each month sectioned off instead into three ten-day periods called *decades*. That works out to 360 days, and the remaining six days in the calendar were worked in as *sansculottides*. Named for *sans-culottes*, the French working class who fueled the Revolution, the *sansculottides* fell at the end of the year, in succession, and each commemorated a different French value: Celebration of Talent, Celebration of Labor, Celebration of Policy, Celebration of Honors, Celebration of Convictions, and "The Revolutionary." When Napoleon seized control of France at the turn of the 19th century, he eliminated the calendar and returned the country to the Gregorian system in 1806.

INTERNATIONAL FIXED CALENDAR

The reason why most calendars are built around a 365-day year is because that's basically how long it takes the earth to make one full trip around the sun. English accountant and financial analyst Moses B. Cotsworth figured that 364 days was close enough, and he formed his International Fixed calendar around that number. Proposed in 1902, Cotsworth suggested a year made up of 13 months of 28 days, but with every day and month permanently fixed to the same weekday. (For example, a date such as January 20 would always fall on a Thursday.) All 12 months from the Gregorian calendar kept their names, with the 13th month coming in the middle of the year, between June and July, and called Sol. No country ever used the calendar (also called the Cotsworth plan), but it did have one adopter: George Eastman made it the official time accounting record of his company, the large and powerful Eastman Kodak. Beginning in 1928, and all the way up until 1989, 57 years after Eastman died, Kodak's internal records were all kept in accordance with the International Fixed calendar.

JUCHE CALENDAR

Juche is the official ideology of North Korea, which combines the political and economic philosophies of communism with a worship of founding father and original leader Kim-Il Sung as a near-supernatural being. As such, in 1997, three years after Kim-Il Sung died from a stroke at age 82, Kim Jong-il, his son and successor as Supreme Leader, instituted the newly created Juche calendar. The year 1912, Kim Il-Sung's birth year, was rebranded as 1; 1941, Kim Jong-il's birth, became year 30. The year 2023 in the Juche calendar is thus 112.

* * *

> "You never know what you got 'til it's gone.
> I wanted to know what I had, so I got rid of everything."
> —Steven Wright

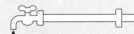

Most of Earth's mass can be attributed to oxygen and iron.

THE WORST TEAMS OF ALL TIME

The Boston Celtics won 10 NBA titles in a row from 1959 to 1969. Tom Brady's New England Patriots captured six Super Bowl victories. The New York Yankees have won the World Series more than two dozen times. The following stories are most definitely not about any of those teams.

TEAM: Charlotte Bobcats (NBA)
SEASON: 2011–2012
STORY: The year got off to a rocky start for the entire NBA. A preseason disagreement between owners and the players' union led to a lockout, shortening the regular season from 82 games to 66. But the Charlotte Bobcats took it especially hard. Missing the playoffs with a 34-48 record the previous season, the not-yet-a-decade-old franchise got even worse. They put up the NBA's worst offense (95 points per game) as well as the worst defense (allowing 110 points per game) and ranked dead last in the league for three-point percentage. Their top scorer, Gerald Henderson, averaged a mediocre 15.1 points per game.

Eliminated from playoff contention a little over halfway through the season, the Bobcats finished the year off terribly, with a 23-game losing streak; in 21 of those games, they lost by at least 20 points. In one of those one-sided contests, rookie Bismack Biyombo blocked a shot from the Toronto Raptors' Rudy Gay during a home game and screamed, "This is my house!" TV cameras picked up Gay's response: "You have seven wins. It's everybody's house." The Bobcats' final record was 7-59, with a winning percentage of .106, the lowest in NBA history.

TEAM: New York Mets (MLB)
SEASON: 1962
STORY: After the New York Giants and Brooklyn Dodgers moved to San Francisco and Los Angeles, respectively, in 1959, Major League Baseball rushed to place a new expansion team in New York City to replace them. The New York Mets began play in 1962, playing in the former home of the New York Giants: the Polo Grounds, a crumbling structure built in the 1890s with a very short outfield that opposing hitters were fully able to exploit. For example, Mets pitchers Roger Craig and Jay Hook sat atop the 1962 list of pitchers who gave up the most home runs (25 and 31), as well as the list of pitchers who lost the most games (24 and 20). The Mets were just as inept at other aspects of the game, ranking last in the league in batting average and fielding percentage.

Last American flying "ace" (a pilot with five combat kills): Steve Ritchie, 1972.

The 1962 Mets were a team of streaks—losing ones. They opened the season with nine losses in a row, and at various times put up losing streaks of 11, 13, and 17 games. When it was all over, the New York Mets' regular season record was 40 wins and 120 losses, the worst of the 20th century and of the modern, 160-game Major League Baseball era. When the New York Mets won 100 games and a World Series just seven years later in 1969, the memory of the woeful 1962 Mets was fresh enough that it helped to inspire a semisarcastic nickname: the "Miracle Mets."

TEAM: Tampa Bay Buccaneers (NFL)
SEASON: 1976
STORY: For their inaugural season as an NFL franchise, the Tampa Bay Buccaneers persuaded five-time Rose Bowl–winning USC coach John McKay to turn pro. However, he couldn't seem to apply his skills or intellectual prowess to that first Bucs squad, which consisted almost entirely of unproven rookies and ready-to-retire veterans that the rest of the NFL had left unprotected in an expansion-team draft. Plagued by injuries throughout the year that left half the squad on the sidelines for at least part of the season, the Buccaneers didn't even score a point until the third game of the season, and didn't score a touchdown until the fourth game. With a 287-point differential (meaning opponents scored 287 more points than they did) that ranked them last in the NFL, the Bucs were also the least successful team in 1976 in terms of points scored and total touchdowns.

The Buccaneers scored zero points in five separate games, almost all of them blowouts, including a 42-0 loss to the Pittsburgh Steelers. The other new NFL team that year, the Seattle Seahawks, won only two games, and one of those was against the Buccaneers. At the end of the season, the Tampa Bay Buccaneers had compiled a 0-14 record, making them the first NFL team to not win or tie a single game in a season. They almost repeated the feat: the franchise didn't record its first win until the 13th game of the 1977 season, but finished that season 2-12.

TEAM: Antigua Barracuda (United Soccer League)
SEASON: 2013
STORY: The small Caribbean nation of Antigua and Barbuda (population: 100,000) sought to compete more effectively on the global stage in the 2010s, and in 2013 formed a professional soccer team to bolster and provide practice for its national squad, the one that would take the field in international tournaments such as the FIFA World Cup. The Antigua Barracuda then joined the United Soccer League, a U.S.-based, lower-tier professional league. The first and only team to originate from outside of the U.S., the Barracuda played just a few matches at its home stadium, an old and converted cricket field; owing to low attendance, they decided to play all

Frozen vegetables have more vitamin C than fresh ones.

games on the road. For the 2013 season, the already poorly funded squad crisscrossed the U.S., perpetually traveling to and from matches in a team bus.

That didn't set the Barracuda up for much success. Over the course of a 26-game season, the Antigua Barracuda amassed an 0-26-0 record. Pro soccer standings are determined on a system where points are awarded for wins and ties, but since the Barracuda didn't win or tie any of its games, it became the first professional soccer team in world history to finish a season with 0 points. It also set a record for goal differential of negative 80, meaning opponents scored 80 more goals then they did, making for an average game score of 3 to 0. The team folded at the end of the season.

TEAM: Indianapolis Racers (World Hockey Association)
SEASON: 1978–1979
STORY: Both the National Hockey League and its now-defunct 1970s competitor, the World Hockey Association, used a point system to determine standings—two points for a win, one for a loss. The lowest point total ever for a North American professional hockey team is 12, a feat achieved by the WHA's Indianapolis Racers in the 1978–79 season. The Indianapolis Racers entered the league in 1974, but by 1978, when it became evident that the WHA was about to fold and the NHL was looking to absorb some of its most successful, Canadian-based teams, Racers owner Nelson Skalbania tried to move the team up north, but to no avail. Stuck with a team running out of money and running out the clock, Skalbania didn't put much of his deep financial resources into the team. Early in the season, he even had to sell the contract rights to his most promising player—a rookie named Wayne Gretzky—to the Edmonton Oilers. (The Oilers would later move into the NHL, and Gretzky, universally regarded as the greatest hockey player of all time, would lead the franchise to four Stanley Cup championships.)

In December 1978, the Indianapolis Racers could go on no more, and they folded in the middle of the season, having played just 25 of their 80 scheduled games. Of those 25 games, they won 5, lost 18, and tied 2.

* * *

SNOW JOKE

South Florida is a tropical place, full of sunny beaches where locals and tourists can walk around in swimsuits almost year-round. It's also a major point of entry for the illegal drug trade: lots of cocaine enters the U.S. through Miami, with some smugglers so bold as to drop it from planes. When a large part of Miami experienced a fine dusting on January 19, 1977, lots of people thought that a cocaine "drop" had gone wrong and a shipment had exploded upon impact, sending the fine white powder everywhere. That was a far more believable notion than what had *actually* happened: it was the first time in recorded history that snow fell on Miami.

U.S. state closest to Africa: Maine.

FORGOTTEN FAD RESTAURANTS

Fast-food burger places, barbecue joints, and Chinese restaurants remain stalwarts on the American food scene, outlasting a lot of other types of eateries that have come...and mostly gone.

FONDUE. While the notion of dipping pieces of bread, meat, and vegetables in hot oil or cheese and calling it a (very filling) meal dates back to 18th-century Switzerland, the trend caught on in America in the late 1960s and 1970s. Fondue became a major food fad, both as an in-home dinner party concept (if you got married in the 1970s, you were probably gifted a fondue set) and as a restaurant theme. Couples or groups would get their own big pot of cheese and stick skewers of food into the bubbling cauldron. Then, for dessert: cookies and cake dipped into melted chocolate fondue. (That doesn't date back to the 1700s—chocolate fondue is a purely American invention.) One of the biggest fondue restaurant chains, The Melting Pot, still operates about 100 locations—far fewer than it did at its peak in the mid-1980s.

PIZZA PARLORS WITH PIPE ORGANS. It seems an arbitrary and inexplicable combination, but in the 1970s and 1980s, every major city in the United States was home to at least one pizza parlor where a live musician played old-timey songs (or movie scores or adapted rock tunes) on a gigantic pipe organ, many of which dated from the 1920s. (Plenty of these establishments salvaged their organs from old, disused silent movie theaters.) Essentially low-cost, easily repeatable dinner theater, "pizza and pipes" joints faded away by the mid-1990s, replaced by another, more up-to-date kind of dinner theater: one with singing animatronics, such as ShowBiz Pizza and Chuck E. Cheese.

"HEALTHY" FROZEN YOGURT. It seems as though every strip mall in the country today is home to a small, self-service, weigh-and-pay frozen yogurt shop, but this is the second wave of yogurt's popularity. Back in the 1980s, thousands of frozen yogurt shops opened up across America, mimicking the ice cream shops of yore—customers went in, and a person behind the counter served them their ice cream. They exploded in popularity because in the health-conscious 1980s, frozen yogurt was marketed as a healthy alternative to ice cream because it had less fat. (It remained, however, just as sugary, and is also full of a lot more preservatives than most ice creams.) While there were plenty of mom-and-pop stores, one chain dominated the fro-yo market: The Country's Best Yogurt (TCBY). Once 2000-locations strong in the early 1990s, there are now just a few hundred left.

COMMENCEMENT NAYSAYERS

Congratulations! You've worked your butt off to graduate from college.
All that's left is to suffer through some smartaleck giving a speech.

"Before I begin, I must point out that behind me sits a highly admired president of the United States and decorated war hero while I, a cable television talk-show host, have been chosen to stand here and impart wisdom. I pray I never witness a more damning example of what is wrong with America today."
—Conan O'Brien

....

"So, what's it like in the real world? Well, the food is better, but beyond that, I don't recommend it."
—Bill Watterson

....

"As you set off into the world, don't be afraid to question your leaders. But don't ask too many questions at one time or that are too hard because your leaders get tired and/or cranky."
—Will Ferrell

....

"You are graduating from college. That means that this is the first day of the last day of your life. No, that's wrong. This is the last day of the first day of school. Nope, that's worse. This is a day."
—Andy Samberg

....

"Every year, many, many stupid people graduate from college. And if they can do it, so can you."
—John Green

"Be wise, because the world needs wisdom. If you cannot be wise, pretend to be someone who is wise, and then just behave like they would."
—Neil Gaiman

....

"And if you remember anything I say today, remember this. Every single thing you see in movies is real."
—Amy Poehler

....

"I didn't go to college. And I'm not saying you wasted your time, or money, but look at me, I'm a huge celebrity."
—Ellen DeGeneres

....

"I don't know if you're tough enough to handle this. You are the most cuddled generation in history. I belong to the last generation that did not have to be in a car seat. You had to be in car seats. I did not have to wear a helmet when I rode my bike. You do. You have to wear helmets when you go swimming, right? In case you bump your head against the side of the pool. Oh, by the way, I should have said, my speech today may contain some peanut products."
—Stephen Colbert

....

"The best advice I can give anybody about going out into the world is this: Don't do it. I have been out there. It is a mess."
—Russell Baker

Hot myth: the spiciness in peppers is in the white flesh, not the seeds.

NATURE NOTES

We write lots of articles about fauna, now let's hear it for flora!

I CAN HEAR YOU

Corn isn't the only plant with ears. A 2013 study at the University of Missouri suggests that some plants can actually "hear" a caterpillar chomping on their leaves. Lead researcher Heidi Appel said scientists used a "cold laser" to record the tiny vibrations a caterpillar makes when it chews on the leaves of a thale cress (*Arabidopsis thaliana*), known as "the lab rat of the plant world"—the cress releases a mustard oil that acts as an insecticide to defend itself against hungry insects. Appel then played the sound within earshot of the cress, and even though there were no caterpillars present, the plant defended itself. "In a second experiment," Appel told NPR, "we played back vibrations caused by a gentle wind on the leaves and also vibrations from a common insect in the plant's habitat, a tree-hopper. And neither of those vibrations stimulated the chemical defense."

SIREN SONG

In 2009, researchers at England's Royal Horticultural Society (RHF) enlisted men and women from the public to read excerpts from famous literary works. Then they played the recordings to tomato plants for a month, "predicting," said RHF Garden Superintendent Colin Crosbie, "that the male voice would be more effective." But the plants exposed to women's voices grew faster and taller—by about an inch. The men's plants didn't fare as well—a few even grew less than the two control plants that grew in silence. Why do they prefer women? "We just don't know," said Crosbie. "It could be that [women] have a greater range of pitch and tone that affects the sound waves that hit the plant." Interestingly, the woman whose voice had the most dramatic effect was none other than Sarah Darwin, the great-great granddaughter of Charles Darwin (one of the founders of RHF). She read excerpts from *On the Origin of Species*, and her tomato plant grew two inches taller than the rest.

YEW GETTING A SEX CHANGE?

Do you know the difference between a male tree and a female tree? Like with humans, it has something to do with nuts and berries. Except for most trees, the females bear seeds and fruits, and the male trees' flowers produce pollen, which finds

First former NBA player to live to be 100 years old: Whitey Von Nieda, in 2022.

its way to the females via wind or insect, then fertilizes the females. One ancient tree in a churchyard in Scotland—known as the Fortingall Yew—has partially changed from male to female, and biologists are baffled. Records of this gnarled, 5,000-year-old tree's growth go back to the 1700s, and in that time, it has never produced berries. Then, in 2015, Max Coleman of Royal Botanic Garden Edinburgh saw that it was growing berries, like a female. "It's a rare occurrence," said Coleman, "rare and unusual and not fully understood." He says the leading theory is something caused "a shift in the balance of hormone-like compounds" within the tree. "One of the things that might be triggering it is environmental stress."

LOOK WHAT SCRAT BEGAT

Remember Scrat, the acorn-obsessed squirrel from *Ice Age*? During a real ice age from the Pleistocene epoch, a real squirrel, patrolling the banks of the Kolyma River in what is now Siberia, buried a cache of seeds dropped by a flowering plant called *Silene stenophylla*. The squirrel damaged the larger, mature seeds—perhaps to keep them from sprouting—but left the smaller seeds intact. About 32,000 years later, in 2012, Russian scientists unearthed those seeds from a layer in the permafrost (which also contained woolly rhinoceros bones). After verifying their age using carbon-dating techniques, the scientists attempted to germinate the seeds. Result: they grew, flowered, and produced new seeds. This is officially the oldest plant life ever regenerated, shattering the previous record of 2,000 years. Who knows what else has been kept preserved in that permafrost?

LIFE ON VENUS

You might think that the main difference between plants and animals is consciousness, but scientists aren't so sure. In 2017, an international team of researchers tested how Venus flytraps (*Dionaea muscipula*) respond to anesthesia. Scientists aren't even exactly sure how compounds such as ether knock out humans, but they know that ether disrupts electrical signals from reaching the brain. Because consciousness is thought to be contained within our nervous system, anesthesia then literally cuts us off from our consciousness. The researchers chose Venus flytraps because the plants respond to touch—using tiny sensory hairs—much in the same way animals do. They don't receive a lot of nutrients from soil, instead getting their nutrients from capturing unsuspecting bugs (and small birds and mammals) that land on—and then are imprisoned by—the plants' spiky leaves.

When a fly lands on a Venus flytrap, the same basic thing happens in the plant that happens in you when a fly lands on your arm: signaling molecules are released

Bee and wasp stings kill Americans 50 times more frequently than alligator attacks.

from the landing spot and then spread throughout the plant, causing the plant's two spiked leaves to close fast. In the study, the anesthetized plant still released the signaling molecules, but those molecules stopped at the source without going anywhere. It's the same way with anesthetized people: pain and touch receptors still activate, but the nervous system doesn't deliver them to the brain. This response suggests that anesthesia has a similar effect on plants as it does on animals. So, if what it does to animals is cut them off from their consciousness, then what is it cutting off in plants if not the same thing? And—just as with animals—when the anesthesia wears off, the Venus flytrap wakes right back up.

Another amazing fact that researchers learned about these increasingly interesting carnivorous plants: they can count. It works like this: When a potential prey (the researchers used crickets) makes contact with a Venus flytrap, the plant doesn't react immediately. It waits for the second touch, and then the leaves close in. After five more touches, it releases digestive enzymes around its meal. (Researchers discovered this by "applying increasing numbers of mechano-electric stimuli.") "The number of action potentials informs the plant about the size and nutrient content of the struggling prey," said lead researcher Dr. Rainer Hedrich of the University of Würzburg. "This allows the Venus flytrap to balance the cost and benefit of hunting." That's one smart plant!

* * *

TAKE ME OUT TO LE BALL GAME

The American pastime of baseball has historically been popular in the mostly French-speaking Canadian province of Quebec, home to the Montreal Expos from 1969 to 2005. Here are the French equivalents for common baseball terms.

- **La balle au camp:** the game of baseball, literally "field ball"
- **L'abris des joueurs:** dugout
- **Le monticule:** mound
- **L'enclos des releveurs:** bullpen ("the pitchers' enclosure")
- **Le but:** base ("goal")
- **Le marbre:** home plate
- **L'avant champ:** infield
- **Le champ extérieur:** outfield
- **La manche:** inning ("sleeve")

- **L'arrêt-court:** shortstop
- **Le voltigeur:** outfielder
- **Le prise:** strike
- **La balle glissante:** slider ("slippery ball")
- **La partie parfait:** perfect game ("perfect part")
- **Le coup de circuit:** home run
- **L'amorti:** bunt ("cushioning")
- **Le retrait:** out
- **La moyenne au baton:** batting average

World's largest golf course: it's in Australian scrub land, and it takes up 848 square miles.

GAME SHOW GOOFS

Being on a game show may look easy from the comfort of your living room, but under those hot television lights, contestants' mouths sometimes disconnect from their brains.

Host: Name something you feel before you buy it.
Contestant: Excited.
—FAMILY FEUD

Host: On *Forbes*'s 2020 list of the 100 highest-paid athletes, at age 50 this active individual sportsman is the oldest.
Contestant: Who is Phil?
—JEOPARDY!

Host: What does the acronym NASA stand for?
Contestant: National Socialist Space Satellite.
—WEAKEST LINK

Host: Name something a rabbit might do in a magician's hat.
Contestant: Fly away!
—FAMILY FEUD

Host: While walking down the beach, I found a message in a bottle. The message said, "I'm trapped on a deserted island with Scarlett Johansson. Please send 'blank.'"
Contestant: Hair.
—MATCH GAME

Host: What is the only planet known to support life?
Contestant: Mars.
—THE CHASE

Host: In what century was the composer J. S. Bach born?
Contestant: The 20th century.
—WEAKEST LINK

Host: Name a tradition that's associated with Christmas.
Contestant: Hanukkah.
—FAMILY FEUD

Host: One of the topics covered in a Major League Baseball course at Arizona State is this player who broke the color barrier in 1947.
Contestant: Who is Babe Ruth?
—JEOPARDY!

Host: Which organ of the human body is used for smelling and breathing?
Answer: The lungs.
—WEAKEST LINK

Host: Name a part of the telephone.
Contestant: The bottom part.
—FAMILY FEUD

Host: The Statue of Liberty is a pale shade of what color?
Contestant: Pink.
—THE CHASE

Austrian author Felix Salten wrote *Bambi* and he was also an ardent deer hunter.

Host: What planet in our solar system takes the least amount of time to orbit the sun?
Contestant: The moon.
—ARE YOU SMARTER THAN A 5TH GRADER?

....

Host: Name a part of the body everybody only has one of.
Contestant: Big toe.
—FAMILY FORTUNES (British)

....

Host: In which city do we find the Kremlin building?
Answer: Russia.
—WEAKEST LINK

....

Host: Name a day of the year where you really want to be with friends.
Contestant: December.
—FAMILY FEUD

....

Host: The asteroid 4238 Audrey is named after which actress?
Contestant: Kim Basinger.
—THE CHASE

....

Host: The salesman said, "That caterpillar must be an athlete. He just bought 100 sneakers and a 'blank.'"
Contestant: Accordion.
—MATCH GAME

....

Host: In the TV series of the same name, who played the pathologist Quincy?
Contestant: Quincy.
—WEAKEST LINK

Host: Name a kind of suit that would be inappropriate at the office.
Contestant: Chicken noodle.
—FAMILY FEUD

....

Host: In what year of the nineties did badminton and basketball become Olympic medal sports?
Contestant: 1984.
—WEAKEST LINK

....

Host: Name something a doctor might pull out of a person.
Contestant: A gerbil.
—FAMILY FEUD

....

Host: What member of the crow family, native to the U.K., has a bare face?
Contestant: Russell Crowe.
—THE CHASE

....

Puzzle: _TAR_ IN THE NIGHT _ _ _
Contestant: Start in the right way.
—WHEEL OF FORTUNE (the actual answer was "stars in the night sky")

....

Host: Name a type of bean.
Contestant: Lesbian.
—FAMILY FORTUNES

....

Host: What does a bat use to facilitate flying in the dark?
Contestant: Its wings.
—WEAKEST LINK

....

Host: What is a herd of elephants called?
Contestant: Cows.
—THE CHASE

Most remote National Monument:
the Mariana Trench, 6,200 miles from the contiguous United States.

RANDOM ORIGINS

*Once again, the Bathroom Readers' Institute asks—and answers—
the question: Where does all this stuff come from?*

FROZEN YOGURT

Ice cream, with all its sugar and cream, has never been something most people can eat as often as they'd like without suffering the fattening consequences. Responding to the rising industry of diet products in the 1960s, New England dairy consortium HP Hood LLC introduced Nuform, a line of low-fat yogurts and milks, and a frozen ice-cream alternative called "ice milk." The line proved so popular that in 1972, the high-end chain Bloomingdale's approached HP Hood about developing a treat for the health-conscious, wealthy, trendsetting women who frequented their in-store cafés; the request prompted the creation of Frogurt, a portmanteau of *frozen* and *yogurt*. The first frozen yogurt in the United States, it had about half the fat and calories (but all the sugar) as ice cream and was dispensed from machines like the ones used by Dairy Queen for its "soft serve" style of ice cream. By the end of the 1970s, defined by a health-food craze in which yogurt was a central player, the idea and appeal of frozen yogurt spread, with the New England dairy Brigham's selling Humphreez, the first frozen yogurt in grocery stores, and yogurt company Dannon introducing frozen raspberry yogurt, covered in dark chocolate, on a stick. The health-food fad of the 1970s gave way to the mass avoidance of fat, and adoption of fat-free products, in the 1980s, providing the opening for a chain of frozen yogurt stores. After retired food industry executive Frank D. Hickingbotham tried some at a café in a Neiman Marcus store in 1981, he purchased the company's wholesale fro-yo supplier and made them a subsidiary of his chain, This Can't Be Yogurt, later known as TCBY. By 1987, there were nearly 1,000 TCBY outlets in the U.S.

PIÑATA

In this traditional party game, blindfolded kids (or adults) take turns using a stick to take a whack at a dangling paper animal or box covered in colorful crepe paper. Eventually somebody's whack succeeds in splitting the thing open, sending candy and trinkets cascading to the ground. The piñata is closely and specifically associated with Mexico, but the toy dates to ancient China. Hollow figures such as cows, oxen, and buffalo were made from clay, filled with seeds, and then hardened. Then they were covered in ribbons and colored paper and hit with sticks as part of New Year celebrations; the seeds that spilled out signified good luck and a good harvest. Marco Polo visited Asia in the 1200s and brought the let's-smash-clay-animals idea back to his native Italy, calling it a *pignatta,* or "clay pot." The toy made its way from

Italy to Spain, and the Chinese New Year custom became a Lenten one. Spanish conquistadores took over large parts of the Americas in the 1500s and 1600s, particularly the Aztec empire, where they found the people had their own piñata-like custom: they'd fill clay jars with crops, seeds, and other offerings to Huitzilopochtli, their god of war, cover them in bird feathers, and then smash them up. Spanish Christian missionaries adapted the local tradition into one of religious significance, fashioning a seven-coned star piñata, with each cone representing one of the seven deadly sins. Breaking the object, the missionaries said, mean that good triumphed over evil, and the candy, fruit, and items inside represented heavenly rewards. Why the blindfold? A reminder to have "blind" faith in one's heart.

THAT ONE DISCO MOVE

"Disco" refers to a style of dance music popular in the 1970s, so named because participants filled clubs called discotheques. Disco is also an umbrella term for the type of dance moves struck on the floor, and perhaps there's no move that instantly screams "disco" quite like the one John Travolta strikes on the poster for the definitive disco movie, 1978's *Saturday Night Fever*. One arm is held at his side in a C-shape, the other is raised to the ceiling. In the movie, Travolta strikes the pose and then takes the skyward arm and points it down to the floor, then up, then down again, in the process inspiring millions of imitators. According to *Saturday Night Fever* cast member Denny Dillon, the film's choreographer, Lester Wilson, came up with the move while shooting a dance sequence at Brooklyn discotheque 2001 Odyssey. "They said it was like taking our money, or a coin, in the air, and putting it in a bus fare slot," Dillon said.

SPORK

Fork-spoon hybrids have existed for centuries, created by inventors lost to history, but they usually took the same approach with a two-ended utensil. On one end of a strip of metal were fork tines, and on the other end, a spoon. They were used by the wealthy and elite of western Europe to eat dessert, as dishes such as candied fruit needed both prodding and spooning. These were an obscure oddity until the late 19th century, when Samuel Ward Francis, a doctor from a prominent New York family who preferred tinkering with inventions and filing patents to seeing patients, improved on the concept by jamming all the functional pieces into the same spot with his "improvement in combined knives, forks, and spoons." Granted a U.S. patent in 1874, Francis's design used a spoon as a launch point, fusing four fork tines to the end of the bowl with a semi-sharp knifelike implement along the side. As plastic wasn't yet a going concern, Francis's tool was to be made of metal. It never entered production, but the idea inspired inventors, such as George Laramy of New Hampshire, who created and patented a "table utensil" in 1907 that resembled Francis's design, albeit with a more prominent knife feature. Around this time, other individuals and

Women are caught shoplifting four times more often than men.

companies started churning out combo utensils without any regard to patents, and the word *spork*, a portmanteau combining *spoon* and *fork*, first appeared in print in 1909. It wouldn't be until plastic emerged as an extremely inexpensive way to mass produce things that the spork would find its place in daily life. Cereal and housewares company Van Brode Milling filed a trademark on *spork* in the late 1960s, roughly the same time that Kentucky Fried Chicken became a fast-food sensation. That company needed to provide customers with utensils, and the cheapest and easiest way to do it was with a plastic all-in-one tool.

BOOM BOX

Music has been portable for about 40 years. Before music was downloadable onto phones or iPods, there was the personal cassette player, most famously the Sony Walkman in the late 1970s and early 1980s—a compact machine that played cassette tapes and pumped the music through headphones. Around the same time, boom boxes hit the scene—fully portable, battery-operated all-in-one stereos with speakers, a radio, and maybe a cassette deck. The very first boom box on the market hit stores in 1966. Manufactured by the Netherlands, the Norelco 22RL962 included in one dictionary-sized package a small speaker, an AM/FM radio tuner, an extendable antenna, and one tape deck that could record onto cassettes from an internal microphone or off the radio. It required (and quickly drained) six D-cell batteries.

COUNTING SHEEP

The oldest known book of fables from Europe is *Disciplina clericalis*, collected by writer Petrus Alphonsi. First written in the 12th century, the book was especially influential on the literature of the country in which its stories originated: Spain. In 1605, Spanish author Miguel de Cervantes produced one of the first popular novels, the adventure tale *Don Quixote*. That book's enormous popularity and longevity popularized the idea of counting farm animals to fall asleep—a focused, monotonous activity that calms down the brain enough to drift off. The idea is referenced in *Don Quixote*, and Cervantes got it from *Disciplina clericalis*. The latter includes a story about a king too wound up from his day of important dealings to fall asleep, so he demands that the storyteller who tells him tales each night stay up late with him to recite more stories. The storyteller wants to go to sleep, too, so he comes up with an interactive story that requires the king to count goats. (It evolved into sheep over the centuries.)

FIGURE SKATING

Archaeological evidence exists of humans skating on ice tens of thousands of years ago, strapping moccasins outfitted with sharpened animal bones on the bottom to traverse icy terrain. Modern skates emerged in a style similar to their contemporary one in the Middle Ages, developed by the Dutch, who forged metal blades and attached them to

Oldest person to finish the Ironman triathlon: Hiromu Inada, at 85 years and 328 days (2018).

their shoes to walk across the many canals that freeze over in the long winter months. It would take another few hundred years before ice-skating was seen as recreational, athletic, or artistic, and not just as a method of personal transportation. The first ice-skating club formed in Edinburgh, Scotland, in the 1740s, followed by numerous others in western Europe in the subsequent decades. As a way of showing off one's abilities to get around the ice while balancing on thin blades, club members would challenge each other to draw pictures, forms, or "figures" in the ice. That became the dominant activity in those clubs, which by the 1800s had formed into national associations and then an international governing body for the activity-meets-sport. The International Skating Union held the first World Figure Skating Championships in 1896; only four men competed. Ulrich Salchow of Sweden won the contest in 1902, debuting a move that would not only become his signature, but a foundational element of figure skating: he jumped into the air and spun around, a move now known as the "salchow." Women were invited to compete more in the early 1900s, and female skaters wore increasingly short ice outfits—at the behest of judges, who couldn't make out their footwork under the long dresses customary in fashion at the time. The shorter costumes allowed for more freedom of movement, completing figure skating's development from picture carving into displays of artistry, combining equal parts athleticism and dance. Figure skating became an Olympic event for men in 1908, and for women in 1924.

DONKEYS AND ELEPHANTS AS POLITICAL PARTY MASCOTS

Instantly recognizable in editorial cartoons and news channel graphics as the symbols of the two major political parties in the U.S., the donkey for the Democrats and the elephant for the Republicans stem from influential *Harper's Weekly* editorial cartoonist Thomas Nast, who wrote and illustrated incendiary political satire for the periodical from 1862 to 1886. An 1874 cartoon called "Third Term Panic" was a response to news that President Ulysses S. Grant would run for an unprecedented third term. That news was actually just a rumor, invented and spread by the Democratic-leaning *New York Herald* to make Grant, a Republican, look bad. Nast, an avowed Republican, depicted the *Herald* as a cowardly donkey presenting itself as a brave lion, wrapped in the skin of that beast, terrifying other animals with the doomful news of a power-mad Grant. Included in the menagerie is an elephant clearly labeled "The Republican Vote," and he's about to fall off a cliff to his doom. The donkey was a Democrat, and the elephant a Republican, imagery Nast took from old sources. A donkey dressed as a lion appears in *Aesop's Fables*, and during the Civil War, the Republican Party used the slogan "See the elephant" on recruiting posters, which was period slang that means "fight with bravery." The cartoon etched itself into the collective consciousness. The Republican Party would eventually adopt the elephant as its official mascot, while the Democrats use the donkey in party imagery despite never making it their official animal.

Northernmost county in the U.S.: Lake of the Woods County in Minnesota.

MAKE YOUR OWN TOILET PAPER

Wouldn't it be great if you could sidestep any future toilet paper shortages by just making your own TP at home? Follow this step-by-step guide and you can! (Note: Please do not actually try to do this. It's a very messy and complicated endeavor.)

WHAT YOU'LL NEED

One to two pounds of junk mail

Big cauldron

One gallon of purified and distilled water

Thermometer

Portable laundry-agitator stick

Water

Large, strong whisk

Large spoon for skimming

Pasta roller and cutter

Oxygenated bleach
(a chlorine-free bleach alternative available at natural markets)

Handheld stick blender

Large screen

Blow-dryer

White school glue

Empty cardboard toilet paper roll

HOW TO DO IT

1. Sort through the junk mail, removing paper from envelopes. Discard all the envelopes, especially the ones with plastic windows, and remove any staples from the papers. (Down the line, you wouldn't want to accidentally wipe with a tiny piece of hard plastic or jagged metal!)

In dogs, hamsters, and Tasmanian devils, cancer is contagious.

2. Tear the plastic-and-staple-free mail into as many tiny pieces as you can.

3. Heat the water in the cauldron on the stovetop until it's lukewarm, reaching a thermometer reading of about 105°F to 115°F.

4. Remove the cauldron of water from the heat and throw in all the torn-up junk mail bits. Aggressively churn it with the agitator for 10 to 20 minutes, or until the mixture takes the form of a watery, oatmeal-like pulpy concoction.

5. Using the large, strong whisk, whip the pulp like you've never whipped anything before. Do this for about 20 minutes—you're trying to introduce as much air into the mixture as possible. Doing so works out the ink particles, which attach to air bubbles and rise to the top of the cauldron.

6. Using the skimmer, carefully remove all the inky foam from the top of the solution and discard it. You're now left with pure paper pulp.

7. Carefully run the pulp through the pasta maker. This will squeeze out the excess water, drying out the soggy pulp to prepare it for the chemical absorption phase. Run the pulp through the pasta machine enough times to make it merely wet to the touch instead of soggy and damp.

8. Place the pulp back in the cauldron (or in another large vessel) and chop it up with the handheld blender. This exposes more surface area for the paper to absorb the cleansing chemicals.

9. Carefully mix in the oxygenated bleach with the pulp. This will turn the pulp from an odd shade of gray into a nice white—the common shade of toilet paper.

10. Run the bleached pulp back through the pasta maker, pressing it through repeatedly until it's flat and holds its shape.

11. Spread the now-flattened and whitened pulp on a screen. Run a blow-dryer over it until the paper is completely dry and delicate to the touch—but not so much that it breaks.

12. Apply a thin layer of glue to the cardboard paper tube.

13. Roll the dried-out paper to the cardboard tube.

14. Use once, then destroy.

The 1976 Tampa Bay Buccaneers sent 21 players to their injured list, and 18 of them needed knee surgery.

LIFE IMITATES ART

Sometimes, a movie or a TV show will predict the future; other times, it directly leads to it.

ON THE SCREEN: In the 1999 animated comedy *South Park: Bigger, Longer & Uncut*, the four kids buy tickets for a PG-rated movie at a multiplex just so they can sneak into an R-rated movie. Reason: the movie is an adaptation of their favorite TV show (*Terrance and Phillip*), which they're excited about because the cursing won't be bleeped.

IN REAL LIFE: Young *South Park* fans were equally excited to see *their* favorite characters uncensored on the big screen. So much so, that, according to the *Los Angeles Times*, "Theater owners reportedly were unusually diligent in trying to keep out the under-17 crowd." They were buying tickets to the Will Smith comedy *Wild Wild West*, then sneaking into *South Park*. Show creators Trey Parker and Matt Stone were not happy about this. Why? They both hated *Wild Wild West* and were none too keen on helping that movie's box office numbers at the expense of theirs.

ON THE SCREEN: In 2009, British comedian Sacha Baron Cohen was making *Brüno*, a guerilla mockumentary about a fashion designer. One scene has "Brüno" bypassing the security at Italy's Fashion Week. Dressed in a ridiculous ensemble, he parades down the runway alongside real, unsuspecting fashion models, and then he wreaks havoc. In the movie, Brüno gets thrown out, arrested, and banned from Fashion Week for life.

IN REAL LIFE: Baron Cohen was thrown out, arrested, and banned from Fashion Week for life.

ON THE SCREEN: In the surreal love story *Eternal Sunshine of the Spotless Mind* (2004), heartbroken Joel (Jim Carrey) goes to Lacuna, Inc. to undergo a "memory erasure procedure" that makes him forget his entire relationship with Clementine (Kate Winslet), who underwent the procedure first.

IN REAL LIFE: PTSD sufferers are being treated with a drug called propranolol that doesn't necessarily erase a bad memory—rather, it suppresses the emotion associated with it. But it is theoretically possible to track down and isolate memories, and then erase them. Researchers at the University of Toronto did this with mice: first, they scared a mouse with a tone that came accompanied by a mild electric shock; then they located the neurons that triggered the bad memory and "stimulated" them with a new (and very sci-fi sounding) technology called optogenetics that uses proteins to render the affected memory neurons sensitive to light. Then the scientists flashed pulses of light directly into the mouse's brain...and were able to switch memories on and off. The mouse literally forgot to be afraid of the tone.

Ocean-based eddies (whirlpools) can grow to as large as 90 miles across.

Wherever this research takes scientists, "These discoveries need to go hand in hand with a real thinking about the ethics involved in potentially manipulating memories in people," says mouse memory researcher Sheena Josselyn. These procedures should be used only in extreme cases where a patient's memory recall can be crippling (not to forget an ex).

ON THE SCREEN: Anne Hathaway played the part of Andy Sachs, an overworked fashion assistant in *The Devil Wears Prada* (2006). Her boss (the titular "devil," played by Meryl Streep) was based on fashion maven Anna Wintour, editor in chief of *Vogue*.
IN REAL LIFE: In 2022, Hathaway attended a Michael Kors fashion show. She must have known that she was going to be seated next to Wintour herself, because Hathaway showed up at the event wearing the same brown leather jacket she wore in *Prada*, and she even re-created her bangs. (It's unclear if Wintour got the reference.)

ON THE SCREEN: On a 2011 episode of the medical drama *House*, written by David Shore and Peter Blake, a patient played by Candice Bergen confounds the diagnostic team: she has heart failure, but her arteries aren't clogged. It's not until she starts displaying neurological symptoms that the sardonic genius Dr. House (Hugh Laurie) has his "eureka!" moment: she has cobalt poisoning that has entered her bloodstream via a corroding hip replacement.
IN REAL LIFE: In 2012, a German doctor named Jürgen Schäfer treated a 55-year-old male patient who also had heart failure but no clogged arties. The patient was also suffering from severe vision and hearing loss. He had already seen three doctors, but none had answers.

Those other doctors obviously didn't watch that particular *House* episode. Dr. Schäfer, a fan of the show (his colleagues even call him "the German Dr. House"), had seen it and noticed the similarities to his patient—whose symptoms began after he was given a ceramic replacement hip to replace a previous replacement hip that had failed. But the surgeons didn't remove all of the old hip, and the new one was grinding away metal every time the man walked. Result: his blood had 1,000 times the amount of cobalt considered safe. The diagnosis not only saved the patient's life but called attention to this issue with transplants. "This demonstrates nicely that well-performed entertainment is not only able to entertain and educate, but also to save lives," said Dr. Schäfer (who comes off as much less grumpy than television's Dr. House).

ON THE SCREEN: The 1999 Disney Channel movie *Smart House* features a kid named Ben (Ryan Merriman) who wins a house that is operated by an artificial intelligence system called PAT (played by Katey Sagal). PAT maintains a pleasant temperature,

Each day, Coca-Cola sells 1.9 billion servings of its various beverages.

turns the TV and appliances on and off, prepares meals, picks out clothes, cleans the house, plays with the dog, and even monitors the family's caloric intake and overall health.

IN REAL LIFE: Less than 20 years later, millions of "smart homes" come with personalized AI (Alexa, Siri, Google Home) that perform many of the same tasks as PAT—including protecting the home from intruders. There are even smart kitchens that use robotic "chefs" to prepare meals. And some of the features that PAT displays (especially after the kid tampers with it) might be on the horizon—like shocking a bully trying to get in. And also like in the movie, there are growing concerns that smart homes are an invasion of privacy—especially when they monitor your health. As the fictional Kevin puts it, "It's like Big Brother is watching you, only Big Brother turns out to be your house."

ON THE SCREEN: *The Terminator*, James Cameron's 1984 sci-fi blockbuster about a time-traveling cyborg, introduced audiences to Skynet, a military system that relies on artificial intelligence. It later becomes self-aware and nukes the world.

IN REAL LIFE: Tempting fate, the British military calls its network of military satellites...you guessed it: Skynet. In a statement to *The Register* in 2020, the defense industry conglomerate BT-Viasat-NSSL, referred to ominously as "The Alliance," says the new AI system "provides leadership in SATCOM, cybersecurity, service delivery, tactical networking, artificial intelligence, and emerging technologies." Let's hope that the AI doesn't get its own ideas on which technologies should emerge. (And don't ever show it *The Terminator*.)

* * *

ALWAYS BE PREPARED

Dolly Parton was being interviewed by RuPaul when the model asked the country singer if she always wears her high heels. Dolly responded, "Do you?"

"No," said RuPaul. "That's the thing: there are similarities in what we do, but I take all that stuff off."

Parton's response: "Well, I don't. I have to always stay ready—street ready, I always say. I have to keep my makeup on and keep my hair done. Like, when I'm in L.A....if we get an earthquake, I'm not running out in the street looking like you look now. I have to be ambulance-ready at all times, if I get sick or something. But I actually do wear high heels most of the time. They're not always as high as the ones I wear for show. But I'm little. I'm short. And I have to wear heels in order to reach my cabinets. But I always enjoy wearing the shoes too, and I just feel more like me. But I can come down, though. I'm comfortable in my own skin; I'm comfortable with my image. I dress for myself more than I do for somebody else."

It's legal to drop something out of an airplane,
so long as it doesn't hit people or damage property.

LOONEY LAWS

Believe it or not, these are real laws, still on the books (but probably not enforced).

- In Florida, it's illegal to pass gas in public after 6:00 p.m. on a Thursday.

- It's against the law to forget your wife's birthday in Samoa.

- Hypnotism shows are legal in Everett, Washington, but the event cannot be advertised on street-posted signs nor at the venue's box office.

- Feeding a pig garbage is illegal in Arizona—without a permit.

- Biting off the limb of another in Rhode Island carries with it a prison sentence of at least one year but no more than 20.

- Men in New Jersey are forbidden from knitting during fishing season.

- Drive-in movie theaters in Delaware are legally barred from showing R-rated movies.

- Shooting fish in a barrel? That's illegal in Wyoming, where killing or wounding a fish with a gun is prohibited.

- Only security guards and police may legally shoot a missile at a bus station in Utah.

- Using an X-ray machine for the purpose of determining another person's shoe size is illegal in Nevada.

- In Oklahoma, it's illegal to trip a horse.

- Whistling underwater violates West Virginia state law.

- Clothesline bans were banned in Vermont—neighborhood associations can't legally tell homeowners not to put them up.

- Checking into a hotel with a fake name is against the law in New Hampshire.

- In Kentucky, it's illegal to dye a duckling blue and then sell it, but if you're selling at least six dyed ducklings, it's fine.

- In Minnesota, it's illegal to cross state lines with a duck perched atop one's head.

- Only residents of North Dakota may sit on the state's Dry Pea & Lentil Council.

- If a frog participating in a frog-jumping contest in California dies during the event, organizers must immediately dispose of the frog, and they're not allowed to eat it.

- The use of confetti is legal in Alabama, so long as it isn't made from plastic.

- Don't throw rocks at trains in Wisconsin, because that's against the law.

- It's illegal to wear slippers after 10:00 p.m. in New York State.

- You can't legally sell dog hair in Delaware (but you can give it away for free).

A MYSTERY OF HISTORY: THE VENUS DE MILO, PART II

In the 1997 animated movie Hercules, the titular Greek god is nonchalantly skipping stones, talking to his new friend Meg, when a rock ends up taking out the arms of a Greek statue. Hercules cringes, while Meg deadpans, "It looks better that way." Surprisingly, that's not the most far-fetched theory as to how the Venus de Milo lost her arms.

PIGMENTS OF THE IMAGINATION

As we told you in Part I (page 55), no one knows for sure what happened to the Venus de Milo's arms, or what they were holding. In fact, we know very little about her appearance when she stood in her niche on the wall of a civic gymnasium around 2,100 years ago. One thing we do know: she was a lot more colorful. It's a common misconception that Greco-Roman art and architecture were white. Venus was painted and adorned with jewelry (proven by traces of pigment and attachment holes on her surface). Her skin had lifelike tones, and her hair and drapery were brightly colored as well. She wore a necklace, bracelets, and earrings, most likely made of gold. That could explain why she was toppled over and why her earlobes are missing: robbers wanted her bling.

But it still doesn't explain the arms. One account says that they broke off in 1820 during a battle for possession of the statue between the French and the Turks, but Olivier Voutier wrote in his notebook that she was armless when the farmer discovered her. What about the hand that was found holding an apple, and the deteriorating arm made of a rougher stone? They were reportedly sent to the Louvre along with the rest of the discovery, but were discarded, perhaps because they were in too rough of shape to be restored. Unlike the discarded plinth, there are no known illustrations of Venus's arms.

BODY LANGUAGE

According to the museum's account of the restoration (which doesn't even mention a hand holding an apple), when the statue was being restored in 1821, curators argued over whether they should restore her missing limbs. First, they'd have to agree on how to position them, but there were numerous options: right arm holding up her slipping drapery, or crossed over her body to inscribe words on a tablet? Left arm holding an apple, or holding a tablet? Or leaning on a post? Or raised to her head?

World's largest producer of bagpipes: Pakistan.

After failing to come to a consensus, the curators ultimately decided to display her without her arms. That fateful decision helped make the mystery of the Venus de Milo as much of a draw as her beauty, and ultimately led to her becoming the best-known ancient Greek statue in the world. For the past two centuries, it's become something of a cottage industry for art historians and laypeople alike to put forth their theories about her arms. Among them:

- Venus's left arm was grazing the shoulder of an adjacent statue, perhaps the god Mars. It was made of a lesser stone because it wouldn't have been visible from eye level.
- Her left arm was holding a shield, a mirror, a bow, or an amphora (a jar with two handles and a narrow neck), and her right arm may have been holding her sheet, or even a baby.
- Her arms were made of ivory, as were those on some similar Greek statues— and they were concealed beneath a fabric top. They disappeared long ago.

We'll never know...or will we? According to a 2021 *Athens News* article, "In 1960, a commission of Turkish archaeologists presented a petition to [French minister of cultural affairs] André Malraux demanding the return of the Venus de Milo." Among the archaeologists' claims came this bombshell that, if ever proven true, would turn the art world upside down: "The arms of the Venus are also buried, and the place of burial is only known to three Turkish families who pass on the secret from generation to generation. But those arms will not come to light until Venus is reintegrated into the homeland." Malraux refused to return the sculpture, calling the Turks' petition "cultural blackmail."

SPINNING A YARN

In her 1994 book, *Women's Work: The First 20,000 Years*, Elizabeth Wayland Barber, a professor of archaeology and linguistics at Occidental College, advocated for a theory first presented in the 1950s by archaeologist Elmer G. Suhr: the woman depicted in the sculpture is "spinning"—meaning spinning fibers to make thread. That would explain Venus's arm placement as well as any other theory would: the left arm would have been holding the top of a staff, while the right arm was pulling the thread. These parts of the statue, says Barber, would have most likely been authentic—made of wood and thread—and were stolen or deteriorated long ago. According to *Smithsonian* magazine, "A distaff, thread, and spindle could have been held in her upraised arms and would have been appropriate for the goddess of love."

If the spinning theory is correct, it opens up another possibility: Alexandros sculpted a "woman of the evening." In ancient Greece, when prostitutes were between

Reinforced concrete lasts only about 50 to 100 years.

clients, some made extra money by spinning thread. The act of spinning itself became associated with sex—as evidenced in other provocative artworks from the period. And the way her drapery is slipping suggests the spinning might have to take a break.

That leaves one final question.

WHO WAS THE VENUS DE MILO?

Or, rather, *what* was she? A god or a human? Greco-Roman gods were often depicted as human, so it could go either way. A positive ID is especially difficult because the arms of ancient statues—how they are positioned and what they are holding—are crucial to telling their story. So, without Venus's arms, we can only guess. The fact that she's made of the finest marble available and is literally larger than life—at six feet seven—points to her being a goddess. And if she was indeed clutching a fruit, that points to her being Aphrodite/Venus, who was famously gifted a golden apple in the *Iliad* story "The Judgment of Paris." However, posits Barber, even if the sculpture depicts a prostitute, it doesn't necessarily mean she isn't also a goddess. And the spinning theory backs that up: "Women create thread, they somehow pull it out of nowhere, just as they produce babies out of nowhere." Quite godlike, indeed.

Even if the statue depicts an immortal being, art historians can't even verify that it's Venus, but she looks enough like other depictions of the goddess of love for Louvre officials to have made that assumption. There's another possibility, however: the statue depicts Amphitrite, the goddess of the sea and wife of Poseidon. This theory makes sense because Amphitrite carried much more clout in the Cyclades than Aphrodite. So, one plausible scenario is that Alexandros of Antioch was commissioned to sculpt Amphitrite for a niche located high on the outer wall of a gymnasium, and a scantily clad prostitute posed for him while she was spinning. (Too bad Alexandros didn't chisel the name of the statue onto the plinth along with his own name.)

LINGERING QUESTIONS

Will the Venus de Milo ever make it back to her home country? There's a decades-long movement by the Greeks—many of whom still refer to the statue as Aphrodite of Melos—to get her back. And if those missing arms ever do show up, will they be displayed beside her...or reattached? Even the Venus de Milo's future is steeped in mystery.

* * *

AN ODE TO THE VENUS DE MILO

"Thou, thou art alive, and thy thoughts are the thoughts of a woman, not of some

There are 21 countries that don't have a military.

strange, superior being, artificial and imaginary. Thou art made of truth alone, outside of which there is neither strength nor beauty. It is thy sincerity to nature which makes thee all powerful, because nature appeals to all men. Thou art the familiar companion, the woman that each believes he knows, but that no man has ever understood, the wisest not more than the simple. Who understands the trees? Who can comprehend the light?"

—Auguste Rodin (1840–1917), sculptor of *The Thinker*

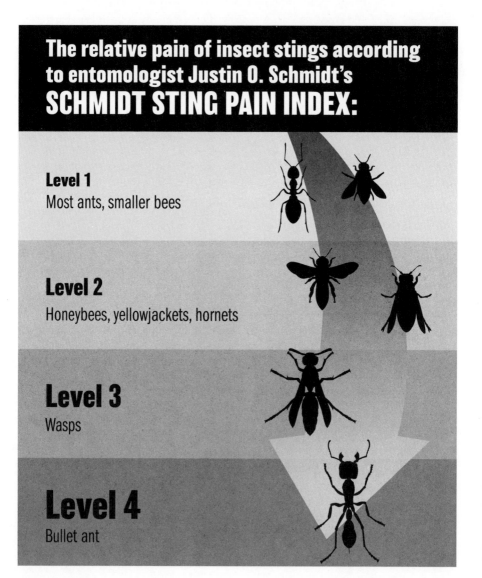

The relative pain of insect stings according to entomologist Justin O. Schmidt's
SCHMIDT STING PAIN INDEX:

Level 1
Most ants, smaller bees

Level 2
Honeybees, yellowjackets, hornets

Level 3
Wasps

Level 4
Bullet ant

Average body fat on a healthy male chimpanzee: 0.002 percent.

UNCLE JOHN'S HOUSEHOLD HACKS

Now for some clever tips and tricks to make your life a tad bit easier.

- To prevent tomato sauce–stained Tupperware, spray the plastic container with cooking spray before adding the tomato sauce.

- Pet hair not coming off the couch? Put on a wet glove and run your hand over it—the hair will stick to it.

- To cut a cherry tomato perfectly in half, place it between two plastic storage lids and use them as a guide for your knife.

- Unsure of how to configure a fitted sheet? Look for the tag: it's designed to go in the bottom right side of the mattress.

- Don't just soak a hard-to-clean pot or pan in hot, soapy water. Add a dryer sheet, and the pan will end up even easier to clean.

- Don't wrestle your pillowcase onto the pillow; turn the pillowcase inside out, reach inside with both hands, and grab each corner. Then, using the pillowcase like two mittens, grab the two corners of the pillow. That makes it a cinch to then pull the pillowcase into position.

- To clean dry paint from a paintbrush, run it under water while using a comb to clean between the bristles.

- Is your salt or pepper clumping? Add a few grains of rice to the shaker to absorb extra moisture and keep the spices flowing.

- If you're hanging a picture with a wire hanger in the frame, after you hammer the nail into the wall, place a fork—tines first—over the nail. Easily guide the wire onto the nail, remove the fork, and your picture is hung.

- If a door lock is sticking, rub the tip of a pencil onto the key. The graphite will make the key glide into place.

- To keep food gunk from building up in your kitchen sink drain, pour some boiling water into it every few days.

- Instead of washing your cutting board with soap and a sponge (which doesn't always penetrate the tiny knife marks where bacteria lie in wait), chop a lemon in half, pour some coarse salt onto the cutting board, and use the inside of the lemon as a scrub brush to scour.

- If you hang your tools on a pegboard, use a Sharpie to outline each one. That way, you and everyone else will know exactly where to put them back.

- Avoid getting blisters from sweeping and mopping by taping a piece of bubble wrap around the broom or mop handle where you hold it.

American cheese is a combination of cheddar, Colby, and washed curd cheese.

WEIRD CANADA

Canada—the land of horse-mounted police, poutine, hockey, Celine Dion,
bilingual street signs...and some really strange news stories.

CHEW ON THIS

In June 2022, thousands of subscribers of Canadian telecommunications company Telus in northern British Columbia were left without cellular and landline phone service and internet access for the better part of a day. An aspen tree fell on a Telus fiber-optic line between two poles in the towns of Topley and Houston. In investigating the outage and its causes, officials from local utility company BC Hydro quickly fingered a suspect: teeth marks at the bottom of the errant tree indicated a beaver (the official national animal of Canada) gnawed on it, causing it to fall into the fiber-optic line. "It's unusual, but it does happen every once in a while," BC Hydro's Bob Gammer said. "So I wouldn't be a rich man if I had a nickel for every beaver outage, but they do happen."

A STICKY SITUATION

Canada is the world's largest supplier of maple syrup (with most of it coming from the province of Quebec) and other maple-based products, and the maple tree is part of the country's identity—a red maple leaf adorns the federal flag. In 2021, global demand for maple syrup inexplicably but significantly leapt by more than 20 percent, and Canadian distributors weren't prepared: they were already faced with shortages owing to an overly warm spring that diminished maple harvesting and production. In November 2021, the co-op Quebec Maple Syrup Producers had no choice but to cut into its emergency strategic stockpile of maple syrup (the world's only such reserve), releasing for sale and distribution 50 million pounds of the sweet and sticky stuff— more than half of its total reserve supply.

A LACK OF ENERGY

The Police Explosives Disposal Unit—aka the bomb squad—responded to a call at the Windsor, Ontario, Mackenzie Hall Cultural Centre. A suspicious, unidentified object was discovered on the premises: a small black box with an exposed red wire and bright blue light. Authorities quickly determined that the strange object was safe and didn't contain any explosives, yet they destroyed it anyway. The Windsor Police Department declined to explain what the black box actually was, but then a representative of the Listowel Paranormal Society took credit—the box belonged to that organization. The item was an EMF detector (or electromagnetic field sensor), a tool that can supposedly

---

First winner of the Claude E. Shannon Award for excellence in information theory: Claude E. Shannon (1972).

detect the energies or presence of spirits. The Listowel Paranormal Society had undertaken a ghost hunt at the reportedly haunted building a few days earlier, and accidentally left the EMF detector behind.

THERE'S LOTS OF SPACE IN CANADA

In 2024 or 2025, American space agency NASA, in association with the Canadian Space Agency and similar organizations from Europe and Japan, will launch its first manned mission to the moon after more than 50 years. The plan is to build a small work colony on the lunar surface, which will be a jumping-off point for both human-led and robotic missions to elsewhere on the moon and over to Mars. With more people on the moon comes more activity—and more criminal activity, theoretically. In April 2022, Canada's parliament approved an amendment to the country's Criminal Code to authorize prosecuting criminal acts committed on the moon. "A Canadian crew member who, during a space flight, commits an act or omission outside Canada that if committed in Canada would constitute an indictable offence is deemed to have committed that act or omission in Canada," the amendment read, meaning that anything that's illegal in Canada is also illegal in space, and will be treated as such in a (Canadian) court of law.

DUDE, WHERE'S MY SIGN?

Guelph Park in East Vancouver features an art installation of a reclining figure. That statue of a "dude chilling" prompted locals and Guelph regulars to nickname the greenspace "Dude Chilling Park." That's not its official name in any way, but park directors went ahead and put up another art installation in 2012, one that closely resembled official signage of the Vancouver Park Board (which didn't sign off) and read "Dude Chilling Park." In 2014, somebody stole the Dude Chilling Park sign. Never recovered, it cost $1,300 to replace. Then in 2018, *that* one was swiped and replaced. And then a crook absconded with another Dude Chilling Park sign in 2021. Not to worry: as of 2022, Guelph Park still has a Dude Chilling Park sign standing.

GAME ON

Severe winter weather is a part of life in Canada, with roads dangerously icing over for several months out of the year in the more northern parts of the country. On the fast-moving, well-traveled Highway 40 near the town of L'Assomption, Quebec, a January 2019 traffic collision quickly ballooned into a massive, multi-car pileup, with nearly 50 cars smacking into one another. The road was closed down for several hours so authorities could clear the debris and safely remove travelers who sustained minor injuries. A couple dozen other people made the most of being stuck on a giant sheet of ice by playing hockey until they got the all-clear. (They apparently had all the gear they needed with them in their cars; hockey is very popular in Canada.)

As of 2022, the *Voyager 1* probe launched in 1977 is 14 billion miles away from Earth.

AMAZING COINCIDENCES

*Whoa, we had an article titled "Amazing Coincidences" in
the last Bathroom Reader! What are the odds?*

FATE SKATES

Sixty-year-old Renée Forrestall of Halifax, Nova Scotia, was looking to switch up
her exercise routine in May 2022 and decided to take up roller-skating, an activity
she'd enjoyed as a child but hadn't undertaken in more than 40 years. After being
underwhelmed by the brand-new skates she purchased, she hit online classified ads
for a pair that looked and felt like the ones she'd used as a teenager. Forrestall found
a listing for skates identical to the ones she'd worn four decades earlier, and arranged
to go to the seller's home nearby to try them on—happily, they fit perfectly. Then as
she was tying the laces, Forrestall noticed a nametag on one of the skates' tongues—
and on it was her own name. They weren't just *like* the skates she'd had as a teenager,
they were the exact same pair, which she'd sold when she was in college. The seller—
whose name happened to be James Bond—said he had a "gut feeling" when Forrestall
contacted him, and told reporters, "I like to think that there are no coincidences."

AUTO PIRATES

Just before dawn one morning in September 2019, police in Jackson, Mississippi,
received a report about a car stolen from a gas station in the south side of the city. That
call came two weeks after a car was stolen from a home in the nearby suburb of Clinton,
in a case that remained unsolved. A few hours after the second theft was noted, police
responded to a crash in downtown Jackson. The two stolen vehicles had crashed into
each other, neither of them anywhere near the sites from where they'd been taken. The
drivers of both cars abandoned their vehicles, but not long after, officers were able to
apprehend the injured man who'd been driving the car stolen from the gas station.

ON THE MARC

In 1967, an art dealer named David Stein sold three watercolors to another New
York City art dealer, who planned to display them in a gallery because they were
purportedly the work of legendary French painter Marc Chagall. However, that same
day, Marc Chagall himself met with the dealer who had just purchased three of what
were supposedly his pieces; the artist quickly confirmed that he had *not* painted the
newly acquired paintings. Stein had made the forgeries himself, the day he sold them.
He was arrested and served more than 20 years in prison.

Only female hornets sting. Male hornets don't even possess stingers.

ONE NIGHTSTAND

A TikTok user identified only as "Valencia" posted a video in 2021 about a pair of nightstands she bought at a Goodwill store—ordinarily a mundane activity, but not in this case. "The weirdest thing just happened, and I'm not making this up," Valencia said. "My heart's like a little trembly. This is really cool." Several scraps of paper remained in the drawers of the secondhand furniture, including a note, written in what appeared to be a child's handwriting, with Valencia's home phone number from the early 2000s, as well as her mother's cell phone number from the same period. Valencia found a girl's first name on another piece of paper and matched it with a last name on another scrap, which turned out to be the name of her childhood friend, with whom she reconnected on Facebook.

A CREEPY LOT

In 1838, poet and horror writer Edgar Allan Poe published *The Narrative of Arthur Gordon Pym*, one of his earliest works and his only novel. Poe claimed the maritime-themed novel was based on true events, but it wasn't really—that was just a spooky angle he made up to promote the book. One part of the story discusses the sinking of a whaling ship, from which only four crewmen survive. The men draw lots to decide which one of them will be killed and eaten by the others, and that fate befalls cabin boy Richard Parker. Fast forward to 1884, when the real-life ship the *Mignonette* got lost at sea and the crew ran out of food. The survivors would later admit to authorities that to avoid starvation, they drew lots and killed and ate the loser: cabin boy Richard Parker.

TAKE NOTE

In 2006, commercial fisherman Mark Anderson was sailing his boat off the coast of Scotland when he caught something other than a fish: a bottle, inside of which was a "message in a bottle" authenticated as 92 years old. That landed Anderson a spot in Guinness World Records, for being the man who discovered the oldest ever message in a bottle. He reportedly frequently talked about this accomplishment, to the point where it annoyed his friends, particularly Andrew Leaper. Six years after Anderson's discovery, Leaper was sailing Anderson's boat off the coast of Scotland, where he found a bottle with a note in it—and the note was 98 years old. Leaper replaced Anderson in Guinness World Records.

PICTURE THIS

The Christmas Day 2007 edition of the *Lewiston Tribune* in Lewiston, Idaho, featured two news stories on its front page. The first concerned a man who stole a wallet containing more than $600 from a holiday shopper. Accompanying the article was a freeze-frame from store security footage depicting a heavyset man sporting a goatee

Sea cucumbers have teeth in their anuses to prevent parasites from taking residence there.

and a blue checkered shirt. Next to that article was an item about Lewiston business owners getting into the holiday spirit, which included a photo of a man hanging lights outside a downtown business. He was a heavyset man sporting a goatee and a blue checkered shirt. It was the same man; newspaper staff didn't notice until the paper was being printed, but hundreds of readers called in to note the connection, too. Michael Millhouse (of Millhouse Signs) was quickly arrested.

THINK OF LAURA

While celebrating her grandparents' 50th anniversary at a party on a farm in Staffordshire, England, in 2001, 10-year-old Laura Buxton decided it would be fun to release a balloon into the sky and see how far it might go. She placed a message inside with her address and instructions to "Please return to Laura Buxton." The balloon wound up flying and bobbing 140 miles away, to a farm in Milton Lilbourne, where the proprietor found the balloon and gave it to his 10-year-old daughter...named Laura Buxton. The girls' parents arranged a meeting, and the two Laura Buxtons had a lot more in common than just their name and age: they both had the same height and eye color, both owned three-year-old female black Labrador retrievers, and both were wearing jeans and pink sweaters when they met.

TOMB WRITER

Amidst heavy combat operations in World War II, archaeologists in the Soviet Union discovered the tomb purporting to be the final resting place of Tamerlane, a descendant of Genghis Khan who, like his ancestor, was a conqueror bent on invading countries and dominating the Eurasian landmass. When the tomb was opened, archaeologists found an inscription that translated: "Whoever opens my tomb shall unleash an invader more terrible than I." The date of the tomb's opening: June 20, 1941. Two days later, the Nazis launched Operation Barbarossa, a multifront, full-scale invasion of the Soviet Union.

TRAGIC TWIST

In 2000, video game publisher Eidos Interactive released *Deus Ex*. Set in the year 2052, the main character is a superhero who works as an agent for a global antiterrorist agency. The action of *Deus Ex* takes place primarily in New York, and designers turned out some highly detailed and realistic skyline shots of the city, only for editors to realize after the game had already been made that the World Trade Center had been accidentally left out. Deciding it would be easier to just make a mention in the game explaining the absence instead of re-rendering graphics, *Deus Ex* explains that the Twin Towers are missing because terrorists destroyed them some years before the events of the game.

On any given day, about 1 in 8 Americans will eat pizza.

THE TITLE NEEDS WORK

The right title tells an audience what to expect from a movie or TV show, but also carries a bit of drama (without being too vague), is marketable, and isn't previously taken. These original title ideas didn't do all that, which is probably why filmmakers and producers opted for other choices over their working titles.

TITANIC:
The Ship of Dreams

EVERYBODY LOVES RAYMOND:
That Raymond Guy

GHOSTBUSTERS:
Ghostsmashers

HAPPY DAYS:
Cool; New Family in Town

FATAL ATTRACTION:
Affairs of the Heart

CAR 54, WHERE ARE YOU?:
The Snow Whites

PSYCHO:
Wimpy

THIS IS US:
36

THE BREAKFAST CLUB:
The Lunch Bunch

GREY'S ANATOMY:
Surgeons

TOY STORY:
Wind-Up Heroes

THE DICK VAN DYKE SHOW:
Head of the Family

SNAKES ON A PLANE:
Pacific Air Flight 121

THE BIG BANG THEORY:
Lenny, Penny, and Kenny

CLOVERFIELD:
Slusho; Chocolate; Cheese

THE GOOD WIFE:
Leave the B******; The Whole Truth

2001: A SPACE ODYSSEY:
How the Solar System Was Won

UNFORGETTABLE:
The Rememberer

AMERICAN PIE:
East Great Falls High; Comfort Food

IT'S ALWAYS SUNNY IN PHILADELPHIA:
Jerks

ANNIE HALL:
Anhedonia

BUFFY THE VAMPIRE SLAYER:
Slayer

PRETTY WOMAN:
$3000

LEAVE IT TO BEAVER:
It's a Small World

Corn sweats. An acre can release 3,000 to 4,000 gallons a day into the atmosphere.

WHILE YOU WERE SLEEPING:
Coma Guy; Coma Girl

LOST:
Nowhere

BASIC INSTINCT:
Love Hurts

SCANDAL:
Damage Control

FRIDAY THE 13TH:
A Long Night at Camp Blood

THE BEVERLY HILLBILLIES:
The Hillbillies of Beverly Hills

LETTERS FROM IWO JIMA:
Red Sun, Black Sand

MANNIX:
Intersect

ALIEN:
Star Beast

NEW GIRL:
Chicks & D****

PULP FICTION:
Black Mask

STRANGER THINGS:
Montauk

THE TEXAS CHAINSAW MASSACRE:
Head Cheese

FULL HOUSE:
House of Comics

BOYS DON'T CRY:
Take It Like a Man

CHARMED:
House of Sisters

HANCOCK:
Tonight, He Comes

HANNAH MONTANA:
Alexis Texas

EDGE OF TOMORROW:
All You Need Is a Kill

MONTY PYTHON'S FLYING CIRCUS:
Ow! It's Colin Plint!; A Horse, a Spoon,
and a Basin; Bunn Wackett Buzzard Stubble
and Boot; The Toad Elevating Moment;
Owl Stretching Time

*   *   *

WHY DOES HITTING THE SNOOZE BUTTON DELAY AN ALARM BY NINE MINUTES?

Most every commercially available alarm clock—and smartphone time-telling app—offers a snooze function, allowing users to sleep just a few minutes longer. That snooze period is almost always nine minutes. It's just tradition now, as that's how long a snooze lasted when it was first offered on the General Electric-Telechron Snooz-Alarm clock in 1956. The engineers who built it intended to make a "snooze" consist of 10 minutes, but they couldn't get the gear teeth inside the clock machinery to line up right. Their most successful options: nine minutes and a few seconds, or 10 and a half minutes. They went with nine and change.

More than 35,000, or about 10 percent, of Canadian Army soldiers
in World War I were Americans.

BADWILL

*Amidst all the clothes, pots and pans, and books donated to the
Goodwill, Salvation Army, and other charity-supporting thrift shops
are some truly weird items. These are definitely the weirdest.*

- Grenade launcher, loaded
- Artificial leg made up to look like it's rotting
- Live grenade
- Crystal ball with a bat floating in liquid inside
- Urn full of cremated human remains
- Pickled baby tiger shark
- Coin purse made from kangaroo skin
- Hollowed-out book filled with $1,000 in cash
- High school diploma in a leather portfolio
- Bag of used diapers
- Lobotomy tool set
- Human skull
- Lock of hair taped to a death certificate
- Hot-dog rollers
- Slurpee machine
- Silicone breast implants
- Live Burmese python
- Garden gnome brandishing the middle finger
- Painting of Chewbacca holding a crossbow and riding a giant squirrel into battle

- Half-inch-tall coffee mug with the name Rick on it
- Toilet disguised as a recliner
- Bag of yogurt-container lids
- Bag of Barbie dolls with the heads removed
- Desk lamp made of doll heads
- Priest's "last rites" kit
- Hard-boiled egg
- Partially taxidermized raccoon
- Live hamster in its cage
- Mickey Mouse gas mask for children
- Coffin
- Dentures
- Plastic shopping bag full of cooked, sauce-less spaghetti
- Japanese soldier's sword from World War II
- An enigma machine, a cipher machine used in World War II
- Suit of armor made of leather
- Wolf trap dating from the 18th century
- Collection of artificial legs with shoes attached
- Jar labeled "Fart, June 1975"

A BARBECUE TOUR OF AMERICA

*At its core, "barbecue" is just meat cooked or smoked over a fire with some
kind of sauce added. How exactly that all comes together varies wildly
throughout the United States, where there's no one single definition of
"barbecue." The one thing the variations have in common: they're all tasty.*

LOCATION: Eastern Carolina
DETAILS: This regional North Carolina style begins with an entire pig cooked in a
pit over wood coals for at least 12 hours, and as long as overnight. It's served with
a barbecue sauce free of tomatoes but heavy on the vinegar and pepper, and used
primarily as a condiment or complement after the meat has been cooked, shredded,
and served. It's traditionally paired with sides such as hush puppies and a slaw made
with mayonnaise.

LOCATION: Western Carolina
DETAILS: Also known as Piedmont or Lexington, after the towns in North Carolina
where the barbecue traditions are particularly strong, pork is the favored meat,
specifically parts such as the shoulder, ribs, and butt. The meat is dressed in a
ketchup-based red sauce with apple cider vinegar, pepper, and sugars added. The
preparation and the sauce are both inspired by Bavarian settlers who adapted an old
dish of pork shoulder slathered in a vinegar-based sweet-and-sour sauce.

LOCATION: South Carolina
DETAILS: In the other Carolina, the preferred meat remains pork, and it's smoked
over a pit, generally atop a grill rack. The sauces are a major costar in South Carolina,
with four main ones found around the state. There's a heavy tomato-based one, a
lighter tomato sauce made with lots of vinegar and pepper, a tomato-free vinegar
and pepper sauce, and the signature condiment of South Carolina barbecue: a tangy
yellow concoction made primarily out of mustard, vinegar, and brown sugar.

LOCATION: Virginia
DETAILS: Local pitmasters claim that Virginia is where modern barbecue originated,
and founding fathers including George Washington participated in outdoor meat
cookouts. The state actually has four different sauce traditions. Virginians prefer
to barbecue (by which they mean "smoke") pork products, particularly bacon, ham,

NASA astronaut with six academic degrees and who flew
on all five Space Shuttles: Story Musgrave.

and sausage, and they top them with different condiments. Northern Virginia utilizes a sweet and aromatics-heavy sauce, central Virginia's signature sauce is sweet and sour and flavored with root beer and peanut butter, the Tidewater area likes a vinegar-tomato-mustard blend, and the Shenandoah Valley prefers a vinegar-based, herb-heavy sauce.

LOCATION: Memphis
DETAILS: The second-largest city in Tennessee has a barbecue system like that of the Carolinas in that they pit-smoke particular cuts of pork: the shoulder, ribs, and butt. They make it their own in Memphis by smoking it in an open pit *very* slowly, for 14 hours or more, with the fired wood sitting directly below the meat. Dry rubs are used, but simple ones consisting of little more than paprika, garlic, and salt, while the sauce is tangy, smoky, and based on tomatoes and vinegar.

LOCATION: West Tennessee
DETAILS: This style of whole-pig barbecuing harkens back to early 20th-century rural life, when hogs were cheaper to raise than cows and one animal fed a large group of people for not a lot of money. The entire animal is smoked over a pit, then becomes pulled pork, mixed with a peppery, acidic sauce, and is always served with slaw.

LOCATION: Alabama
DETAILS: Alabama isn't far from Memphis or the Carolinas, so there are traces of both style in Alabama barbecue, where the meats are usually pork shoulder or whole chickens. The meat tends to be the star of the show, where sauce is used sparingly so as not to detract from the experience of the low-and-slow-cooked meat, smoked for around eight hours at no more than 300 degrees. The meat is drizzled in a unique sauce: a white barbecue sauce made with mayonnaise and vinegar.

LOCATION: Florida
DETAILS: Nestled in the South below the Carolinas and closer to the Caribbean than any other mainland state, Florida's barbecue sauces mix the vinegar-forward elements of Carolina blends with the citrus, spiky, and tropical parts of Cuban and West Indies cooking. Floridians add it to the meat as it cooks and smokes, basting whatever meat they like, which might be a signature, locally caught fish, the striped mullet.

LOCATION: Kentucky
DETAILS: The barbecue method of Kentucky can be found other places—smoking over coals made from hickory wood—but the meats and sauces are unique. In the

Cost of a U.S. Army standard-issue M67 grenade: $45.

eastern part of Kentucky, the traditional protein used is mutton, while in the west, turkey and cured ham are smoked, sliced, and served on sandwiches. One might also find shredded pork in a tomato-based sauce in Louisville, pork butt basted in pepper-vinegar sauce in the south-central part of the state, and mutton served with a sauce comprised mainly of vinegar, pepper, and Worcestershire sauce.

LOCATION: Kansas City

DETAILS: Large populations of emancipated slaves from the Carolinas and Tennessee resettled in Kansas City, Missouri, bringing the barbecue traditions from those areas with them to what was once a major meatpacking-industry town as well as a waypoint between western livestock farms and eastern population centers. Thus, pork, brisket, and ribs are all part of Kansas City barbecue, but the signature dish is burnt ends, or beef brisket points, cooked extremely slowly, smoked for 15 to 17 hours. Kansas City barbecue sauce is the sweetest regional sauce, made from tomato, molasses, and brown sugar and used as a complement rather than a marinade.

LOCATION: East Texas

DETAILS: Southern influences are present, but Texas is a beef-forward state where hard hickory wood is used to impart a palpable smokiness in the meat as it cooks at a low temperature over indirect heat for half a day. The preferred meat medium in East Texas is beef brisket, chopped up and served on sandwiches and covered in hot sauce or a sweet, tomato-based barbecue sauce.

LOCATION: Central Texas

DETAILS: The beef industry is dominant in the middle part of Texas, particularly in and around Austin, and barbecue masters here allow the meat to speak for itself, where it's generally served naked (except for a salt-and-pepper rub) with no sauce to dilute the sweet, charred, fatty flavors of the beef. In Central Texas, brisket is cooked with horizontal convection over pecan wood or oak, with lateral air flow making the beef moist. It's then carved or sliced like a roast.

LOCATION: South Texas

DETAILS: Down by the Mexican border, Texas barbecue is culinarily intertwined with hallmarks of Mexican food. The same conquistadores of Spain who settled what is now Mexico and the U.S. Southwest in the 1500s also brought the outdoor fire-roasting of meat preparation called *barbacoa* to the New World. *Barbacoa* became *barbecue*, and in southern Texas, the traditional style is dying out, with only one authentic restaurant left in the area—probably because the meats used aren't

Vintners spray milk on grapes. It prevents mildew.

widely popular with modern Americans, including goat and the tongue, head, and diaphragm of a cow. The cuts are smoked slowly in fully underground pits and then served with guacamole, salsa, and a sweet, molasses-based barbecue sauce.

LOCATION: St. Louis

DETAILS: Residents of the St. Louis area consume more barbecue sauce per capita than anybody else in the U.S., and they use a sweet, sticky, tomato-based sauce (free of smoke flavor) to thoroughly cover their meats before, during, and after cooking (which is grilling rather than smoking). St. Louis was a longtime major meatpacking zone, and pork is king, particularly pork steaks and St. Louis–style pork spareribs.

LOCATION: California Central Coast

DETAILS: The middle part of the large West Coast state that's now a prime wine production region was traditionally the home of large cattle ranches. In the 19th century, thousands of Swiss and Italian immigrants arrived in the area to work the dairy farms in and around Santa Maria and San Luis Obispo, and they brought European culinary traditions with them and blended them with native ideas. Today, California barbecue means a tri-tip beef roast cooked over locally available red oak coals, prepared with a dry rub of salt, pepper, and garlic salt, or it means a rib-eye steak served with grilled artichokes or french fries. The tri-tip or the steak is then carved and sliced and served with pinquito beans and tortillas, or garlic bread and pasta with a light butter sauce.

LOCATION: Hawaii

DETAILS: The best-known Hawaiian contribution to the American food landscape is the plate lunch, a concept that can trace its origins to a local barbecue tradition that similarly combines indigenous, Asian, and colonial European ideas. A plate lunch consists of rice, macaroni salad, and a heaping portion of protein, usually chicken or pork, quick grilled over an open fire to get a char. The meats—be they barbecue pork, Korean-style short ribs, kalua pork, or huli-huli chicken—develop a flavorful crust thanks to a sweet and tangy marinade that begins with a blend of soy sauce, sugar, garlic, and ginger.

* * *

GOING NOWHERE FAST

U.K.-born driver Victor "Al" Pease competed on the Formula 1 circuit of racing from 1967 to 1969. He competed in just three major events, including the 1969 Canadian Grand Prix, from which he was disqualified and kicked out for driving too slowly—the first and only time that's happened in a Formula 1 race.

Each year, $140 million worth of Starbucks gift cards go unused.

THE ARTICLE OF THE CENTURY

"Trial of the century" was (and still is) a hyperbolic designation given to numerous high-profile court cases. First applied to the treason trial of former vice president Aaron Burr in 1807, a few dozen big trials were declared the "trial of the century" throughout the 20th century.

1901: The murder trial of anarchist Leon Czolgosz, assassin of President William McKinley. Immediately caught and tried, Czolgosz was executed via electric chair within six weeks of the crime.

1906: Coal and railroad scion Harry Thaw was convicted of murdering prominent architect Sanford White, who allegedly assaulted Thaw's girlfriend.

1907: Bill Haywood, a high-ranking member of the Socialist Party of America and founder of the Industrial Workers of the World union, was tried for the bombing murder of anti-union Idaho governor Frank Steuenberg. Prosecutors couldn't come up with enough compelling evidence and Haywood was acquitted, but he was later jailed for protesting World War I during the anti-communist Red Scare in 1918. Out of prison by 1921, he defected to the Soviet Union.

1921: Sacco and Vanzetti—Nicola Sacco and Bartolomeo Vanzetti—were Italian immigrants and anarchists arrested for the murder of a shoe factory paymaster and a security guard. Both were found guilty of murder and sentenced to death, despite the protests of socialist and anarchist groups who alleged that the defendants had been railroaded and maligned for their political views, and despite an organized criminal named Celestino Madeiros confessing to the crime.

1921: The trial of early movie star and comedian Roscoe "Fatty" Arbuckle for the assault and murder of actress Virginia Rappe. After two mistrials, Arbuckle was acquitted, but his reputation and career were ruined, and he barely worked in Hollywood again.

1924: In a grim, salacious, headline-grabbing act, Nathan Leopold and Richard Loeb, two well-off University of Chicago students, kidnapped and killed a teenager in 1924 because they believed themselves to be superior citizens who could plan, execute, and get away with a murder. Loeb's family hired famous attorney Clarence Darrow, who, despite arguing against the merits of capital punishment in a 12-hour closing statement, couldn't prevent his clients from receiving life sentences. (Loeb was murdered in prison, Leopold was paroled in 1958.)

1925: Tennessee public school teacher John Scopes was fired and then arrested for teaching the theory of evolution, which had recently been made illegal in that state (in

A whale shark's throat is only about as wide as a quarter.

favor of creationism). Scopes was found guilty and paid a $100 fine; the verdict was later reversed on a technicality while the statute was upheld by the state supreme court.

1935: A German immigrant who worked for famous American aviator Charles Lindbergh was arrested for the kidnapping and murder of Lindbergh's infant son; he was found guilty and sentenced to death.

1946: The Nuremberg trials were a series of 13 international military tribunals carried out in Nuremberg, Germany, against the surviving high-ranking officers in the Nazi Party that started World War II and exterminated millions of Jewish people. Out of 177 defendants, 25 were acquitted, 98 received nominal prison sentences, 20 were sentenced to life in prison, and 24 received the death penalty.

1951: Americans Julius and Ethel Rosenberg were found guilty of (and subsequently executed for) high crimes of espionage, for passing on nuclear secrets to the Soviet Union.

1961: Nazi official Adolf Eichmann was tried in Israel for 15 counts of crimes against the Jewish people for his role in creating and seeing out the "Final Solution," or the Jewish Holocaust via a network of concentration camps during World War II. After an eight-month trial, Eichmann was found guilty on all charges and was hanged in 1962.

1969: Seven anti–Vietnam War protestors, including Abbie Hoffman and Jerry Rubin, associated with the hippie counterculture movement were involved in what turned into a riot outside the 1969 Democratic National Convention. They were arrested, charged by the federal government on charges of crossing state lines with intent to riot, and tried collectively in a heavily publicized trial characterized by Hoffman and Rubin's rebellious outbursts. Five of the so-called "Chicago Seven" were convicted, later overturned on appeal.

1970: Charles Manson and his "family" of followers were tried for two August 1969 mass murders in Los Angeles in which they killed a total of seven people, including pregnant actress Sharon Tate. Manson and three associates were found guilty and sentenced to the death penalty, with those sentences later commuted to life in prison when California briefly did away with capital punishment.

1989: Ousted as the Communist leader of Romania, Nicolae Ceaușescu and his wife, Elena, were tried in a court-martial by the newly formed government on charges that they okayed a genocide of opposition forces. (They were found guilty and executed.)

1995: O. J. Simpson, football star turned sportscaster and actor, was put on trial for the murder of his former wife, Nicole Brown Simpson, and her friend Ronald Goldman. After a televised trial, Simpson was found not guilty.

1999: President Bill Clinton was impeached (but not convicted) on charges of obstruction of justice and perjury to a grand jury.

Every Traveling Wilburys member is in the Rock & Roll Hall of Fame, but the Traveling Wilburys are not.

DUMB CROOKS

Here's proof that crime doesn't pay.

QUICK! COVER ME!

"Here at the Belfast (Maine) Police Department, we have seen some crafty ways of hiding from the Police. This unfortunately is not one of them." The May 2022 Facebook post went on to describe a call the department had received the night before about a suspicious man at the Admiral Ocean Inn. Responding officers found Philip Dulude, who was quite drunk. They removed him from the premises and informed him that if he came back, they'd arrest him. He came back. Police came back, too. That's when they discovered a mysterious, person-sized lump—covered by a blanket—sitting on a chair in front of a room. Big surprise: the lump was Dulude. Hopefully, they gave him a new blanket while he slept it off at the jailhouse.

GIVE AND TAKE

In October 2020, two Florida men named Robert Hobby, 41, and Marcus Reeves, 23, went on a burglary spree in and around the city of Ocala. After stealing lottery tickets and cigarettes from a convenience store, the men left behind one of their shoes...and their break-in tools...and Reeves's wallet...which contained his driver's license. The next day, officers showed up at the suspect's house to tell him they found his wallet. Both men were arrested and, according to the police, "are now in the Gold Star Hotel" (which we're assuming means jail).

INTO THE LION'S DEN

1. In May 2021, at around 10:00 p.m. in New York City, six kidnappers ambushed a 19-year-old victim who, earlier that day, had agreed to sell them his car. They pointed a fake gun at him, forced him into another car, and blindfolded him. Then they used the victim's phone to call his cousin and demand $10,000 for the victim's safe return. The tech-savvy cousin traced the call and determined the victim's location: right next to an NYPD training facility. The cousin called 911, and then, reported the *New York Post*, "Officers from the 62nd and the 63rd precincts, along with city Parks Department police, rushed to the area and arrested the alleged kidnappers."

2. Monaghan's Pub is less than a block away from the Baltimore County Police Department District 2, but two would-be robbers—Joseph McInnis III, 21, and Tyree McCoy, 22—decided to rob the pub anyway in August 2017. What they didn't count on: police holding a retirement dinner in the pub's back room. After the masked men held a bartender at gunpoint and made away

with an undisclosed amount of cash, the bartender ran over and told the dozen or so cops, who all ran out and apprehended McInnis and McCoy within a few minutes.

WHAT A BLOCKHEAD

When you're driving your Audi A1 on England's A2 freeway, while in possession of what London police describe as "a large amount of cannabis," you might not want to be swerving around traffic at high speeds. That's exactly what a 21-year-old man (unidentified in press reports) was doing in February 2022. The ensuing 25-mile chase from London to Kent included dozens of cops from two forces, along with a helicopter, and ended when the assailant ran out of gas. The stupidity didn't end with driving recklessly in possession of illegal contraband: the police were especially amused by the young man's driver's license. It had been issued to him 19 years earlier at the LEGOLAND amusement park when the then-two-year-old successfully navigated a car made from LEGO bricks through "traffic lights, roundabouts, LEGO policemen, and even a speed camera." If only the real policemen had been as impressed as that LEGO cop.

DUMBEST. POST. EVER.

In February 2015, Andrew Hennells, 31, of Norwich, England, posted a selfie of him holding a knife with the caption "Doing. Tesco. Over." Fifteen minutes later, he showed up at the Tesco supermarket, brandished the knife, and demanded cash. With £410 in his pocket, Hennells ran out and stole a car (that belonged to a retired couple who were using the cash machine), then drove it to a nearby pub. Officers joined Hennells a few minutes later…after spotting the car he'd *just* stolen. Police later said they didn't even need his incriminating Facebook post to make an arrest—he'd made enough other mistakes, such as not wearing a mask and not ditching the knife. Hennells was sentenced to four years in prison, and Police Sgt. Pete Jessop called the case both "bizarre and unusual."

FENDER BENDER

In October 2018, the driver of a delivery truck was navigating a crowded Brooklyn street when he sideswiped a parked Honda CR-V—barely scratching it—and then parked to deliver some boxes of baby food and medical supplies. Before he opened the door, from "out of nowhere" came Francisco Jimenez, 24, and Rondell Halley, 33. They told the driver he had to pay them $40 to make the scratch "go away." The driver (who mistakenly assumed the CR-V belonged to them) said he didn't have any money, so the men took him hostage at gunpoint and all three left in the delivery truck. When they got to a parking lot in Queens, they called the driver's boss and

Number of times Mao Zedong brushed his teeth in his lifetime: zero.

demanded $700 if he wanted to see his driver or his truck again. The boss played along and told the kidnappers to meet him at a Manhattan bank. The boss called police, who instructed him to pay the kidnappers as planned.

A few hours after the fender bender, Jimenez, Halley, and their hostage arrived at the bank in a stolen BMW. As soon as the boss handed over the $700, officers swarmed the area. Jimenez sped away and crashed on a sidewalk just a few seconds later. He was arrested. Halley ran through a school courtyard and then scrambled up a fire escape; he was arrested on the eighth floor. No one was injured in what NYPD Captain Timothy Malin called "one of the strangest cases" of his 18-year career, but both perpetrators received prison sentences. The lesson: if you're going to attempt a grand-theft/extortion/kidnapping scheme, it's best not to wing it.

SEASON'S GREETINGS

Whoever wrote this Facebook post for the Medford, Oregon, police department in December 2021 was really in the Christmas spirit:

Dear Mr. Giovanni Solis,

We realize holiday shopping is stressful, and it appears you have several to shop for when you grabbed 8 pairs of Juicy Couture sweatpants from JC Penney. But here is the problem, you forgot to pay for them! Employees tried to tell you but you must [have] got confused and took off running. In all the commotion you dropped your phone, you big goof. So we have that if you'd like to swing on by the department, and get this cleared up! It looks like your phone has a lot of information you probably need as you seem to be very active in selling property online. Oh and be sure not to sell those sweatpants, or that could land you in more trouble (selling stolen property and all). Case 21-20610. Hope to hear from you soon! Merry Christmas.

*   *   *

SIX QUARTERBACKS SELECTED
BEFORE TOM BRADY IN THE 2000 NFL DRAFT

#18 Chad Pennington (New York Jets)

#65 Giovanni Carmazzi (San Francisco 49ers)

#75 Chris Redman (Baltimore Ravens)

#163 Tee Marin (Pittsburgh Steelers)

#168 Marc Bulger (New Orleans Saints)

#183 Spurgon Wynn (Cleveland Browns)

#199 Tom Brady (New England Patriots)

Lyndon Johnson didn't run for reelection in 1968 because he was convinced he'd die within the next four years...

CLASS ACTS

*To balance out intensive classes such as
advanced calculus, medieval literature, and organic chemistry,
many schools offer a few oddball courses like these.*

WASTING TIME ON THE INTERNET
University of Pennsylvania

"We spend our lives in front of screens, mostly wasting time: checking social media, watching cat videos, chatting, and shopping. What if these activities— clicking, SMSing, status-updating, and random surfing—were used as raw material for creating compelling and emotional works of literature? Using our laptops and a Wi-Fi connection as our only materials, this class will focus on the alchemical recuperation of aimless surfing into substantial works of literature. Students will be required to stare at the screen for three hours, only interacting through chat rooms, bots, social media, and listservs."

ARGUING WITH JUDGE JUDY
University of California, Berkeley

"TV 'Judge' shows have become extremely popular. A fascinating aspect of these shows from a rhetorical point of view is the number of arguments made by the litigants that are utterly illogical, or perversions of standard logic, and yet are used over and over again. The seminar will be concerned with identifying such apparently popular logical fallacies on *Judge Judy* and *The People's Court* and discussing why such strategies are so widespread. It is not a course about law or 'legal reasoning.' It is not about the application of law or the operations of the court system in general."

WORDPLAY: A WRY PLOD FROM BABEL TO SCRABBLE
Princeton University, New Jersey

"This course brings together interesting reading, thoughtful scholarship, and hands-on revelry in the exploration of the ludic side of language. We will consider the formal features, aesthetic pleasures, and societal roles of wordplay from a wide temporal and geographical perspective by reading poetry, stories, and novels both familiar and unfamiliar, having fun with scripts besides our own, and regularly trying to produce decent examples of 'constrained writing' ourselves. In the end we will arrive at a better understanding of how language works and how these workings can be bent in unusual ways to produce striking effects."

...he passed on January 22, 1973, two days after his term would've ended.

PATTERNMAKING FOR DOG GARMENTS

Fashion Institute of Technology, New York

"Learn to work with various dog body types to produce a pattern for a dog coat that fits. This primary level course does not require patternmaking experience."

AMERICAN PRO WRESTLING

Massachusetts Institute of Technology

"This class will explore the cultural history and media industry surrounding the masculine drama of professional wrestling. Beginning with wrestling's roots in sport and carnival, the class examines how new technologies and changes in the television industry led to evolution for pro wrestling style and promotion and how shifts in wrestling characters demonstrate changes in the depiction of American masculinity. Students may have previous knowledge of wrestling but are not required to, nor are they required to be a fan."

THE SOCIOLOGY OF MILEY CYRUS: RACE, CLASS, GENDER, AND MEDIA

Skidmore College, New York

"Using Miley as a lens through which to explore sociological thinking about identity, entertainment, media and fame, including core issues of intersectionality theory, looking at race, class, and gender, as well as taking a feminist critique of the media."

STUPIDITY

Occidental College, California

"Stupidity is neither ignorance nor organicity, but rather, a corollary of knowing and an element of normalcy, the double of intelligence rather than its opposite. It is an artifact of our nature as finite beings and one of the most powerful determinants of human destiny. Stupidity is always the name of the Other, and it is the sign of the feminine. Stupidity, which has been evicted from the philosophical premises and dumbed down by psychometric psychology, has returned in the postmodern discourse against Nation, Self, and Truth and makes itself felt in political life ranging from the presidency to Beavis and Butt-Head."

BIOLOGY OF JURASSIC PARK

Hood College, Maryland

"Even though they are extinct, dinosaurs can serve as models to understand many biological principles, including patterns of biodiversity, evolution, extinction, community ecology, homeostasis, and behavior. To understand these principles, we will answer questions such as: How many species of dinosaurs were there? Are birds really dinosaurs? Did dinosaurs show parental care?"

On average, there are 53 supernovas in space exploding every second.

HIGHER LEARNING?

You don't need a college degree to get these jokes.

Q: How many fraternity brothers does it take to change a light bulb?
A: That's what pledges are for.

Q: What do you call a test tube with a college degree?
A: A graduated cylinder.

I knew a manicurist who went back to college to become a veterinarian. She was trying to give a pet a cure.

Q: What's a liberal arts major's favorite board game?
A: Trivial Pursuit.

My old girlfriend wanted me to do her college algebra homework. But frankly, I didn't want to solve for ex.

Q: How many grad students does it take to change a light bulb?
A: Just one, but it takes five years. The good news is that, after graduation, the grad student can get low-priced replacement bulbs with their employee discount at Lowes.

Did you hear about the cat that went to college? It majored in string theory.

Did you hear about the dog that went to college? It was trying to get its pedigree.

Q: How do you know that you've been in college too long?
A: Your parents are running out of money.

Jean: How'd you do on your carpentry exam?
John: Nailed it!

Q: What was the most expensive streaming service during the pandemic?
A: College.

Thank you for getting me through college, student loan. I don't how I can ever repay you.

Q: What do you call a horde of college students after they graduate?
A: The walking debt.

In college, I was so poor that I couldn't pay my electric bill. Those were the darkest days of my life.

Student: Dad, great news! Remember that $500 you promised me if I made the dean's list?
Dad: I certainly do!
Student: Well, you get to keep it!

Diner: What's the usual amount to tip?
Waitress: I'm not sure. This is my first day. I'm just a lowly college student trying to pay for my expensive textbooks. But I don't expect much. The other waiters told me that the patrons of this café don't tip that well—that I'd be lucky just to get a dollar. I mean...if you can spare it.
Diner: A dollar? We'll show them who tips well. Here's a tenner! By the way, what's your major?
Waitress: Applied psychology.

Q: Why is a circle so smart?
A: It has 360 degrees.

First Lady Eleanor Roosevelt regularly held female-reporters-only press conferences.

YOU'RE MY "MAN"SPIRATION

Just like "You're My Inspiration," but more manly, bro!

FIGHT CLUB

The idea for the 1996 novel about a disillusioned businessman who starts an underground fight club came to Chuck Palahniuk after a camping trip. "Other people who were camping near us wanted to drink and party all night long, and I tried to get them to shut up one night, and they literally beat the crap out of me," he said. He arrived back at work with his face *looking* like someone beat the crap out of him, but no one said anything. "If you looked bad enough," he realized, "people would not want to know what you did in your spare time. They don't want to know the bad things about you. And the key was to look so bad that no one would ever, ever ask. And that was the idea behind *Fight Club*." (Like the book's narrator, Palahniuk actually went out at night, trying to get in fights. "Yeah, it hurts a little. But I lived through it.")

BORAT SAGDIYEV

British comedian Sasha Baron Cohen is known for his shtick of affecting a fake persona and interviewing unsuspecting people. "I was struck by the patience of some of these members of the upper class," he said, "who were so keen to appear polite—particularly on camera—that they would never walk away." He found the perfect interviewer character while on vacation in Russia: Baron Cohen was at the hotel pool, and there was an eccentric doctor making a fool of himself. Borat, the Kazakhstani journalist, is an impression of that doctor.

BARNEY STINSON

Years before Neil Patrick Harris played the smarmy womanizer on *How I Met Your Mother*, the 18-year-old star of *Doogie Howser, M.D.* got invited to his first real Hollywood party at the home of Bob Saget, whose squeaky-clean TV persona on *Full House* couldn't be further from real life. "I walk in," Harris said, "and there in the middle of this giant room, under a crystal chandelier, surrounded by a hoard of topless girls...is Bob Saget wearing nothing but a pair of women's thongs on his

Bupkis, meaning "worthless," is a Yiddish word that means "as valuable as goat turds."

head and the biggest...smile...I've ever seen." One of the women threw her panties at Harris, and Saget said, "Suit up." Saget's persona—and that catchphrase—became the foundation for Barney Stinson.

CHEECH MARIN

When Richard Anthony Marin was only a few days old in 1947 (he was "Bo-orn in East L.A.!"), his uncle looked at him in his crib and said, "Ay, *parece un chicharrón.* Looks like a little *chicharrón,* you know?" And that's how Cheech came to be named for a fried pork rind.

DIE HARD

This 1988 action movie revolves around an NYPD detective who tries to reconcile with his separated wife while also thwarting a terrorist takeover of a Los Angeles building. The movie is based on the 1979 Roderick Thorp novel, *Nothing Lasts Forever,* about a retired NYPD cop who's trying to save his daughter from a similar threat. While Jeb Stuart was working on the screenplay, he got into a fight with his wife and drove away in a huff—nearly hitting an empty refrigerator box in the driveway. He stopped the car and had a sudden burst of inspiration: "It's not about a 65-year-old man whose 40-year-old daughter gets dropped off a building. It's about a 30-year-old guy who should have said he's sorry to his wife, and then bad stuff happens."

* * *

EAT LIKE A BIRD

For his 1807 cookbook *L'almanach des Gourmands* ("The Almanac for Gourmands"), French chef Alexandre Balthazar Laurent Grimod de La Reynière invented an opulent dish called *Rôti Sans Pareil,* or "Roast Without Equal." Ever heard of (or eaten) a turducken, a feasting dish that consists of a chicken stuffed inside a duck stuffed inside a turkey? The Rôti Sans Pareil is like that, but it requires the use of 17 birds. How to make it: take a bustard and into it stuff a turkey stuffed with a goose stuffed with a pheasant stuffed with a chicken stuffed with a duck stuffed with a guinea fowl stuffed with a teal stuffed with a woodcock stuffed with a partridge stuffed with a plover stuffed with a lapwing stuffed with a quail stuffed with a thrush stuffed with a lark stuffed with an ortolan stuffed with a garden warbler stuffed with an olive stuffed with an anchovy stuffed with one caper—and don't forget to place a stuffing made of chestnuts and bread between each bird layer.

RIDE ON!

A rider is a part of a performer's contract that includes a list of that artist's backstage demands. The promoter must provide these items, or else the performer might not go on. Here are some real excerpts from real riders.

Beyoncé: A 78-degree dressing room, rose-scented candles, and baked chicken legs "heavily seasoned" with cayenne, salt, pepper, and fresh garlic.

Adele: Tea accoutrements, including bottles of spring water, an electric kettle, mugs, teaspoons, and honey, as well as a pack of Marlboro Lights cigarettes and a disposable lighter.

Rihanna: A dressing room outfitted with a humidifier, dark blue or black drapes covering the room with "icy blue chiffon draped nicely on top," and five AC power outlets.

Katy Perry: Freshly cut pink flowers in her dressing room, such as hydrangeas, roses, peonies, and orchids, but "absolutely no carnations"

Eminem: A set of 25-pound dumbbells, two loaves of bread, and six Lunchables packs.

The Smiths: The band's lead singer, Morrissey, needed a tree backstage, specifically a "young sapling no less than four feet but no higher than six feet."

Bush: Miniature chocolates, a special room for massages, and a request that "no less than 10 percent of all security personnel" be women.

Mötley Crüe: A 12-foot-long boa constrictor, a submachine gun, and the address of a place where band members can attend an Alcoholics Anonymous meeting.

Jay-Z: Access to a Maybach luxury car, either the Maybach 57 or Maybach 62 model, with tinted windows. (To purchase such a vehicle would cost $400,000.)

Korn: Access to a doctor, dentist, masseuse, chiropractor, and lawyer, all of whom are "rock friendly."

Deadmau5: The DJ requires "one inflatable animal of at least five feet in height and fully inflated" in his dressing room.

DJ Steve Aoki: Two "medium-sized cakes" decorated with the words "DIM MAK."

Bloodhound Gang: "One refrigerator magnet of local interest."

Grace Jones: Two dozen oysters along with an oyster knife, because she preferred to shuck them herself.

Pharrell Williams: A photo of one of his heroes, astronomer and *Cosmos* author Carl Sagan, set up in his dressing room.

Axl Rose: The Guns N' Roses singer asks for a square melon.

Rae Sremmurd: In addition to four bottles of champagne and one of cognac, the hip-hop duo needs 24 chicken wings, two spicy Doritos tacos from Taco Bell, some beach balls, Super Soaker water guns, and a 15-passenger van outfitted with a stripper pole to take them to the airport after the concert.

There's an average of about 20 total gallons of urine in the typical busy public swimming pool.

THE ALIEN FILES

*Deep in the research vaults at the Bathroom Readers' Institute is a
mysterious file simply marked "Aliens." Let's investigate it.*

🚽 THE INDIGO CHILDREN

Boriska Kipriyanovich was born in Russia in 1996 or, as he would later put it,
"reborn." His parents later claimed that their son was born a genius—he mastered
talking and reading at a little over a year old, and he displayed an uncanny
knowledge about space, especially the planet Mars, before he even went to school.
On a camping trip when Boriska was seven years old, he had his family gather
'round the fire and told them quite a tale: In his former life, he lived on Mars.
He'd been sent to Earth in human form to help keep us from destroying ourselves
with nuclear weapons...just as the Martians had done to themselves thousands of
year ago. He, along with the few other Martian survivors, live on Earth today as
"Indigo Children." They were seven feet tall on Mars, but here, they look like us.
And they will stop aging at 35.

Kipriyanovich said in a 2020 interview, when he was 23, that he remembers
"that time when I was 14 or 15 years old" on Mars. "The Martians were waging
wars so I would often have to participate in air raids with a friend of mine." Then
there's this: "We could travel in time and space flying in round spaceships, but
we would observe life on Earth on triangular aircraft. Martian spaceships are
very complicated. They are layered, and they can fly all across the Universe." But
these days, Kipriyanovich and his fellow Indigo Children are here to save us from
ourselves. But will they succeed? Stay tuned!

🚽 A DATE WITH E.T.

It was 1980. *Star Wars*, *Star Trek*, and *Close Encounters of the Third Kind* were all the
rage. Like a lot of people, 32-year-old Granger Taylor wished that he could travel to
space himself. And he actually did something about it. Known in his small town on
Vancouver Island, British Columbia, as a shy man who smoked pot and tripped on
LSD, Taylor told a friend that aliens were communicating with him telepathically.
Why him? He'd built his own "flying saucer" (that he sometimes slept in) out of
large satellite dishes on his parents' farm. He'd also restored an old steam engine
locomotive and a World War II airplane. One night, a strong November storm blew
through town. The next morning, his parents woke up and found this note (spelling
and punctuation in the original maintained here):

29 11 80

Dear Mother and Father

I have gone away to walk aboard an alien space ship. As reocurring
dreams assured a 42 month intersteluar voyage to explore the vast
universe, then return

I am leaving behind all my possesions to you as I will no longer will
require the use of any. Pelase use the instructions in my will as a guide to help

Love,

Granger

There was no sign of Taylor. He'd drawn a crude map on the back of the letter, but it was incomplete. The 42 months came and went with no return. Six years later, in the mountains not too far from where Taylor lived, a forest worker found what was left of his Datsun pickup. All indications are that it exploded.

The bizarre case is still being investigated today by alien enthusiasts, but none of the numerous articles and documentaries have been able to determine exactly what happened. Did Taylor fake his own death and start a new life, as some of his friends believe? Did he kill himself, as the police believe? He reportedly had dynamite with him (used to blast tree stumps), and bone fragments were found near the scene. Perhaps he used the storm as cover so no one heard his suicidal explosion. Conspiracies persist that the aliens themselves either killed Taylor...or faked his death and took him away on their spaceship.

UNDER THE SEA

In 2014, a meteorite plunged into the Pacific Ocean off the coast of Papua New Guinea. But this was no ordinary meteorite—and no one would have even known about it had a Harvard University astrophysicist named Avi Loeb not decided to go looking for it. "I found the catalog that the government compiled of meteorites that were detected by government sensors [from] our missile warning system," he told NBC Boston. "I asked my student to check if any of the meteors, the fastest moving meteors, could have arrived to Earth from outside the solar system." Based on this particular object's speed and trajectory, the U.S. Space Command reported a "99.999 percent confidence level" that it "came from outside the solar system." The data also showed that the object took much longer to burn up in the atmosphere than most meteors, pointing to it being made of a much stronger material than iron. With that revelation, said Loeb, "I realized that we found an object from a technological origin that was produced elsewhere."

At the time of this writing, Loeb had raised half of the $2 million required to recover traces of the object, which most likely broke into tiny fragments. Loeb's plan

is to trawl a huge magnet along the ocean floor where the object is calculated to have landed. If any of the fragments are found, whether they were made by aliens or not, "This would be the first time that humans put their hands on the material that makes an object that came from another star...It will change our perspective about our place in the universe."

📷 HAVE YOU SEEN A UFO?

If you'd like to report a close encounter—or are simply curious about others people's encounters—visit the National UFO Reporting Center's website at https://nuforc.org. There are thousands of firsthand accounts sorted by date. Three examples:

- *Athens, Georgia (May 10, 2022, 6:10 p.m.):* "While driving home east bound on Lexington Road, my wife and [I] noticed a large round, flat light. It was approximately 10,000 feet in the air. We watched it for a few seconds and then it disappeared. A few minutes after military aircraft flew by in the same direction as the object."

- *Kihei, Hawaii (April 21, 2022, 8:35 p.m.):* "I noticed a diamond shape floating nearby the roadside may[be] easily 100–150 ft. in the air. I pulled over to investigate and started filming on my phone. By then it was no longer diamond shaped but rather a disk emitting bright white and green lights. The[n] I noticed there was another one on the opposite side of the road. There was no sound coming from them and the[y] were hovering then one started moving very slowly northbound. At that point, I lost track of the other one, it appeared to have left the area. I know what I saw and they were not planes or helicopters. I was so excited I was shaking."

- *San Antonio, Texas (October 29, 2020, 9:00 p.m.):* "It was 3 bright yellow lights in the shape of a triangle about 300 feet in the sky (wild guess) high in the sky so it/they were close. I at first thought the lights were stadium lights because they were in the distance but as I got closer in my car I just started freaking out, was on the phone with a friend at the time and I just started babbling. I followed it down the street a ways and ended up losing sight of it when it changed direction suddenly. At one point the lead light detached from the triangular formation and began to move in a tethered manor. Really freaky s***...It really sucks because I can never really tell anyone as it immediately ruins my overall credibility. Anyway I thought I'd put this here in case one day we get definitive proof, then I can say I told you so."

Your brain is 80 percent water.

YOU WORKED THERE HOW LONG?

Having to go to work sucks. Unless, of course, you happen to like your job.
Here are some folks who stuck it out for the long haul—along
with their secrets to living a long and happy life.

THE EMPLOYEE: In 1938, 15-year-old Walter Orthmann got a job as a shipping assistant at a textile company called Industrias Renaux S.A. (now called RenauxView) in Santa Catarina, Brazil. Eighty-four years later, the 100-year-old man claimed the Guinness World Record for longest time worked at a single company. He'd started there as a teenager, he said, after his family had fallen on hard times. Because Orthmann could speak German, he was promoted to a sales position in the 1950s and spent the next seven decades traveling all over Brazil. He said he made a lot of friends along the way, but earning a world record is his proudest accomplishment.

WALTER'S SECRET: "I don't do too much planning, nor care much about tomorrow. All I care about is that tomorrow will be another day in which I will wake up, get up, exercise and go to work; you need to get busy with the present, not the past or the future. Here and now is what counts. So, let's go to work!"

THE EMPLOYEE: Bette Nash has been a flight attendant for so long that she remembers when complimentary cigarettes were handed out to passengers. In 2022, Nash was recognized as the longest-serving flight attendant in the world. For 65 years, she worked the New York–Boston–Washington, D.C., route for American Airlines (called Eastern Airlines when she started at 21 years old). The Boston woman said she chose that route so she could be near her son, who has disabilities. As of this writing, her son still lives with her, and she's still a flight attendant.

BETTE'S SECRET: "As long as I have my health and I'm able, why not work? It's still fun."

THE EMPLOYEE: When 11-year-old Anthony Mancinelli started cutting hair in 1922—only two years after arriving in the U.S. from Italy—the cost of a haircut was a quarter. When he retired in 2019 at age 108—after spending 96 years as a barber—the cost of a haircut was $19. "I cut them all: long hair, short hair, whatever was in style—the shag, the Buster Brown, straight bangs, permanents." He owned a barbershop in New Windsor, New York, for 40 years (only taking a couple of years off to serve in World War II), and then worked in various barbershops for the rest of his life. In 2007, Guinness World Records recognized him as the oldest living barber...12 years before he finally retired.

Unlike most people over 100 years old, Mancinelli still had a steady hand, good eyesight, all of his teeth, and most incredibly, he'd never been on any medication in his entire life. "He never calls in sick," his boss, Jane Dinezza, told the *New York Times*. "I have young people with knee and back problems, but [Mancinelli] just keeps going. He can do more haircuts than a 20-year-old kid. They're sitting there looking at their phones, texting or whatever, and he's working."

ANTHONY'S SECRET: He never smoked or drank in excess. Also, "I eat thin spaghetti, so I don't get fat."

THE EMPLOYEE: Johnnie "Spider" Footman fled segregated Florida when he was a teenager, landed in New York City, and started driving a taxi cab in 1937. He's never looked back (except to check traffic before changing lanes). "I don't know anything else," he said in 2012, when he was informed that, at 92, he was the oldest taxi driver in the Big Apple—where he'd become a legend. Always dressed in a dapper hat and his trademark suit and tie, and with a cigar hanging out of his mouth, he'd tell stories from his 75 years of driving cabs—like when he had Rock Hudson and John Wayne as fares, or how much the city's changed. "We used to trust each other. I'd leave the cab downstairs and take people's bags upstairs, get paid, and go on with my business. Now as soon as you leave the cab, someone breaks in."

SPIDER'S SECRET: "I drive more slowly now." If someone's in a hurry? "I tell them they need a faster cabby—this one's too slow. I do things my way."

THE EMPLOYEE: Angelo Cammarata retired from bartending in 2009 at 95 years old. He served his first beer in 1933 at his father's grocery store. Cost of the beer: 10 cents. He was 19 years old, and Prohibition had ended a few minutes earlier. When the boy's dad realized they were selling more beer than groceries, he converted the grocery store into a bar. Cammarata served beers and shots (except for a quick jaunt to fight in World War II) for the next 70 years, eventually owning his own joint—Cammarata's Cafe—in West View, Pennsylvania, just outside of Pittsburgh. He lived in an apartment above the bar for decades and raised a family there. What's the biggest change since he started out? "There are now more women bartenders than men."

ANGELO'S SECRET: He always followed his father's advice: "Beer is made to sell, not drink. Don't be your best customer."

THE EMPLOYEE: Herman Goldman, who goes by Hy, vowed never to quit his job, despite the fact that he was 101 in 2014 and had been working at the same New Jersey lighting company for the past 73 Years. Starting out as a stock boy, he spent most of his time at Capitol Lighting repairing damaged lighting figures. And he says as long as his hands and eyes keep working, he'll keep fixing lights.

HY'S SECRET: "Working gives me a reason to get up in the morning and go."

Cleopatra (69–10 BC) lived closer to the construction of Las Vegas's pyramid-shaped Luxor Hotel & Casino than to the construction of the Great Pyramid of Giza.

BOB'S BURGERS, PART II: MEET THE BELCHERS

For the origin of the animated Fox series Bob's Burgers, turn to page 139. Otherwise, order up!

WHY "BELCHER"?

Bob's Burgers cocreator Loren Bouchard said he likes the obvious joke: that a burger joint is run by a family that burps a lot. He also likes "Belcher" because it's vaguely ethnic: "My name is French-Canadian and we wanted them to have some ethnicity but couldn't settle on what." Before he decided on the name Belcher, Bouchard almost went with Boygas. One of the most endearing aspects of the Boygas...er, Belcher family is that each member has a unique, quirky personality. Let's get to know them.

BOB BELCHER (44 YEARS OLD)

The character: Bob comes across as grumpy, but he's just exasperated. While the show doesn't hammer this point home, chef Bob is a genius at both inventing and grilling burgers—which makes the fact that his restaurant is perpetually struggling all the more frustrating. An artist through and through, Bob loves foreign films and progressive rock, and every morning he comes up with a new punny name for an elaborate new (but delicious) burger-of-the-day creation. Examples: "Hit Me with Your Best Shallot Burger," "Eggers Can't Be Cheesers," and "Let's Give 'Em Something Shiitake 'Bout."

The quirk: Like any artist that talks to their canvas, Bob carries on full conversations with his burgers and cooking equipment, and he provides their responses with funny voices. His annual relationship with the Thanksgiving turkey borders on creepy: "Okay, looking good in your little brine bath, buddy. And tomorrow, somebody's going to be the most delicious Thanksgiving turkey ever! *Is it meee?* Sure is, pal."

The actor: "I knew I wanted him as the dad, and we built the family around him," said Bouchard about voice-acting legend H. Jon Benjamin, who's worked on most of Bouchard's shows (*Dr. Katz, Lucy,* and *Home Movies*). Somehow, Benjamin uses the same deadpan voice for Bob as he does for his equally famous super-secret spy character on *Archer.* "I had no intention of ever doing voice-overs," said Benjamin in his defense, who got his start in a live improv troupe with David Cross. "I wasn't opposed to voice-overs; I just didn't have any particular knowledge of how or why people do that."

LINDA BELCHER (44 YEARS OLD)

The character: With her pointy red glasses, thick black hair, and even thicker New York–ish accent, Linda is the very definition of outgoing. She's passionate to a fault

Sharks have been around longer than trees.

(sometimes annoyingly so), whether its making elaborate costumes for the kids' play (and then muscling her way in to direct) or forcing unwilling customers to engage in small talk.

The quirk: Linda makes up funny, odd little songs for everyday situations, like, "Goin' to the accountant / Gonna do our taxes / at the last minute / We're adults—responsible adults! Yeahhh!"

The actor: John Roberts invented the character that would become Linda in a series of early YouTube videos that starred him in a black wig doing an impression of his mom. The videos went viral, and before Roberts knew it, he was doing the character—as Jimmy Fallon's mom—on *Late Night with Jimmy Fallon* in 2009. That's where Bouchard first noticed Roberts, and he knew Roberts could play the perfect foil to Benjamin's grumpy Bob. Roberts came up with the voice, but he credits Linda's success to the show's writers. Not that he doesn't have some input: "There are some elements straight from my mother, like when Linda says she wants to throw her ashes in Tom Selleck's face."

TINA BELCHER (13 YEARS OLD)

The character: It's tough to say there's a "breakout character" on an ensemble show where every cast member has fans, but Tina—with her thick glasses and monotone voice—has the most. As with most young teens at the onset of puberty, Tina still likes kid things such as rainbows, unicorns, and horses, but she finds herself getting excited by the boy band Boyz 4 Now in ways she doesn't quite understand. It's even worse with her school crush, "Regular Sized" Rudy...and with butts. Tina really likes butts. She daydreams about them, draws them, and even writes "erotic" butt fiction.

The quirk: The Tina groan. Whenever she's nervous, sad, or confused, out comes a guttural, several-songs-long groooooooooan. (Do yourself a favor and don't watch the supercut video of all of Tina's groans spliced together. It's the stuff of nightmares.)

The actor: The only cast member not handpicked by Bouchard, stand-up comedian Dan Mintz was recommended by Benjamin to play the oldest brother, Daniel. Mintz was known as much for his droning cadence as for his material. Bouchard loved the voice so much that, after Fox told him to change the oldest brother to an oldest sister, he kept Mintz on and had him do the exact same voice for Tina. "I thought it was insane," he said. "But when they showed me a clip of me talking as Tina, I was like, wow, that actually works."

What does he think about Tina being the breakout character? "I think what draws people to Tina is her complete acceptance of herself and all her quirks. Which is just inspiring to the rest of us who feel like we have to hide who we are." Tina also knows how to ask for exactly what she wants: "Dear Lord Santa, this year, please bless me with a calendar of Australian firefighters holding puppies in casual settings."

During the "Snowball Earth" period 650 million years ago, it's thought that Earth resembled the icy planet Hoth from *The Empire Strikes Back*.

GENE BELCHER (11 YEARS OLD)

The character: Gene looks like his father but acts more like his mother—he shares her love for music and lack of a filter. And he's as comfortable in his own skin as Tina is awkward in hers. Gene's at his funniest when the plot doesn't revolve around him and he gets to comment—often inappropriately—on the proceedings as a casual observer, prompting the one-word admonishment from his father: "Gene." (Bob: "It's not a race, Linda. It's a war." Gene: "It's a race war!" Bob: "Gene.")

The quirk: Making fart sounds on his Casio SK-5 keyboard. And dressing up in a burger costume. And writing a musical based on the villain Hans Gruber from *Die Hard*. Actually, there's not a lot about this kid that isn't quirky: "I'm gonna take a nap under a warm tortilla and then eat my way out when I wake up."

The actor: Stand-up comedian Eugene Mirman was born in Russia and moved to Massachusetts when he was four. After Bouchard became a fan of Mirman's stand-up routine, he cast him in *Home Movies* and *Lucy: The Daughter of the Devil*. And then Bouchard basically turned Mirman into a cartoon character to create Gene. Mirman describes his alter ego as a "lovable, goofy savant," a "42-year-old kid" who's "wiser than he seems but not as wise as he wants to be."

LOUISE BELCHER (9 YEARS OLD)

The character: The youngest Belcher is the one most likely to get a lifetime ban from local arcade Family Funtime. Scratch that—she's the Wagstaff School student most likely to get the ban. At her most content when she's orchestrating some grand scheme or prank involving anything from candy to revenge, Louise, more than anyone else on the show, resembles your typical bratty kid. She's also the only Belcher who routinely walks toward danger, like the time she approached a crime scene and told the cops, "Hi, my name's Louise. I would like to donate a piece of my personal chalk, in case you need to outline a body."

The quirk: The pink bunny ears. Louise never appears without them. According to Bouchard, they were inspired by another clever trickster, Bugs Bunny, as well as a character from the Japanese Manga series *Tekkonkinkreet* who wears bear ears. For the first 12 seasons of the show, Louise's bunny ears went unexplained. Then came *The Bob's Burgers Movie*. If you haven't seen it and want to find out about the ears that way, skip to the next section. Otherwise...in the movie, it's revealed that Linda made the bunny ears from a hat that Bob's mother used to war. She gave the bunny ears to Louise on her first day of preschool to help her be brave. It worked.

The actor: Yet another stand-up comic, Kristen Schaal was awarded "Best Alternative Comedian" in 2006. She'd also worked with Eugene Mirman on HBO's *Flight of the Concords*. Bouchard was a fan, and he liked her breathy voice—"I knew she would be an incredible little girl." He cast her and Mirman at the same time. "They felt like siblings to me already."

Schaal explains *Bob's Burgers* lasting appeal: "A lot of people say it's good for their mental health...I think selling a comfort that's genuine, something that's happy, that feels real—it is very difficult to achieve. And with jokes, it's special."

SUPPORTING CAST

What Springfield is to *The Simpsons*, the Belchers' hometown is to *Bob's Burgers*—it's a coastal tourist town in New Jersey (the same part of New Jersey where MTV filmed the reality show *Jersey Shore*), which Bouchard first referred to as Seymour's Bay during a Comic-Con event in 2015...Anyway, the Belchers live in a town like the Simpsons', where they're surrounded by a rich tapestry of characters:

- The pathetically loveable Teddy (Larry Murphy), the restaurant's only regular customer, who desperately wants to be Bob's best friend. "I like to play with a yo-yo, so something comes back to me."

- The Belchers' flamboyant, uncaring landlord, Mr. Fischoeder (Kevin Kline). Casting an Oscar winner like Kline was a big get for Bouchard, and it happened only because Kline's kids are fans of Eugene Mirman's stand-up comedy. Mr. Fischoeder: "If there's one thing I learned from that week I was married its when to walk away."

- The ineffectual guidance counselor, Mr. Frond, played by voice-acting veteran David Herman (who played Michael Bolton in *Office Space*). Mr. Frond: "I will often do divorce counseling for kids whose parents aren't divorced because, you know, I can see who's not going to make it."

BATHROOM HUMOR

Has any other TV show tapped into the humor potential of the bathroom as much as *Bob's Burgers*? We think not. And somehow it manages to do so without ever resorting to "gross-out" humor, such as in the episode when Tina is a school reporter trying to find the scoop on a kid leaving poop in the hallway; she insists on calling the culprit "the Mad Pooper," whereas Linda insists on "the BUTT-ler." Or when Gene befriends a robotic toilet voiced by John Hamm (Gene: "That's what I call easy money!" Toilet: "Playing artist 'Eddie Money'"). Or when Bob lands an interview with a local food magazine that he almost misses because he's glued to the restaurant's toilet seat. (In a prank war, Louise had intended for Gene to sit on it.) This being *Bob's Burgers*—a cartoon that at any moment can become a musical—Bob starts singing a song called "Bad Stuff Happens in the Bathroom." He's right...but the great thing about *Bob's Burgers* is that it always works out in the end.

The gray-headed albatross can fly around the planet in a month and a half.

THE TRUTH ABOUT LICORICE

Some facts about licorice as dark as licorice itself.

- What's the difference between black licorice candy and red licorice? The latter isn't technically licorice at all. Black licorice candy contains extracts from the root of the licorice plant. Red licorice is flavored with fruit and spices to create an approximation of a light licorice flavor—but it doesn't contain any real licorice root derivatives.

- Red Vines and Twizzlers, the most popular and famous licorice products in the U.S., aren't licorice and can't legally claim to be. They're labeled as "twists."

- Some mass-produced black licorice candy brands (meaning the cheaper ones) also don't use genuine licorice root products. They're made from fennel or anise seed oil, which taste like licorice but are not actually related to licorice at all.

- There are three main varieties of licorice all related to one another, and which developed separately in North America, Europe, and China. The European variety is the one most used in black licorice candy.

- Chinese licorice root is most associated with traditional natural medicine, used for hundreds of years as the active ingredient in concoctions to treat respiratory and digestive ailments.

- Licorice flavor comes from a compound called *anethole*, created and found in the roots of a licorice plant. Also found in the roots: *glycyrrhizin*, a natural sweetener that's 30–50 times as sweet as cane sugar.

- Consuming glycyrrhizin medicinally or recreationally can be a slippery slope. While it can help relieve an upset stomach or help with minor cardiovascular issues, it can also wreak havoc on the body. Too much glycyrrhizin (literally "sweet root" in Latin) can lead to water retention, a noted reduction in potassium levels, and an increase in blood pressure. That, in turn, can cause heart arrythmia (irregular heartbeat), which can trigger a heart attack or kidney failure.

- According to the FDA, those possibly fatal or hospitalization-requiring health conditions can manifest in people over the age of 40 who eat two ounces of black licorice every day for two weeks.

Watch your step: there are more than 600 species of venomous snakes.

- To further limit the risk, the FDA regulates glycyrrhizin levels in licorice candy sold in America. Black licorice in the U.S. can consist of no more than 3.1 percent glycyrrhizin.

- People do die from licorice poisoning. In 2020, the *New England Journal of Medicine* documented the case of a 54-year-old man who checked into Massachusetts General Hospital after suffering a heart attack. The next day he died from kidney failure, right after doctors determined the cause of his issues: for the previous three weeks, he'd eaten a large bag of black licorice candy every day.

- Salty licorice, or *salmiakki*, is a popular candy in Scandinavia and the Netherlands. It's not just black licorice with some salt added. The candy is made by combining licorice root, sugar, and other ingredients with ammonium chloride, salt created by combining hydrogen chloride with ammonia. It's food-safe, but results in a licorice that tastes sugary, spicy, and extremely salty.

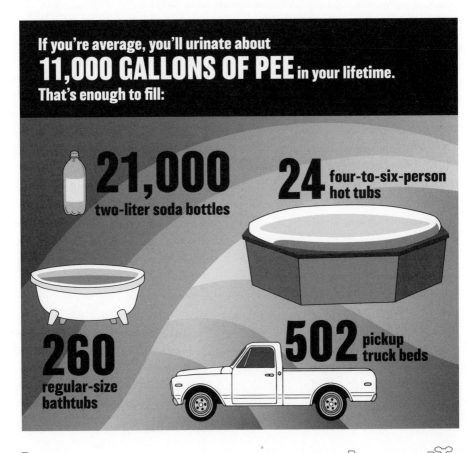

If you're average, you'll urinate about **11,000 GALLONS OF PEE** in your lifetime. That's enough to fill:

21,000 two-liter soda bottles

24 four-to-six-person hot tubs

260 regular-size bathtubs

502 pickup truck beds

Count 'em yourself: there are about 35,000 works of art on display at the Louvre.

WELCOME TO THE BIG WINDY EMERALD

Most big cities have at least one nickname.
Here's where they came from.

CITY: Chicago

NICKNAME: Windy City

DETAILS: Situated along the shores of often-stormy Lake Michigan, Chicago is presumed to be a blustery place, with the lake winds ripping off the water and into the city. However, Chicago isn't particularly windy, with average wind speeds topping out at 10 miles per hour. But in 1876, it was *extremely* windy there once—a tornado ripped through town—by which time Chicago politicians had already acquired a reputation as being full of bluster and empty promises. They were windbags—or, in other words, were windy. In 1876, the *Cincinnati Enquirer*, the paper of record for the city that positioned itself as a rival with Chicago, nicknamed the temporarily literal and often metaphorical city of wind the Windy City, and the name stuck.

CITY: New York

NICKNAME: The Big Apple

DETAILS: The first reference in print to the nickname for America's biggest and busiest city came in 1909, and it was as a cutting insult. In *The Wayfarer in New York*, Edward Sanford Martin wrote that the image midwestern Americans had of New York was one of "a greedy city," and in using a tree metaphor, he said that the average person "inclines to think that the big apple gets a disproportionate share of the national sap." The phrase would emerge more than a decade later in the work of *New York Morning Telegraph* horseracing columnist John J. Fitz Gerald, using "the big apple" as a synonym for New York City itself. After being repeatedly asked what, exactly, it meant, Fitz Gerald confusingly wrote, "The Big Apple. The dream of every lad that ever threw a leg over a thoroughbred and the goal of all horsemen. There's only one Big Apple. That's New York." "Big Apple" subsequently entered regular usage but fell out of favor by the 1950s. It was revived in the 1970s in a tourism campaign designed to attract people to a financially destitute New York.

Poll results: one in three Americans experienced "serious loneliness" during the COVID-19 pandemic.

CITY: New Orleans

NICKNAME: The Big Easy

DETAILS: New Orleans is one of the most fruitful development and performance spots for blues and jazz music, and it has been since the 1920s, adding to a vibrant culture of countless bars and music halls, and a distinctive food scene. The want and need to have a good time became central to the New Orleans way of life, and early 20th-century residents, particularly jazz and blues musicians who moved there, referred to that ease by nicknaming the city "the Big Easy," a conscious play on the much more busy and intense New York that called itself "the Big Apple." The nickname was musician slang until the 1960s, when *New Orleans Times-Picayune* columnist Betty Guillaud began frequently using the phrase in her articles and popularized it among the general public.

CITY: Seattle

NICKNAME: Emerald City

DETAILS: Prior to the 1980s, the largest city in the Pacific Northwest had a few semi-memorable nicknames—like Queen City, Gateway to Alaska, and Jet City (it's the home of plane maker Boeing)—but none were anything the city's tourism department felt it could use. In 1981, the Seattle Convention and Visitors Bureau held a contest to give Seattle its official (and eminently more marketable) nickname. The winning entry: Emerald City. Reflecting how Washington state is nicknamed the Evergreen State for its abundance of dense forest land, Seattle is similarly lined with and surrounded by trees, particularly those of a rich, emerald shade of green.

CITY: Baltimore

NICKNAME: Charm City

DETAILS: By the early 1970s, crime, urban blight, and abandoned buildings contributed to Baltimore falling into great decline. Seeking to revitalize the city and subsequently its image, in 1975 Mayor William Donald Schaefer recruited figures—Dan Loden and Stan Paulus of VanSant Dugdale & Co., and Herb Fried and Bill Evans of W. B. Donor—from big Baltimore advertising agencies to devise a quick and effective way to make the city seem more attractive to tourists and to businesses and individuals looking to move. Paulus and Evans struck on the idea of playing up the hidden, unexpected charm of Baltimore, realized only after living there for a while. Evans came up with a line of copy: "Baltimore has more history and unspoiled charm tucked away in quiet corners than most American cities out in the spotlight." That bit got cut down until it was just "Charm City."

NASA astronaut Chris Hadfield says *Apollo 13* is the most realistic space-travel movie of all time.

TIME TO CLEAN THE EAVES TROUGHS, EH?

Most Canadians and most Americans speak English, but that doesn't mean they always use the same words. Here are some common things that are known by different names in Canada than they are in the U.S.

In the U.S.: Eraser
In Canada: Rubber

In the U.S.: Bachelorette party
In Canada: Stagette

In the U.S.: Permanent marker
In Canada: Jiffy marker

In the U.S.: Counter or window
In Canada: Wicket

In the U.S.: Sweatpants
In Canada: Joggers

In the U.S.: American cheese
In Canada: Processed cheese

In the U.S.: Elementary school
In Canada: Public school

In the U.S.: Substitute teacher
In Canada: Supply teacher

In the U.S.: Community college
In Canada: College

In the U.S.: College
In Canada: University

In the U.S.: Rain gutters
In Canada: Eaves troughs

In the U.S.: Gas station
In Canada: Gas bar

In the U.S.: Cigarettes
In Canada: Darts

In the U.S.: Gyro
In Canada: Donair

In the U.S.: Studio apartment
In Canada: Bachelor apartment

In the U.S.: Fined
In Canada: Dinged

In the U.S.: Powdered sugar
In Canada: Icing sugar

In the U.S.: Non-dairy creamer
In Canada: Whitener

In the U.S.: Utility bill
In Canada: Hydro bill

In the U.S.: Evicted
In Canada: Turfed out

In the U.S.: Poster board
In Canada: Bristol board

In the U.S.: Silverware
In Canada: Cutlery

In the U.S.: Kickball
In Canada: Soccer baseball

In the U.S.: Teasing
In Canada: Chirping

In the U.S.: Take a test
In Canada: Write a test

In the U.S.: Proctor a test
In Canada: Invigilate a test

In the U.S.: Round-trip ticket
In Canada: Two-way ticket

In the U.S.: Briefs-style underwear
In Canada: Gotches

In the U.S.: Popsicles
In Canada: Freezies

In the U.S.: Adirondack chair
In Canada: Muskoka chair

In the U.S.: Bathrobe
In Canada: Housecoat

In the U.S.: Food truck
In Canada: Chip truck

In the U.S.: Napkin
In Canada: Serviette

In the U.S.: Welfare
In Canada: Pogie

In the U.S.: Brown-noser
In Canada: Keener

In the U.S.: Knit cap
In Canada: Tuque

In the U.S.: Backpack
In Canada: Knapsack

In the U.S.: Recycling bin
In Canada: Blue box

In the U.S.: Macaroni and cheese
In Canada: Kraft Dinner

As of June 2022, 50 movies have grossed over $1 billion worldwide.

FIGHTING LIKE ANIMALS

Horses, dogs, homing pigeons, pack animals...sure,
those can be put to use by the military. But what about arming animals
and enlisting them to fight your human enemies? It's a tradition
that dates back almost as far as the idea of war itself.

DOLPHINS

The U.S. Navy started training bottlenose dolphins for military purposes in the 1960s. Exploiting the animals' intelligence and echolocation abilities, naval personnel trained the dolphins to emit squeaks, which echo back when they see something underwater that doesn't belong there, such as bombs or mines dispatched by enemy combatants. Then they mark the spot of the difficult-for-humans-to-see object with a buoy line. Mine-spotting dolphins were used extensively by the U.S. Navy during the Persian Gulf War in the early 1990s and the Iraq War in the 2000s, with the sea mammals credited for safely clearing out the mines that the Iraqi military had placed throughout the Umm Qasr port. In the latter conflict, military personnel were able to train sea lions to accomplish similar tasks.

BEES

In ancient Greece, bees were a commonly employed implement of war. When armies would attempt invasion of fortified city-states, one of the first lines of defense involved catapulting hives full of agitated bees over the walls, right into the enemy hordes. In 72 BC, the Greek city of Themiscyra, a major honey-production area, defended itself against an invading Roman army by sliding bees up through underground shafts dug underneath its outer walls.

In the Vietnam War in the 1960s, guerillas from the Viet Cong routinely scoured the jungle for hives of the Asian giant honeybee, a particularly large and aggressive species of bee, and would place them on trails used by American forces on patrol. When U.S. troops approached the hidden hive on the path, a guerilla would toss a firework at the hive to upset the bees, which would then attack the Americans.

Jim Carrey underwent CIA torture endurance training to learn how to tolerate the makeup and prosthetics he had to wear for *How the Grinch Stole Christmas.*

SCORPIONS

A 198 BC Roman siege of the city of Hatra (in modern-day Iraq) was thwarted by a scorpion-based defense. The Hatrenians figured out how to temporarily disarm the insects—they'd spit on their tails, which would neutralize the poison stingers long enough so the scorpions could be picked up, moved, and placed into clay pots with dozens of their brethren. Then, the defenders threw a whole bunch of those scorpion-filled pots at charging soldiers, at which time the angry, no-longer-neutralized insects would repeatedly sting any flesh they touched.

ELEPHANTS

Gargantuan, awe-inspiring, and capable of wreaking mass destruction just by walking, elephants have understandably been used for warfare around the world for centuries, notably during the Punic Wars. The two seats of power in Europe in the 3rd century BC were Rome and Carthage, and they clashed in a series of wars for decades, fighting for dominance in the area that is now Spain and Italy. In 218 BC, Carthaginian general Hannibal took his troops through the Alps with more than three dozen elephants, soldiers riding and controlling them as if they were horses. Only one animal survived the treacherous journey, but Hannibal stepped up the elephant-based aggression in 201 BC. After Romans expelled the Carthaginian army from Italy and pursued them back to Carthage, Hannibal staged his final stand in Zama. This time he had 80 elephants at his disposal. Romans could see the elephants slowly stampeding toward them, and general Scipio Africanus devised a novel defense: he ordered soldiers to bang on their mess pots and shout when the elephants came near. Frightened and upset by the chaotic noise, the elephants threw off their riders and ran in every direction, trampling both Romans and Carthaginians.

PIGS

A surprising counteroffensive to the gigantic, destructive war elephant: the small and scrappy pig. In 275 BC, Greek king Pyrrhus sent elephants with his troops on an invasion of Rome. The Romans responded with a grotesque onslaught of living bombs—according to ancient historian Claudius Aelianus, defenders covered the pigs in highly flammable tar, set them on fire, and set them off running into the hordes of elephants. The terrifying sight of flaming, sprinting pigs—and the sound of their relentless squeals of pain—caused the elephants to turn around and retreat. Another

Nighty night: more than 100 compounds have anesthetic effects on people.

attack was repelled by loud, fiery pigs about a decade later. In 266 BC, Macedonian ruler Antigonus II Gonatas ordered a siege of the Greek city of Megara. Megarians, who possibly learned the technique from the Greek defeat in Rome, drove flaming pigs toward the Macedonian war elephants, who were so spooked they threw off, trampled, and killed their own riders and troops.

MONKEYS

That less-than-respectful treatment of pigs wasn't restricted to ancient Europe, or to pigs. In a series of wars between the Jin Dynasty and the Song Dynasty in China in the 12th century, Song warriors turned monkeys into living projectile bombs. The animals were evidently an ideal middle-of-the-road weapon, as catapults and bows and arrows both proved inaccurate. So, soldiers would outfit the monkeys in little coats made of straw, then dip them in flammable oil, light them on fire, and launch them into enemy field camps. The creatures were so panicked and in so much pain that they'd run around the camp, lighting on fire the tents and anything else they touched.

More than 800 years later, monkeys still have a use in the Chinese military. In 2020, while planning a huge military parade in commemoration of the 80th anniversary of China's entry into World War II, organizers predicted that migrating birds would fly into the engines of planes performing flyovers. The military recruited macaques to climb trees along the parade route and near the air force bases from where the planes would launch. Each monkey could dismantle, on average, seven nests a day, and so the migratory birds weren't an issue.

CATTLE

Cows are gentle, lumbering creatures, natural plant eaters who don't have any prey—unless they're spooked into stampeding. In 1591, troops from Morocco invaded the west African territory of the Songhai Empire, and the fight came down to the Battle of Tondibi. As the Moroccans advanced, the Empire's military released 1,000 cattle, which charged right into the assembled army. This had been the method with which the Songhai Empire had successfully defended itself against multiple invasions over the past century, but this time it didn't work: unlike the Moroccans, none of the animal aggressors had guns. The Moroccan troops didn't necessarily shoot that many cattle; they just fired their weapons into the air. That spooked the cattle into a stampede...back from whence they came, killing the majority of the Songhai Empire's assembled troops.

A dog named Donald Trump in the *Crazy Rich Asians* novel had his named changed to Rockefeller for the movie.

BATS

Soon after the United States was pulled into World War II by the Japanese attack of Hawaii's Pearl Harbor, the U.S. Army worked on a top-secret retaliation project, a bombing of multiple cities in Japan. Officially approved by President Franklin Roosevelt in 1942 and allocated $2 million, army scientists got to work on the "bat bomb" project. What looked like a regular missile was actually filled with 1,000 live bats, each outfitted with a small incendiary device. Once the missile was dropped and opened, it wouldn't explode but would release those bats into a Japanese city. Army scientists theorized that the bats would then seek out roosting spots in homes and buildings, and when they rubbed against wooden ceilings and walls, it would start a fire—a thousand times over. The army conducted multiple bat bomb tests, with most of the bats flying away or dying upon the initial impact of the vessel. The plan was never put into action in an actual combat situation.

MOSQUITOES

In 1943, late in World War II, Italy switched from the Axis Powers to the Allies, and the country was vulnerable enough that German Nazi troops invaded and took it over. They focused on fortifying the Pontine Marshes, south of Rome, which had been drained of their water in the 1920s. The Nazis switched the pumps off and the marshes refilled with water, attracting back millions of mosquitoes that had left the area years earlier. As the water got deeper and muddier and full of waterborne disease, the mosquito population grew, and did exactly what Nazi scientists thought they'd do: spread deadly malaria. Allied forces and the Nazis battled it out in the infested swamps, but the mosquitoes failed to remain loyal to their Nazi masters and bit thousands of troops on both sides. That created a small, mosquito-based malaria epidemic, until the Allies eventually secured the area.

TURKEYS

Almost every war in recorded history used animals in some way, generally as support staff—pack animals to carry in large amounts of supplies, food, and ammunition to the battlefield, or to help carry out the wounded and the dead. During the Spanish Civil War, a group of pilots aligned with the fascist Nationalist faction were called in to airdrop supplies to an allied Catholic monastery under siege by rebel combatants. Unable to secure parachutes, the pilots improvised and attached small parcels of food and medicine to a group of turkeys. Turkeys can sort of fly, so after they were pushed

"Thank you for submitting your tape of 'U2' to RSO...we feel it is not suitable for us at present." —RSO Records, rejecting U2 in 1979

out of planes with their payload, the birds would flap their wings and slowly, safely descend to the ground. And then the turkeys could serve as supplies themselves—after the birds arrived at the monastery, the monks and priests inside cooked and ate them.

CHICKENS

The American military response to Iraq's invasion of Kuwait in 1990 and 1991 happened so fast that there weren't time or resources available beforehand to research how Iraq may use chemical warfare, in the form of poison gas. After the U.S. Armed Forces had already arrived in the Middle East, high-ranking officials determined Iraq would likely use weaponized gas, and some on-field commanders developed an unofficial program called Operation Kuwaiti Field Chicken. The birds have a respiratory system far more sensitive than that of humans, and the theory was that if the birds were dispatched to a possibly gassed area and died immediately, gas was in the air, and troops would have the time to put on their masks. Operation KFC (that pun *was* intended) failed when all the chickens died one night, not of gas but from freezing to death in the chilly desert night. When the U.S. military returned to the Middle East for the Iraq War in 2003, troops once again relied on chickens as poison gas testers, many of whom died in the line of duty, giving human soldiers fair warning to mask up. Grateful soldiers buried them in the deserts of Iraq, where tiny tombstones note the names of fallen chickens including "Captain Popeye" and "Lance Corporal Pecker."

* * *

ROLLING RIGHT ALONG

Anglian Water runs the plumbing and sewers in and around Ipswich, in eastern England. They also deal with some of the most clogged sewers in the Western world—Anglian's legion of plumbers deal with about 30,000 sewer blockages each year, an average of about one every 15 minutes. The main culprits: fat, oil, grease, and other things flushed down toilets that don't break down in the sewers, primarily wet wipes and feminine-hygiene products. In February 2019, Anglian faced one of its strangest and most difficult industrial-level clogs yet: somebody dumped huge amounts of Yorkshire pudding directly into a sewer in Ipswich. A Yorkshire pudding, if you're not familiar, is a spongy, eggy roll, oftentimes served with the traditional British Sunday roast beef dinner. There were so many of them in the sewers that it led to a backup in the sewers that prevented sewage from draining. (Yuck!) Anglian Water issued several public pleas to get people to stop flushing anything that isn't biological waste.

Ouh là là! Napoleon removed the *Mona Lisa* from the Louvre and hung it in his bedroom.

MOUTHING OFF

MUSIC LESSONS

*Quiet, please. These renowned musical artists from the past
and present will now share their secrets of success.*

**"ALWAYS BE SMARTER
THAN THE PEOPLE
WHO HIRE YOU."**
—Lena Horne,
American singer

**"To get your playing
more forceful,
hit the drums harder."**
—Keith Moon,
English drummer

"Set your guitars and
banjos on fire and before
you write a song smoke a
pack of whiskey and it'll
all take care of itself."
—Beck,
American singer

**"You can't complain
about your dressing
room or you'll look like
Celine Dion."**
—Adele, English singer

"WHEN AN INSTRUMENT FAILS ON STAGE,
IT MOCKS YOU AND MUST BE DESTROYED."
—Trent Reznor, American singer

"There are two golden rules
for an orchestra: start
together and finish together.
The public doesn't give a
damn what goes
on in between."
—Thomas Beecham,
English conductor

*"Only become a musician if
there is absolutely no other
way you can make a living."*
—Kirke Mechem,
American composer

"Do it again on the next verse, and
people think you meant it."
—Chet Atkins,
American guitarist

"In order to compose, all you need to do is remember
a tune that nobody else has thought of."
—Robert Schumann, German composer

BEHIND THE HITS

Here's another edition of a longtime Bathroom Reader *favorite—
the secret stories and facts behind popular songs.*

THE SONG: "Smooth" (1999)

THE ARTIST: Santana featuring Rob Thomas

THE STORY: Santana—the name of the psychedelic-Latin-jazz-rock fusion band fronted by guitar legend Carlos Santana, the only permanent member—was a dominant act in the early 1970s with hits such as "Evil Ways," "Black Magic Woman," and "Oye Como Va." Santana took a long hiatus after a flop 1992 album and had faded into obscurity by 1997, which is when his kids pointed out that they never heard their father's old songs on the radio. That prompted Carlos Santana to get back in the game, so he called his old Columbia Records boss, Clive Davis (by that time head of Arista Records), invited him to a concert, and told him he wanted to record an album for him. Davis, noticing the breakthrough of Latin pop acts during the late 1990s, thought he could capitalize with a Santana pop album, finding inspiration in a 1997 B. B. King record that teamed the blues great with contemporary artists. Songwriter Itaal Shur of the band Groove Collective pitched a song about a hotel room tryst called "Room 17," but Davis gave it to Rob Thomas, singer and songwriter for the pop-rock band Matchbox 20, to rewrite into something less salacious. Thomas, inspired by his Puerto Rican girlfriend, turned the song into "Smooth," a lament about a wild and difficult Latin woman. He recorded a demo, intending for Davis to hire George Michael to sing lead. But Santana liked Thomas's take and his vocal impression of Michael. The final recording of "Smooth," with Thomas on vocals and Santana playing lead guitar, was the biggest hit of both musicians' careers, and pretty much everyone else's in music history. It spent 12 weeks at #1 in 1999 and 2000, and in 2021, *Billboard* named it the third-biggest hit of all time.

THE SONG: "Cherish" (1966)

THE ARTIST: The Association

THE STORY: After releasing two flop singles in 1965, California pop-rock band the Association was looking to change up its sound. They were primarily a group that played lighthearted, danceable, up-tempo songs, but lead singer and songwriter Terry Kirkman wanted to write a serious, earnest, bombastic ballad, much like "You've Lost That Lovin' Feelin'," a #1 hit in 1964 for the Righteous

Brothers. While Kirkman's result was earnest, his execution wasn't—he wrote the slow love song "Cherish" in about half an hour. The Association added it to their set list, and Mike Whelan loved it so much that he got his band, vocal group the New Christy Minstrels, to record it. To get their version out to record buyers first, the Association had to rush to record their own version of "Cherish," laying down the track at a garage studio owned by Columbia Records engineer Gary Paxton. One problem: when it was done, it was well over three minutes long, and thus not likely to get added to the playlists of American pop radio stations. After speeding up the song and removing a few lines near the end, the song was still 3:15; the band decided to just list the run time on the label as "3:00" anyway. Radio programmers didn't notice (or care about) the discrepancy, and "Cherish" went all the way to #1.

THE SONG: "St. Elmo's Fire (Man in Motion)" (1985)

THE ARTIST: John Parr

THE STORY: After playing with various bands in his native England in the 1970s, John Parr was hired as a songwriter by music publisher Carlin America. He wrote songs for Meat Loaf and Roger Daltrey before scoring his own top 40 hit with "Naughty Naughty" in 1984. After Parr's successful tour opening for Toto, superstar soft-rock producer David Foster hired Parr to write and record the theme song for the 1985 drama *St. Elmo's Fire*. But after watching a rough cut of the movie, Parr didn't feel very inspired to write a song directly about the movie's plot, about a bunch of directionless college graduates hanging out in their favorite bar (named St. Elmo's Fire). Instead, Foster introduced Parr to the story of Canadian wheelchair athlete Rick Hansen, who in 1985 set off on his Man in Motion World Tour, eventually a 26-month-long charity marathon across four continents intended to raise awareness for accessibility. That was the inspiration Parr needed. He composed and recorded "St. Elmo's Fire (Man in Motion)" about Hansen. The song went on the *St. Elmo's Fire* soundtrack, and went to #1. It likely would have received an Oscar nomination for Best Original Song, but Parr disqualified it from competition, telling the Academy of Motion Picture Arts and Sciences that the song wasn't really about the movie, but about Hansen.

* * *

"The child had his mother's eyes,
his mother's nose, and his mother's mouth.
Which leaves his mother with a pretty blank expression."
—Robert Benchley

What do crabs, snakes, and turtles have in common? They have no ears.

STRANGE LAWSUITS: THE MOON DUST BAG

Now for the story of some otherworldly dust that was put into a bag that was put into storage and then loaned out and then mislabeled and then seized and then sold and then seized again and then sued for...and that's just the first page! Confused? You'll still be after reading this head-scratching tale about some trace amounts of history.

THE CONTINGENCY COLLECTOR

On July 20, 1969, a moment before Neil Armstrong became the first human being to step foot on another world, he stood on the lunar module's ladder and described the Moon's surface as "very fine grained, almost like a powder." The main objective of Armstrong's first Moon walk was to gather some of that powder as a contingency plan in case something went wrong and they had to get out of there. (Having never actually been to the Moon in person, NASA scientists weren't sure what to expect.) Seven minutes after hopping off the ladder, Armstrong used a stick (because the bulky space suit prevented him from bending down) connected to an 11.5-inch zippered "Teflon contingency sample return container decontamination bag" to scoop up some of the gray dust. Then he closed the bag and put it in his pocket. Buzz Aldrin later joined Armstrong on the surface and together they collected 48 pounds of dust and rocks.

Over the next three years, Apollo astronauts would land on the Moon five more times and bring back more than 800 pounds of material, nearly all of which is still owned by NASA. (A few other countries have sent unmanned missions to collect lunar samples as well.) But no lunar dust on Earth has more worth—historic *and* monetary— than the 1,014 grams that Armstrong collected on his very first Moon walk.

ON LOAN

Back at the Johnson Space Center in Houston, Texas, the dust was removed and then set aside for analysis at NASA's Lunar Sample Laboratory Facility. The bag itself— which still contained trace amounts of Moon dust—was put in storage. Forty years later, the space agency loaned the mostly empty bag, along with some other space artifacts, to Cosmosphere, a museum in Hutchinson, Kansas.

What happened next isn't exactly clear. At some point, while on loan, the bag was mislabeled when someone mixed it up with a similar—and much less historic—bag from a later Apollo mission. In 2006, Max Ary, the founder and former director of the museum, was imprisoned for money laundering, fraud, and theft of government property. In 2015, in order to pay Ary's restitution, the Justice Department obtained a court order to auction several items from the museum's collection—including Armstrong's bag, now mislabeled as "flown zippered lunar sample return bag with lunar dust." The auction was conducted by the U.S. Marshals Service in Texas on the website www.forfeiture.gov.

CHANGING HANDS

The winning bid went to Nancy Lee Carlson, a corporate and real estate attorney from Palatine, Illinois. She paid $995 for a museum lot that contained a head rest from a command module, a launch key for the Soviet Soyuz T-14 spacecraft, and the mislabeled lunar sample return bag. Not a bad deal for three historical artifacts. Carlson had a feeling that the dusty bag might be the most valuable. But before she could sell it, she had to verify its authenticity, so she sent it to the Johnson Space Center, where Ryan Ziegler, NASA's Apollo 11 curator, analyzed it. Not only did he confirm that the residue inside the bag was indeed Moon dust, but that this was Neil Armstrong's Apollo 11 contingency bag. With that revelation, NASA decided to keep it.

After repeated requests to get her Moon bag back were denied, Carlson filed a lawsuit—naming the United States of America, NASA, and Ziegler himself as defendants—demanding the return of her property. The suit was filed in Texas, where the bag was being held, and in Kansas, from where it had been forfeited. A NASA spokesperson said that because the bag had been stolen, the space agency had "never relinquished ownership," adding, "This artifact was never meant to be owned by an individual...It belongs to the American people and should be on display for the public."

Kansas-based U.S. District Court Judge J. Thomas Marten acknowledged in his ruling that "NASA was a victim in this case, not a wrongdoer." Nonetheless, he ruled in favor of Carlson; it was within the Justice Department's right to auction the incorrectly labeled bag, and Carlson had purchased it "in good faith." The Texas judge ruled similarly, and the space agency reluctantly returned the bag to Carlson, but it wasn't in the same condition.

DAMAGED GOODS

At some point during Ziegler's analysis, the fabric had been ripped. Not only that, but he used five small pieces of "carbon tape" to remove dust particles for testing. Those

samples were not returned. By this point, the lawsuit had gained traction in the press, and Carlson told the *Chicago Tribune* that she wasn't sure what she would do with her Moon bag. She'd been keeping it in her bedroom closet and was receiving up to 50 messages per day from people who either wanted to buy it, or who told her she should return it to NASA. She said she thought about holding on to it and leaving it for her grandchildren. "I'm thrilled we won," she said. "This is like the Holy Grail, but I'm trying to be as anonymous as possible."

Carlson decided to sell the dust. The bag, labeled "Flown to the Moon on Apollo 11," became the star item at a 2017 Sotheby's Auction on the 48th anniversary of Armstrong's Moon walk. It was estimated to sell between $2 million and $4 million, but it brought in only $1,812,500, including the auction house costs. Disappointed, Carlson claimed that the negative publicity from the lawsuit—along with the fact that the bag had been torn—hurt its value. On her behalf, her Kansas City law firm, Wyrsch Hobbs & Mirakian (WHM), filed a second suit against NASA, claiming their examination diminished the value of their client's property, causing her "humiliation, embarrassment, emotional stress, and anxiety." She sought damages and the return of the five samples, or a monetary award matching their estimated worth.

Carlson won a second time: NASA settled for $50,000 and once again reluctantly relinquished the lunar samples. Now Carlson owned five pieces of dusty tape that had been mounted onto five aluminum disks and then set into a small display case just a few inches long.

THE FINE PRINT

In 2020, after the legal battle had been won, Carlson assumed she'd paid off WHM in full—to the tune of $50,000—but the law firm informed her in an email of "WHM's entitlement to compensation from any future sale or other disposition of the carbon tapes." They informed Carlson that she would owe them 28.5 percent of the money she made from selling the samples. Or else, she would have to pay them for "lost revenue" if she decided not to sell. WHM also insisted that Carlson have the pieces of tape analyzed to verify that they contain dust from Armstrong's first walk on the moon. In an affidavit, Carlson responded, "I was not advised at any time that [WHM] would be taking any kind of lien or interest in the tapes, and I never consented to them doing so."

Ultimately, Carlson decided to sell the carbon tapes through Bonhams Auction House in New York. In 2022, after the trace amounts of dust had been reverified, the item was labeled "Scanning Electron Microscope aluminum sample stubs, each topped with approximately 10mm-diameter carbon tape containing Apollo moondust." When the item went up for auction in May of that year, it was billed as "the only Apollo sample that can be legally sold." Expected to bring in between $800,000 and $1.2 million, the winning bid was only $400,000. It's unclear from press reports how much, if anything, Carlson paid to her former lawyers, but she was finally free of the Moon dust.

DUST IN THE WIND

Throughout the prolonged legal battle, NASA never wavered from its stance that Moon dust belongs to everyone. In similar cases of lunar samples going astray, the space agency has managed to get them back from private owners, but not this time. (Good thing the agency still has 800 more pounds of the stuff.) Press reports also didn't mention who bought the Moon dust bag or the carbon tapes, so it's possible we haven't heard the end of this out-of-this-world tale.

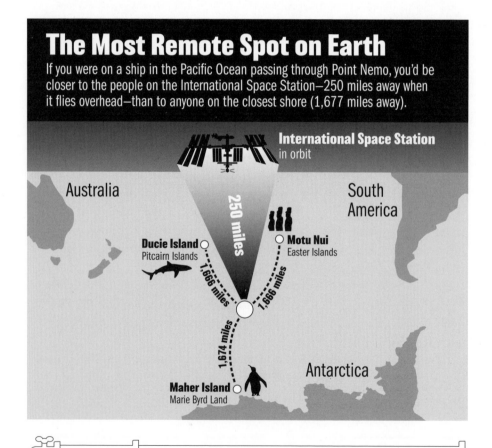

The Most Remote Spot on Earth

If you were on a ship in the Pacific Ocean passing through Point Nemo, you'd be closer to the people on the International Space Station—250 miles away when it flies overhead—than to anyone on the closest shore (1,677 miles away).

International Space Station
in orbit

Australia

South America

250 miles

Ducie Island ○
Pitcairn Islands

○ **Motu Nui**
Easter Islands

1,666 miles

1,666 miles

1,674 miles

Antarctica

Maher Island ○
Marie Byrd Land

If your brain didn't filter out the end of your nose, you'd see it all the time.

WAG BAGS AND CROTCH ROT

Whether you're a day hiker, a backpacker, or a "one time, I walked from
my car to a viewpoint" kind of outdoor enthusiast, you might want to
brush up on your hiking lingo so you don't come off like a glonk.

Alpine: A high-elevation area "above the tree line" where trees don't grow.

Alpine start: Waking up well before dawn in order to hike to a high elevation before the heat of the day kicks in.

Aqua blazing: Floating down a river that runs alongside the trail.

Base layer: The clothing layer closest to your skin, which needs to be light, airy, insulating, and waterproof to keep you warm in the cold and cool in the heat.

Bear bag: A sack for your tasty food that you hang from a tree, out of the reach of a hungry bear.

Bear box: A metal food-storage container at a campsite that's difficult for bears (and some people) to open.

Bear burrito: A hammock.

Bear fortune cookie: A tent.

Blaze: A small mark or arrow on a sign, tree, or rock indicating the official route of a trail.

Bliss index: How enjoyable or worth it a hike is; a bliss index of 10 means it was a fantastic hike with fantastic views and few glonks.

Blowout: When your hiking boots have had all they can take and literally come apart at the seams.

Brown blazing: Leaving the trail and finding a place to dig a cat hole and read *Uncle John's Briefs*.

Camel up: To drink as much as you can from a water source before filling up your water bottle.

Cat hole: A hole you dig in the woods to bury...not a cat, but something else you deposit.

Cobbknocker: The hiker in front who clears the trail of spider webs.

Cowboy camping: Sleeping under the stars without a tent; also called groundling.

Crotch rot: The mugginess that sets in down there after you've logged a lot of trail miles.

Death march: A long slog of a hike through uninteresting scenery in less-than-ideal weather.

Ditty bag: A small bag easily accessed on backpacking trips that holds important items.

Flip-flop: A backpacker that changes direction.

Gear Acquirement Syndrome (GAS): The ongoing desire to have the newest, latest equipment.

Getting off: Taking a break from a thru-hike with the intention of returning to it.

Glonk: An inexperienced or rude hiker who fails to yield the right of way to uphill hikers.

GORP: Trail mix—"good ol' raisins and peanuts."

Gram weenie: A hiker who obsesses over the weight of their gear.

Gray water: Dirty water left over after washing your dishes and yourself.

Hiker funk: The pungent aroma that sets in after a few days of backpacking.

Hiker midnight: When backpackers go to sleep, usually around 9:00 p.m.

Best-selling poster of all time: the Snellen eye chart, invented in 1862.

Hiker tan: What you think is a tan, but when you wash your skin off you realize it was just dust and dirt clinging to your sweat.

LNT: Leave no trace. Tread lightly, and pack out what you packed in.

MacGyver: To fix damaged gear with random objects, just like the titular character on TV's *MacGyver.*

Misery index: How unenjoyable or not-worth-it a hike is. A misery index of 10 means the weather was lousy and trail was full of ruts and dog crap and unyielding glonks who forced you into the dog crap.

Mountain money: TP.

MUDs: Mindless up and downs. A trail with unnecessary inclines just to make it harder.

Privy: A small outhouse near the trail exclusively for number two.

Rutabaga: A still-warm privy seat.

Scat: Animal poop.

Scree: Loose rocks on a slope that require you to scramble; also talus (like scree but a bit smaller).

Shelter rat: A hiker who camps in trail shelters, which are only meant to be brief rest stops.

Shuttle: Getting a ride to or from a trailhead to your car, so you can hike a trail in one direction.

Slackpacking: Carrying only a few personal items while a mule or porter carries the rest.

Speed hiking: Fast walking, or even running on a trail to try to beat a time record.

Stick snake: A stick that turns out to be a snake; also called danger noodle, nope rope, and snek.

Stump bear: You thought it was a bear, but it's just a stump.

Stupid light: You wanted so little weight in your pack that you failed to bring enough essentials to stay fed and warm.

Sweep: The final hiker in a group.

Three-season: Clothing and gear that keeps you warm, except on really cold nights, when you'll need four-season gear.

Thru-hiker: A backpacker hiking from one end of a long trail to the other. The three major U.S. thru-hikes are the AT (Appalachian Trail), CT (Continental Divide Trail), and PCT (Pacific Crest Trail).

Town food: The occasional perishable treat, such as fruit or takeout.

Trail angel: The townie who provides your town food, which is one example of "trail magic." (Not all townies are trail angels.)

Trail candy: An attractive hiker who draws your eye away from the scenery.

Trail legs: Muscles gained after hiking for a few days.

Tramper: Neither rain, nor sleet, nor snow will keep the tramper from tramping along the trail.

Vitamin I: Ibuprofen.

Wag bag: When you can't leave it in a cat hole, you carry it out in a wag bag.

Walk-up: A mountain you can "summit," or hike to the top of, without rock-climbing gear.

Widowmaker: A tree snag or weak limb that you avoid hiking under and never sleep under.

Yard sale: What it looks like when you've spread your gear around you at your campsite.

Yogi-ing: Named after Yogi Bear, it's the fine art of allowing someone to offer you their food so you don't have to beg for it, which is bad trail etiquette.

HOW TOO WRITE GOOD

Every so often, we run an article pointing out common language goofs.
After spending three minutes on the internet,
we decided that it's time for a refresher.

IT'S ALL IN THE USAGE

The first mistake a lot of people make when complaining about grammar is thinking that "grammar" is a catchall term for any language mistake. *Grammar* specifically refers to a set of rules for writing that govern things such as sentence structure and subject-object agreement. So, a run-on sentence can be grammatically incorrect. But misspelled words and improper punctuation marks are not grammar goofs, they're spelling goofs and punctuation goofs.

A lot of the time, when people complain about "poor grammar," they're actually describing poor *syntax* or *usage*. *Syntax* is like grammar in that it deals with word order, but it has more to do with communicating your point clearly than adhering to a strict set of rules. A sentence can have poor syntax but still be grammatically correct, as in: "After John went to the bathroom, it felt great." This isn't wrong, per se, but it's unclear exactly *what* felt great—John or the bathroom. To correct the poor syntax, you might rewrite it like this: "After John went to the bathroom, *he* felt great." *Usage* has to do with using specific words correctly, such as *irony* versus *coincidence* or *further* versus *farther*.

So, if you desire to be a better writer—or you don't want to come off sounding like a language dunce by incorrectly "correcting" someone—here are some of the most common offenses and how you can fix them.

- **Unnecessary Quotation Marks:** If you're making a sign or a menu and you suddenly feel the urge to put quotes around a word, it's usually a bad idea. We recently saw this on a sign:

  "FRESH" PRODUCE

  Uh-oh. In writing, quotation marks can designate several things: that someone is speaking, that something is a title, or that something isn't what it says it is—this is how we express sarcasm. Quotation marks should never be used to add emphasis to a word. (That's what bold, italics, and underlines are for.) Because this sign might be implying that the produce is indeed not fresh, we kept our distance.

- **Misplaced Commas:** One mistake nonwriters (and some writers) make is thinking that a comma indicates a dramatic pause: "John slowly opened, the

Before Edgar Allan Poe settled on a raven for his famous poem,
he was going to feature a parrot.

bathroom door." Bad comma! You do not belong there! A subject (the noun part of the sentence) and a predicate (what that noun is doing) should be separated by a comma only if there's a dependent clause.

- **Never-Ending Dependent Clauses:** Another common comma goof is leaving out the second comma of a dependent clause. What's a dependent clause, exactly? It's just what it sounds like: dependent—as in, it *depends* on that second comma or it ceases to be a clause! Use a dependent clause when your subject and predicate need a bit more explaining. For example, here's a sentence without a dependent clause: "John ran to the bathroom." No comma needed. But if you want to tell your readers *why* John was in such a hurry, you might write, "John, having just eaten a pound of haggis, ran to the bathroom." For some inexplicable reason, that second comma is often left out of dependent clauses (even in major media outlets): "John, having just eaten a pound of haggis ran to the bathroom." Lots of people miss that second comma, but now you won't!

- **Conjunction Junction:** *And* and *but* are the most common conjunctions, and a lot of people are confused when it comes to punctuating them. In the case of *but*, the word tells the reader that a twist is coming. Add a comma before *but* if what follows it includes both a subject and a predicate. Correct: "I was about to go in there but had no air freshener." Also correct: "I was about to go in there, but I had no air freshener." The addition of "I" gives the second part of the sentence a subject, making this a complete sentence: "I had no air freshener." This is incorrect: "I was about to go in there but I had no air freshener." Write the same sentence with *and*, and the same rules apply. And, this sentence is punctuated incorrectly. You do not add a comma after *and* or *but* unless there's a dependent clause. And now on to the next one.

- **Capital Gains:** Some People Feel The Need To Capitalize Every Word In A Sentence. (Or they Capitalize Random words.) Capitalizing every word is called *title caps.* The practice should be used only for titles, formal announcements, and signs. Otherwise, you need to capitalize only proper nouns.

- **Here's Some Disagreements:** *Here's* is a contraction of *here* and *is*. You wouldn't say, "Here is some examples." You would say, "Here *are* some examples." This falls under usage, and it has to do with singular-plural agreement. If the second part is plural, the first part must be, as well. This is correct: "Here are some examples." This is also correct: "Here is a list of examples." The best way to remember this is to look at the word right after *here* or *there*. If it's *a*, that's singular, so use "here is." If it's *some*, that's plural, so use "here are."

All of the "crows" in the 1994 movie *The Crow* were played by ravens.

- **Its vs. It's:** The confusion surrounding this common goof is understandable. If a word is possessive, the rule states that it gets an apostrophe before the *s* if singular (John's golden toilet), and after the *s* if plural (the writers' outhouse). But when it comes to an "it" owning something, leave off the apostrophe: "The dog lifts its leg." Use "it's" only as a contraction of *it* and *is*. Correct: "It's funny when the dog lifts its leg." If you're unsure, say "it is" out loud followed by the word. If it doesn't make sense—"The dog lifts it is leg"—no apostrophe is needed. If it still makes sense—"It is funny"—add the apostrophe: "It's funny."

- **Possessed:** This common goof shows up most often when someone posts a photo online and titles it "Last Nights Sunset." Even though the night is not a living thing, the sunset belonged to it, so the statement requires an apostrophe: "Last Night's Sunset." Without it, the word "nights" is simply plural, and it makes the caption read weirdly.

- **Dollars to Dollar Signs:** This common mistake can suck the credibility out of an otherwise cogent point. If you use a dollar sign, you don't need to add the word "dollars" after the amount. Incorrect: "Congress wasted $2 million dollars on a toilet-paper study." It's just "$2 million" (and that might be a worthwhile study).

A FEW COMMON SPELLING MISTAKES TO AVOID

- As an adjective, the word *loose* means "not tight"; as a verb, it means "to make less tight" or "to let free." *Lose* is a verb meaning "to not win" or "to misplace." You can loose a knot, but you can't loose weight.

- Use *than* for comparing, as in "smellier than thou," and then use *then* for everything else, especially if it follows a clause using *if*.

- *Farther* implies a physical distance that could be measured ("I ran farther away from the bathroom than ever"); *further* is figurative ("It couldn't be further from the truth").

- You're not supposed to use *your* when you mean "you are." So if you write "Your wrong" to tell someone they're incorrect, then you're wrong.

* * *

BLAZING MOVIE TRIVIA

When director Mel Brooks screened his soon-to-be-classic comedy *Blazing Saddles*, most of the Warner Bros. executives didn't laugh once during the vulgar, racially charged Western spoof. They threatened to "bury" the movie indefinitely. Undeterred, Brooks set up a second screening—this time for the "regular Joe" workers at the studio lot. They hardly stopped laughing...and the executives changed their minds. Result: *Blazing Saddles* was the biggest hit of 1974 for Warner Bros.

First movie released on DVD: *Twister.*

ASK UNCLE JOHN

Some questions have no answers. Others, like these, do.

GET A GRIP

Dear Uncle John, why don't birds fall off branches when they sleep?

A: Because of the potential danger from predators, weather, and people, birds are very light sleepers. Some even sleep with one eye open. But they could still fall off a branch, if not for a built-in fail-safe mechanism: Once a songbird lands and places weight on its feet, the tendons and muscles in the legs automatically tighten, which bends the legs and closes the clawed toes (or talons, in raptors) around the branch, thus securing the bird to its perch. This grip remains until the bird is ready to fly away.

I DON'T REALLY SOUND LIKE THAT, DO I?

Dear Uncle John, why does everyone hate the sound of their own voice?

A: There are two reasons for this phenomenon. One has to do with the physics of how you hear your voice compared to how others hear it. Because your voice emanates from within you, you hear two versions of it: The one that everyone else hears is the one that comes out of your mouth and travels to your inner ear via the eardrum. The other, that only you hear, emanates from the vocal cords and enters the inner ear via the skull bones. This internal air conduction boosts lower frequencies—giving your voice more bass and timber (from your perception, anyway). Result: when you hear a recording of your voice, it sounds like a tinny, high-pitched version of you.

That's the physical part. The psychological reason most people don't like the sound of their recorded voice is because it's...a little off. At first, you recognize it as your own, but that slight difference between your perception and reality is disconcerting. It's you, yet it's not you.

REDUCING POWER

Dear Uncle John, how famous do you have to be to be assassinated?

A: It's not necessarily how famous you are but what you do for a living—and also, why you were killed. An assassin is a killer who specifically targets a person in power—be it political or corporate—and offs them for political reasons. It's always predetermined,

An average of three UFOs are reported in Canada every day.

and the goals range from removing them from power to settling a past grievance to inciting terror. So technically, you don't have to be *that* famous to be the target of an assassination—you just have to have some kind of power that will give your death a broader political meaning. That means if a head of state is killed for a personal grievance, or in a robbery, that person's death is classified as murder. But what about when former Beatle John Lennon was gunned down in 1980? You'll often see the word "assassinated" before Lennon's name, but, by definition, he was murdered.

THAT MOON IS LIT

Dear Uncle John, how come you never see a full moon in the daytime?

A: The reason you can see the moon at all in daylight hours is because the sunlight reflecting off our celestial neighbor is 100,000 times brighter than any star or planet; it's even brighter than the sky itself. If you think you saw a full moon during the day, you didn't. You saw the waxing gibbous or waning gibbous, which, on the days before and after a full moon, reveal about 99 percent of the lunar surface facing us.

You see, the moon's phases aren't calculated by its visibility to people on the ground, but by its position in its orbit around Earth. The full moon occurs at the precise moment that the side facing Earth is drenched in 100 percent sunlight. For that to happen, the moon must be on the opposite side of Earth from the sun. If this moment occurs during your daytime, then you won't see it because you're on the wrong side of the planet. Every once in a while, a nearly full moon will appear on the horizon just before sunrise and after sunset—but if you see it before sunset or just after dawn, it's not actually full.

WEARING YOUR DESSERT

Dear Uncle John, how come so many cakes are named after fabrics?

A: Standardization in cooking measurements for cups, teaspoons, and the like didn't come about until a century and a half ago; before that, it wasn't easy to share recipes. And in those days, women did most of the cooking and baking. Without standard terms for different food textures, women drew from one of their other household tasks: making and repairing clothes. So when trying to explain what the final product should look and feel like in the mouth, women used words they knew, which is why we have lemon chiffon cake, red velvet cake, French silk cake, black satin cake, chocolate layer tweed cake, ermine frosting, and lace cookies.

If you shift each letter of *cheer* seven letters ahead in the alphabet, you get *jolly*.

ALTERNATE TV GUIDE

Some actors are so closely associated with their specific roles or TV series that it's hard to imagine they weren't necessarily the producers' first choice.

8 SIMPLE RULES FOR DATING MY TEENAGE DAUGHTER, STARRING JOHN GOODMAN

After *Roseanne* ended in 1997, costar John Goodman moved on to a successful movie career, but was soon ready to return to an ABC sitcom. Producers of the family comedy *8 Simple Rules for Dating My Teenage Daughter* pursued Goodman for the lead role of Paul Hennessy, a nervous, overprotective dad. They were just about to sign him when their actual first choice, John Ritter, became available. Ritter got the job.

FAMILY GUY, STARRING WILLIAM H. MACY

In 1998, Fox gave the greenlight to *Family Guy*, a crude and wacky animated comedy created by 24-year-old Seth MacFarlane. He voiced several characters in the pilot, including abrasive dad Peter Griffin, lascivious neighbor Glenn Quagmire, and genius baby Stewie Griffin. Fox talked MacFarlane into letting William H. Macy, recently nominated for an Oscar for *Fargo*, portray the show's cynical voice of reason, talking dog Brian Griffin. At the last moment, MacFarlane nixed it, deciding to add Brian to his character list. "I look back and I'm like, how cocky and arrogant must I have been at 24 to have Bill Macy audition for Brian and go, 'You know what? I don't think it's working and I'm going to do it myself,'" MacFarlane later said.

SCHITT'S CREEK, STARRING ABBY ELLIOTT

When assembling their Canadian sitcom, stars and creators (and father and son) Eugene Levy and Dan Levy quickly cast *Saturday Night Live* star Abby Elliott as Alexis Rose, the spoiled, party-girl daughter of the family stripped of their wealth and forced to live in a motel in the small town of Schitt's Creek. Elliott joined her father, Chris Elliott, already cast as town mayor and lout Roland Schitt. When the younger Elliott had to drop out of the series because she booked a part on an American TV show, the role of Alexis went to Annie Murphy instead.

THE GOOD WIFE, STARRING HELEN HUNT

The Good Wife was a high-profile CBS drama about a woman who returns to her abandoned profession as a defense attorney after her husband, a high-powered Chicago politician, cheats on her. CBS and producers wanted a big movie star to

A hummingbird has more bones in its neck than a giraffe.

portray main character Alicia Florrick, so they pursued Academy Award winner Helen Hunt. She said no, and so did the next big name on the list, Ashley Judd. Their third choice, Emmy Award–winning *ER* star Julianna Margulies, got the role—but she almost said no when she found out she'd been so far down on the list.

HOMELAND, STARRING HALLE BERRY

When Showtime developed an American remake of the Israeli espionage drama *Homeland*, they eyed Academy Award winner Halle Berry to play bipolar, jazz-loving CIA operative Carrie Mathison. Creators Alex Gansa and Howard Gordon wrote the role with Claire Danes in mind, however. After weeks of feuding and negotiating, Showtime agreed to the creators' suggestion, and Danes said yes.

SEINFELD, STARRING CHRIS ROCK

Seinfeld was created by comedians Jerry Seinfeld and Larry David, and they based the two main characters, stand-up comic Jerry Seinfeld and fussy loser George Costanza, on themselves. Seinfeld played himself on the show, but David wasn't interested in portraying a fictional version of himself, so the two cast a wide net for someone to play George, auditioning Broadway stars David Alan Grier and Nathan Lane, indie movie actor Steve Buscemi, and stand-up comedians like Brad Hall, Larry Miller, and Chris Rock, and ultimately offered the part to TV and movie veteran Danny DeVito. He passed. In the end, then-little-known actor Jason Alexander got the part.

WINNING TIME, STARRING WILL FERRELL

Winning Time, the television dramatization of the Los Angeles Lakers' 1980s dominance of the NBA, was produced by Adam McKay, longtime creative partner of movie star Will Ferrell. Together the pair wrote and made comedies such as *Step Brothers* and *Talladega Nights: The Ballad of Ricky Bobby*, and started the comedy website Funny or Die. They ended their professional partnership and friendship because McKay didn't cast Ferrell as Lakers owner Jerry Buss in *Winning Time*. Ferrell grew up in Los Angeles as a huge Lakers fan and lobbied hard for the role, which instead went to his *Step Brothers* and *Talladega Nights* costar John C. Reilly. McKay didn't tell Ferrell he'd cast their friend and collaborator, and Ferrell was so miffed the two stopped speaking.

KILLING EVE, STARRING MAYA RUDOLPH

Phoebe Waller-Bridge is best known for her comedic work, such as the Emmy-winning British series *Fleabag*. She also created the cat-and-mouse spy show *Killing Eve* for BBC Three and BBC America, and when she was looking to cast the role of Eve Polastri, an MI5 analyst who engages in a mutual obsession with an Eastern European assassin, she sought out another entertainer known for funny things: *Bridesmaids* and *Saturday*

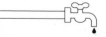

Bob Hope's final TV appearance: a 1997 Kmart commercial.

Night Live star Maya Rudolph. Even though she was a big fan of *Fleabag*, Rudolph said no. "There was no way I was about to move to Europe for months" of filming, she told *The Hollywood Reporter*, because she felt like she couldn't be away from her four children for such a long time. Sandra Oh wound up with the role instead.

THE O.C., STARRING CHRIS PINE

The hottest teen show of the early 2000s: Fox's *The O.C.*, about Ryan Atwood, a juvenile delinquent from a poor family who moves in with a kind and wealthy family in fancy Orange County, California. Ben McKenzie got the role, launching a long career in TV, but he edged out future *This Is Us* star Justin Hartley and *Star Trek* and *Wonder Woman* movie actor Chris Pine. According to casting director Patrick Rush on an O.C. podcast, Pine's audition was terrific, but his appearance disqualified him—he had severe acne at the time, and producers rejected him.

THIS IS US, STARRING OLIVER HUDSON

For the role of patriarch Jack Pearson on the time-hopping family saga *This Is Us*, producers narrowed down their choices to Milo Ventimiglia (best known for *Gilmore Girls*) and Oliver Hudson (coming off the sitcom *Rules of Engagement*). Ventimiglia won the part by default because Hudson took himself out of the running: when producers wanted to see him for a screen test opposite already-cast Mandy Moore as Rebecca Pearson, Hudson had left Los Angeles for a long-planned fishing trip.

GREY'S ANATOMY, STARRING YUNJIN KIM

In the lead-up to the 2004–2005 TV season, Yunjin Kim was up for two roles on two different ensemble dramas for ABC. Producers of the hospital soap *Grey's Anatomy* liked Kim's audition and asked her to come try out again for the role of young surgical intern Izzie Stevens, right around the same time that J. J. Abrams told her that he wrote a role on his mysterious sci-fi show *Lost* just for her. Kim decided to play Sun-Hwa Kwon on *Lost*, leaving the door open for Katherine Heigl to star on *Grey's Anatomy*.

THE COSBY SHOW, STARRING JALEEL WHITE

Jaleel White became one of the biggest TV stars of the late 1980 and early 1990s for his work as ultra-nerd Steve Urkel on the sitcom *Family Matters*, but he almost found fame and success on another family comedy from the same era. In 1984, the eight-year-old actor auditioned to play Rudy, the youngest Huxtable kid on *The Cosby Show*. White's agent told him and his family that he'd secured the role, and that he only needed to jump through one more hoop—getting NBC executives to sign off on the casting. But while he waited for that audition, show star and creator Bill Cosby decided he wanted Rudy to be female because the youngest of his five real-life children was a girl, too. Kiesha Knight Pulliam got the gig.

Migrating frigate birds sleep in the air in 10-second naps for about 45 minutes per day.

BATHROOM NEWS: POLITICS EDITION

*Here at the Bathroom Readers' Institute, we're always sad
to see our favorite room get dragged into contentious political debates.
But at least it makes for good bathroom reading.*

FLUSH OUT THE VOTE

In the fall of 2020, the contagious COVID-19 virus made in-person voting a
dangerous venture, which led to several U.S. states adopting mail-in voting. After
President Donald Trump expressed concern that these new measures could lead
to voter fraud, one of his supporters in Michigan (whose name and address were
withheld) decided to express their distaste by placing a porcelain toilet on their front
lawn, along with a sign that read "Place mail in ballots here."

Not everyone was amused. Democrat clerk of Ingham County, Barb Byrum, said,
"Elections…are to be taken seriously, and there are many people who are voting by
mail for the first time this election." She was concerned that the toilet might confuse
them, and it happens to be a federal crime to impersonate a voting booth. Byrum's
attempts to get the resident arrested fell short after county prosecutor Carol Siemon
(also a Democrat) declined to press charges, citing "no evidence of an intent" to break
election laws. "Instead, this seemed to be an effort to make a humorous political
statement," said Siemon.

THE SITTING PRESIDENT

President Donald Trump was hosting a meeting with business leaders at the
White House in December 2019, talking about the negative effects that the U.S.
Environmental Protection Agency's regulations were having on innovation. Trump
took direct aim at low-flow technology, designed to reduce water use:

> We have a situation where we're looking very strongly at sinks and showers
> and other elements of bathrooms where you turn the faucet on—and in areas
> where there's tremendous amounts of water, where the water rushes out to
> sea because you could never handle it, and you don't get any water. You turn
> on the faucet and you don't get any water. They take a shower and water
> comes dripping out. Just dripping out, very quietly dripping out.

**With more than 15,000 hours of his playing on tape, the Grateful Dead's
Jerry Garcia (1942–95) is the most recorded guitarist of all time.**

Then came the worst part: "People are flushing toilets 10 times, 15 times, as opposed to once."

The remarks predictably made the rounds in the media, with most people wondering what exactly the president was attempting to flush that it was taking him that many tries. According to Politico, which quoted former campaign manager Corey Lewandowski's book, *Let Trump Be Trump*, it might have something to do with his diet: "a full McDonald's dinner of two Big Macs, two Filet-O-Fish sandwiches, and a small chocolate shake—a total of 2,430 calories."

BEYOND THE BOUNDS OF DECENCY

In October 2021, four members of an immigrants-advocacy group called LUCHA (Living United for Change in Arizona) protested the voting record of U.S. Sen. Kyrsten Sinema (D-AZ) by going to Arizona State University, where the lawmaker was teaching a class (called Advanced Fundraising). When Sinema left the room so she could move her car, the activists followed her down the hall, filming her while one of them told a story about their family's immigration history. Sinema didn't engage and then ducked into a women's restroom. Two activists followed her inside and continued to film as she went into a stall and closed the door. The activists kept hounding the senator until she emerged from the stall, washed her hands, and left the restroom without saying a word.

Afterward, Sinema said in a statement that the activists (who weren't identified in press reports) had "entered a locked building" to hold a protest that was "not legitimate." She reportedly told officers that she entered the restroom because it's illegal in Arizona to film someone in there without their consent. The university's police department agreed, and urged the county prosecutor to charge the LUCHA members with felonies. (Technically, that law forbids the filming of someone who is "urinating, defecating, dressing, undressing, nude," or engaged in intimate relations; it's unclear from the video if Sinema was doing any of those things.) As of last report, no charges had been filed. A LUCHA spokesperson said they only went to the university because Sinema had earlier declined to meet with them. In fact, they said the only real response they'd received from their senator was an Instagram photo in which she's sipping a sangria and displaying a ring that says, "F*ck Off." (There's no definitive evidence that Sinema's photo was directed at the group.)

* * *

*"Who wants to see a movie about
a talking tree and a raccoon?"*
—**Amanda Seyfried,**
on why she turned down a role in *Guardians of the Galaxy*

The shortest distance over an MLB fence for a home run: 250 feet. The longest: 355 feet.

WEIRD FESTIVALS

As the saying goes: there ain't no party like a small-town party,
'cause a small-town party is downright bizarre.

Event: MATTOON BAGELFEST

Location: Mattoon, Illinois

Details: In 1984, Kraft Foods bought the company that makes Lender's Bagels and opened three new processing facilities, including one in Mattoon. When looking to hire new employees, Kraft realized that the small town in central Illinois wasn't familiar with bagels, a traditionally Jewish boiled-and-baked breakfast bread. So, one Saturday morning in July 1985, they set up a bunch of tables downtown and handed out hundreds of free Lender's bagels, both to familiarize Mattoon with the product and to recruit workers. The next year, Mattoon Bagelfest proper began. It's grown into a celebration of bagels (particularly Lender's, as its last American plant is the one in Mattoon), including a carnival, live bands, the Bagelfest Parade, the Bagel Baby Contest, and the Miss Bagelfest beauty pageant. On the fourth and final day comes the event that started it all: the Free Bagel Breakfast.

Event: GRUMPY OLD MEN FESTIVAL

Location: Wabasha, Minnesota

Details: While the idea of a festival dedicated to cranky codgers, complete with a pageant and parade, sounds hilarious, this Grumpy Old Man Festival is devoted to a different humorous display of elderliness—the 1993 comedy *Grumpy Old Men*, starring Walter Matthau and Jack Lemmon. The film, which took place over a chilly Minnesota winter and was filmed in nearby towns, was only a modest success and is largely forgotten everywhere except Wabasha. The itinerary for the Grumpy Old Man Festival consists of events inspired by stuff the grumpy old men did in *Grumpy Old Men*, including ice fishing, a bingo tournament, and a cribbage tournament.

Event: TWINS DAYS FESTIVAL

Location: Twinsburg, Ohio

Details: Amidst the summerlong celebration of America's bicentennial in 1976, the town of Twinsburg, Ohio, devoted one day to honor its namesake: twins. After an initial Twins Day Festival consisting of little more than the dedication of some new public buildings and a flag ceremony, things really took off in year two (appropriately enough), with food stands, dancing, and a buggy parade for kids. It was a lot like

A line in William Butler Yeats's 1928 poem "Sailing to Byzantium" inspired the title *No Country for Old Men*.

other small town summer festivals except for all the doubles: 38 sets of twins showed up as honored guests. By 2020, more than 77,000 twosomes had attended (including a delegation of nine twin pairs from the U.S.S.R.). Nowadays, Twins Days lasts a weekend, and each year has a theme ("Two-Player Mode," or video gaming; "Twinsfinity and Beyond," or space) to which twins theme their lookalike costumes. There's even a Double Take Parade, twin volleyball, and a twin talent show.

Event: LOWER KEY UNDERWATER MUSIC FESTIVAL

Location: Looe Key Reef, Florida

Details: Each year, thousands of people visit the Florida Keys National Marine Sanctuary near Big Pine Key to enjoy an extensive coral reef. To raise awareness of the need to protect the reef while also enjoying it, an area radio station holds the Underwater Music Festival. They send out a bunch of boats that drag speakers under the surface of the water, which blast ocean-themed songs like "Yellow Submarine" and "Under the Sea." Meanwhile, scuba divers hang around under the water and dress in mermaid costumes and mime playing those songs on instruments, giving off the impression of an underwater concert.

Event: THE MOONING OF THE AMTRAK

Location: Laguna Niguel, California

Details: The Mugs Away Saloon in Laguna Niguel in Orange County is home base for the Mooning of the Amtrak, a festival held the second Saturday of each July. The bar sits along a passenger train track, and at the appointed time, the thousands who have gathered head outside, drop their pants, and show off their bare bottoms to the unsuspecting Amtrak passengers. The lead-up to the big moment is decidedly and similarly adult- and nudity-oriented, with lots of drinking, beads tossed to women who flash their bare chests, and wet-clothing contests.

Event: FESTIVAL OF NEAR-DEATH EXPERIENCES

Location: Galicia, Spain

Details: A town straddling the Spain-Portugal border attracts thousands of visitors every July 29 to commemorate those who died...but then didn't. One part religious pilgrimage, one part celebration of the triumph of life over death, the most fervent participants arrive inside of coffins, carried by their relatives in a procession following an effigy of Santa Marta, sister of Lazarus, who rose from the dead in the Bible. (She's also the patron saint of Galicia, and the patron saint of death.) Then everyone gathers and talks about how they almost died but lived to tell the tale.

The *SS Minnow* on *Gilligan's Island* that stranded the castaways
was a 1964 Wheeler...which could travel only about 40 miles from the coast.

THE BETTY WHITE TIMELINE, PART III

Everyone talks about Betty White's "big comeback" in the 2000s, but she never went anywhere. She did, however, have a string of flops after The Golden Girls that brought up questions of her retirement. White's response: "I'm so pleasantly surprised when I get asked to do something, I always say yes. Retirement is not in my vocabulary. They aren't going to get rid of me that way." (Part II is on page 109.)

1993 Following the success of *The Bob Newhart Show* and *Newhart*, the third time's not a charm for Bob Newhart's *Bob*, which is canceled in its second season right after Betty White joins the cast as Bob's new boss. Newhart and White met way back in 1960 when they were both guests on *Tonight Starring Jack Paar*. Newhart's advice in 2021 to all the "young people starting out in the business, all they have to do is just be Betty White, and they've got nothing to worry about. The good ones make it look easy."

1995 White is inducted into the Television Hall of Fame and is honored with a star on the Hollywood Walk of Fame, right next to her late husband Allen's star. Also a prolific author, White releases another memoir, *Here We Go Again: My Life in Television 1949–95*, a follow-up to 1987's *Betty White in Person*. These books are among many she wrote in her lifetime, some about animals (*Betty & Friends: My Life at the Zoo*, *The Leading Lady: Dinah's Story*, and *Together: A Story of Shared Vision*) and another memoir (*If You Ask Me: And of Course You Won't*).

1996 A sitcom actor without a sitcom, White, now pushing 80, becomes a "special guest star" on a bevy of shows, including *Yes, Dear*; *Suddenly Susan*; and *The Practice*—with each appearance garnering Emmy nominations. She wins a fourth Primetime Emmy for a memorable episode of *The John Larroquette Show*. Playing herself, White is recruited for a musical version of *The Golden Girls*. She not only reunites with McClanahan and Getty but with some of the creative team behind their hit show. From her acceptance speech: "I not only appreciate all the people on that stage but that wonderful gang of writers, some of them from *Golden Girls*, who really saw into the true Betty."

1999 In a nod back to *Life with Elizabeth*, White guest stars on yet another dream-sequence show, *Ally McBeal*. She plays therapist Dr. Shirley Flott. After Ally (Calista Flockhart) divulges that her own daydreams have turned into hallucinations, she looks wantonly at the therapist. Flott smiles, and after a bit of a pause, says, "What I'd like to do...is put you on Prozac." When Ally protests, Flott says, "I'm on it!" And then comes this bit of wisdom, as only Betty White can deliver it: "I've been a therapist since before you were born. You won't find happiness through love, or by turning to God. It comes in a pill!" Then Flott starts giggling about how the pills come in "suppository form" and it "gives me a little wriggle." Cue: look of horror on Ally's face.

2001 White's first main role since the short-lived *Maybe This Time* (ABC, 1995, canceled after 18 episodes), is on CBS's *Ladies Man* (canceled after 30 episodes). White will spend the 2000s as a talk-show regular and perennial "special guest star" on shows such as *The Simpsons*, *Family Guy*, *My Name Is Earl*, *That '70s Show*, *Malcolm in the Middle*, *King of the Hill*, and *Boston Legal*, but her search for another juicy main role like Sue Ann or Rose remains elusive.

2006 The lack of a steady job gives White more time to focus on her charity work. At the Los Angeles Zoo, she receives the official title "Ambassador of the Animals," with a commemorative bronze plaque next to the gorilla exhibit. "I'm not sure what I'm going to do as ambassador except to love the animals as I have all my life."

2006 White once again proves her dramatic chops as Ann Douglas, the long-lost mother of fashion matriarch Stephanie Forrester on *The Bold and the Beautiful*. Appearing in 22 episodes, Ann's bittersweet storyline of redemption is much heralded by soap fans. "For years," Ann pleads to her estranged daughter, "you have denied me a place in my own family. Well, I've done my penance. I have grandchildren and great-grandchildren—who like and appreciate me. Why should I give that up?"

2009 Snickers candy bars launches its "You're not you when you're hungry" ad campaign with a commercial starring White, seemingly as herself, playing tackle football against a bunch of men...and struggling. One of them yells at her: "Mike, you're playing like Betty White out there!" She claps back, "That's not what your girlfriend said last night!" Then "she" eats a candy bar and turns back into Mike. The commercial takes #1 on the fan-voted "Super Bowl Ad Meter" and helps raise Snickers from #7 in candy bar sales to #1. It is also heralded as the moment Betty White makes her comeback. "It's been phenomenal, but everybody keeps congratulating me on my big comeback. I haven't been away, guys. I've been working steadily for the last 63 years."

2009 White makes a memorable appearance as a randy grandma in the romantic comedy *The Proposal*, starring Sandra Bullock and Ryan Reynolds. (Rumors of an off-screen romance between Reynolds and White turn out to be false.) White is nominated for "Best WTF Moment" at the 2010 MTV Movie Awards, for a scene in which she gropes Bullock. (She loses to Ken Jeong, who jumps out of a car naked in *The Hangover*.) At the ceremony, White says to Bullock, "Sandy, you're a national treasure, which I know a thing or two about, since my ovaries were recently named national monuments." Bullock's reply: "I want your life."

2010 On the heels of a Screen Actors Guild Life Achievement Award ("Thank you from the bottom of my heart, and from the bottom of my bottom!"), more than half a million Facebook users mount a campaign to get White to host *Saturday Night Live*. At 88, she becomes *SNL*'s oldest host ever and brings in the highest ratings of the season. And she wins her fifth Primetime Emmy, this one for Outstanding Guest Actress in a Comedy Series. From her *SNL* monologue: "In 1952, I starred in my first live sitcom, which was *Life of Elizabeth*, and of course, back then we didn't want to do it live, we just didn't know how to tape things. So, I don't know what this show's excuse is."

2010 White is invited to the pilot of a TV Land sitcom called *Hot in Cleveland*. Unsure if she wants another series, she agrees to the pilot only if she doesn't have to make a long commitment. White ends up sticking around for all five seasons, appearing in 124 episodes as Elka Ostrovsky and earning yet another Emmy nomination. And her salary–$75,000 per episode–has risen considerably from the $10 per week she made for *Grab Your Phone*. The show doesn't break much new ground, with most critics comparing it to *The Golden Girls*: Wendie Malick plays the Dorothy character, Jane Leeves is Blanche, Valerie Bertinelli is Rose, and Betty White has aged into Sophia. Once again, White delivers the laughs. Elka, to Joy (Leeves): "You're too old and creaky to be robbing the cradle." Joy: "*I'm* old! Was Ohio even a state when you were born?" Elka: "They were talking about it."

2010 The "Year of Betty White" is capped off with her being named Honorary Park Ranger by the National Park Service. At the ceremony, wearing the trademark tan hat (like her dad used to) and standing next to Smokey Bear, White beams, "In my heart I've been a forest ranger all my life, but now I'm official!" She's more than earned the title. According to the Morris Animal Foundation, for which White served from 1971 to 2009, she sponsored 30 animal health studies and established the Betty White Wildlife Fund following the Deepwater Horizon oil disaster in the Gulf of Mexico. "Betty always put the animals first," said friend and former Morris director Dr. Rob Hilsenroth. "In the 1990s, she suggested pain management should be an area of future research and funded the first few studies. Today, if a veterinarian performs an elective surgery, like a spay or neuter without using pain management, she/he could face a malpractice charge. You can thank Betty White for that revolutionary change in the way we practice all phases of veterinary medicine today."

2011 In a *Reuters* poll, White beats out Tom Hanks, Sandra Bullock, Oprah Winfrey, Taylor Swift, and Morgan Freeman to be named "Most Trusted Personality." She'll win it the next two years as well. Never too old to take on a new kind of role, White stars in *The Lost Valentine*, a "finding long-lost love" Hallmark Hall of Fame movie that brings Hallmark its highest ratings in four years. White nearly turns the role down because of other projects but changes her mind after reading the script. "It's such a beautiful love story. And when you've had a love like that in your life, it's an awful temptation to revisit it."

2011 Coming in at #1 on the Dance Club Songs chart is a remix of Luciana's "I'm Still Hot" with 89-year-old Betty White rapping new lyrics (for a social media campaign for the federal Lifeline Program). The music video has a blinged-out White seated on a throne surrounded by shirtless muscular men: "I'm smokin' hot in the world / I'm still a golden girl. / I may be a senior, so what / I'm still hot!" Not surprisingly, White's not a half-bad rapper.

2012 NBC's star-studded *Betty White's 90th Birthday: A Tribute to America's Golden Girl* generates such huge ratings (and fun) that the following year, the network airs *Betty White's 2nd-annual 90th Birthday*. White also receives her first and only Grammy Award for Best Spoken Word for the audiobook recording of *If You Only Ask Me*, full of nuggets of wisdom like this: "Animals don't lie. Animals don't criticize. If animals have moody days, they handle them better than humans do."

Ahem—we were saying...You spend about half of your waking hours daydreaming.

2012 White meets her doppelganger at Madame Tussauds Hollywood wax museum. "I'm the happiest old broad on two legs," she says at the ceremony, dressed in the same hot-pink sweatsuit (trimmed with rhinestones) as the wax figure. "But why did they have to wait to do this until I was 90!" (There was going to be a wax replica of all four Golden Girls in the late 1980s, but Bea Arthur said no, so it was canceled.)

2013 White is invited to the GLAAD media awards to speak about the praise she's garnered from the gay and lesbian community. "I was going to say I'm 'GLAAD' to be here. But that would be corny. But when have I ever missed a chance to be corny? I'm GLAAD to be here!" At an earlier event, White explained that the adoration from the gay community began in the 1980s when *The Golden Girls* aired on Saturday nights: "Our show would come on, and all the gay bars would shut the music off and stop the dancing...and they'd watch our show, and then the show would end, and they'd turn the music and dancing back on."

2014 *Betty White's Off Their Rockers* is a hidden-camera show where the practical jokers are senior citizens...and their marks are young people. White serves as host, introducing segments such as an elderly widow asking a "hot girl" to help pour her late husband's ashes into a garbage can, and an old couple helping themselves to other people's meals at a restaurant. *Off Their Rockers* lasts three seasons...and White is nominated for three Emmys. From the trailer: "When I heard about all these television shows on the air today that are about 'hyper-sexual beings' that don't age and live forever, I was surprised to find out that all these shows are about vampires! I thought they were finally making *The Betty White Story*."

2015 After being recognized by Guinness World Records as "Longest TV career by an entertainer (female)," White wins the Daytime Emmy for Lifetime Achievement. In all, she wins eight Emmys and receives more awards and honors than we can fit in here. Her advice to other stars who feel they're "past their prime": "Make yourself as useful as possible so that they'll find a place for you, too! And don't complain—try to accentuate the positive rather than the negative. If you're complaining, you're not fun to be around, and fun is the name of the game." (Proving her point, she makes headlines after giving heartthrob Bradley Cooper a long, passionate kiss in a soap-opera parody sketch on her final *Saturday Night Live* appearance.)

2017 One award that White never receives is an Oscar, which makes sense when you look at the movies she appeared in. Despite this, at age 95, White becomes the oldest new member of the Academy of Motion Picture Arts and Sciences.

2018 After appearing on nearly 120 television shows, White makes her final sitcom appearance on Freeform's *Young & Hungry*, playing an old lady who teaches a young woman (Emily Osment) about men. According to Osment, "She's got a mouth on her!"

2018 The PBS documentary *Betty White: The First Lady of Television*, premieres. White quips: "I've worked nearly 80 years in television, and finally I made it to PBS."

2019 White's final film appearances are voiceover roles for two animated movies, *Trouble* and *Toy Story 4*, which has her playing a tiger toy named Bitey White. These are just two of a dozen movies White lent her vocal talents to, the most notable being Grammy Norma in *Dr. Seuss' The Lorax*, an environmentally themed parable. "It's all the things that I believe in and love. And I think it's a great message to send out to kids to get the thing across about appreciating trees."

2020 The COVID-19 pandemic puts everything on hold, including White's career. She meets it with her usual verve, saying, "Since I am turning 99, I can stay up as late as I want without asking permission." But after a year and a half in quarantine—which White takes very seriously—her agent tells TMZ that White is lonely. She doesn't have any pets, so she spends her days doing crosswords and enjoying the company of two ducks that live on her property.

2021 White suffers a stroke on Christmas and dies on New Year's Eve, just two and a half weeks before she would have turned 100. In a final video (made shortly before the stroke) to her 1.9 million Instagram followers, her voice sounds very, very old, but her smile and the spark in her eyes are as bright as ever. "I want to thank you all for your love and support over the years. Thank you so much, and...stick around." The video was going to be played at her birthday celebration, which turns into a memorial as tributes pour in all over the world. According to her old friend Carol Burnett, White's last word was the name of her late husband: "Allen."

2022 Shortly after what would have been White's 100th birthday, the #BettyWhiteChallenge Facebook/Instagram charity event is a huge success, bringing in donations from more than 390,000 people for a total of $12.7 million. The benefactors: animal shelters and rescues all across the United States.

The U.S.A.'s first metal detector was made in 1881 by Alexander Graham Bell to find a bullet lodged in President James A. Garfield's chest.

FORMAT FLOPS

For every successful video delivery method such as DVDs or VHS cassette, there are a lot more that sit on the shelf and gather dust.

VIDEO CD (1993)

DVDs would supplant VHS cassettes as the standard home video distribution method in the late 1990s and early 2000s, but they weren't the first digital disc on the market. In 1993, European electronics giant Philips created the Video CD. As Philips, Sony, and Toshiba all worked together to develop DVDs, Philips marketed the VideoCD to bridge the transition to digital video. About the only place where Video CD performed well was in southeast Asia, where the extreme humidity in the region rapidly left VHS tapes unusable, and the discs were a cheap way for consumers to replace them. Once DVDs—which could hold six times as much data and thus present a much better picture quality—came along, film studios lost interest in putting their movies on Video CDs. It also didn't help the format much that Video CDs could be easily pirated with common computer CD burners.

TELEVISION ELECTRONIC DISC (1975)

In the early days of videotape (used mostly by TV stations and cost prohibitive for everyone but the wealthy) in the early 1970s, Teldec and Telefunken, two West German electronics companies, pooled their resources to come up with another way for consumers to record and play back materials at home: the Television Electronic Disc, a flexible, metallic eight-inch-wide disc. Marketed primarily as a way to record TV programs, the discs worked like records, writing video and audio data onto the disc's grooved surface. (One millimeter contained 130 to 150 grooves; a record has about 12 in the same area.) They recorded on a vertically oriented machine, and an electrified crystal translated the grooves into a video signal as it played at a speed of 1,500 revolutions per minute. The big problem with TED: one disc could hold a maximum of 10 minutes of video footage. Only a few thousand units sold, and Teldec and Telefunken discontinued TED in 1978.

COMPACT LASERDISC (1986)

When compact discs first became available in the mid-1980s, they cost about twice as much as records and cassettes. Pioneer Artists gambled on the idea that people wealthy enough to drop a bunch of cash on a new CD player and CDs would buy an even more luxurious entertainment system: Compact LaserDiscs. A combination of the emerging audio CD with the emerging LaserDisc high-fidelity video format, the 12-inch discs offered very high-quality sound as well as music videos for some of the songs, if available, and if the machine was hooked up to a TV. (For the tracks on which there wasn't any accompanying video, the screen just displayed an image of the album cover.) Pioneer could obtain the rights to release just seven albums in the Compact LaserDisc format, which, at a foot wide, weren't compact at all. They didn't last a year on the market.

SLOTMUSIC (2008)

Apple launched its iTunes Music Store in 2003, and it quickly transformed the way Americans bought music. The ability to download songs and easily transfer them to an Apple iPod or iPhone led to the rapid cratering of music sales on physical media, such as CDs. In 2008, SanDisk, a company that makes removable and portable storage drives, unveiled slotMusic, memory cards that would plug into computers and play the factory loaded music. SanDisk secured the rights to manufacture slotMusic cards featuring musicians from the four major record companies (Universal, Sony BMG, Warner, and EMI), but only 14 albums were ever released on the format. Artists objected to slotMusic's highly touted lack of "digital rights management," meaning the songs on the cards could be infinitely shared and copied to as many computers as the consumer wanted.

SOUND TAPE CARTRIDGE (1958)

The technical trade name for the music format commonly known as the tape is the Compact Cassette, introduced by Philips in 1962. It got its name in part because it was a successor by four years to another, similar, and substantially larger magnetic reel-to-reel system encased in a plastic shell, RCA's Sound Tape Cartridge. It looks almost identical to the Compact Cassette, except that it's four times as large, which made it sort of as portable as its marketing materials promised, and more so than vinyl records, the only widely used format for prerecorded music in the late 1950s. STC decks offered stereo sound and an auto-reverse function, so users didn't have to remove and flip over the tape after one 30-minute side played out. RCA released the cassette at virtually the same time that stereo vinyl records hit the market, which could be played on preexisting sound systems and didn't require a whole new player like the STC tapes did. Those cassettes were also *really* expensive—one Sound Tape Cartridge cost $4.50, four times as much as a record. (Adjusted for inflation, that's more than $40.) RCA kept producing the cartridges for a limited audience until the Compact Cassette overwhelmed it into discontinuation by the mid-1960s.

* * *

"To truly laugh, you must be able to take your pain and play with it!"
—Charlie Chaplin

Liquid mercury is so dense that an anvil will float in it.

LET'S TALK ABOUT URANUS

Oh, so many "Uranus" jokes. Do we really need to keep making fun of Uranus? It's Uranus after all, and it should be celebrated. So settle into your seat as we share all the details of Uranus.

Uranus Is Vast. How vast? Uranus is so vast that 63 Earths could fit inside it. With a circumference of nearly 100,000 miles, the seventh planet from the Sun is the third largest in our solar system; only Saturn and Jupiter are larger.

Uranus Is Far, Far Away. How far? About 1.6 billion miles from Earth at its closest, and nearly 2 billion at its farthest (due to its elliptical orbit). And Earth is "only" 93 million miles from the Sun. To put this in perspective, if the Sun was home plate, and Earth was the pitcher's mound, Uranus would be located over the fence, outside the stadium, in the back of the parking lot.

Uranus Has Had a Long Year. What do Isaac Newton, Benjamin Franklin, Salvador Dali, Pope John Paul II, and Estelle Getty have in common? They all lived for 84 Earth years, the time it takes Uranus—at an average distance of 1.8 billion miles from the Sun—to complete one orbit. The planet's low density makes it rotate faster than Earth—giving it a sidereal day that's only 17 hours long. But because of the planet's 90-degree tilt, the same side of Uranus faces the Sun for half a Uranian year (42 of ours) as it rotates in its orbit. This gives Uranus two seasons: summer and winter. During the summer, the Sun appears to travel in circles. It will remain in the sky until the other side of the planet faces the Sun, bringing on a long, cold, dark winter. It will be 15,340 Earth days until the Sun rises again on Uranus.

Uranus Is Leaking Gas. When NASA's *Voyager 2* spacecraft whizzed past Uranus in 1986, it flew through a plasmoid, a "coherent structure of plasma and magnetic fields" that measured 127,000 miles long. The plasmoid was emanating from the planet's atmosphere and shooting out into space—taking some of Uranus's gases with it. Astronomers didn't even learn about this until the late 2010s while reviewing *Voyager's* data. They have no idea what unseen force is extracting gases from Uranus.

Uranus Is Sideways. And no one knows why. The other seven planets all spin on an equatorial axis parallel to their orbit around the sun. (Earth and Mars have a slight tilt to their axes, however, which is why they have four seasons.) Something happened

The singer Prince, who was 5'2", owned 3,000 pairs of custom-made high-heeled shoes.

to Uranus that makes it rotate at a nearly 90-degree angle to the Sun—so the poles are where the equator would be.

Uranus Has an Odd Magnetic Field. Every planet has a magnetosphere that extends out from its core. On Earth, the magnetic north and south poles line up pretty closely with their geographic counterparts. Not so on Uranus—the magnetic poles are halfway around the planet, and their axis doesn't go through the center. Even weirder, the magnetosphere is stronger than Earth's on some parts of the planet, and weaker in others. One theory as to why: Uranus (along with Neptune) doesn't have a solid core, so its magnetic field emanates from deep within the planet's salty inner oceans. Maybe in the not-too-distant future people will be able to take a vacation to Uranus to watch the most spectacular display of aurora in the solar system.

Uranus Is as Cold as Ice. The eight planets in our solar system consist of four rocks (we're on the third), two gas giants (Saturn and Jupiter), and two ice giants (Uranus and Neptune). Even though Neptune is the farthest from the Sun, Uranus boasts the solar system's lowest temperatures. Why? It's almost nothing but ice. Jupiter, Saturn, and the inner planets have solid inner cores that generate heat. Neptune and Uranus have very small cores, and they consist of hydrogen, helium, and methane—but Neptune has more methane, a greenhouse gas that, despite the planet's greater distance from the Sun, keeps it warmer than the extremes of Uranus—which is ice, ice, ice, almost all the way down to its core. That's why you can't walk on the surface of Uranus: the ice particles aren't very dense. That low temp, by the way, is -371°F.

Uranus Almost Wasn't Called Uranus. In 1781, when British astronomer William Herschel had a gander at Uranus through his telescope, he mistook it for a comet. But when Herschel and other astronomers, including Germany's Johann Elert Bode, deduced that it *was* a planet—the first discovered since antiquity—Herschel wanted to name it Georgium Sidus (literally "George's Planet") after King George III. Bode, first to track the planet's orbit, suggested naming it after the Greek god of the sky, Uranus. That makes Uranus the only planet named after a Greek god rather than a Roman god. (His logic: Saturn was the father of Jupiter, so he chose Uranus, the father of Saturn.) Uranus didn't become the planet's official name until 1850.

Uranus Has a Ring around It. Thirteen rings (discovered so far), but they're so hard to see that no one even knew Uranus had rings until the 1970s. Unlike Saturn's rings—which consist of large, school-bus sized rocks surrounded by trillions of pebble-sized rocks—most of Uranus's rings are lacking the tiny rocks. Ranging from golf-ball-sized stones to large boulders, the rings' icy rocks are the shade of charcoal, so they reflect hardly any light. Just as the leaking gas is a mystery, astronomers don't know what swept away all the dust from the rings of Uranus.

NFL field goal kickers' success rate in 1970: 59 percent. In 2020: 85 percent.

Uranus Has 27 Moons. At least 27—there may be more waiting to be discovered. Oberon and Titania (named after Shakespeare characters), then Ariel and Umbriel (named for characters in the Alexander Pope narrative poem "The Rape of the Lock"), were the first four to be discovered. The remaining moons are all named after more Shakespeare characters. The largest, Titania, is nearly 1,000 miles in diameter—about half that of our Moon—whereas the smallest, Cupid, is only 11 miles wide. The moons are mostly dark-colored, like the rings. And they're made of a combination of rock and ice (except Miranda, which is mostly ice).

Uranus Has the Blues. The two ice giants are different shades of blue—cyan for Uranus, and azure for Neptune. Both get their hues from the methane in the upper atmosphere, which absorbs the red light from the Sun and reflects the blue lights. Astronomers aren't sure why Uranus is slightly lighter—most likely because there's more atmospheric haze.

Uranus Requires Deeper Study. Admit it: before you read this article, you probably hadn't thought about Uranus that much. Except for its accidentally vulgar name, this pale, blue dot isn't steeped in lore like the other planets. And with no real surface and an unwelcoming methane sky, Uranus hasn't been high on the "we've got to go there" list. But that started to change in the 2020s thanks to new discoveries by powerful telescopes that can detect exoplanets (planets in other solar systems). Lo and behold, ice giants are by far the most common type of planet in our galaxy. "There is obviously something important about planets like Uranus and Neptune," said British astronomer Leigh Fletcher in 2022. "And crucially we have two great examples of them, the galaxy's most common planets, right here in our solar system. Yet their composition, their nature, and their origins remain a relative mystery. It is time to put that right."

Ur Saying It Wrong. It's not "Your Anus," Beavis. When astronomers pronounce the planet (probably to keep from chuckling), they put the emphasis on the first syllable and shorten the A sound: "YUR-unus."

*　*　*

Fry: Oh, man, this is great! Hey, as long as you don't make me smell Uranus.

Leela: I don't get it.

Farnsworth: I'm sorry, Fry, but astronomers renamed Uranus in 2620 to end that stupid joke once and for all.

Fry: Oh. What's it called now?

Farnsworth: Urectum.

—*Futurama*

Un-real estate: one in six homes for sale in the U.S. is purchased by an investor.

MODERN MYTHOLOGY

In ancient Greece, they had heroes like Hercules and Pegasus. Today we have new "heroes," like the San Diego Chicken and the GEICO Gecko.

KEEBLER ELVES

German immigrant Godfrey Keebler opened a bakery in Philadelphia in 1853 and formed a network with other bakeries in Pennsylvania and elsewhere; by 1927, it had grown so large that those hundreds of companies merged into the United Biscuit Company of America. After operating multiple major regional bakeries, the company went back to using Keebler in 1966 as an umbrella label for everything; in order to quickly establish a national brand identity, they hired the Leo Burnett Worldwide ad agency to develop a character campaign. Creative director Bob Noel struck on the idea of elves who live in a hollowed-out tree and use magic to bake the many Keebler cookies, crackers, and chips, led by head elf J. J. Keebler. (That character would later be renamed Ernie, and animator Sig Bogowitz, who devised the initial image of the elves, drew him to look like Noel.) In 1968, the Keebler Elves made their debut, not in TV commercials but in a classroom film called *Show and Sell*. Claiming the film was a look at the animation process and how ads are made, Leo Burnett Worldwide shipped it to schools specifically to get kids interested in the Keebler Elves. The characters' commercials debuted in 1969 and have run for more than 50 years, with the character base expanding to include wrapper Fast Eddie, peanut-butter specialist Sam, fudge supervisor Zack, accountant Flo, artist Leonardo, and dough-master Elwood.

JOVNY THE VLASIC STORK

Since the mid-1970s, the Vlasic jarred pickle company has advertised its products with animated TV commercials featuring a laid-back stork who speaks in a thinly veiled Groucho Marx impression, emphasizing his points by gesturing with a pickle he holds in his "hand" the way Marx used a cigar. What's the connection between storks and pickles? Pregnancy. When Vlasic launched the campaign in 1974, the birth rate in the United States was on a steep decline for the first time in decades, and it was a big news story that alarmed plenty of Americans. Using the old bit of folklore that storks deliver newborns, Vlasic positioned Jovny as an underemployed baby-delivery bird — there were so few babies being born that he had to find a job delivering pickles, which are also associated with pregnancy because they're understood to be a common craving for expectant mothers. "I deliver pickles since babies are in such short supply!" Jovny says in one commercial.

Twenty-five percent of shoplifters are kids.

THE NOID

A pizza-craving, pint-sized, nonsense-spewing crazed gremlin in the vein of the McDonald's hamburger-stealing Hamburglar, Domino's 1980s advertising character the Noid was conceived by advertising agency Group 243 and executed by Will Vinton Studios, just after the Claymation-pioneering studio created the commercial-mascots-turned-pop-culture-phenomenon the California Raisins. As they began to battle with rival Pizza Hut for pizza-delivery market share, Domino's took the angle of speed, guaranteeing delivery to customers in 30 minutes or less. The Noid was part of that campaign, with ads claiming that the red-spandex-unitard-clad mini-monster, who frantically grabs at his bunny-like ears, is always lurking in the vicinity of the chain's restaurants and delivery vehicles. Customers were warned to be on alert and "avoid the Noid," lest he speedily steal that delicious hot pizza. Despite being a villain, the Noid was a cultural hit; Noid T-shirts and toys flew off of shelves, he starred in two video games (*Avoid the Noid* for the Commodore 64 and *Yo! Noid* for the Nintendo Entertainment System), and he appears in Michael Jackson's experimental 1988 film *Moonwalker* in a segment produced by Will Vinton Studios. In 1989, Domino's abruptly retired the character after an ugly real-life incident: a man named Kenneth Noid, who was diagnosed with paranoid schizophrenia, became convinced that the character was a personal attack on him, and he held two employees hostage at a Domino's outlet in Georgia. The resulting bad press meant the end of the Noid.

MAYHEM

In 2003, Allstate began airing commercials featuring 24 actor Dennis Haysbert delivering stern warnings about the need for insurance protection. But with cut-rate providers such as GEICO and Progressive infringing on its business with humorous and memorable commercials (starring the GEICO Gecko and retro saleslady Flo, respectively), Allstate added the darkly comic Mayhem ads in 2010. Actor Dean Winters portrays "Mayhem," the human embodiment of chaos who gleefully causes trouble for drivers by unleashing bad weather, a distracting puppy, and roadside hazards. Winters usually gets beaten, battered, bloodied, and bruised, a warning to viewers to get themselves insured. Created by the Leon Burnett Worldwide advertising agency, the character tested well with young viewers, but ad writers looked to older commercials for inspiration. Mayhem is the latest in a line of ad bad guys who cause trouble until they're eradicated by the advertised product, like Crest's Cavity Creeps. Winters took his inspiration for how he plays the character—a taciturn, mischievous tough guy—from Harvey Keitel's portrayal of Mr. White in the 1992 crime thriller *Reservoir Dogs*.

Tiniest book in the world: Canadian artist Robert Chaplin's *Teeny Ted from Turnip Town* (2007) is 0.07 mm x 0.10 mm.

THE PREHISTORIC SISTINE CHAPEL

From our "Accidental Archaeologists" files, here's the remarkable tale of France's Lascaux Cave, home of the world's best-preserved Paleolithic wall art. (At least, it used to be.)

DOWN THE RABBIT HOLE

The modern story of Lascaux cave began sometime in the late 1930s, when a tree fell in a French forest. The uprooted trunk opened a small hole in the ground that led to a system of tunnels and caverns that had previously been hidden from human eyes for untold thousands of years.

In September 1940, an 18-year-old mechanic's apprentice named Marcel Ravidat was exploring those woods—which overlook the village of Montignac in the Dordogne region of southwestern France—when his dog Robot chased a rabbit into that very same hole. (Or it might have been a fox. The accounts vary.) It was only after Marcel and three of his friends—Jacques Marsal, Georges Agniel, and Simon Coencas—returned to that spot four days later that the details come into focus.

The teenagers were hoping to find a buried treasure, or maybe even the secret tunnel to the area's famed Lascaux Chateau they'd heard about through local legend. After using a knife to widen the small opening, Marcel shimmied in first and slid down a pile of scree to the rocky floor. A kerosene lamp lit his way as he ventured down a tunnel, his younger friends following close behind. After about 50 feet, the tunnel opened up into a cavern. Marcel raised the lamp. The walls were covered with paintings of animals: there was a bear, several bulls, and some horses—including a headless stallion and, for lack of a better description, a unicorn. These "action shots" could have been painted yesterday: they had bold outlines, lifelike shading, and rich hues ranging from deep, dark browns to bright reds and yellows. And the flickering light of the oil lamp made it seem as if the animals were in motion. As Coencas later recalled, "It was like a dream."

BACK TO REALITY

The teenagers' discovery occurred less than a year after World War II began ravaging Europe. Only three months earlier, Germany had invaded France and turned it into a near police state. Two days after the discovery, 13-year-old Coencas and his Jewish family fled to Paris, hoping to be hidden by relatives. Coencas avoided deportation to a concentration camp, but his parents didn't. He spent the rest of the war hiding in an attic and didn't reunite with his Lascaux codiscoverers for 46 years.

On Twitter, KFC follows 11 people: six men named Herb and the five members of the Spice Girls. (Get it? They're "11 herbs and spices.")

Agniel, 16, was only visiting Montignac at the time and had to go back to Paris, leaving the care of the cave with Ravidet and Marsal (the youngest at 14). The boys kept their find a secret at first, but then they started charging their friends to see it. The first adult to go in was one of Marsal's former teachers, Léon Laval, who initially thought the teens were pranking him because of his affinity for prehistoric artwork (he was a bit nervous that they were going to trap him in the cave). But once Laval saw the paintings, the mood turned serious. He instructed the boys not to allow anyone else in the cave. The teacher was mostly worried about vandalism, but an even greater threat had already started to creep in.

THE GUARDIANS OF LASCAUX

Marsal's parents gave him permission to pitch a tent at the cave's entrance. He stayed there, day and night, for a week. Meanwhile, Laval had sent word of the discovery to the esteemed French archaeologist Henri Breuil, a Catholic priest who was hiding from the Nazis not too far away in France. Father Breuil made a clandestine trip to Montignac to see the cave animals for himself. "My God," he exclaimed. "This is a prehistoric Sistine Chapel!"

But this chapel would not open to the public anytime soon—the war made sure of that. Ravidat and Marsal spent most of their free time during the following fall and winter guarding the cave entrance; then the landowners installed a door with a lock. Both boys joined the French Resistance, which later stored munitions and supplies inside the cave. It wasn't until 1948, three years after World War II ended, that Lascaux cave finally opened to the public. By this point, Marcel Ravidat and Jacques Marsal were in their 20s, and became tour guides. Marsal never moved away from Montignac; he was known locally as the "Guardian of Lascaux" until his death in 1989.

MARCH OF THE MOUTH BREATHERS

It's unfortunate that Lascaux cave wasn't discovered until the 21st century, now that scientists are finally figuring out how to properly protect such a fragile environment. Back in the 1950s, when Lascaux was operated by the French government, a constant flow of visitors—as many as 1,500 per day—viewed the cave art. The moisture from all the breathing, not to mention the exhaled carbon dioxide, combined with the bright, steady lights, quickly started to fade the bold lines and vivid hues. As early as 1958, Ravidat and Marsal were complaining to the curators about algae growing on the cave walls, but it was another five years—with millions more visitors—before Lascaux was finally closed to the public in 1963. But the damage had been done.

THE TIME MACHINE

What made Lascaux so special? Hundreds of caves have been discovered containing prehistoric animal paintings, but most of the art has faded from water, minerals,

Gallup poll results: Americans rank "nursing" as the profession with the most ethical people.

and light that leaked in over time. Until that tree fell in the 1930s, Lascaux had been sealed in darkness—and a layer of clay in the topsoil kept moisture out—for up to 17,300 years, which is how old these paintings are thought to be. (Archaeologists don't even know where the prehistoric entrance to the cave was.)

The cavern that the four teens discovered—now called the Hall of Bulls—had changed little in all that time. And that area was just the beginning of a sprawling cave system that researchers have since divided into seven sectors, including the Axial Gallery, the Passageway, the Nave, the Chamber of the Felines, the Apse, and the Shaft. All told, there are approximately 600 paintings and 1,500 engravings in Lascaux.

ABOUT THE ARTISTS

They used to be called Cro-Magnon. The term was coined in 1868 after the discovery—made only 15 miles from Lascaux—of five prehistoric skeletons in a shallow cave along a cliff. (*Cro* means "cavity" and *Magnon* was the name of the landowner on whose property the cave was located.) Today, they're also referred to as early modern human (EMH). Like us, these people were *Homo sapiens*, but they were stockier and more robust, with larger teeth and a more prominent brow and jaw line—you know, cavemen. After traveling north out of Africa, these early humans spread throughout Eurasia during the Upper Paleolithic period (50,000–12,000 years ago).

Their art supplies were mainly mineral pigments consisting of ocher (iron oxide), a clay material known for its red and yellow hues. They also used bone marrow, animal fats, blood, urine, lime, and charcoal (for shading). Brushes were made from moss, fur, and hair. And they used small, hollow bones to blow paint onto the walls. This technique was used for the hundreds of stenciled handprints found in Lascaux, made by people of all ages. Many of the paintings are so high above the cave floor that the artists would have needed some type of scaffolding (not unlike Michelangelo when he painted the Sistine Chapel). The walls in some places were too rough to paint on, so the artists used sharp stones to etch pictures into the surface, revealing the colors beneath. When Pablo Picasso viewed Lascaux's artworks in 1948, he reportedly declared, "We have invented nothing."

But there's no archaeological evidence that any humans ever lived in Lascaux, suggesting that the caves were purely ceremonial. Their true purpose remains a mystery, but there are some compelling theories.

STONE AGE GIFS

Most of the illustrations depict game animals—horses, bison, deer, big cats, rhinoceroses, bulls (including one that's more than 16 feet long), and mythical creatures. (Strangely, no woolly mammoths or reindeer.) There is one lone humanoid in Lascaux: a stick figure of a dead hunter lying beneath an aurochs, a now-extinct

That sucks: the first vacuum cleaners were so large that getting them from house to house required a horse-drawn cart.

grazing animal. The hunter has the head of a bird and an erect phallus. Was he a god, a cautionary tale, or graffiti?

While the caves were most likely used for religious ceremonies, they might have also been a subterranean schoolhouse—a safe place where young hunters were taught about game animals. Or the caves might have been akin to going out to the movies. Picture a group of prehistoric people being led from room to room, following a storyteller who's spinning yarns about legendary hunts. Now picture this: the animals on the walls are moving!

"Paleolithic artists," wrote researcher and filmmaker Marc Azéma in 2012, "invented the principle of sequential animation, based on the properties of retinal persistence. This was achieved by showing a series of juxtaposed or superimposed images of the same animal." The element that brought them to life: the flickering light of a fire. Not unlike today's animated GIFs, this made some of the cave animals look like they're running, wagging their tails, or opening their mouths. Adding credence to this theory: more than 100 stone lamps (that most likely burned an oil derived from animal fat) were among the few types of objects found in the cave system.

That's why, in 1940, the cavern appeared so dreamlike to the teens with their flickering oil lamp. Sadly, the cartoonish effect was lost on the millions who toured the cave under harsh, steady light from 1948 to 1963. "At the time," said Azéma, "archaeologists did not consider how the brightness and the location of lights altered how the paintings would have been viewed. In general, archaeologists have paid considerably less attention to how the use of fire for light affected the development of our species, compared to the use of fire for warmth and cooking."

FROM PERIL TO BALANCE

Lascaux has been a UNESCO World Heritage site since 1979. UNESCO (United Nations Educational, Scientific and Cultural Organization) seeks to protect "cultural and natural heritage around the world considered to be of outstanding value to humanity," especially those sites in danger of being lost forever. And Lascaux was most certainly "in peril," said Luiz Oosterbeek, secretary general of the International Union of Prehistoric and Protohistoric Sciences, in 2008. A few years earlier, torrential rains had fallen during a restoration, when the cave was especially vulnerable to moisture. That, in conjunction with an ill-advised new air-conditioning system, caused black lines of a destructive fungus called *Fusarium solani* to spread on the walls. For the next few years, Lascaux was closed to everyone—save for a handful of scientists, wearing hazmat suits, who went in once a week to take measurements.

Oosterbeek admitted in 2009 that it would be "impossible" for the cave "to return to a hypothetical original condition," but in 2020, Lascaux's conservation

Until the 1850s, umbrellas were used only by women.

manager, Muriel Mauriac, reported that the fungus has been eradicated and the environment is once again "in balance." And they intend to keep it that way. "Lascaux has been a victim of its own success," she said. "After the different microbiological crises that it has been through, we can see that it is doing better. It is still fragile, vulnerable, and a very complex ecosystem."

THE NEXT BEST THING

Today, the original site is open to visitors, but the cave art is off limits. Good news: there are replicas. The first one, called Lascaux II, opened in 1983 just a few hundred yards from the cave, and today small groups of visitors can tour with a reservation. Lascaux III was an international traveling exhibit that ran from 2013 to 2020. In 2016, a state-of-the-art facility, Lascaux IV: The International Centre for Cave Art, opened in Montignac, built into the base of a hill. The $70-million project used more than "10,000 tons of concrete and 30 artists to re-create—with accuracy faithful to the millimeter—hundreds of images of cave paintings on artificial walls." Every care has been taken to transport visitors back in time. From the description:

> Inside the cave facsimile, the atmosphere is damp and dark, re-creating the humidity within the caves. Sounds are muffled...This sequence is dedicated to contemplation, allowing people an experience of the sanctuary that once was. Lights flicker just as the animal fat lamps of Paleolithic times did, revealing the layers of paintings and engravings on the surface of the walls.

Another French archaeological site with similarly impressive Paleolithic art, Chauvet Cave, was discovered in 1994. Thanks to the hard lessons learned at Lascaux, it has never been open to the public. And like Lascaux, there's a replica of Chauvet that you can visit.

In September 2020, on the 80th anniversary of the four teenagers' discovery, a three-mile trail opened up from the village to the spot where they first entered Lascaux Cave. Earlier that year, Coencas, the Holocaust survivor, became the last of the discoverers to pass away. "We were hoping to find a treasure," he'd often said. "We found one, but not the one we thought."

*   *   *

"Scientists have just built the world's biggest supercollider
and they're doing experiments to see what makes up protons.
I hope that if the experiment's successful, the whole of our reality will dissolve
and a big sign will come up that says: 'Level Two.'"

—Frankie Boyle

Web MD: ancient Greek physicians used spider silk for bandages.

PIRATE MYTHS

Near everything ye scalawags think ye know
about the pirate life be wrong. Argh!

"WALKING THE PLANK" WAS THE FAVORED METHOD OF PIRATE EXECUTIONS.

There are a handful of documented instances of pirates doing this in the 18th and 19th centuries—forcing vanquished foes to slowly walk out on a board extended out over the ship until they fell in the sea and drowned. But it wasn't their idea. It's written about in *The Canterbury Tales* (1387–1400) and for hundreds of years, European navies used the process as punishment for mutiny. Often, if pirates wanted to kill somebody, they'd either shoot them or just throw them overboard.

PIRATES DRANK NOTHING BUT RUM.

Then as it is now, drinking rum all day isn't a recipe for getting much done. Pirates usually consumed a semimedicinal concoction called *grog*, made of rum diluted with water (or low-alcohol beer, which was cleaner and more portable than regular water) with sugar added for flavor and lime juice added to prevent scurvy.

PIRATE SHIPS WERE GIGANTIC, SAIL-POWERED VESSELS.

That type of ship is called a galleon; pirates usually sailed around in galleys, moderate-sized ships that ran on rows of human-powered oars instead of sails. The advantage of such a ship is that it can be rowed in any direction and can change course quickly—both vital needs of a pirate operation.

PIRATES TALKED LIKE, WELL, PIRATES.

Pirates hailed from all over the world, so they spoke in a variety of languages and dialects. The "pirate voice" with which we're all familiar dates back about 70 years. Actor Robert Newton starred in a bunch of popular pirate movies in the 1950s, including *Treasure Island*, *Long John Silver*, and *Blackbeard the Pirate*. He spoke in a West Country English dialect, made more grizzled with folksy turns of phrase that he and filmmakers invented, such as "scurvy dog" and "argh," and replacing "is" and "are" with "be."

A PARROT WAS A STANDARD PASSENGER ON A PIRATE SHIP.

Because pirates traveled in tropical locations where parrots are native, the occasional pirate ship may have taken a bird on board, but the idea was popularized in Robert Louis Stevenson's 1883 adventure novel *Treasure Island*.

Before anesthesia, surgeons were trained to block out the noise of screaming patients.

THE PIRATE FLAG, A.K.A. THE "JOLLY ROGER," DEPICTED A SKULL AND CROSSBONES.

Ships of all kinds used flags for long-distance communication and identification. Pirate vessels might carry many flags, such as a British flag to trick British naval ships into letting them come close (then board and pillage). On the rare occasion they would display their pirate flag (rare because they didn't want to self-identify as criminals), it might be blank or have any illustration, not necessarily a skull or crossbones. The flag of the notorious Blackbeard came close—it depicted a skeleton with a bleeding heart.

PIRATES STOLE TREASURE—BIG CHESTS OF GOLD, COINS, JEWELS, AND GEMS—AND THEN BURIED IT ON REMOTE ISLANDS.

Extremely rare and valuable money, bullion, and other such items weren't transported via ship on the open sea in the age of high seas piracy. (Pirates went after more practical, easily sellable, or personally usable goods: food, water, alcohol, spices, weapons, clothing, slaves, and ship equipment.) So not only would such treasure be rare, but pirates would've also had no need to bury it in some remote spot where they likely wouldn't even sail again for months or even years.

LIFE AS A PIRATE WAS SO FULL OF VIOLENT COMBAT THAT MANY LOST A HAND OR LEG AND REPLACED THEM WITH A PROSTHETIC—A HOOK FOR A HAND, OR A PEG LEG, FOR EXAMPLE.

In the 17th and 18th centuries, when piracy was at its historical height, antibiotics hadn't yet been discovered, so if a pirate on a very unsanitary ship was unfortunate enough to lose a hand or a leg, it's likely the wound would've quickly become infected, spread, and killed the individual. If someone did survive the loss of a limb and avoided fatal infection, their days as a pirate were over—they wouldn't have been capable of all the hard work it takes to operate a ship without all their appendages intact. The myth of hook hands and peg legs comes from pirate literature; pirates in works such as *Treasure Island* and *Peter Pan* were given false appendages to make them seem more frightening and battle-experienced.

PIRATES LIVED ON THE FRINGES OF SOCIETY BOTH METAPHORICALLY AND LITERALLY—CRIMINALS FOREVER ADRIFT AT SEA, WANTED BY GOVERNMENTS WHOSE LAND THEY HAD TO AVOID.

Many pirates had spouses and families that they'd visit in between voyages, much like sailors working for a legitimate navy. Larger pirate organizations had communication networks in place, anchored by boats that would deliver mail from home and pass along dispatches from the sea. Those same boats would also hustle away sick or retiring pirates, offering safe passage to their final destinations.

Oprah Winfrey's mansion includes an Oprah Winfrey–shaped bathtub that fits two people.

FINAL ACTS

*Pop culture phenomena come and go. Tastes change, and so do the times.
And thus, what once was hot and dominant eventually fades away.
Here are some last gasps from some once-major entertainment forces.*

The Last Sherlock Holmes Case. Sir Arthur Conan Doyle wrote 56 short stories featuring the genius detective work of Sherlock Holmes (and his assistant, Dr. John Watson). Doyle retired from writing about the character in 1927 with *The Case-Book of Sherlock Holmes*, a collection of 12 stories that had appeared in magazines earlier in the decade. The very last written, and published, Sherlock story: "The Adventure of Shoscombe Old Place," which found the detective investigating a case set in the world of horse racing.

The Last Ice Capades show. The most famous of the traveling arena-ice-skating spectaculars, Ice Capades was a popular attraction from the 1940s until the early 1990s, when Olympic figure skater Dorothy Hamill took over in an attempt to save it. By then what was known as Dorothy Hamill's Ice Capades sent out one last show, called *The Magic of* MGM, a tribute (on ice!) to old MGM movie musicals. It was the last show before the Ice Capades shut down.

The Last *American Bandstand* Performance. After 37 years, Dick Clark stepped down from hosting the nationally syndicated musical showcase in 1988. About a year later, the show moved to the USA cable network, with comedian David Hirsch hosting. The new incarnation of *Bandstand* lasted six months, airing its final episode on October 7, 1989, which featured dance-pop group the Cover Girls performing "We Can't Go Wrong" and "My Heart Skips a Beat."

The Last *Soul Train*. The premier weekly program featuring soul, R&B, funk, and hip-hop acts, Don Cornelius's *Soul Train* aired new episodes regularly from 1971 until 2006. After the March 25, 2006, episode, *Soul Train* adopted a "best of" format of old footage. That last new installment, number 1,117, featured performances by the singers Lorenzo Owens and Goapele.

The Last Shows on The WB and UPN. In September 2006, fledgling broadcast networks The WB and UPN merged to become The CW. The WB's final night of programming consisted of the very first episodes of the network's biggest hits: *Felicity*, *Angel*, *Buffy the Vampire Slayer*, and, finally, *Dawson's Creek*. On the same night at the same time, UPN aired the pro-wrestling show WWE *SmackDown!*

Ellie Kemper's high school drama teacher: a pre-fame John Hamm.

The Last Saturday Morning Cartoon. By 2014, The CW was the only broadcast network still airing cartoons on Saturday mornings, in the form of "Vortexx," a block of Japanese-produced action cartoons. In September 2014, the network announced plans to get rid of the cartoons in favor of government-mandated educational programming. On September 27, 2014, cartoons aired on a network on Saturday morning for the last time, with the last show being a series called *Yu-Gi-Oh! ZEXAL.*

The Last Primetime Variety Show. In the 1960s and 1970s, primetime TV was loaded with glitzy, cheesy music variety shows, which offered some singing, some host banter, some comedy sketches, and some more singing. The format petered out in the early 1980s when *Barbara Mandrell & the Mandrell Sisters* was canceled in 1982.

The Last Movie Serial. Before television made serialized screen entertainment a regular, if mundane, occurrence, movie theaters included episodes of ongoing sagas—most of them Westerns or science-fiction—in their programming, particularly during weekend matinees aimed at kids. Commonplace in the 1940s and 1950s, the very last serial was the 15-part Western *Blazing the Overland Trail.* It was the 57th and final movie serial made by industry leader Columbia Pictures.

The Last Warner Bros. Cartoon. Movie package deals, both for kids and adults, might include a few cartoons. Warner Bros. had two concurrent series, *Merrie Melodies* and *Looney Tunes*, that ran in movie theaters from 1931 up until 1969. By that time, television had proved an ideal outlet for the cartoons featuring the likes of Bugs Bunny and Daffy Duck. The last of the movie-theater kind was the *Merrie Melodies* short "Injun Trouble," released to theaters on September 20, 1969. (Due to some suggestive content and ugly stereotyping of Native Americans, not to mention the slur in the title, it's never been shown on TV or released on video.)

The Last Movie with a Built-In Intermission. An intermission of 10 to 15 minutes added into the actual print of a movie was common in the golden age of cinema in the mid-20th century, when epics such as *Gone with the Wind* and *The Ten Commandments* wore on for three or four hours or more, and the audience needed a chance to stretch their legs and use the restroom. As films got shorter over the decades, the intermission necessarily disappeared, too. The final time an intermission was officially employed in a Hollywood film was in the 2003 Civil War epic *Gods and Generals,* to break up the four-hour running time.

The Last X-Rated Movie. The Motion Picture Association of America rates movies according to audience appropriateness, doling out a G, PG, PG-13, or R rating. They also used an X rating, designated for films appropriate only for adults. Used

Long before Meghan Markle married Prince Harry, the struggling actress was a calligrapher; she did the invitations for Robin Thicke and Paula Patton's wedding.

occasionally for artsy and edgy movies (such as the 1969 Oscar-winning *Midnight Cowboy*), it was co-opted by the adult film industry in the 1970s and 1980s. In 1990, the MPAA ditched the X in favor of the more legitimate-sounding NC-17, for "no children under 17" admitted. The final movie to receive the X rating was Spanish director Pedro Almodóvar's provocative (but not pornographic) 1989 movie *Tie Me Up! Tie Me Down!*

The Last Black-and-White TV Series. The broadcast networks went full color at the start of the 1966–1967 season, but PBS precursor National Educational Television would take a little longer to make the switch. The first season of *Mister Rogers' Neighborhood* in 1968 was the last black-and-white program.

The Last Inaccurately Tallied Chart-Topping Album. Ever since its May 25, 1991, issue, *Billboard* magazine has used a digital point-of-purchase system called SoundScan to compile its various album and singles charts. SoundScan provides an accurate count of the music people are actually buying. In the decades before that, *Billboard* editors used a fairy imprecise and easily fudged system: they would simply call record stores around the country and ask what they thought was selling. The first SoundScan-generated #1 album in the U.S.: Michael Bolton's *Time, Love, & Tenderness*. The last chart topper in the pre-SoundScan era: R.E.M.'s *Out of Time*.

The Last Dr. Seuss Book. Over a publishing career that spanned six decades, Theodor Seuss Geisel, a.k.a. Dr. Seuss, wrote and illustrated many classic children's books, including *The Cat in the Hat*, *Green Eggs and Ham*, and *How the Grinch Stole Christmas*. His 51st title was published in 1990, just before his death; it's one geared not toward kids but young adults, and has subsequently become a perennial best-seller and popular graduation gift: *Oh, the Places You'll Go!*

The Last Catskills Resort. Each summer in the mid-20th century, thousands of people in the Northeast—predominantly Jewish American families from New York City—would decamp to the Catskill Mountains and spent a week (or six) at one of the many all-inclusive resort hotels collectively referred to as the "Borscht Belt." Meals and lodging were provided, as were activities such as swimming, recreational classes, and nightclub-style entertainment in the evening from major musical acts and comedians. By the 2010s, only one Catskills resort remained: Kutsher's Hotel and Country Club. After a woman fell off a roof and died on the premises in 2013, the whole thing shut down, and the property was sold off and mostly demolished in 2014.

Now for some Hawkeyeliner: Jeremy Renner got his start in Hollywood as a makeup artist.

ANOTHER PROVINCE, EH?

Canada consists of 10 provinces (which are sort of like states) and three territories. If activist groups, separatist movements, and lawmakers had all gotten their way, there'd be a whole lot more than 10.

BUFFALO

The North-Western Territory was once an extremely vast area of British-controlled land in North America. Comprising more than 1.3 million square miles, it was incorporated into Canada in 1870 and eventually split into three modern territories (which still aren't provinces): Northwest Territories, Yukon, and Nunavut. In 1904, the North-Western Territory included the moderately sized cities of Edmonton, Calgary, Saskatoon, and Regina. That year, North-West Territories premier Sir Frederick Haultain proposed breaking off the southernmost regions of the area to form a new, well-populated, and economically powerful province called Buffalo. The plan didn't get much support; leaders in Calgary, Edmonton, and Regina squabbled about which city would get to be the capital of the new province, and in 1905 Canadian Prime Minister Wilfrid Laurier rejected Haultain's proposal. Concerned that the Conservative Party would control one new large province (Laurier was from the Liberal Party), he instead saw to the creation of *two* new provinces made out of the same land that would've comprised Buffalo: Alberta and Saskatchewan.

ATLANTIC UNION

Canada's three easternmost provinces—Nova Scotia, Prince Edward Island, and New Brunswick—are also known as the "maritimes" because of their sea-centric geographic features and fishing-based economies. They're also among the least populated areas in all of Canada, and thus aren't allowed many representatives (or much power) in the national parliament. As early as 1863, the ruling U.K. government considered unifying the three colonies into one, but the plan fell apart. Politicians floated the idea again throughout the 20th and 21st century—most recently in 2012, when three senators, one from each of the provinces in question, unsuccessfully introduced legislation to formally create a new province called the Atlantic Union, what would have been Canada's fifth-largest province by population.

MONTREAL

Canada is officially a bilingual nation, but around 90 percent of its French speakers live in Quebec. In 1995, Quebecois (residents of Quebec) rejected a referendum to secede from Canada entirely, upsetting English speakers in the province. In Quebec's largest city, Montreal, English and English-language culture is dominant, and so

If you're like most people, your right nostril is your dominant daytime smeller; the left takes over at night.

when Quebec separatists planned to get out of Canada, an anglophone movement developed to create the Province of Montreal. Had the Quebec separation vote passed, the city and its surrounding metropolitan area would have remained a part of Canada, and become a new province.

POINT ROBERTS

Point Roberts is a political anomaly. A peninsula, surrounded on three sides by water, it's part of the state of Washington (and, thus, also part of the United States) but connects to land only at the city of Delta, British Columbia—Canadian territory. To get to anywhere else in Washington (and, thus, anywhere else in the U.S.) by car, Port Roberts residents have to make their way through a border crossing into Canada, and then another crossing back into the United States. In 1949, Point Roberts leaders and residents got so tired of this arrangement that they discussed eliminating all the trouble and just joining Canada, either as an extension of British Columbia or as their own province. With a population of just over 1,000, it would've easily been the least populous province in the Canadian Confederation. Point Roberts never did leave the U.S., although city leaders raised the idea again in 2020 after the closure of the Canadian border during the COVID-19 pandemic essentially imprisoned residents on the peninsula.

ICELAND

When a 2013 financial and banking crisis nearly destroyed the national economy of Iceland, a group of the country's citizens looked across the Atlantic Ocean for a bailout. They started a political campaign called "Invite Iceland In," urging the Canadian government to admit Iceland as a province. That campaign failed (neither Canadian leaders nor the Icelandic populace gave it much serious thought), so the Invite Iceland In leaders instead urged the Icelandic government to abolish the Icelandic krona and adopt the Canadian dollar as its currency. Prime Minister Jóhanna Sigurðardóttir publicly commented favorably on the idea, but it never took hold.

BERMUDA

Canada and Bermuda enjoy a few historical and cultural connections. Both are independent nations that are part of the Commonwealth of Nations, an alliance of former British overseas territories, and four of the largest Methodist church congregations in Bermuda are members of the United Church of Canada. The Salvation Army territory that covers maritime Canada also includes Bermuda. In 1949, Bermuda's Trade Development Board president Henry Vassey petitioned the island's House Assembly to establish an official political alliance with Canada with an eye toward becoming the larger country's eleventh province. The parliament said no.

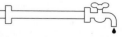

BLOCKED AND MANGLED

Imbibing alcohol is a big part of the social culture in Northern Ireland. Part of the United Kingdom politically, but sharing the island of Ireland with the Republic of Ireland, Northern Ireland is its own unique place, with its own unique drinking slang seldom heard anywhere else. Here are all the terms that mean "drunk" in Northern Ireland.

- Steaming
- Stocious
- Four sheets to the wind
- Pished
- Ballicksed
- Blocked
- Mangled
- Polaxed
- Wrote off
- Paralytic
- Ballbagged
- Steamboated
- Wrote
- Slaughtered
- Lamped
- Heads in the shed
- Rubbered to the cupboard
- Toastered
- Goosed
- Rodgered
- Stoven
- Blitzed
- Mingin'
- Half cut
- Cut
- Trimmed
- Clean rote

- Juiced
- Canned
- Jarred
- Trolleyed
- Bin bagged
- Steamin' Willy Beaming
- Stonkied
- Racked up
- Pie-eyed
- Swallied
- Full as the Boyne
- Souped
- As full as a fireman's water boot
- Well-oiled
- Monkeyed
- Pastie-bapped
- Wingdinged
- Panelled
- Like a Thunderbird with half his strings
- Polluted
- Spannered
- Banjoed
- Ga'gad
- Seized
- Tombstoned

- Doomed
- Welded
- Full as a shuck
- Buckled
- Gassed
- Legless
- Full as a bingo bus
- Langered
- Locked
- Bladdered
- Bevvied
- Blootered
- Muntered
- Scootered
- Banjaxed
- Snookered
- Airlocked
- Squiffy
- Stinkered
- Numptied
- Wanked
- Bluttered
- Cabbaged
- Snattered
- Leaning over the railings
- Splootered
- Oranged

The only movie Gwyneth Paltrow acted in that she says she can watch:
The Royal Tenenbaums.

IF THE QUOTE FITS...

Do these quotations about footwear have a lot of "sole" in them? Shoe enough, they do.

"Shoes are the first adult machines we are given to master."
—Nicholson Baker

"If your hair is done properly and you're wearing good shoes, you can get away with anything."
—Iris Apfel

"To wear dreams on one's feet is to begin to give a reality to one's dreams."
—Roger Vivier

"Be comfortable in your skin, and more importantly, be comfortable in your shoes."
—Octavia Spencer

"It's better to buy one good pair of shoes than four cheap ones."
—Cary Grant

"I like Cinderella, I really do. She has a good work ethic. And she likes shoes. The fairy tale is all about the shoe at the end."
—Amy Adams

"High heels can always put you in a good mood. The more depressed you are, the higher the heels you should wear."
—Anna Dello Russo

"I firmly believe that with the right footwear one can rule the world."
—Bette Midler

"When the feet are comfortable, so is the mind, body, and soul."
—Donald Pliner

"A woman with good shoes is never ugly."
—Coco Chanel

"When a shoe is freaking fabulous, it may be worth a subsequent day of misery. Soak in Epsom salts and take comfort in the fact that you're better than everyone else."
—Clinton Kelly

"The average woman falls in love seven times a year. Only six are with shoes."
—Kenneth Cole

"Shoes are the quickest way for women to achieve instant metamorphosis."
—Manolo Blahnik

"Life is short, your heels shouldn't be."
—Brian Atwood

"You are either in your bed or in your shoes, so it pays to invest in both."
—John Wildsmith

"The shoes always tell the story."
—Ruta Sepetys

"Sometimes that's all you get out of life. Great shoes."
—Pepper Phillips

Population of the United States when it was founded in 1787: 4 million.

MORE WORD ORIGINS

*Ever wonder where certain words come from? Here are the
interesting stories behind some of them.*

BOGUS

Meaning: Fake, unacceptable

Origin: "When *bogus* first laid claim to some English ground, it was a noun;
specifically, a machine for counterfeiting coins. This type of machine was also called
a *bogus press*. The noun version of the word *bogus* also eventually referred to any
counterfeit coin. However, by the mid-eighteenth century, the connotations of the
bogus machine gave birth to *bogus*, the adjective." (From *The Complete Idiot's Guide to
Weird Word Origins*, by Paul McFedries)

SCRATCH

Meaning: The launch point, as in to "start from scratch" or "bake from scratch"

Origin: "To begin any enterprise, investigation, search, or other activity from the
very beginning, often with no precedent as a guide; to begin at the beginning; to take
the first step. Actually the expression is derived from the sporting world, from a race
in which *scratch* designates the line or mark [drawn on the ground] that is to be the
starting point. Hence, he who starts from scratch starts from nothing." (From *2107
Curious Word Origins, Sayings & Expressions from White Elephants to Song & Dance*, by
Charles Earle Funk)

LUNCH

Meaning: A midday meal

Origin: "*Lunch* was originally a variant of *lump*, referring to a lump or chunk of bread.
The first use of lunch is as a translation of Spanish *lonja*, a noon meal—which may
therefore be the source. Certainly the form if not the meaning of luncheon (as it
changed from a large lump of bread to a meal) is influenced by *nuncheon*, the much
earlier word for noon meal." (From *Dictionary of Word Origins*, by Joseph T. Shipley)

NIMROD

Meaning: A wildly unintelligent person

Origin: "Playground bullies might still call somebody a 'nimrod.' Anyway, Nimrod is
an actual name. He was the great-grandson of Noah and the man responsible for the

Tower of Babel, which, according to the Bible, created the world's diverse languages. By the fifteenth century, *nimrod* became a generic term for tyrant. In the twentieth century, thanks to Bugs Bunny, nimrod has come to mean idiot. On occasion, he would call his arch-nemesis, Elmer Fudd, a nimrod." (From *The Terrible Meanings of Names*, by Justin Cord Hayes)

HIPPOPOTAMUS

Meaning: A large animal found in rivers in Africa

Origin: "Etymologically, a hippopotamus is a 'river horse.' The word comes, via Latin, from late Greek *hippopotamos*, a lexicalization of an earlier phrase, 'hippos ho potamios,' literally 'horse of the river.' Other English descendants of *hippos* (a relative of Latin *equus*, 'horse') include *hippodrome*, from a Greek compound that meant originally 'horse-race' and the name Philip, literally 'lover of horses.'" (From *Word Origins*, by John Ayto)

JEOPARDY

Meaning: Serious trouble

Origin: "The early spelling of jeopardy was *iuparti*. The word comes from Old French *ieu* (modern *jeu*) *parti*, an evenly divided game, and was originally used in chess and similar games to mean a problem or position in which the chances of winning or losing were evenly balanced. This led to the modern sense 'a dangerous situation' and the legal use 'danger arising from being on trial for a criminal offense.'" (From *The Oxford Dictionary of Word Origins*)

NOSTALGIA

Meaning: Bittersweet recollections of "the good old days"

Origin: "Nostalgia is remembering a happy moment, a person, or a place from your past. You might even feel a little bit sad that you can't experience it again. It was originally translated into modern Latin from the German *heimweh*, or 'homesickness.' The translation was formed of the Greek *nostos*, meaning 'homecoming,' and *algos*, meaning 'pain or grief.'" (From *Once Upon a Word*, by Jess Zafarris)

DRUTHERS

Meaning: One's preferred state of a situation, or how events would unfold

Origin: "Druthers, probably a contraction of either 'would rather' or 'had rather,' very likely from a Southern pronunciation of the phrase, means 'preferences, wishes'; it is informal and conversational." (From *The Columbia Guide to Standard American English*, by Kenneth G. Wilson)

Established in India in 250 BC, the first known nursing school did not allow women to attend.

QUIZ

Meaning: A short exam, or to issue a short exam

Origin: "It is said that this word came into use in the 1780s when Mr. Daly, a Dublin theater manager, had a bet that he could introduce a new word into the language within 24 hours. Somehow he came up with this word and had it chalked all over Dublin. *The Oxford English Dictionary* dates the word at 1782 with the now rare meaning 'an odd or eccentric person,' but it is not far from the Latin interrogative pronoun *quis* ('who?' or 'what?') and also resembles the second syllable of the word 'inquisitive' (from the Latin *inquisitere*, to acquire) which was current by the 16th century." (From *Cassell's Dictionary of Word and Phrase Origins*, by Nigel Rees)

PERSON

Meaning: A human being

Origin: "In Greek and Roman theater, actors played more than one role during a performance simply by donning a *persona* ("mask") to change character. Eventually, *persona* came to mean the role an individual assumes in life and, later, the individual himself." (From *So That's What It Means!* by Richard Lederer)

UMPTEEN

Meaning: An absurdly high and indistinct number

Origin: "'I'll go to bed and I'll not get up for umpty-eleven months.' You know the feeling. The speaker here is war-weary Bill, a character in Patrick MacGill's early 20th-century novel *The Great Push*. His 'umpty' originated as military slang around 1905 and stood for an indefinite number, generally largish. (It was probably created by analogy to actual numbers such as 'twenty.') Soon, there followed 'umpteen,' blending 'umpty' and '-teen.'" (From *The Merriam-Webster Dictionary*)

HITCHHIKE

Meaning: Soliciting free rides to a destination

Origin: "The expression is thought to have originated in America in the 19th century to describe how two men could travel with only one horse. One man rode ahead an allotted distance, then hitched the horse to a tree and continued on foot. When the second reached the horse at the end of his *hike*, he rode it until he overtook his companion, and so the sequence went on." (From *Word Origins*, by Dhirendra Verma)

* * *

"Normal is an illusion. What is normal for the spider is chaos for the fly."

—Charles Addams

The tetrapod (four-legged vertebrate) with the shortest lifespan:
Labord's chameleon, which lives four to five months...

BEE PLUS

The workers and droners of the Bathroom Readers' Institute hive mind were buzzing around all day to bring you these facts about bees and honey.

🐝 Everybody knows that bees make honey, but how? They pollinate flowers, attracted by the plants' nectar. The bees take that nectar, bring it back to their colony (or hive), and save it in hexagonal honey cells. Then they dry out that nectar by running their wings over it, which creates a warm wind. When it's dry, they seal it up with a fine layer of beeswax, which their bodies naturally create and excrete from a gland.

🐝 That wing flapping is actually what makes the bees' signature "buzz" sound. Those wings can move back and forth about 11,000 times per second.

🐝 Bees make honey to feed the members of their community, particularly the young. But they make too much, and that's what humans collect (if they do it correctly).

🐝 An eight-ounce jar of honey is the collective result of the work of a *lot* of bees: it takes about a million visits to flowers for the nectar to fill that jar.

🐝 Bees pollinate 50 different cash crops in the U.S., directly responsible for about $20 billion of the economy. And $2.5 billion of that alone comes from bees pollinating almond plants in California.

🐝 That must have been a painful, noisy boat ride: bees aren't native to North America but were brought over by European settlers in the early 1600s.

🐝 There are three main types of bees: the queen, drones, and workers. There's only one queen in a hive, and it's her job to mate with drones to create new bees. The worker bees may be delegated to different tasks. While the job of most is to create honey, there's a subtype called scout bees, who go out and find new places for a bee colony to build a new hive (which it needs if the colony feels it's getting overcrowded in its present location). In 2012, scientists discovered the first soldier bees in a colony of Jatai bees in Brazil—bigger and heavier than the other workers, they guard the entrance to the hive. About 1 percent of drone and worker bees may change jobs, segueing into the removal of dead bees from the hive.

🐝 Bees alert their colony to danger by releasing a powerful, odiferous pheromone. It smells exactly like bananas, which is why high-volume beekeepers try not to eat those.

🐝 The rarest and most naturally pure honey on the planet is Pitcairn honey. It's found only on the remote, volcanic Pitcairn Island in the South Pacific Ocean, the lowest-populated occupied place on Earth, with less than 50 residents. (It was settled by mutinous British sailors in the late 19th century.) Because Pitcairn Island is so small and so sparsely populated, there's almost no pollution, leading to nearly completely pure honey made by the area's bees out of several different species of native wildflower.

Honeydew honey isn't honey made by bees pollinating honeydew melon plants. Ants, aphids, and mealybugs may feed on the soft parts of flowers and plants, but, unable to digest the naturally sweet substances inherent in them, they barf it up, right there near where they fed. Bees then swoop in, collect it, take it back to the hive, and use it to make honeydew honey; it's the sweetest honey in existence, made of 90 percent sugar and comprised of 27 different types of sugar.

Heather honey is the honey that's the hardest to get. It's made by bees that visit the vast swaths of heather that's native to Scotland—but the plant blooms for just a couple of weeks each year, and those weeks fall when the honeybees have just about completely gone dormant for the winter. The perfect conditions for creating and harvesting heather honey are an overlap between plant and bee readiness that lasts a mere two or three days.

Himalayan bees, native to China and Nepal, are the world's largest bees (average length: 1.1 inches). They create a powerful substance known variously as red honey, crazy honey, or mad honey. The bees make it in part with the flowers of a local rhododendron, which contains *grayanotoxin*, a neurotoxin that can causes dizziness and powerful hallucinogenic effects when consumed through honey by humans. (That honey can also lead to nausea, diarrhea, and loss of consciousness.) It's harvested, or rather foraged, from a single hive, the biggest in the world.

Bees can make honey out of anything their bodies can process, which means there's such a thing as vulture bees. Also named carrion bees, they're found in the rain forests of Costa Rica, and, while they can feed on plant nectar, the microbiomes in their stomachs are much more effective at handling the meat of dead animals. The acid-favoring gut bacteria let the bees digest meat and turn it into honey, and give them immunity to the otherwise toxic substances found on rotting or rotten flesh. Vulture bee honey is harmless when consumed by humans, though it's rarely harvested because it's extremely viscous, and thus hard to collect. And those who know say it tastes downright weird—a combination of sweet, smoky, and salty.

The cowpox virus, also called *vaccinia*, gave us the word "vaccine."

FAILED SPORTS LEAGUES

*These big-time sports organizations wanted to be like
the NFL, NBA, WNBA, MLS, MLB, or NHL, but they just couldn't
make it in a highly competitive sports business world.*

AMERICAN BASKETBALL LEAGUE

Abe Saperstein helped popularize basketball in the United States with his
barnstorming Harlem Globetrotters—before they rebranded as a stunt/entertainment
squad, they were an all-star squad who'd play local teams. The Globetrotters were
wildly popular decades before the NBA was formed, and they helped the nascent
league catch on, playing doubleheaders at early NBA events. Saperstein claimed
that he was promised the rights to an NBA expansion franchise in Los Angeles in
the late 1950s, but just in case he didn't get it, he started planning an NBA rival
league in 1959. Saperstein met with potential owners in eight cities to finance teams
and, along with semi-pro team owner Paul Cohen and future New York Yankees
boss George Steinbrenner, cocreated an association called the American Basketball
League. Indeed, the NBA didn't give Saperstein his Los Angeles team—authorizing the
Minneapolis Lakers to move to California instead—and Saperstein sprang into action,
with the ABL starting play in 1961. The League came apart as quickly as it came
together. The Los Angeles Jets, despite NBA legend Bill Sharman as coach, folded
halfway through the season. Cohen and Steinbrenner couldn't use their connections
to amateur basketball leagues to lure any talent. The ABL folded midway through the
1962–1963 season. Its most lasting legacy: it was the first basketball organization to
introduce a three-point shot, adopted by the rest of the basketball world decades later.

WORLD BASKETBALL LEAGUE

By the late 1980s, the NBA was one of North America's most popular and financially
successful sports leagues. A high-end professional league hadn't gone head-to-head
with the NBA since the American Basketball Association folded in 1976, so the time
was right for the International Basketball Association. Founded under that name
in 1987 by basketball Hall of Famer and Boston Celtics legend Bob Cousy, ex-NBA
referee Norm Drucker, and businessman Michael Monus, the organization changed its
name to the World Basketball League just before its first season in 1988. Teams were
largely centered in cities in the U.S. and Canada without NBA teams, and included
the Vancouver Nighthawks, Calgary 88's, Fresno Flames, Las Vegas Silver Streaks, and
Youngstown Pride. The big difference between the NBA and the WBL: player size.
Super-tall athletes were barred from the WBL—it had a height limit of 6'5" (later altered

Honk, honk! Harpo Marx (the "silent" Marx Brother) coined the phrase "in the hot seat."

to 6'7"). With games played in concert halls, auditoriums, and convention centers and broadcast on second-tier cable sports networks in the U.S. and Canada, the handful of permanent WBL teams played one another as well as all-star teams from Italy, the Bahamas, Estonia, Finland, and the U.S.S.R. The WBL couldn't compete with the NBA and lost millions of dollars for each of the four years of its existence, folding in 1992; the remaining Canadian franchises formed the National Basketball League, which fell apart after two years. But what really tanked the WBL was a financial scandal. Cofounder Monus embezzled $10 million from Phar-Mor, his chain of drug stores, in part to finance the league. He served nine years in prison for financial crimes.

GLOBAL HOCKEY LEAGUE

Hockey was one of the most widely played and viewed sports in both North America and Europe by the early 1990s, around the time that the Eastern Bloc of communist nations fell apart and opened large swaths of Europe to the West. Seeking to exploit the wealth of newly available talent, Michael Gobuty (a former owner of the NHL's Winnipeg Jets) and Dennis Murphy (founder of the World Hockey Association, a defunct 1970s NHL competitor) created the Global Hockey League. Gobuty and Murphy were excited and ambitious with their plans, announcing the league in February 1990 and planning to begin play in November of that year, just nine months later. The plan was for the GHL to initially consist of six North American teams, and within a year expand to 10 teams in the U.S. and Canada and another 10 in Europe. The style of play would be different, too: the goals would be moved out from the walls, creating a smaller rink space; games would consist of two 30-minute periods (versus three 20-minute periods in the NHL); and fighting—one of the main reasons many people watched hockey—would be downplayed and eliminated thanks to heavy player fines. Local ownership groups got on board for teams in Hamilton and Saskatoon in Canada, as well as in Albany, Providence, Sacramento, and Los Angeles in the U.S. The Albany and Los Angeles teams quickly folded, and the league couldn't attract top-tier talent away from the NHL, Europe, or even amateur leagues in Canada. While teams in the European cities of Lyon, Prague, Milan, Rotterdam, and Berlin took hold, financial issues were too overwhelming, and in June 1990, Murphy announced that the GHL's debut would come in 1991, not late 1990. And then it never happened at all.

NATIONAL PROFESSIONAL INDOOR BASEBALL LEAGUE

During the first wave of baseball's popularity in the 1880s, people didn't want to stop playing when rain, wind, snow, and other winter weather phenomena prevented outdoor games from taking place. So indoor baseball independently took off in numerous cold northern U.S. cities in the late 1880s. An amateur association was formed, and the Spalding corporation made a special ball for indoor baseball—larger

For every 100 decisions you make, 95 of them come from your subconscious.

and softer, and not able to travel as far as a baseball. The game became especially popular among women, and, when moved back outside, became known as softball. But indoor baseball, as a game for men, persisted, and the rules were codified in the early 20th century. It was to be played in a hall or gymnasium measuring 40 by 50 feet with seven men to a team (just one player in the "outfield," instead of the three required by baseball). Basepaths were to be 60 feet (not 90), and the ball was to be 12 inches in circumference. In 1939, Major League Baseball star Tris Speaker so loved indoor baseball, which he played during the offseason, that he formed the National Professional Indoor Baseball League and served as its first (and only) president. Speaker worked to place 10 teams, all in Major League Baseball cities, hoping to recruit players from the local big-league teams for the NPIBL affiliates. That didn't work, and the new league was virtually barred from hiring male softball players because the Amateur Softball Association, formed in 1933, threatened to strip players of their membership should they turn pro. The Chicago franchise folded before the 104-game scheduled season began, and the other nine teams all folded when the league itself went bust after only a month of play.

* * *

RARE CONDITIONS

Twins: For reasons that scientists can't quite figure out, the rate of twins born worldwide has nearly doubled over the past 100 years. In 1915, about one in every 50 births included two babies. Today, a two-for-one birth happens in about one out of every 30 live pregnancies.

Albinism: This is a skin condition in which a person lacks most, if not all, pigment in their skin, eyes, and hair. It's very rare in the United States and Europe, with only about one in every 20,000 babies diagnosed with albinism. It's still rare but about three times as common in Africa, where one in every 5,000 babies has the condition.

Tails: Millions of years ago, a tail was a standard feature of human beings. Today, tails are considered "vestigial," meaning there are traces of them in human anatomy—a developing one is visible on embryos, but usually it doesn't form all the way and merely presents as some lumps in the tailbone. But in the past 150 years, there have been two dozen recorded cases of humans born with tails.

Webbed fingers and toes: The technical name for this is syndactyly. The hands and feet first form as flat shapes in the womb before differentiation takes hold, when they develop into individualized fingers and toes. If that doesn't go according to plan, the fingers come out slightly webbed. Scientists aren't sure why this happens, and it's correctable with surgery. About one out of 2,000 babies is born each year with syndactyly.

The root *-bert*—as in Albert, Robert, or Herbert—comes from Indo-European *bherg*, which means "bright and shining."

POINTLESS PARTS

The brain controls the heart. The heart pumps blood. The blood sends nutrients all over the body. Those things all have clear functions. But there are several elements of human anatomy for which scientists haven't quite yet figured out a purpose.

PART: Appendix

DESCRIPTION: It sits between the large intestine and small intestine, both of which are involved in the digestive system. Yet the appendix doesn't serve any purpose in processing food, at least for modern humans.

EXPLANATION: You probably won't ever even notice it or think about it unless it gets inflamed or ruptured and has to be removed in an emergency surgery called an appendectomy. Some scientists think it helped with digestion of fibrous, inedible plant material thousands of years ago, back when humans ate a diet consisting primarily of plants.

PART: Body hair

DESCRIPTION: All the other kinds of hair on the human body have an obvious purpose: eyebrows keep brow sweat from running into the eyes and stinging them; facial hair is a throwback to the days of early humans, a sign of maturity and virility in men.

EXPLANATION: As for body hair—the thin layer of the stuff that can grow almost everywhere, such as on the arms, the legs, and the back—scientists remain baffled. It's not thick enough to have provided any warmth, and experts can't seem to locate an evolutionary advantage of having a few dark and wispy hairs on one's back.

PART: Wisdom teeth

DESCRIPTION: Around the age of 20, after all your baby teeth have fallen out and been replaced by adult teeth, along comes a third wave of teeth, an extra set of molars called "wisdom teeth" because they arrive after the onset of adulthood and subsequent alleged maturity.

EXPLANATION: As soon as they come in, dentists extract them, because their mere presence is painful, pushing other teeth out of alignment. Wisdom teeth are so useless to modern man that there's evidence evolution is doing away with them: as of the 21st century, about a third of adults worldwide won't develop wisdom teeth.

PART: Darwin's point, also known as Darwin's tubercle

DESCRIPTION: It's named after Charles Darwin, who first documented this feature in his 1871 book *The Descent of Man, and Selection in Relation to Sex*, noticing that it was a commonality among different primate species that had pointy ears. It's a small fold of skin that grows on the upper ear in about 10 percent of humans worldwide.

EXPLANATION: Scientists think it's a holdover from when early humans needed that skin flap. It may have been something like a joint made of cartilage that allowed the ear to fold down over itself as a means of protection, keeping out dirt, bugs, and other unwelcome objects.

PART: The *palmaris longus* muscle

DESCRIPTION: Place the back of your wrist down on a flat surface, and then hold your thumb to your pinky. If you're average, a narrow, ropy muscle will rise up out of your wrist. That's the *palmaris longus* muscle, and it's vestigial.

EXPLANATION: About three million years ago, that muscle aided humans in their efforts to grip onto trees as they climbed them. We're now slowly losing it—about 10 percent of people never develop the *palmaris longus*.

PART: Auricular muscles

DESCRIPTION: They're found on the outer ears, the oval-shaped protrusions on the side of your head that most people just refer to as the ears. Some mammals have them, and they're used to move the ears to better hear a sound.

EXPLANATION: In humans, the auricular muscles don't move at all... unless you can "wiggle" your ears. Those are your auriculars that you're wiggling.

PART: Coccyx

DESCRIPTION: It's colloquially referred to as the tailbone, a clue to its former purpose hundreds of thousands of years ago.

EXPLANATION: Humans used to have tails, and the coccyx, found at the very bottom of the spinal cord, helped aid in balance while walking (and not tripping over that tail). People evolved away from needing tails, but the tailbone stayed.

PART: Nipples

DESCRIPTION: Women's nipples serve an obvious biological purpose—they're ducts through which babies may acquire nutritious breast milk early in life. But men don't make milk, meaning male nipples are totally pointless.

EXPLANATION: They're leftover from gestation, or the period when a human baby is growing and developing in the womb. Fetuses develop nipples just a few weeks into the process, well before their gender-determining genitals grow in.

If you have all your teeth, you have eight incisors, four canines, eight premolars, and 12 molars (including four wisdom teeth).

THE MATILDA EFFECT: ROSALIND FRANKLIN AND DNA

British chemist Rosalind Franklin (1920–58) has been called the poster child of
the Matilda Effect, a systemic bias that denies women scientists their due credit
(page 101). And while it is true that three men won the Nobel Prize on the heels
of Franklin's game-changing discovery, she was one of many key players in the race
to determine what DNA actually looks like, and in doing so, to discover...

THE SECRET OF LIFE

Today, it's common knowledge that DNA, short for *deoxyribonucleic acid*, is a self-replicating material that exists in all living creatures. But that knowledge is relatively new, and it took many years for scientists to come to the consensus that DNA contains genetic codes that instruct an organism how to grow. The three most cited names in the discovery of DNA are Friedrich Miescher, a Swiss-born biochemist who in 1869 isolated the phosphate-rich chemicals that came to be known as nucleotides, and James Watson and Francis Crick, who in the April 1953 edition of *Nature* published the first academic article that described this long molecule's "twisted ladder" double-helix structure. "It has not escaped our notice," Watson famously wrote, "that the specific pairing we have postulated immediately suggests a possible copying mechanism for the genetic material."

Einstein's theory of relativity, along with Watson and Crick's double helix model, are arguably the two most important scientific discoveries of the 20th century. Just as relativity launched the era of space travel, the DNA breakthrough changed not just biology but medicine—finally allowing researchers to construct a genetic map, or genome, that can be used to treat and even prevent genetic disorders. In 1962, Watson, Crick, and Maurice Wilkins were awarded the Nobel Prize in Physiology or Medicine for "discoveries concerning the molecular structure of nucleic acids and its significance for information transfer in living material." Wait—Maurice *who*?

CAMBRIDGE VS. KING'S COLLEGE

Maurice Wilkins, a New Zealand–born British biophysicist, oversaw the DNA studies at the Medical Research Council Biophysics Unit at King's College London. In 1950 (a year before Rosalind Franklin would be hired at the school), Wilkins and a British PhD student named Raymond Gosling made a major breakthrough when they discovered how to crystalize DNA so it could be photographed via the process of X-ray crystallography. That brought them one step closer to identifying the structure of DNA, and in doing so, unlocking its secrets.

Originally, Fenway Park's 37-foot-tall "Green Monster" was built to
prevent fans at nearby restaurants from watching baseball games for free.

Wilkins presented these findings at a lecture that was attended by Watson. Inspired, the American chemist joined the DNA project. He teamed up with Crick, a British molecular biologist, at the University of Cambridge's Cavendish Laboratory (about 60 miles north of King's College). Their process involved a great deal of theorizing and plugging variants into mathematical formulas, and then building physical models of proteins and phosphates. But exactly how these proteins and phosphates fit together was eluding them.

MEET ROSALIND

Meanwhile, over at King's College, Wilkins's team was trying to solve the problem with X-ray crystallography—which is too technical to describe here, but it involves carefully placing crystallized proteins onto a microcamera slide in such a way that when the proteins are bombarded with X-rays for a long duration, the electrons are refracted. Then, a researcher measures the angles of spots created by the X-rays and plugs the data into complex formulas. Before computers, these equations had to be done by hand. And there were few people in the world better at it in 1951 than Rosalind Franklin. That's why the head of the department at King's, John Randall, hired her away from her postdoctoral laboratory duties in Paris.

Born in West London's famous Notting Hill district to well-to-do Jewish parents, Franklin excelled in school. After graduating from Cambridge in 1941, she gained a reputation for her work in identifying the molecular structures of virus molecules. During World War II, the British government hired Franklin to classify different forms of coal by studying their porosity to determine which coals burn the best and which types make the most effective filters for gas masks. That research—the first of its kind—earned Franklin a PhD.

By most accounts, Franklin was a fun-loving young woman in her early 30s who was just as content studying viruses as she was hiking the French countryside, or traveling to America to have drinks and laughs with friends.

A HOSTILE WORK ENVIRONMENT

But not by all accounts. It was no secret that some of Franklin's scientific contemporaries—Wilkins and Watson especially—didn't like her. Watson made that abundantly clear in his best-selling 1968 memoir *Double Helix*. He significantly downplayed Franklin's contributions and mockingly called her "Rosy" (a nickname he knew she didn't like). He called her "belligerent" and even complained about her looks: "There was never lipstick to contrast with her straight black hair, while at the age of thirty-one her dresses showed all the imagination of English blue-stocking adolescents." He also wrote, "The best home for a feminist was in another person's lab." And, "Clearly, she had to be put in her place."

There is no doubt that Franklin intimidated men. She always spoke her mind while making direct eye contact. That made for a difficult two years at King's College,

Flossing your teeth regularly can help prevent a heart attack.

which Franklin called "an old boys' club" where women weren't even allowed in the Senior Common Room.

Making matters worse, Professor Randall had informed Franklin in a letter that she would be in charge of the lab, and that Gosling would be her assistant. She arrived at King's when Wilkins was on vacation. When he returned, he assumed that Franklin had taken it upon herself to use his microcamera that he had ordered, and that she stole his grad student. Gosling later admitted that he was uncomfortable being put in the middle, especially because he and Franklin worked so well together. He blames the "misunderstanding" on the head of the department, Randall: "He definitely subscribed to the divide and rule principle, as lots of people did. He thought it would make them competitive and improve their work."

"YOU'RE WRONG"

Franklin's first big breakthrough at King's College was identifying that DNA comes in two types, which she and Gosling called A and B. She presented these findings at a lecture that Watson attended, but he didn't quite understand the chemistry behind it, which she let her colleagues know in no uncertain terms when Watson and Crick invited her, Gosling, and Wilkins to view some new models they'd constructed in their lab. The night before, Watson had been bragging at the pub that he'd found "the meaning of life!" But when Franklin walked in to the lab and saw the model, she blurted out, "You're wrong—and you're wrong for the following reasons: one, two, three, four." That's how Gosling remembered it. "The boys had built a model with the phosphate linkages going up the middle of the thing, which gave it, of course, rigidity, and so you could hang all the nucleotides and things off the ends of the ionic chain. That must be wrong, because we knew that the water went into that phosphate-oxygen group...so those phosphate groups had to be on the outside."

Watson was apparently so embarrassed by Franklin's verbal beatdown that he painted her as the villain in his book, *Double Helix*. After that debacle, Wilkins started spending more time at Cambridge, often complaining to Watson and Crick that Franklin stole his grad student and got access to the best gene samples and lab equipment. The rift between Wilkins and Franklin widened. "On the one side was a quick, single-minded young woman with a passion for argument," wrote Franklin biographer Brenda Maddox. "On the other an exceedingly reserved man with a hesitant, circumlocutory manner and an aversion to direct eye contact."

EUREKA!

Building on Gosling's earlier imaging successes, and after more than a year of experimentation, in early 1953, Gosling and Franklin finally had the humidity level just right, the precise placement of the gene sample (ram sperm) on the slide, and the

The U.S.A. contains 4 percent of the planet's population but is responsible for 20 percent of its garbage.

correct angle of the lighting. After a 100-hour exposure, they developed the now-famous image, dubbed Photo 51, that shows an X-ray diffraction pattern of DNA. (We recommend you google "Photo 51" to see the groundbreaking image for yourself.) Though it may be difficult for us laypeople to see, the X shape in that fateful image provided the missing piece of the DNA puzzle: the double helix.

By this point, Franklin had announced she was quitting King's College and was making the transition to a new job at Birkbeck College, University of London, where she'd have less funding but more support. At King's, Franklin had only a grad student and no seasoned peers to bounce theories off of. Because of that, she didn't get the opportunity to present her findings as she wanted to; instead, she managed only to write an unpublished paper for the project donors outlining her findings. When Franklin left King's in March, Photo 51 and her unpublished article stayed behind. After landing at Birkbeck, she received a letter from King's informing her that she could no longer work on "the DNA problem." She shrugged it off and continued working on her data and helping Gosling with his PhD.

As for Wilkins, he was less concerned with school rivalries than he was in finding answers, and knew that the King's data could help the Cambridge team with its models, so Wilkins invited Watson to his office and showed him what they had. As Watson wrote at the end of his and Crick's historic *Nature* article, seeing Photo 51 "stimulated" their process.

Ironically, a month later, when Franklin was invited to the Cavendish lab to have a look at Watson and Crick's new double helix model, she was impressed by their progress without knowing that they'd had access to her work.

SLOW AND STEADY LOSES THE RACE

As is the case with scientific discoveries, the credit doesn't always go to who did the most work or made the most crucial discoveries, but to whoever publishes first. There were three articles about the double helix discovery in that April 1953 issue of *Nature*—the one that made history was Watson and Crick's, even though it didn't include any experimental data, just deductive reasoning. But King's administrators "pulled some strings" to get two other articles in the issue that would "support" Cambridge's findings—one authored by Wilkins, and one by Franklin and Gosling that included Photo 51. But Franklin wasn't ready to formally present their research.

Why not? She felt that men had the luxury of being wrong, as evidenced by another innovator with questionable integrity, Thomas Edison, who famously said, "I have not failed 10,000 times—I've successfully found 10,000 ways that will not work." As a woman, Franklin had less leeway for error. Result: she was still configuring her findings when Watson and Crick got all the glory. "We are not going to speculate,"

The French word *debacler* ("to free or unbar ice on a river") gave us the English word *debacle*.

she wrote in a letter, "we are going to wait, we are going to let the spots on this photograph tell us what the [DNA] structure is."

To be sure, Watson and Crick deserve their accolades—according to Maddox, it was they who discovered that "chains are linked by complementary pairs of base pairs [that] run in opposite directions." But would they have come to that conclusion had they not been shown Photo 51? Decades later, Watson said in a speech that it certainly spurred them along.

> There's a myth which is that, you know, that Francis and I basically stole the structure from the people at King's. I was shown Rosalind Franklin's X-ray photograph and 'Whooo! That was a helix!,' and a month later, we had the structure...Wilkins should never have shown me the thing. I didn't go into the drawer and steal it. It was shown to me, and I was told the dimensions, a repeat of 34 angstroms, so, you know, I knew roughly what it meant and it was that the Franklin photograph was the key event psychologically, it mobilized us back into action.

ROSALIND, MEET MATILDA

It's tough to say how much the Matilda effect affected Franklin. Sadly, she never got the chance to defend her work or her character. In 1958, ovarian cancer cut her life short at only 37. After working on DNA, Franklin's next and final project was mapping the tobacco mosaic virus. That work earned her partner, Aaron Klug, a Nobel Prize in 1982. Watson and others have suggested that Franklin would have been a corecipient. Why wasn't she nominated for her DNA work in 1962? The Nobel committee had a strict rule banning posthumous awards.

The Nobel Prize went to Watson, Crick, and Wilkins three years after Franklin died. Wilkins was included because, as head of the department at King's, he'd spent years collecting and refining the data that proved the double-helix model, and he was instrumental in the DNA diffraction work that Franklin later perfected. It also took nine years because many in the scientific community were hesitant to accept that DNA did indeed hold "the secret of life."

At the ceremony, Watson accepted on behalf of Crick and Wilkins, and he didn't mention Franklin by name, but did acknowledge, "I knew many people...who thought I was quite unbearable."

As for Crick, he stayed by Franklin's side when she was dying of cancer. In 1993, he acknowledged that they "always had a patronizing attitude towards her." And for the rest of Wilkins's life, a cloud hung over his Nobel Prize...that many believed (and still do) should have gone to Franklin instead.

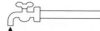

It's a bat's world: out of the 5,400 species of mammals, 1,400 are bat species.

WEIRD WORLD RECORDS

This just in: this article just set a new world record for Silliest List of Useless, Frightening, or Baffling Accomplishments. Congrats to us!

Tallest Toilet Paper Pyramid: In 2018, a Meijer store in Wisconsin hosted paper company Kimberly-Clark's efforts to build a pyramid out of rolls of TP. They're in Guinness World Records now for a pyramid that measured 14'3" at its tallest point.

Biggest Flag Made of LEGO: A person can make virtually anything out of LEGO blocks, and the employees of the LEGOLAND Discovery Centre in Toronto built a Canadian flag—a red maple leaf on a red and white background. It took 248,062 bricks to construct the 11'5" by 21'2" flag.

Worst Kidney Blockage: In 1999, a man (name withheld from news reports) entered a hospital in Saudi Arabia and was diagnosed with an enlarged kidney. That was the result of a urinary flow obstruction—once that cleared, doctors removed 5.8 gallons of urine from the organ.

Longest Functional Golf Club: At a golf center at the MGM Grand resort in Las Vegas in 2018, a team of companies (Callaway, Fujikura, Topgolf, Liquid Light, What's Inside?) showed off a collaborative project and publicity stunt: the longest golf club in history that can also be used to actually hit a golf ball. Actor and comedian Anthony Anderson (*Black-ish*) did the honor, swinging the club that measured 37 feet long.

Most License Plates Torn in a Minute: Bill Clark is a professional strongman—so strong that in Binghamton, New York, in 2018, he ripped 23 metal car license plates in half in 60 seconds' time.

Widest Tongue: In 2014, Byron Schlenker had his tongue measured by Guinness World Records representatives, and it turned out to be the widest for a man in recorded history, measuring 3.37 inches across. On the same day at the same event, the record for widest tongue on a woman was set, too—Schlenker's daughter, Emily, has one almost as big as her father's, at 2.89 inches.

Most Pinkie Pull-ups: At an October 2018 event in Italy, performance artist Tazio Gavioli made 36 consecutive chin-ups on a bar, holding onto the bar with only his two smallest fingers.

Most Push-ups with a Sword in the Throat: German man Franz Huber completed 20 push-ups at the 2017 Tattoo and Piercing Expo in Eggenfelden, just after sliding a standard-length sword down his esophagus.

There are more Panda Express restaurants than pandas.

Most Surgeries: South Dakota man Charles Jensen was born with a genetic disorder that caused him to prolifically develop noncancerous facial tumors throughout his life. From 1954 to 1994, Jensen endured 970 tumor-removal operations.

Highest Blood Glucose Level: A normal, healthy blood sugar reading is anywhere between 80 and 120. Significantly higher than that, and the individual probably has diabetes. In 2008, seven-year-old Michael Buonocore was admitted to an emergency room in a Pennsylvania hospital where he was diagnosed with diabetes after producing a blood glucose reading of 26,656.

Most Kidney Stones Passed: Canadian man Donald Winfield spent most of August 2006 passing a succession of kidney stones, most of which were the size of a grain of sand. When he finally rid himself of the last one, Winfield had passed 4,504 stones.

Longest Length of Finger Inserted into Nose: Josh Werner stuck his entire pinkie finger—all 2.25 inches of it—all the way up his nose.

Farthest Propelled Arrow Fired by Feet: Brittany Walsh trained herself to stand on her hands so she can load and shoot an archer's bow with her feet. In 2018, she fired an arrow 40 feet, four inches (and almost got a bull's-eye).

Longest Fart, and Loudest Fart: London man Bernard Clemmens is in Guinness World Records for sustaining a rear-end blast for two minutes and 40 seconds. Alvin Meshits of Texas holds the record for the fart with the highest volume—his fart in 1972 lasted one-third of a second, but registered at 194 decibels, which is louder than a jet taking off.

Biggest Spatula Collection: At a Washington state cake show in 2017, Renee Wesberry was confirmed to be the keeper of the world's largest assemblage of spatulas. Over the previous 19 years, Wesberry had collected 1,636 spatulas made of metal, plastic, and wood.

Quickest Mouth Origami Boat Constructer: Gao Guangli of China is a master of the art of paper folding, taking just three minutes and 34 seconds to make a paper boat in 2017—and he did it with just his tongue, teeth, and lips.

Most Stuff Stuck in a Beard: Joel Strasser of Lacey, Washington, holds two Guinness records for long, skinny objects jammed into his thick and fluffy facial hair. In 2019, he set the record for straws, sticking 312 into his beard. That came a year after he inserted 3,500 toothpicks into that beard; that task took more than three hours to complete, and per Guinness rules, the toothpicks had to stay in place for a minimum of 10 seconds.

When George Lucas got married in 2013, Prince played at his wedding.

NUDES AND PRUDES

Nudity can be shocking...and so can prudery.
Which side of the fence do you fall on?

NUDE... For decades, a handful of beaches in the resort town of Nantucket, Massachusetts, were known by locals and frequent visitors to be unofficially "clothing optional." In a May 2022 referendum, residents voted by an overwhelming margin (327 to 242) to make that status official for all beaches. Voters at the annual Nantucket town meeting approved the "Gender Equality on Beaches" measure, which says that "any person shall be allowed to be topless on any public or private beach within the town of Nantucket," regardless of whether they're male or female. "This bylaw would not make beaches nude beaches. This bylaw would allow tops to be optional for anyone that chooses to be topless," seventh-generation Nantucket resident and pleasure educator Dorothy Stover told reporters. Before the bylaw went into effect, men could go topless on beaches, but if women disrobed from the waist up, they could face a $300 fine.

PRUDE... Spoiler alert if you haven't seen the 2021 political satire movie *Don't Look Up*: A comet destroys Earth, and the only survivors are a privileged few who jet off in escape pods and land on a paradise planet. Among the survivors is the U.S. president, played by three-time Academy Award winner Meryl Streep, who appears nude and with a huge tattoo. Even though a body double was used, *Don't Look Up* costar Leonardo DiCaprio was adamantly opposed to Streep seeming to appear nude. "Leo just views Meryl as film royalty. He didn't like seeing her with the lower back tattoo, walking for a second naked. He said something to me like, 'Do you really need to show that?'" director Adam McKay recalled. "But [Streep] didn't even blink. She didn't even bring it up."

NUDE...A series of institutions, including NASA's Jet Propulsion Laboratory, want to utilize a scientific information repository called arXiv to communicate with any intelligent life-forms that may be lurking in the far reaches of the Milky Way galaxy. Their 2022 proposal suggested beaming out binary code that could be translated into images of the basics of life on planet Earth, including drawings of an atom's structure, a global map, DNA structure, and two illustrations of human figures, one male and one female, both fully naked. Those drawings "can easily be considered one of the most important parts of the message," the proposal stated, arguing the nude pictures "would certainly be of compelling interest" to aliens. Amazingly, there's precedent for this. In 1972, the Pioneer 10 space probe was launched into space with

The word *blockbuster* comes from a WWII–era bomb capable of destroying an entire block.

much information about Earth and its location, and it had onboard a gold plaque embedded with images of a nude man and a nude woman.

PRUDE... Alina Fazleeva is a Russian yoga instructor and Instagram personality, and in May 2022 she did a nude (but tasteful) photo shoot comprising yoga poses and positions in front of a 700-year-old weeping paperbark tree that stands on the grounds of a temple on the Indonesian island of Bali and is considered sacred to locals. After she posted the photo to her Instagram account, Fazleeva received negative comments and backlash from Balinese followers. Reported to local authorities, Fazleeva was threatened with a six-year prison term and a $100,000 fine, were she to be found guilty of violating Balinese pornography and obscenity laws. She deleted the picture, publicly apologized, and was subsequently forcefully deported from Bali and barred from reentering Indonesia for six months.

NUDE... Two Austrian repositories of art, the Albertina and the Leopold Museum, endured criticism and repercussions in 2021 for posting items from their collections on online social accounts—because those items featured nudity, and sites such as Instagram and Facebook have strict zero-tolerance policies when it comes to overt displays of flesh (even artistic renderings of it). "These artworks are crucial and important to Vienna," said Helena Hartlauer, spokesperson for Vienna's tourism board. "If they cannot be used on a communications tool as strong as social media, it's unfair and frustrating." The solution: Vienna's tourism board went to bat for its museums by opening an account on OnlyFans, a site where amateurs may post their own explicit or graphic content and charge subscribers to view it. The Vienna tourism council charged $3 a month for readers to see paintings and sculptures that featured nude people.

PRUDE... In July 2022, Scottish couple Sadie Tan and Colin Unsworth were participating in a charity bike ride, pedaling their tandem bicycle on the trip from John O'Groats to Lands End. Along the way, a man drove past the couple in his car, and then turned around and swerved into them, knocking both riders to the ground. "You're a f****** prostitute!" the female passenger yelled before the car sped away. Tan and Unsworth are naturists (which is what nudists call themselves), and they spend most of their time in the buff, even in public and while riding their bike. The incident was caught on video and local police sought out the perpetrators of the attack, which Tan believes was a deliberate act and a violent statement against their clothes-free lifestyle. "Clothes feel like putting on layers of expectations and pressures of modern life, they feel like putting on layers of anxiety," Tan said. "Being naked for me is a relief from those anxieties and I feel completely in my element. My social anxiety almost ceases to exist."

What will you do 4.2 million times this year? Blink.

FREAK ACCIDENTS: CELEBRITY EDITION

Let these tragic stories of bizarre deaths serve as a reminder to not take life for granted, because—famous or not—we're all just one minor miscalculation away from meeting our maker.

ANTON YELCHIN (1989–2016)

CLAIM TO FAME: The Russian-born American actor starred in such films as *Fright Night*, *Charlie Bartlett*, and *Odd Thomas*, and, most famously, had starred as Ensign Pavel Chekov in the *Star Trek* reboots.

BACKGROUND: One of the hardest-working actors in Hollywood, 27-year-old Yelchin had appeared in 16 movies between 2013 and 2016 and had six more coming out when it all came to a screeching halt on June 19, 2016. He was leaving his Studio City, California, home on a Saturday night, but not to go party. He had an 11:00 p.m. rehearsal.

CAUSE OF DEATH: After driving through his security gate, Yelchin parked his 2015 Jeep Grand Cherokee on his steep driveway and got out to get his mail. The 2.5-ton SUV slipped out of gear and rolled backward. According to TMZ, it "pinned [Yelchin] against the gate with such force, it bent the metal." The medical examiner later said that Yelchin might have been alive for a minute or two before succumbing to "blunt traumatic asphyxia."

After he failed to show up at rehearsal, his friends drove to his house and discovered what police ruled a "freak accident." But could it have been avoided? Yelchin's parents sued Fiat Chrysler, claiming that the Jeep shouldn't have rolled. Initially, the auto company put the blame back on Yelchin for not engaging the emergency brake. But after it was revealed that Fiat Chrysler had issued a recall of that very vehicle two months earlier—because the gear shifter could slip and cause the vehicle to roll—the auto company settled out of court. The money went to charity and to fund a documentary of the actor's short but extraordinary life.

NATASHA RICHARDSON (1963–2009)

CLAIM TO FAME: The daughter of acting royalty (director Tony Richardson and actress Vanessa Redgrave) and wife of action star Liam Neeson, the English actress won a Tony Award for *Cabaret* and appeared in such films as *Nell*, *Maid in Manhattan*, *Patty Hearst*, and *The Parent Trap*.

BACKGROUND: Normally, dying while skiing wouldn't count as a freak accident because of the inherent dangers of the sport. But Richardson, 45, was taking beginner lessons at a Montreal resort on March 18, 2009, and wasn't even going fast enough to warrant wearing a helmet...or so she thought.

CAUSE OF DEATH: It was at around noon at the bottom of a "gentle slope" where Richardson slipped on her skis and hit her head on the packed snow. Her instructor asked if she needed to see a medic; Richardson joked about her clumsiness and said she was fine. A few minutes later, the instructor contacted ski patrol, who decided to call an ambulance. But Richardson insisted she was fine and just needed to rest. She signed a waiver declining medical attention and walked back to her room.

What Richardson didn't know: she was suffering from a rare type of brain injury known as "talk and die" syndrome. The initial trauma causes an epidural hematoma, where blood slowly starts pooling up between the skull and the brain—after which there's a "lucid interval" before the blood begins to put pressure on the brain. That's why it's important to seek medical treatment before it's too late. But again, Richardson didn't know that.

Back at her room, she called her husband (who was filming the movie *Chloe* in Toronto) and told him, "Oh, darling. I've taken a tumble in the snow." Not long after that call, and only two hours after the fall, Richardson complained of a splitting headache and seemed confused. Another ambulance came and transported her to a nearby hospital by 3 p.m. Her vital signs were stable, but she was slipping in and out of consciousness, so they decided to send her to a better-equipped hospital in Montreal. After the two-hour drive, it was too late to save her.

By the time Neeson made it to his wife's side that evening, she was brain dead. "Sweetie," he told her, "you're not coming back from this. You've banged your head. It's—I don't know if you can hear me, but that's—this is what's gone down." Richardson died two days later in New York, where the lights were dimmed on Broadway in her memory. An organ donor, she helped save three strangers' lives.

CHARMAYNE "MAXEE" MAXWELL (1969–2015)

CLAIM TO FAME: Born in Guyana, Maxwell was a member of the popular girl band Brownstone, best known for its Grammy-nominated top-10 song, "If You Love Me" (1994). After a solo career in the 2000s never took off, Brownstone reunited in 2013 for the reality show *R&B Divas: Atlanta*.

When a baby giraffe is born, it falls six feet to the ground and lands on its head.

BACKGROUND: Two years later, Maxwell, 46, was living in Los Angeles with her husband, a producer named Carsten "Soulshock" Schack, and their 11-year-old son, Nicholas. While Schack was at work, Maxwell took Nicholas to a soccer game. After they returned, the boy went to his room and Maxwell poured herself a glass of wine.

CAUSE OF DEATH: While walking in the kitchen, she slipped and fell. The wineglass hit the floor first and shattered. A shard of glass landed in such a way that when Maxwell fell on top of it, she received "two fatal puncture wounds in the back of the neck." At around 9:00 p.m., Schack arrived home and found his wife unconscious on the floor in a pool of blood, but she still had a pulse. He put pressure on the wound and called an ambulance, but she died en route to the hospital. Police ruled it a freak accident.

BOB SAGET (1956–2022)

CLAIM TO FAME: As a TV actor, Saget was the wholesome dad from *Full House* and the corny host of *America's Funniest Home Videos*; as a stand-up comedian, he was among the filthiest in the business.

BACKGROUND: Saget, 65, was on a stand-up tour, staying by himself at a hotel in Orlando. On the afternoon of January 9, 2022, after not responding to calls from worried friends and associates, the comedian was found dead in his bed, lying face up. There were no apparent wounds or other clues pointing to a cause of death. That didn't stop the rumors from flying: some said he'd been robbed, others that he got into a fight and was hit in the head with a bat.

   The truth is much more mundane. After performing in Jacksonville the previous night, Saget drove two hours to Orlando, and—as security footage confirms—no one but Saget entered his room. In his final social media post, he wrote, "Okay, I loved tonight's show…Really nice audience. Lots of positivity…I had no idea I did a two hour set tonight. I'm back in comedy like I was when I was 26. I guess I'm finding my new voice and loving every moment of it."

CAUSE OF DEATH: It's unknown exactly what happened. Police ruled out foul play. The most likely scenario: Saget had just taken a shower and was getting into bed when he hit the back of his head on the padded headboard. These hotel headboards are often harder than they appear, as there's only a thin layer of fabric covering a hard, wooden surface. According to the medical examiner: "This report shows that the… brain suffered trauma which led to skull fractures, bruising of the brain and actual bleeding in the space around the brain. This blood can compress the brain and cause death. The coroner determined that this trauma was most likely caused by an accidental fall backward." There were no drugs or alcohol in Saget's system; it's likely he fell right asleep after hitting his head and never woke up.

But if the freak accident hadn't taken Saget, the Grim Reaper might not have been far behind. Not only was he COVID-19 positive at the time of his death, but the medical report revealed that he had an enlarged heart and several other heart conditions. Fittingly, when ABC broke in to programming to announce the news of Saget's death, the show it broke into was *America's Funniest Home Videos*.

TV Shows with the Highest Body Counts

BLACK MIRROR
387,100

GAME OF THRONES
174,400

HUMANS
110,100

24
16,100

BATTLESTAR GALACTICA
10,900

German musical notation subbed H for B natural, so Johann Sebastian Bach composed his "musical motif" as B flat, A, C, H—his own last name.

LOS HECHOS DE MÉXICO

Most Americans know muy poco (diddly-squat) about their neighbors to the south, so here are some Mexico facts courtesy of Tío Juan.

- Mexico's top three languages are Spanish, Nahuatl, and Yucatec Maya. The word *México* comes from Nahuatl: *metztli* ("moon"), *xictli* ("center"), and *co* ("place").

- The ancient city of Tenochtitlan, which had an estimated 200,000 people in 1519, existed on an island in Lake Texcoco. The lake was later drained, and is now the location of Ciudad de México (Mexico City). Population: 8.85 million.

- Result of building a city on top of a drained lake: Mexico City is sinking six to eight inches each year.

- The official name of Mexico—which turned 200 years old in 2021—is Estados Unidos Mexicanos ("United Mexican States").

- The Jarabe Tapatío is the national dance of Mexico. It's a courtship folk dance wherein the woman wears a long skirt and the man throws his hat on the floor.

- Originally founded in 1551, the National University of Mexico is the oldest college in North America.

- First minted coins used internationally: Mexican silver pesos—also known as "pieces of eight"—were viable currency in Spain, the Caribbean, and Southeast Asia.

- Two Mexican inventions: color television (Guillermo González Camarena, 1940) and oral contraceptives (a.k.a. "the pill," Luis Miramontes, 1951).

- Top 5 tourist destinations: 1. Mexico City; 2. Puerto Vallarta; 3. Cancún; 4. San Miguel de Allende; 5. Chichén Itzá.

- First Mexican in space: Rodolfo Neri Vela. He was a payload specialist on the space shuttle *Atlantis* in 1985.

- Highest-grossing Mexican movie: *No se Aceptan Devoluciones* (English title: *Instructions Not Included*). Released in 2013, the comedy-drama was directed by and starred Eugenio Derbez and grossed $100 million worldwide.

According to a 2014 study, the catchiest song of all time is the Spice Girls' "Wannabe."

- Highest-grossing movie in Mexico: *Avengers: Endgame* (2019), which made $920,425,545.

- The states, bodies of water, and countries that border Mexico: California, Arizona, New Mexico, Texas, the Gulf of Mexico, the Caribbean Sea, Belize, Guatemala, and the Pacific Ocean.

- The five largest countries in the Americas: Canada (3,854,083 square miles), United States (3,617,827), Brazil (3,287,086), Argentina (1,073,234), and Mexico (758,249).

- All of Texas, California, Nevada, and Utah—and parts of Arizona, Colorado, New Mexico, and Wyoming—were once a part of Mexico.

- The longest border in the world is between the United States and Canada (3,987 miles); the second longest is between the United States and Mexico (1,954 miles).

- Celebrities born in Mexico: Guillermo del Toro, Frida Kahlo, Salma Hayek, and Carlos Santana.

- Roughly 80 percent of Mexico's petroleum is exported to the United States.

- There are 32 Mexican states: Aguascalientes, Baja California, Baja California Sur, Campeche, Coahuila, Colima, Chiapas, Chihuahua, Durango, Mexico City, Guanajuato, Guerrero, Hidalgo, Jalisco, State of Mexico, Michoacán, Morelos, Nayarit, Nuevo León, Oaxaca, Puebla, Querétaro, Quintana Roo, San Luis Potosí, Sinaloa, Sonora, Tabasco, Tamaulipas, Tlaxcala, Veracruz, Yucatán, and Zacatecas.

- Chihuahua dogs were named after the state of Chihuahua.

- In southern Mexico, children have to wait until January 6 to get their Christmas presents. That's the date of Epiphany, when the Three Wise Men brought gold, frankincense, and myrrh to the Baby Jesus.

- Wildlife: there are 200,000 animal species in Mexico, making it fourth in biodiversity in the world.

- Nightlife: there are 16,000 bars and cafes in Mexico.

- Foods that come from Mexico: avocados, pumpkins, popcorn, cacao, vanilla, chewing gum, and chili peppers.

- What do Mexico and Oregon have in common? All of the beaches are public.

Over the hill: the brain begins to slow down at around 24 years old.

NICE STORIES

*Every now and then we like to lock our inner cynics in a box
and share some stories with happy endings.*

TURNING SILVER INTO GOLD

There wasn't a lot of fanfare after Maria Magdalena Andrejczyk of Poland won a silver medal in javelin at the 2020 Olympic Games. Few outside her home country knew her sad backstory: she had missed out on medaling at the 2016 games by mere centimeters, and then she was sidelined by a shoulder injury, and *then* she got bone cancer: just three weeks after her cancer surgery, she was training for the 2020 games. Rebounding after all of that adversity, and then winning the silver medal, made for a great feel-good story...but only if you tuned in.

However, a few weeks after the games, Andrejczyk made international headlines after posting on her Facebook page that she was auctioning off her silver medal. Why? An eight-month-old Polish baby she didn't even know needed urgent, life-saving heart surgery in the United States. Andrejczyk explained that when she heard about the fundraiser for the child's care, and that it was falling far short of its goal, she knew that her silver medal put her in a unique position to help. The auction was held right there on Facebook. The winning bid: $125,000, by Zabka, a Polish convenience store chain. "We were moved by the beautiful and extremely noble gesture of our Olympia girl," read a company statement. "So we decided to support the collection of funds for the benefit. We also decided that the silver medal from Tokyo will stay with Ms. Maria, who showed how Great the Champion is." Not only did Andrejczyk save the baby boy's life, she got to keep her silver medal after all.

BRAYDEN AND DARLA

Brayden Morton got hooked on drugs when he was a teenager. "I was the hopeless addict who was never supposed to get better," he told the *Washington Post*. But after several stints in rehab, he finally kicked his fentanyl habit in 2015. He became a volunteer at that very same rehab center he'd attended and a few years later got a job as a clinical drug and alcohol interventionist. He's since started a free service called Find the Right Rehab.

In June 2021, Morton was upstairs in his Vancouver, BC, Canada, home. His loyal dog Darla, a three-year-old Chinese shar-pei, was lounging on the porch in their fenced backyard. Morton heard a commotion outside, and when he looked out the window, his dog was gone. He darted downstairs and saw a

The blue jeans trademark expired in 1890, but Levi Strauss & Co. still owns
the trademark for their stitching pattern and orange thread.

pickup truck speeding away...with Darla in the back. Morton called the police and shared his predicament on Facebook, offering a $4,000 reward—which was everything he could spare. "I love my dog," he wrote. "This isn't stealing a bike out of my garage; this is much more serious."

The post went viral, and one of the people who saw it was a 20-year-old woman (name not released), who, with two other people, had stolen Darla. Overwhelmed with guilt, she called the tip line and said, through tears, that she had his dog. Morton told her that he'd messed up a lot in his life, too, and people had forgiven him. He agreed to meet her—with the reward money.

When Morton showed up, there was the slender young woman—still crying—with Darla on a leash. Based on his own experience, Morton could tell that she was a fentanyl addict. "I know if I give you this money," he told her, "I'm going to hear about you dead in the next day or two." He shared his own troubled past and said that the money should go toward her rehabilitation, so he put her in touch with a 90-day rehab program that would cost $22,000. Morton offered to support the woman in the meantime, and the rehab director pledged to seek additional funding to ensure that she got treatment.

Judging by the young woman's state, Morton probably saved her life. She had been living on the streets and feeding her drug addiction through sex work. And she'd been "terrified" to seek help (fentanyl withdrawal is a very painful ordeal). Call it fate, or a bit of good luck, but the young woman just so happened to steal a dog from someone who was in a unique position to help her. "One day," he said, "I hope she looks back on this story and it motivates her to help somebody else."

YOUNG AT HEART

What's the secret to a long life? Maybe it's carrying a five-gallon bucket full of gas to your daddy's tractor in the field, and then catching frogs in the creek on your way back to the farmhouse. That was a typical day in the 1930s for three Beardsley, Kansas, sisters—Julia, Lucy, and Frances. In December 2021, they became a feel-good news story when the youngest sister, Frances Kompus, turned 100 years old. The middle sister, Lucy Pochop, was 102, and the oldest, Julia Kopriva, was 104. The sisters, all long-since widowed, have remained close their entire lives, and they all live within walking distance of one another. They credit their longevity to "family and faith," walking a lot, and simple foods such as "homemade bread, just plain potatoes, and gravy and meat." But it was growing up during the Great Depression and the Dust Bowl that toughened them up for life. "The younger generation don't believe what we went through," said Julia. "We work today, but we worked harder in those days."

The office chair's four fathers: Charles Darwin (wheels), Thomas Jefferson (swivel), Thomas E. Warren (combined wheels and swivel), and Otto von Bismarck (marketed it).

1920s SLANG

Time to crank up that Model T and talk like an egg from the Roaring Twenties, when booze was outlawed, gangsters patrolled the streets, and jazz ruled the nightlife.

JAKE EXPRESSIONS

The bee's knees: (Also, hotsy-totsy or the cat's pajamas) An extraordinary person, place, or thing.

"I gotta iron my shoelaces": "I gotta go to the bathroom."

"Ya follow?": "Do you understand?"

"Phonus balonus!": "Nonsense!"

"Applesauce!": "That's BS!"

"Everything is Jake.": "It's all good."

"Whoopee!": "Yay!"

RAGS & CHEATERS

Cockdollager: An important event.

Rags: Clothes.

Cheaters: Eyeglasses.

Blower: Telephone.

Rattler: Train.

Bucket: Car.

Hayburner: A gas guzzler.

TOMATOES & EGGS

Egg: A person, often of means, who can either be a good egg or a bad egg.

Bimbo: An unintelligent, brutish man.

Rube: A naive simpleton.

Wise head: An intelligent person.

Dewdropper: An unemployed young man.

Tomato: A pretty lady.

PINS & PEEPERS

Noodle: Head.

Puss: Face.

Kisser: Mouth.

Beezer: Nose.

Peepers: Eyes.

Pipes: Throat.

Bubs: Breasts.

Pins: Legs.

SUGAR & SCRATCH

Mazuma, voot, sugar, scratch, spinach, rhino, jack, lettuce: Money.

Two bits: $25, or 25 cents.

Clam: A dollar.

C: $100 (a pair of Cs: $200).

JAWING & MAKING WHOOPEE

Jawing: Talking.

Snap a cap: To shout.

Hotsy-totsy: Good-looking.

Making whoopee: Making out with a romantic partner.

Getting the icy mitt: When the whoopee is declined.

Fire extinguisher: A chaperone that ensures the whoopee will be declined.

"Bank's closed!": "Stop that whoopee!"

TIGER MILK & PANTHER PISS

Chew: Eat.

Tiger milk: Liquor.

Panther piss: Homemade whiskey.

Tip a few: Have a few drinks.

Whale: A heavy drinker.

Nevada gas: Cyanide.

NIPPERS & MEAT WAGONS

Packing heat: Carrying a loaded gun.

Chopper squad: Men with machine guns.

Pump metal: Shoot a gun.

Chicago lightning: Gunfire.

Meat wagon: Ambulance.

Copper: Cop, police.

Nailed: Caught by the cops.

Nippers: Handcuffs.

Under glass: Incarcerated.

Pop, bop: To kill.

Pooped, zotzed: To be killed.

Step off: To be hanged.

Casey, Illinois, is home to the world's largest rocking chair. It's 56 feet high, and it actually rocks.

HAIRSTYLE ORIGINS

Why does your hair look like that?
Here's why.

MOPTOP

When Beatlemania hit England in 1963 and the rest of the world in 1964, the Beatles' style of haircut became almost as popular as their music. The Beatles' cohesive look of four guys in matching suits also included matching "moptop" haircuts—moderately long, draping over the head, and with prominent bangs. In the early 1960s, the Beatles decamped to Hamburg, Germany, and were befriended by Jürgen Vollmer and Astrid Kirchherr, a couple of young, hip photographers. Kirchherr dated Beatles' roommate and collaborator Klaus Voormann, and Kirchherr deployed the haircut on Voormann to hide his large and ungainly ears. Then-Beatle Stuart Sutcliffe asked Kirchherr to style and cut his hair (it was already long, so he didn't have to grow it out) in the same way. One by one, each Beatle acquiesced to letting Kirschherr give them the same 'do.

MULLET

Also known as "hockey hair," because players of that sport favored the style in the 1980s, the mullet is commonly associated with party animals of all kinds—gaining it the unofficial slogan "business in front, party in the back" (meaning it's cut short around the face, giving someone the appearance of being clean-cut when viewed head-on, and left to grow long over the neck). While artistic renderings of individuals with mullets date back thousands of years, the style was popularized (without any particular name attached) in the mid-1970s, when it was worn by most of the major rock stars of the day, including Paul McCartney, Keith Richards, Rod Stewart, and David Bowie in his "Ziggy Stardust" alien persona. Mullets were part of the culture by the 1980s for young men in the U.S., U.K., and Australia, as well as in the LGBTQ community, where cultural anthropologists say it became a visual shorthand for lesbians to identity one another in countries where being publicly "out" was not okay. In discussing the haircut and the kind of guys who have it in the 1994 song "Mullet Head," rap-rock group the Beastie Boys coined and popularized the name; they likely acquired it from Henri Mollet, a French fashion figure and underground culture icon who wore the style in the early 1970s.

Pikachu! The most expensive Pokémon card (as of 2022) was sold
to wrestler Logan Paul for $5.275 million.

BEEHIVE

In 1960, Chicago hairstylist Margaret Vinci Heldt was one of several prominent salon managers approached by the editors of the hair-industry trade magazine *Modern Beauty Shop* to create new hairstyles that they could write about, photograph, and suggest to readers as a way to boost their business. In searching for inspiration, Heldt examined a black velvet fez she often wore. It was decorated with beads that resembled bees and Heldt liked wearing it because it was so tall and spacious that it didn't flatten her hairdo when she had it on. That gave her the idea to create a tall hairdo that kept its shape, and the bee associations led her to a specific strong, conical structure: a beehive. Heldt devised the beehive hairdo, and since it was featured in *Modern Beauty Shop*, hundreds of hairdressers around the country simultaneously embraced and recommended it to their more daring clients. The beehive, tall and narrow with hair piled all the way up, took a long time to create but was virtually effortless to maintain: Heldt recommended women sleep in a scarf and just tuck in any loose strands upon awakening.

THE RACHEL

Brand-new twentysomething-oriented sitcom *Friends* was the hottest show on TV in the 1994–1995 season, and by April 1995 it was pulling in 25 million viewers a week. That was right around the time that breakout star Jennifer Aniston, as coffee shop server Rachel Green, unveiled a new hairdo. A modified version of the decades-old shag 'do, Aniston's hairstyle was more layered with several waves of hair framing her face, and then highlighted to create slight variances in color. In 1995 and 1996, hundreds of thousands of American women went to their hairstylists and salons, copies of magazines with Aniston on the cover in hand, and demanded a replica of the unnamed cut, quickly christened "the Rachel." It all started when Aniston asked her hairdresser, Chris McMillan, for something that was "a bit different"; McMillan recalled that he came up with the style in the spur of the moment, devising it as he cut and styled. The hairstyle didn't last much longer than a year, because as women tried it out, they found it difficult to maintain. The Rachel was a *style* more than it was a cut, and a professional had to set the 'do in a salon to give it the right look. Aniston dropped the style after about a year of wearing it and has since worked hard to dissociate herself from the Rachel, calling it "the ugliest haircut I've ever seen" and "cringey."

* * *

"You can sing a song to 85,000 people and they'll sing it back for 85,000 different reasons."

—Dave Grohl

Have you noticed? The smile arrow in the Amazon logo goes from a to z—as in, the company sells everything.

HAIR IT IS

Off the top of our heads, we got this idea for a page of quotes about hair (or the lack thereof), so we combed through the archives and came up with these.

"The worse the haircut, the better the man."
—John Green

"A woman who cuts her hair drastically is set to make some decisions."
—Weike Wang

"In my youth, the athletes had crew cuts and the hippies had long hair. Now the athletes have long hair, and the hippies are bald."
—Harley King

"You're only as good as your last haircut."
—Fran Lebowitz

"There's a reason why 40, 50, and 60 don't look the way they used to, and it's not because of feminism, or better living through exercise. It's because of hair dye."
—Nora Ephron

"Anyone can be confident with a full head of hair. But a confident bald man—there's your diamond in the rough."
—Larry David

"Gorgeous hair is the best revenge."
—Ivana Trump

"I wish I were taller and thinner, but the hair you can do something about."
—Hillary Clinton

"Nobody is really happy with what's on their head. People with straight hair want curly, people with curly want straight, and bald people want everyone to be blind."
—Rita Rudner

"Showing up is like 90 percent of the battle, and just make sure your hair is really cute."
—William Belli

"There is one thing about baldness—it's neat."
—Don Herold

"I think that the most important thing a woman can have—next to talent, of course—is her hairdresser."
—Joan Crawford

"It doesn't matter if your life is perfect as long as your hair color is."
—Stacy Snapp-Killian

"Hairs are your aerials. They pick up signals from the cosmos and transmit them directly into the brain. This is the reason bald-headed men are uptight."
—Bruce Robinson

"People who worry about their hair all the time, frankly, are boring."
—Barbara Bush

The digestive enzyme pepsin is the source of the brand name Pepsi, which was originally called Brad's Drink.

SWEET FANNY ADAMS!

Many common expressions are built around names—either a first name or a last name, or the whole thing. Here are the stories of the real people who inspired their namesake phrases.

PHRASE: Sweet Fanny Adams
MEANING: Something substandard or subpar; nothing
ORIGIN: In 1867, the mutilated and dismembered body of eight-year-old Fanny Adams was discovered in a field near Alton, England, and a clerk named Frederick Baker was arrested for her murder. The case was salacious, widely reported and discussed, and absolutely shocking to Victorian England, and the victim was invariably pitied in print and conversation as "sweet Fanny Adams." By the 1880s, the phrase was such a part of British vernacular that sailors in the Royal Navy began using it to refer to their meager and questionable canned meat rations, comparing it—in a darkly comic way—to human remains. By the 20th century, the phrase's meaning had evolved into a euphemism for "f*** all," meaning "nothing." "F.A." was a more polite way of delivering the phrase, and as those initials also represent "Fanny Adams," the latter came to mean the same thing.

PHRASE: Murphy's Law
MEANING: An unofficial but widely-believed-to-be-truthful axiom that states if something *can* go wrong, it probably *will* go wrong
ORIGIN: Prior to the 20th century, the concept was referred to variously in Europe and North America as Sod's Law, Finagle's Law, or Reilly's Law. All those are Irish names, reflecting anti-immigrant, anti-Irish sentiment pervasive in the 1800s—that things going wrong *had* to be the fault of the Irish somehow. Murphy's Law replaced all of those in common usage. Again, Murphy is an Irish name, but one that has a specific historical figure attached to it: in the 1940s, Captain Edward A. Murphy served as an aerospace engineer in the U.S. Air Force. Purported to be a grump and a perpetual pessimist, he frequently lamented how projects never seemed to unfold correctly, as if things that *could* be done incorrectly *would* be done so. That developed into air force slang, "Murphy's Law," which entered general usage by the early 1950s.

PHRASE: Peeping Tom
MEANING: An individual who derives tremendous pleasure from secretly viewing others, without their knowledge, during undressing or other physically intimate activities
ORIGIN: Lady Godiva was a real person who lived in England in the 11th century, but the most famous story about her might be a legend. According to lore, spotty historical records, and sketchy translations, Lady Godiva took a horseback ride around

Coventry, totally naked, as a form of protest against her husband, the local ruling lord who had passed taxes that were economically crushing to the city's poorer residents. Authorities implored the townsfolk to ignore Lady Godiva and to not look at her, but a man named Tom took a peek...or a peep, hence he became the first "Peeping Tom." However, this figure wasn't mentioned (or named) in accounts of Lady Godiva's ride until much later: in 1773, when Coventry, as part of its annual celebrations of the event, constructed a new effigy for the lusty looker known only as "Tom the Tailor."

PHRASE: The real McCoy
MEANING: The real thing; unassailably genuine
ORIGIN: Linguists theorize that the most likely origin story is some kind of corruption of the name MacKay. In Scotland in the late 19th century, the family-owned MacKay distillery produced a top-shelf whiskey so different from and superior to that of competitors that they marketed it as "The Real MacKay." That advertising catchphrase was itself a pun. The MacKay family originally hailed from Reay, Scotland, making that group "the Reay McKay."

PHRASE: The full Monty
MEANING: The whole thing; all the way
ORIGIN: The phrase is most associated with (and was internationally popularized by) the 1997 hit movie *The Full Monty*, about a group of unemployed Sheffield, England, steel workers who form an all-male stripping revue and promise to go "the full Monty," meaning completely nude. That expression was of local origin. In the early 1900s, Sir Montague Burton opened a chain of men's clothing stores in England, including a big store in Sheffield. One of the signature deals at Burton's was the "full Monty" (short for Montague), which was a full, formal three-piece suit.

PHRASE: Davy Jones's locker
MEANING: The ocean, specifically as the final resting place for sailors and pirates who die at sea
ORIGIN: "Davy Jones" first appeared in print in the 1751 novel *The Adventures of Peregrine Pickle*, as a horned, tailed, smoke-breathing monster who serves as both a grim reaper and devil of the ocean, presiding over hurricanes, shipwrecks, and other maritime calamities. His name combines linguistic elements of two belief systems. In the Caribbean (where pirates were quite active), a ghost was called a *duppy* or *duffy*. That was anglicized to "Davy," while the "Jones" is a corruption of Jonah, the biblical figure who was thrown overboard from a ship and spent some time in the belly of a sea monster. That's "Davy Jones." "Locker" comes from use of the word by pirates to describe whatever personal storage space they had on board a ship.

When they learned how much bagel-making equipment cost, Ben Cohen and Jerry Greenfield switched gears and created Ben & Jerry's Ice Cream.

LEGALLY BLONDE, STARRING CHRISTINA APPLEGATE

Some roles are so closely associated with a specific actor that it's hard to imagine he or she wasn't the first choice. But it happens all the time. Can you imagine, for example...

BRITNEY SPEARS AS ALLIE HAMILTON (*THE NOTEBOOK*, 2004)

The Notebook, based on the 1996 Nicholas Sparks romance novel, follows two young lovers in the 1940s. Steven Spielberg was originally going to direct, with Tom Cruise in mind for the lead (the part went to Ryan Gosling). After Spielberg and a few other directors passed, the studio brought in Nick Cassavetes. Final auditions for the part of Allie came down to Rachel McAdams and Britney Spears (after Ashley Judd and Reese Witherspoon were considered). Spears had tried to break into acting before, most notably in Shonda Rhimes's 2002 comedy, *Crossroads*, which got a 15 percent rating on Rotten Tomatoes. McAdams's biggest part to date was in the raunchy Rob Schneider comedy *The Hot Chick* (21 percent). Spears was at the height of her fame, so her presence in the movie would have no doubt helped at the box office. Casting director Matthew Barry said it was a "close call," but in the end, they decided to go with the actual actor: McAdams. That part, plus *Mean Girls* (which came out the same year), turned McAdams into a leading lady. Spears's acting career never took off, but in 2021, her *Notebook* screen test with Gosling was auctioned on eBay for an undisclosed amount (but the starting bid was $1 million).

PETER COYOTE AS INDIANA JONES (*RAIDERS OF THE LOST ARK*, 1981)

Coyote read for the part of the adventuring archaeologist in front of the two hottest filmmakers in Hollywood: George Lucas and Steven Spielberg. Needless to say, Coyote—who had a political theater background—was nervous. So much so that he tripped over a lighting cord before he even read his first line. He didn't get a callback for *Raiders*, but Spielberg liked his "presence" and later offered him another role: the friendly government agent, Keys, in *E.T. the Extra-Terrestrial*. (Coyote later became the narrator for all of Ken Burns's PBS documentaries.)

HEATH LEDGER AS LLEWELYN MOSS (*NO COUNTRY FOR OLD MEN*, 2007)

While adapting Cormac McCarthy's book into what would become an Oscar-winning instant classic, the Coen brothers had one actor in mind to play an everyman who is hunted by a sadistic killer: Heath Ledger, whose star seemed to rise with every movie he appeared in. Ledger was reportedly interested in the role, but he'd done five movies in the past two years and had a baby daughter at home, so he decided to take a break from acting (his next film: *The Dark Knight*). Josh Brolin really wanted the part, so while he was filming *Planet Terror*, he enlisted directors Quentin Tarantino and Robert Rodriguez to film a screen test on a million-dollar camera. The Coens' only feedback: "Who lit it?"

As Brolin tells it, "I was much bigger and I had a goatee, but it had nothing to do with the physicality. They just didn't see it. It's not what they were looking for at that moment." But thankfully, "I have a brilliant agent who just became a persistent pest and just said, 'Meet him, meet him, meet him, meet him.' Not, 'He's perfect for the part.' Not, 'You're making a mistake.' Just, 'Meet him.'" The Coens met Brolin...and cast him.

CHRISTINA APPLEGATE AS ELLE WOODS (*LEGALLY BLONDE*, 2001)

From the beginning, first-time director Robert Luketic wanted Reese Witherspoon to play the plucky blonde law student from Amanda Brown's novel. "I wanted someone with gravitas and brains," he said. But the MGM studio bosses—who initially thought it was going to be a raunchy sex comedy instead of the women's empowerment tale it ended up as—were turned off by Witherspoon's stuck-up persona in the satire *Election*, so they brought in other actresses. The first one offered the role was Tori Spelling of *Beverly Hills, 90210* fame. She declined. Luketic still pushed for Witherspoon. Then Christina Applegate was sent the script, but, "I had just gotten off *Married...with Children* and I thought it was too close to what I had been doing." (Years later, she admitted, "What a stupid move that was, right?")

Luketic again: "How about Reese Witherspoon?" MGM: "How about Gwyneth Paltrow?" She declined. The studio also courted Charlize Theron, Alicia Silverstone, Milla Jovovich, Katherine Heigl, and Jennifer Love Hewitt. No, no, no, no, and no. The studio considered Britney Spears but changed their mind after a "disastrous *Saturday Night Live* performance." Meanwhile, Luketic continued to push for Witherspoon. As she remembers, "My manager finally called and said, 'You've got to go meet with the studio head because he will not approve you. He thinks you really are your character from *Election* and that you're repellent.' And then I was told to dress sexy." Witherspoon had to audition several times before she was finally cast in what would become her most impactful role: "I think Elle just inspired people to be themselves."

JOAQUIN PHOENIX AS DOCTOR STRANGE (*DOCTOR STRANGE*, 2016)

Comic book fans had been clamoring for years for Benedict Cumberbatch to play the brilliant neurosurgeon turned superhero. *Doctor Strange* cowriter and director Scott Derrickson also wanted Cumberbatch. And Marvel Studios—which had considered Tom Hardy and Jared Leto—was also onboard with Cumberbatch. One problem: the

Need some exercise? Become a nurse. During a 12-hour shift, you'll walk between four and five miles.

British actor was playing Hamlet on stage, and the run wouldn't be done in time for the movie's production. Thankfully, the filmmakers' second choice, Joaquin Phoenix, hemmed and hawed, saying, "I don't want a multi-picture deal," and, "It wouldn't be fulfilling" with "too many requirements...against my instincts for character." That pushed the movie's release date back.

Meanwhile, Marvel considered Ewan McGregor, Ethan Hawke, Ryan Gosling, Oscar Isaac, Matthew McConaughey, Jake Gyllenhaal, Colin Farrell, and Keanu Reeves for the character of Doctor Strange. Ultimately, they decided to wait for Cumberbatch's Hamlet to breathe his last breath ("Goodnight, sweet prince"), and he took the Doctor Strange role to great acclaim.

Phoenix would go on to play a comic book villain in the gritty drama *The Joker*, which did let him follow his acting instincts. Good move: he won the Academy Award for Best Actor. Phoenix had signed on to the role thinking *The Joker* was going to be a standalone movie...but he later agreed to two sequels when Warner Bros. offered him $50 million.

LEONARDO DICAPRIO AS ANAKIN SKYWALKER (*STAR WARS: EPISODE II— ATTACK OF THE CLONES*, 2002)

As soon as *Star Wars: Episode I–The Phantom Menace* was released in 1999—which featured child actor Jake Lloyd as Anakin Skywalker, the future Darth Vader—rumors began to fly about which 20-something actor would make the transition to the Dark Side and play Anakin in the franchise's next installment. George Lucas was writing the second prequel about forbidden love, and he wanted 26-year-old Leonardo DiCaprio, who became a megastar in another story of forbidden love, *Titanic*. "I did have a meeting with George Lucas," recalled DiCaprio. "I just didn't feel ready to take that dive. At that point."

Paul Walker auditioned; he later said it's the one part he didn't get that he really wanted. (He'd go on to star in the *Fast & Furious* franchise.) Heath Ledger was considered, but never read for the part. Jonathan Brandis also auditioned, as did Colin Hanks, who was pretty obviously not right for the part, but he did like the fact that "suddenly they were saying 'Tom Hanks's son in the running to play Darth Vader!' That might be the only press clipping I ever put up on my fridge." *Cruel Intentions* star Ryan Phillippe nearly got the role but, at 27, was deemed too old. The part ultimately went to 21-year-old Hayden Christensen, who'd been nominated for a Golden Globe Award for his supporting performance in the 2001 drama *Life as a House*. "When Hayden came for his first meeting, I opened the door, and I just suddenly became flushed, because I knew," said casting director Robin Gurland. "I literally picked up the phone and called George (Lucas) and said, 'Anakin just walked in.'"

Written in 1857, "Jingle Bells" was originally a Thanksgiving song about a sleigh race.

UNCLE JOHN'S PAGE OF LISTS

More random tidbits from our bottomless files.

Top 10 Video Games of All Time (IGN, 2022)

10. *Disco Elysium*
9. *Half-Life 2*
8. *Red Dead Redemption 2*
7. *Super Mario 64*
6. *Mass Effect 2*
5. *Super Metroid*
4. *The Legend of Zelda: A Link to the Past*
3. *Portal 2*
2. *Super Mario World*
1. *The Legend of Zelda: Breath of the Wild*

12 Countries That Abolished Their Monarchies

1. France (1792)
2. Mexico (1867)
3. Brazil (1889)
4. Portugal (1910)
5. Russia (1917)
6. Germany (1918)
7. Turkey (1922)
8. Italy (1946)
9. Bulgaria (1946)
10. Romania (1947)
11. Greece (1974)
12. Nepal (2008)

10 Romance-Novel Subgenres

1. Young Adult
2. New Adult
3. Adult
4. Erotic
5. LGBTQ+
6. Fantasy
7. Paranormal
8. Sports
9. Romantic Suspense
10. Romantic Comedy

15 Parts of a U.S. Presidential Motorcade

1. Sweepers on motorcycles
2. Lead police cars
3. Presidential limo
4. Decoy presidential limo
5. Secret Service vehicles
6. Doctor vehicle
7. Electronic defense vehicle
8. Control and Support vehicle
9. Counter-assault team
10. Intelligence team
11. Hazardous materials unit
12. Press van
13. Satellite communications SUV
14. Ambulance
15. Rear police cars

8 Foot Fashions that Start with "S"

1. Shoes
2. Socks
3. Sandals
4. Slippers
5. Stilettos
6. Sneakers
7. Snowshoes
8. Steel-toe boots

5 Major Types of Anxiety Disorders

1. Generalized anxiety disorder
2. Obsessive-compulsive disorder (OCD)
3. Panic disorder
4. Post-traumatic stress disorder (PTSD)
5. Social phobia

8 Parts of the Digestive System

1. Mouth
2. Pharynx
3. Esophagus
4. Stomach
5. Small intestine
6. Large intestine
7. Rectum
8. Anus

Rubik's Cube is the best-selling toy of all time (over 350 million sold).

THERE'S A MUSEUM FOR THAT!

Museums—they're not just for paintings and historical artifacts anymore.

LEEDS CASTLE DOG COLLAR MUSEUM

Location: Broomfield, England

Background: The Leeds Castle Dog Collar Museum displays collars used from the 1400s to the 1800s, particularly those that served as defensive attire for man's best friend. Europe was once heavily covered in forests full of wolves and bears that would attack hunting dogs, prompting their masters to outfit pooches in thick iron collars adorned with sharp metal spikes that acted as predator deterrent. Many of those collars are on display at the Dog Collar Museum, as well as samples from the latter Baroque and Victorian periods, when the collar became more about fashion than purpose, and was frequently made of leather and embellished with metal and velvet flourishes.

Be Sure to See...A collar from the 19th century made completely out of silver.

MUSEUM OF MINIATURE BOOKS

Location: Baku, Azerbaijan

Background: Before opening this museum in 2002 to display her collection, Zafira Salakhova spent 30 years collecting tiny books—novelties, limited press runs, or reprintings of well-known books. Small books were a fad in Russia in the early 20th century, and these comprise a large portion of the Museum of Miniature Books displays, which amount to 6,000 books in 65 languages.

Be Sure to See... The oldest item in the building is a Koran dating to the 1600s.

AMERICAN VISIONARY ART MUSEUM

Location: Baltimore, Maryland

Background: The museum sits on a space that organizers got for free from the city of Baltimore, on the condition that they clean up pollution from the defunct whiskey warehouse and paint factory that used to stand on the location. That's an apt origin for this clearinghouse of "outsider" or "raw" art, paintings and sculptures made by untrained, amateur artists outside the art mainstream who work with found, repurposed, and nontraditional media and materials, such as tin cans, gum wrappers, cut-out pieces of cloth, or discarded dolls, used to present pieces with titles including "10 Things to Be Happy About" and "Theaters of the 13th Dimension."

Be Sure to See... Devon Smith's "First Recycled Family," a bunch of homemade robots that the artist made out of junk.

In 2008, the BP oil company spent $211 million on a logo redesign.

MUSEUM OF SALT AND PEPPER SHAKERS

Location: Gatlinburg, Tennessee

Background: Proudly proclaiming itself "the only museum of its kind," the Museum of Salt and Pepper Shakers sits just outside of the Great Smoky Mountains and is home to 20,000 sets of those little seasoning containers found on virtually every dinner table in America, offering a history lesson on how people have slightly spiced up their food since the 16th century (the age of the oldest specimens on exhibit). The museum consists of one brightly lit room, lined with shelves, onto which thousands of salt and pepper shakers made of wood, plastic, ceramic, and metal, from Europe and the Americas, sit jammed and jockeying for space. Admission is $3 a person, but that's applied as a credit to purchasing souvenir salt and pepper shakers in the substantial gift shop.

Be Sure to See... The special section devoted to pepper mills.

LE MUSÉE DES VAMPIRES

Location: Les Lilas, France

Background: Translated to English, "The Museum of Vampires" looks at the cultural history of vampires and celebrates humanity's fascination with the fictional bloodsuckers and their place in the collective consciousness. In a private home and open by appointment only, the museum features paintings and sculptures of vampires throughout history and literature, autographed pictures of every actor who has ever played Dracula in a movie, and a mummified cat.

Be Sure to See...A painting by Nicolas Claux, a French serial killer known as the "Vampire of Paris" because he drank his victims' blood.

UMBRELLA COVER MUSEUM

Location: Portland, Maine

Background: After collecting so many umbrella covers, Nancy Hoffman heeded the advice of family and friends and opened the Umbrella Cover Museum. This isn't an umbrella museum, it's an umbrella *cover* museum—showcasing the little slipcover, sheath, or tube that holds a new umbrella, made from the same material as that umbrella. Hoffman has hundreds of them, mostly in solid, normal, and totally mundane colors.

Be Sure to See... Hoffman herself. She conducts guided tours of her museum, all while playing the accordion.

KAFKA MUSEUM

Location: Prague, Czech Republic

Background: Franz Kafka was born in Prague in 1883 and buried there in 1924; in between, he became one of the most influential writers of the 20th century, penning bleak, nightmarish works about the cruelty and pointlessness of life, including *The*

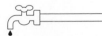

The Coca-Cola logo is recognizable to 94 percent of the world's population.

Trial and *The Metamorphosis*. The hometown museum in his honor tries to evoke the spookiness of Kafka's works, with darkly lit and creepy hallways lined with artifacts such as first editions of the author's work, letters, diaries, and drawings, accompanied by a haunting original soundtrack playing on speakers.

Be Sure to See... The sculpture of two men urinating into a pool shaped like the Czech Republic. They're animatronic, and their pee can spell out words sent by visitors via text message.

MUSEUM OF HANGOVERS

Location: Zagreb, Croatia

Background: College student Rino Dubokovic was out drinking with friends in Zagreb one night when they started telling stories about their worst and most memorable hangovers. Dubokovic got the idea to collect stories about drunken nights, and the consequences, and display relics of them in a building. Six months later, next door to the bar where the idea manifested, the Museum of Hangovers opened. The exhibits are a rotating array of 40 to 50 objects and mementos of getting drunk and paying the price the morning after, such as objects people found in their possession after sobering up that they have no recollection of acquiring.

Be Sure to See... The interactive "Beer Goggles" exhibit, where visitors can simulate what it feels like to be drunk.

MUSEUM OF ICELANDIC SORCERY AND WITCHCRAFT

Location: Hólmavík, Iceland

Background: According to local legend, Strandir, the eastern coast of Iceland, was once rife with wizards, warlocks, and magical activity. Between 1652 and 1963, 17 people from Strandir were burned at the stake on suspicion of being witches, and this museum commemorates those tragedies while also celebrating witchcraft as a real and powerful concept. Curated by Sigurdur Atlason, who claimed to be a sorcerer, the museum features a re-creation of a reanimated zombie crawling out of the ground (the crime one of the witches is said to have committed) and an exhibit on using magic to turn invisible—there are full instructions on how to do it, along with an invisible child supposedly on display.

Be Sure to See...*Nabrok*, an enchanted pair of pants made from the skin of a dead man. In Icelandic witchcraft lore, these "necropants" are said to produce endless money for whoever puts them on. (The ones on display here are a non-magical replica, however.)

* * *

> *"It means nothing to me. I have no opinion about it, and I don't care."*
> —**Pablo Picasso, July 1969,** when asked about the Moon landing

Who sold more CDs in 2016 than Adele, Drake, and Beyoncé combined? Mozart.

SYNONYMOUS BAND NAME QUIZ

Sure, they're your favorite rock and pop groups of all time, but can you spot them when we've renamed them with words that mean the same thing as their actual name? (Answers are on page 405)

1) The Moss Non-Gatherers

2) Heavy Hydrogen Balloons

3) Concurrence

4) The Automobiles

5) Her Majesty

6) The Marijuana Siblings

7) Smooch

8) Origin

9) Hurry

10) The Cops

11) Blood-Pumper

12) Windy City

13) Larry, Curly, and Moe

14) Quest

15) And Yourself As Well

16) Birds of Prey

17) Two Types of Electricity

18) Impish Fairies

19) The Medicine

20) The Walking Dead

21) Dark Sunday

22) Thick Milk

23) A Terrible Place to Work

24) Flying Limbs

25) The Not-Plants

26) Woodworkers

27) Big Scary Dinosaur

28) Terrible Pinkies

29) Doughy Loaf

30) Armed Conflict

31) Trash

32) The Makers

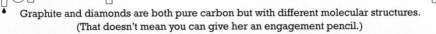

Graphite and diamonds are both pure carbon but with different molecular structures. (That doesn't mean you can give her an engagement pencil.)

LIFE AFTER THE BOMB

There's obviously nothing great about a nuclear bomb that kills millions of people and upends life as we know it. If there's any good news to be had about a theoretical nuclear war, it's that it will be over quickly. The bad news? We'll have to survive in a world where society has crumbled and the air, land, and water are fatally toxic. Here are some tips on how to make it through the early days in a post-apocalyptic nuclear wasteland.

GET PREPARED

It's unlikely that a nuclear strike is going to happen completely suddenly and with no widespread warning that doom is imminent. There are only so many countries on earth with nuclear weapons, and if the U.S. descends into a serious disagreement, tricky political situation, or war with one of those nations, it's definitely time to start considering the nuclear possibility. That means you've got some time to prepare and stock up on the essential supplies that will sustain you and your family and keep you safe in the immediate aftermath of bombs dropping.

Stock up on foods that will last the longest, both in terms of time and nutritional content. Nonperishables, such as anything canned or loaded with carbohydrates, won't spoil for a year or longer and will provide a lot of densely packed energy. Think oats, dry pasta, rice, beans, honey, sugar, dried fruits and vegetables, and powdered milk; for protein, load up on canned meat and fish. (Don't forget to store a can opener with your stash.)

Drinking water is even more important than food. Accounting primarily for drinking and for using small amounts for washing (reserved for removing radioactive particles from your clothing or skin, if necessary), a good rule of thumb is one gallon of water per person per day. Space considerations in your bunker, basement, or garage means there's only so much water you can hold in storage, so pack away some bleach and potassium iodide to purify potential drinking water you encounter after the apocalypse.

GET MORE PREPARED

Beyond food and water, pack away a first aid kit (with sterile gauze, latex gloves, antibiotic ointments, alcohol wipes, tweezers, and other essentials), vital or required medicines (such as an inhaler for asthma sufferers or insulin for diabetics), a solar-powered radio (for electricity-free news and safety updates, should they be forthcoming), a flashlight with batteries, and N95 masks or ventilators, for when you eventually venture out into the wastelands to replenish your supplies or survey the damage.

Fastest record to go platinum (sell a million copies on Billboard):
Post Malone's *Beerbongs & Bentleys* (2008), in four days.

However, before you start shopping for end-of-the-world supplies, assess the likelihood of your area being one that gets hit. Do you live near a military base, airfield, or major airport, or within a large population center, particularly one on a coast? If so, you might be better off evacuating and driving as far away as possible as quickly as possible. But if you're not in one of those hot zones, you're probably going to be fine—for now.

THE FIRST MOMENTS

If you're anywhere inside of a half-mile radius of the atomic bomb's point of impact, it is extremely unlikely you're going to live. You'll probably be killed by either the destruction of the bomb itself, flying debris, or the immediate, intense burst of atomic energy. The farther away you are from the bomb, the greater your chances of survival. Between one-half mile to one mile away brings a 50 percent chance of surviving the bomb, a mile to a mile and a half increases your odds to 85 percent, and a mile and a half to two miles out brings survival odds of 97 percent. If you're more than two miles away, it's highly unlikely the atomic bomb itself will make you meet your end.

Regardless of how far away you are from the dropped bomb, it's important to brace for impact. Experts say your chance of injury or death in the immediate blast decreases if you hit the deck: fall to the ground, face-down, and up against a sturdy building, if at all possible; failing that, fall into a ditch or gutter. You're far less likely to be tossed into the air from that position, or to be hit by flying shrapnel or broken glass or to sustain flash burns from the bomb's enormous heat wave. If you're inside when all this is going on, falling flat on a basement floor is the best option, followed by lying along an inside wall, or under a table or bed. Avoid windows, and no matter where you drop flat, burrow your face into your arms, with the most vulnerable parts—your eyes—buried into the crook of your elbow.

INITIAL RADIOACTIVITY

In the immediate aftermath of a nuclear bomb attack, the blast and heat waves are far more likely to kill or injure than the first wave of radiation, or initial radioactivity. Rays are expelled quickly and explosively and then burn out immediately. Radiation delivered in this way is an intense and directed concentration of what comes from an X-ray machine or from the sun, so it's not necessarily deadly—but your location at the moment of impact certainly determines how much sickness (or death) that radioactivity may cause. Even with buildings and other objects blocking or absorbing some radiation, people within two-thirds of a mile of an explosion will endure a fatal dose.

The terms "pop music" and "rock 'n' roll" originated in the 1920s but weren't widely used until the 1950s.

However, if you're within that diameter of danger and don't die immediately from radiation, there's a chance you will shortly. Signs of moderate to severe radiation poisoning don't present for a while, and the less radiation you soaked up, the longer it may take for symptoms to show. For example, you might experience nausea and vomiting a few hours after the blast, or two weeks later notice that all your hair suddenly falls out. But this is not necessarily fatal: if you've survived this long, you'll probably survive your bout of radiation poisoning in the long run.

STOP THE RADIATION

Also known as *fallout*, residual radiation is the toxic, radioactive material produced after the bomb hits. The bomb creates a deep crater wherever it lands, and in the process displaces dust, dirt, and debris, sending it shooting up hundreds of feet into the air. That stuff goes up, and so it must come down, and when it does, it's been completely infected with radiative particles, transforming into a black soot, or "black rain." It's hot and will contaminate whatever it falls upon or comes in contact with. It also lingers, just hanging out in the atmosphere like smoke, pollution, or pollen—but much more unpleasant and killing a lot faster.

There are three kinds of radiation particles, classified by what kind of materials can resist or block their absorption. Alpha particles are stopped by skin and clothes but can cause damage if inhaled. Beta particles can travel through wood and intensely burn skin. Gamma rays can penetrate anything short of lead. This means that if you want to survive your new life in a radiation-poisoned atmosphere, you're going to need to live in a shelter that can block all three types of particles. To reduce radiation penetration down to nominal, unharmful levels, the walls of your (preferably underground) shelter need to be made of 21 centimeters of steel, 70 centimeters of rock, 66 centimeters of concrete, 3 meters of wood, or a meter of soil. At any rate, get into the shelter as quickly as possible after the moment of the bomb's impact, then stay inside, completely sealed, for at least 48 hours; the lingering radiation is at its most intense levels during the first two days after a blast.

TIME TO FORAGE

When you're all out of food, and you've got to find more food, it's important to be careful about what fresh food you eat and how. First, protect yourself when heading out into your radioactive neighborhood. Wear as much clothing as possible, covering every part of your skin. That prevents radiation absorption, particularly from the alpha and beta particles still floating around, and painful burns from the betas. Dress

From 1912–48, Olympic medals were awarded to artists and musicians who created the best artwork and songs about sports.

in layers, wearing gloves, thick boots, a mask that covers as much of your face as possible, sunglasses, and a hat, preferably one that fits over your ears to protect them.

Plan on hunting for fresh meat to replenish or supplement your canned tuna? That's fine, and it's even relatively safe to eat the flesh of animals that have been wandering around, absorbing up radioactive particles. After killing an animal in the manner you see fit, prepare it for consumption: carefully skin it with a sharp knife, making sure that the skin does not touch the increasingly exposed meat underneath, if you can help it. The skin is full of poisonous radiation, so discard it. Also, don't eat the organ meats, particularly the heart, liver, and kidneys, as that's where radiation concentrates and festers. Avoid eating meat close to the bone, too, because radiation also seeps into the marrow.

Wild-growing plants are edible, but after a while in a radioactive environment, not a lot of palatable food sources will grow well. It's not a bad idea to make yourself a little garden focused on root vegetables: potatoes, carrots, turnips, parsnips, and the like grow underground, where they aren't as subject to absorbing those toxic particles floating around.

And should you find any water, such as in an open stream or river, it's likely fine to drink, provided you boil it first to get rid of various bacteria and microorganisms in addition to radiation. Well water, or other underground water sources, are objectively safer in this case, but whatever water you find, boil it first, or at least purify it. Two to four drops of bleach can purify a gallon of water, while five drops of iodide make a gallon of dirty water safe.

* * *

18 REAL CRYPTOCURRENCIES

Haha Coin	BitCoen
PonziCoin	Unobtanium
JRR Token	FUNK Coins
Cthulhu Offerings	CAT Token
PotCoin	Useless Ethereum Token
TrumpCoin	FuzzBalls
PUTinCoin	Mooncoin
Coinye	Garlicoin
WhopperCoin	Jesus Coin

Each year, American businesses buy 16.5 million chairs, while 900 million tons of office furniture go to landfills.

APOCALYPSE JOKES

Serious question: if you're reading these jokes during the actual apocalypse, are they still funny?

So what if I don't know what *apocalypse* means? It's not like it's the end of the world.

People are making end-of-the-world jokes like there's no tomorrow.

I used to make really bad end-of-the-world jokes, but Armageddon better at it.

A lunar eclipse happens when Earth is between the sun and the moon. A solar eclipse happens when the moon is between Earth and the sun. Apocalypse happens when the sun is between Earth and the moon.

Q: What is the safest room to be in during a zombie apocalypse?
A: The living room.

Q: What is a zombie's favorite shampoo?
A: Head & Shoulders.

Q: What's the funniest way to prepare for the impending zombie apocalypse?
A: Have the world's undertakers tie all the corpses' shoelaces together.

What do you call a redneck apocalypse?

Armagit-r-done. Okay, how about a cheesy apocalypse? Parmegeddon.

I met a horse who keeps talking about the apocalypse. He told me the end is neigh.

Porgy: Did you see that movie about all that cattle at the end of the world? It's called *Apocalypse Cow.*
Bessie: They weren't cows; they were pigs, and it's called *Aporkalypse Now.*

Why hasn't the zombie apocalypse happened already? Someone's really been dragging their feet on this.

In case of an actual zombie apocalypse, your best bet is going to a Costco. They have tons of food and thick concrete walls, and the zombies can't get in without a membership.

I met a woman in southern Mexico who kept going on and on about the end of the world with her Acapulco lips.

Q: Why did the alarm clock go to the ruler during the apocalypse?
A: Desperate times called

for desperate measures.

Q: What's the best soda to drink while getting ready for the apocalypse?
A: Dr Prepper.

At the end of the world, they arrived—one had laryngitis, one had strep throat, one had a bad cold, and one had yelled too much during a concert the previous night: the Four Hoarse Men of the Apocalypse.

If a zombie apocalypse were to happen in Vegas, would it stay in Vegas?

Based on my history with trying to open a Capri Sun, I don't feel like I'd be able to stab a zombie during the apocalypse.

I asked the hotel checkout girl, "Do you provide turndown service?"
She said, "Sure. I wouldn't go out with you if you were the last guy on earth after the zombie apocalypse and your saliva contained the antidote."

Q: What's the last thing you'll see at the end of the world?
A: The letter *d*.

Sour notes: 5 percent of the population has a biological condition called musical anhedonia that causes them to dislike music in any form.

AMAZING LUCK

If you're interested in reading heartwarming stories about good
fortune changing people's lives, you're in luck!

OOP$IE

LaQuedra Edwards had placed $40 in cash into a California Lottery self-service kiosk at a Vons supermarket in the Los Angeles area in November 2021, intending to select and purchase a round of scratch-off tickets. As she reached out to the touchscreen, someone walking by bumped into her, causing her to push the wrong selection. She wound up with a $30 200X Scratcher, instead of the collection of cheaper tickets she'd intended to buy. Annoyed, Edwards took her ticket to her car and scratched it off—and it won her the $10 million jackpot.

THE MOST COMFORTABLE COUCH

In June 2022, Vicky Umodu moved into a new home in Colton, California, and scoured Craigslist to find inexpensive or free furniture with which to furnish the place. She found a family that was giving away all the furniture that belonged to a deceased relative, and she arranged to pick up a couch on offer. Once she had it home and set up, she noticed one of the cushions didn't feel right; feeling something rigid and rectangular underneath, Umodu figured it was a heating pad. It wasn't—it was a stack of envelopes containing a total of $36,000 in cash. Umodu immediately called the family that had given her the sofa and returned the money; as a reward, they gifted her $2,200 and bought her a brand-new refrigerator.

DOUBLE OR NOTHING

Kevin Lewis of Cincinnati entered a monthly $1,000,000 raffle at the local Horseshoe Casino. And then another, different Kevin Lewis, also of Cincinnati, entered the same drawing. Both Kevin Lewises were in the house at the time the winner was announced, and the winner was...Kevin Lewis of Cincinnati. Actually, the *wrong* Kevin Lewis came up to get his check in front of the TV cameras, and Horseshoe Casino officials realized it later on. Owing to the confusion caused by two identical entrants, the casino gave the other Kevin Lewis $1,000,000, and also let the first Kevin Lewis keep his prize.

AN EYE FOR ART

Robin Darvell, a retired eye surgeon, went to a low-key auction in London in 2003 and placed a winning bid of $50 for a nondescript box of what looked like random junk. Of the contents, he did, however, like a small oil painting about the size of a postcard and adorned with a faded, illegible artist signature. Darvell thought it resembled the work of famous painter John Constable, which his family thought was ridiculous. Darvell threw the painting in a drawer and forgot about it. Ten years later, his son found the art; just for fun, he took it to get appraised on the British TV series *Treasure Detectives*. That postcard painting was, in fact, a Constable original, and it was worth just under $400,000.

ROADSIDE ASSISTANCE

Sara Berg and her cousin, Lisa Meier, were driving on a Minnesota highway when one of their tires popped, forcing them to pull over. One problem: they had no idea how to change a tire. As they were standing helpless at the side of the road, a man named Victor Giesbrecht came by and gave them assistance. They were back on the road for less than five minutes when they came upon Giesbrecht's vehicle pulled to the side of the road—the man's wife explained that he'd suffered what they thought was a heart attack while driving and didn't have a pulse and wasn't breathing. Meier called 911 while Berg, a certified nursing assistant, performed CPR. That got his heart beating again, and Giesbrecht eventually made a full recovery.

HAS A NICE RING TO IT

Passing a Kansas City homeless man holding out a cup for spare change donations one day, Sarah Darling obliged—but as the coins fell in, her engagement ring slipped off, too. She didn't realize it for hours, and figured the ring was gone forever as it might be difficult to track down the homeless man, Billy Ray Harris. He went and got the ring appraised at a jewelry store, which offered him $4,000. Harris resisted the windfall and, the next day, returned to the spot where he'd met Darling. She came by and she got the ring back, and then she set up an online crowdfunding page to help Harris. Seeking $1,000 in donations, Darling's campaign raised $190,000, which Harris used to buy a car and make a down payment on a home. Additionally, the media attention the story received put Harris back in touch with his family, whom he hadn't seen in more than 15 years.

* * *

"If you have any young friends who aspire to become writers, the second greatest favor you can do them is to present them with copies of *The Elements of Style*. The first greatest, of course, is to shoot them now, while they're happy."

—Dorothy Parker

Where did artists store their oil paints before the paint tube was invented in 1841? In pig bladders.

DUBIOUS SPORTS ACHIEVEMENTS

Every athlete dreams of making it to the big leagues, and then making it into their sport's record books. They probably didn't plan on setting records in the following ways, however.

LEAST-EFFECTIVE SCORER IN THE NBA

The NBA uses a statistic called "player efficiency rating" (PER) as a metric to determine just how effective players are on the offensive side, regardless of the number of minutes played. By these criteria, the long-term player who made the least impact on the NBA is Greg Kite, who played in 680 games over 11 seasons (1983–1995) with seven teams. He averaged 2.5 points and 0.5 assists per game, leading to a PER of 6.5. (For the sake of comparison, Michael Jordan had the highest PER ever: 27.9.)

BIGGEST DRAFT BUST IN THE NBA

Almost as bad on paper as Greg Kite was Darko Milicic, a center who racked up career averages of 6 points and 4.2 rebounds over a career that lasted 10 seasons (2003–2013). Plenty of players have produced similarly mediocre results, but Milicic's lack of accomplishments stands out because he didn't deliver on his promise. The 2003 NBA Draft class is one of the most stacked ever. Among the top five selections: future Hall of Famers LeBron James, Carmelo Anthony, Chris Bosh, and Dwayne Wade. The Detroit Pistons drafted Milicic at number 2, behind James and in front of all those other superstars.

WORST FREE THROW SHOOTER

Ben Wallace is a member of the Naismith Memorial Basketball Hall of Fame because he's one of the NBA's all-time best defenders—he was the Defensive Player of the Year a record four times. On offense, Wallace wasn't so great, particularly at the free throw line. On those supposedly easy, stand-and-shoot post-foul shots, he made 1,109 out of 2,679, for a career free throw shooting percentage of just 41 percent, the NBA's worst ever.

PRO BASEBALL PITCHER WHO LOST THE MOST GAMES

The Major League Baseball pitcher who lost the most games for his teams is also the pitcher who won the most games: Cy Young, who finished his career with a 511-315 record, and played in the 1890s and 1900s, when teams used a three-man pitcher rotation (today they use five). The pitcher with the most lopsided win-loss record is Jim Hughey. He pitched in 145 games (1891–1899), and was credited for 29 wins and

Levi Strauss named his invention "waist overalls" in 1873.
"Blue jeans" didn't catch on until the 1960s.

80 losses, a winning percentage of .266. In his final season, he set a record for most losses in a season with 30—and the record still stands today.

STATISTICALLY WORST MAJOR LEAGUE BASEBALL PITCHERS

Major League Baseball determines a pitcher's efficiency with a stat called "earned run average." The lower the number, the better the pitcher, because the figure accounts for how many opposing runs the pitcher is directly responsible for, amortized across a nine-inning game. As of 2022, 22 Major League pitchers fared so poorly in their brief stints, allowing so many runs through bad play and easily hit balls, that they have an infinite earned run average. The most recent is Zach Weiss, who, after toiling in the minor leagues for eight years, got called up to the Cincinnati Reds: he pitched in one inning in which he didn't secure any outs and allowed four runs off two hits and two walks.

WORST ALL-AROUND PLAYER IN BASEBALL HISTORY

This honor could reasonably be bestowed on a forgotten early Major Leaguer named John Gochnaur. He managed to eke out a three-year career in the big leagues, playing for the Cleveland Naps and the Brooklyn Superbas despite routinely putting up terrible numbers on both offense and defense. His lifetime batting average was a paltry .187, and he never hit a single home run. On the field as a shortstop, he bumbled the ball constantly, committing 146 errors in his short career—98 of them coming in his third and final year.

WORST GOALTENDER IN NHL HISTORY

The NHL was strapped for talent in the mid-1940s, as vast numbers of Canadian and American players left their teams to fight for their countries in World War II. The New York Rangers lost all their goalies, and hired Ken McAuley, a man with minimal hockey experience and who had already fought in and returned from military service, to tend goal. In the 1943–1944 season, McAuley set a still-standing NHL record when opposing teams scored an average of 6.24 goals against him each game. (That figure is inflated only a little by a 15-0 loss to the Detroit Red Wings.) Over his brief career, McAuley won 17 games, lost 64, tied in 15, and finished with a goals-against average of 5.61.

LEAST-EFFICIENT SCORER IN THE NHL

Ken Daneyko spent his entire 19-year NHL career with the New Jersey Devils, where he set a team record for most time spent in the penalty box (2,516 minutes). He played the position of defenseman, a title he took very seriously, because he went years without ever scoring a goal. Between 1999 and 2002, a period of more than three seasons, he set an NHL record for most consecutive games without scoring (255). In six seasons, he didn't score any goals, and he also holds the NHL record for lowest point-per-game average.

It can take between 12 hours and two weeks for oil paints to dry.
Acrylic paints: between 10 minutes and two hours.

MOST-SACKED QUARTERBACK

The quarterback sack—in which a defender pulls the opposing QB to the ground before the QB has the chance to throw the ball—is a rare and exciting occurrence in an NFL game. Sacks started being recorded as a statistic in 1963, and since that time, legendary quarterback Tom Brady has achieved the record for being sacked the most (565 total in regular and postseason games)...but with a career spanning more than two decades, he also holds the record for most games started as a quarterback, so he's averaged fewer than two sacks per game.

MOST NASCAR RACES WITH NO WINS

J. D. McDuffie raced in NASCAR's top-level Winston Cup series for a long time, from 1963 to 1991. He started in 653 races, and finished most of them, and finished most of them well, landing in the top-10 more than 100 times. However, in all that time, McDuffie never actually *won* a race. (And he died in an on-track crash in 1991.)

MOST SOCCER OWN-GOALS

It's hard to score a goal in a professional soccer game, and it's even harder to score on one's own net. Richard Dunne holds the record for most "own goals" in the century-plus history of England's high-profile Premier League. In 432 games, he somehow kicked the ball into his own goal, past his own goalie, 10 times.

LEAST WINNINGEST PROFESSIONAL GOLFER

With a limited field of only a few hundred golfers competing in any given season, eventually every long-term member of the PGA Tour eventually wins at least one tournament. Well...everyone except Brett Quigley. He participated in more than 400 tournaments in the 1990s and 2000s, but the closest he ever got to winning were his five second-place finishes. (He fared slightly better on lower-tier Nationwide, Buy.com, and PGA Tour Champions circuits, winning one tournament in each of those.)

WORST PERFORMANCE IN A GOLF TOURNAMENT

Mike Reasor played in the PGA Tour's Tallahassee Open in 1974 and shot terribly on both days of the weekend tournament. On day one, he racked up 123 strokes (that's 51 shots over par) and the next day, improved slightly to 114 (42 over par).

MOST LOPSIDED TENNIS CHAMPIONSHIP

Professional men's singles tennis uses a fixed scoring system: a player wins if they're the first to score six points in three sets. In the final, championship match of the 1881 Wimbledon tournament, William Renshaw easily won in three straight sets, beating John Hartley 6-0, 6-1, 6-1. That quick vanquishing still holds a pro-tennis record for quickest championship round, as it took Hartley just 36 minutes to bow out.

Vice President Kamala Harris's parents are Jamaican and Indian immigrants.

IRONIC, ISN'T IT?

*There's nothing like a good dose of irony to put the problems
of day-to-day life into proper perspective.*

CONTINUING THE CYCLE OF IRONY

In an effort to urge their government to "drastically reduce emissions," a group of French climate activists disrupted the 2022 Tour de France by running onto the course. The race was delayed for 15 minutes. Their message about lowering emissions might have been better received had they attempted this at a car race instead of a bike race.

IRONIC ANTIDOTE

After a ruler from Asia Minor (modern-day Turkey) named Mithridates (120–63 BC) waged an unsuccessful war against Rome, he retreated to the lands north of the Black Sea to build a new army. But this ruler's ruthless tactics proved too much for the locals to take, so they revolted. With the angry mob closing in, Mithridates tried to kill himself with some poison that he kept in his satchel. But he didn't die. Why not? He'd been so paranoid that his foes would poison him that he'd been drinking small amounts every day to build up immunity. So, the poison failed to kill Mithridates, but it *did* make him too weak to kill himself with his sword instead. The angry locals showed up and finished the job for him.

GROUNDED IRONY

In June 2022, after a record number of flight delays and cancellations marred Memorial Day weekend for travelers, U.S. Secretary of Transportation Pete Buttigieg met with airline industry officials and told them to hire more customer-service workers. Afterward, Buttigieg drove to New York because his flight there had been canceled.

63×246=IRONY

During a heat wave in the summer of 2022, the Oxfordshire City Council in England issued a 491-page environmental report detailing plans to "make Oxfordshire greener, fairer, and healthier due to the relationship between transport, quality of life, health and the environment." However, in an attempt to be "inclusive" (because not everyone on the council likes to read reports online), a copy was printed for every councilmember, whether they requested one or not. Let's do the math: There were 63 councilors, and each 491-page report used 246 sheets of paper. That totaled 15,498 pieces of paper. "Looking round the chamber, I see many councilors looking tired and weary," commented Conservative member David Bartholomew as he held up his report. "It's not just the heat, it's having to carry this around."

IRONIC CLAIM

In May 2019, a company called Answers in Genesis sued its insurance company for refusing to cover the damages caused by a flood at the Noah's Ark Museum in Kentucky.

WHIPPING UP MORE IRONY

The Black Death pandemic, which killed up to 200 million Europeans in the mid-14th century, consisted of two types of plague: bubonic, a bacterial infection that spreads from person to person via fleas; and pneumonic, a bacterial lung infection that spreads via airborne saliva droplets. But the flagellants believed that the Black Death was a punishment from God. Large groups of these religious zealots walked from town to town while flogging one another. Their message: stop sinning to stop the Plague. Ironically, all the flagellants' flogging (which sent the fleas flying) and preaching (which sent the saliva flying) only contributed to the spread.

WHO STOLE MY IRONY?

In 2018, thieves pulled off a carefully planned job in Winnipeg, Manitoba: in the predawn hours, they infiltrated a movie location and stole a van containing a quarter-million dollars' worth of film equipment. The heist delayed the production of the movie *Vandits*, about teenagers "pulling off a ridiculous heist." Said director Stu Stone: "The irony is not lost on us that we got heisted before our first day of shooting."

THE EFFECTS OF LONG EXPOSURE TO IRONY

In 2021, the Dutch Authority for Nuclear Safety and Radiation Protection (ANVS) issued a warning to consumers who bought Energy Armor–brand bracelets, necklaces, and sleeping masks, which the company claimed can "block the harmful effects" of 5G mobile networks. Numerous studies have found no harmful effects of 5G. But if you do happen to own an Energy Armor bracelet, necklace, or sleeping mask, you should know that ANVS tests revealed that these trinkets are radioactive: they can cause severe health effects after prolonged use. "Don't wear it any more, put it away safely, and wait for the return instructions," stated ANVS.

SONGS OF IRONY

- During an Eagles concert at London's Hyde Park, several men and one woman in the VIP section were removed from the venue after a brawl broke out while the band was singing their hit "Take it Easy."
- Chad Gray, frontman of the heavy metal band Mudvayne, was at a Tampa, Florida, concert singing the song "Not Falling"...when he fell off the stage.

The wheelchair was invented in 1869; the folding wheelchair, in 1933.

HISTORY'S MOST PILFERED PAINTING, PART II

*In part I of the story (see page 37), Adoration of the Mystic Lamb, a 15th-century
12-paneled painting of religious art by brothers Jan van Eyck and Hubert
van Eyck, endured multiple thefts and multiple theft attempts. As the 20th
century dawned, it wouldn't be spared from the chaos of war. Here's the next
chapter in the tale of the most frequently stolen painting of all time.*

ALL OVER EUROPE

Nine years after acquiring *Adoration of the Mystic Lamb*'s six side panels as one of
the chief attractions for an art museum intended to rival other great collections of
Europe, Prussian king Frederick William III saw his plan come to fruition with the
1830 opening of the Konigliche National-Gallerie in Berlin. He died in 1840, and the
building was renamed the Kaiser-Frederick-William Museum in his honor in 1904;
the *Adoration of the Mystic Lamb* panels continued to draw huge crowds. By this time in
the early 20th century, art historians were calling it the most influential painting of all
time because of how it inspired a shift in Europe toward the use of oil paints.

Nevertheless, the Berlin museum displayed the panels incorrectly: they split them
vertically and arranged them horizontally, in a row. As for the rest of *Adoration of
the Mystic Lamb*, most of the remaining panels stayed intact in Ghent at Saint Bavo's
Cathedral as a valuable draw in art tourism, which was a bourgeoning industry after
the various Napoleonic wars calmed down and before the 20th century dawned.
At this point in time, *Adoration* existed in three separate pieces, thousands of miles
apart: the main sections in Ghent, which was now part of Belgium; the side panels in
Berlin; and the long-removed Adam and Eve panels pulled from storage in Ghent and
sent across the country for display at a museum in Brussels.

DON'T GIVE IT AWAY

Fast forward to 1914, and the dawn of World War I. While the conflict began
with the assassination of the archduke of Austria-Hungary, Germany (which, by
1914, included the formerly independent nation of Prussia) quickly asserted itself

If every human being were squeezed together into a ball,
it would have a diameter of less than one mile.

as the main aggressor, taking advantage of Europe's state of political turmoil to begin an imperial march to dominate the continent. German troops advanced, making clear their intention to invade, occupy, and annex Belgium, and striking fear and concern into the heart of Gabriel Van den Gheyn, the cleric or *canon* in charge of overseeing the well-being of the art and treasures at Saint Bavo's Cathedral in Ghent.

With mere days before troops would arrive in Ghent, Van den Gheyn met with local magistrate Émile Braun to determine how to protect *Adoration of the Mystic Lamb*, knowing that the Germans would most certainly want to plunder the portions of the painting not already housed in Berlin. Braun suggested appeasement—leave the painting in the cathedral and just let the Germans have it. If their chief object of desire was gone by the time they arrived, Braun theorized, the Germans would be so mad they'd burn Ghent to the ground.

INSIDE OUT

Van den Gheyn, appalled that the magistrate wanted the church and the town to not fight back at all, devised a different plan. With the assistance of Antoon Stillemans, the Bishop of Ghent, he decided to smuggle the painting out of the cathedral and hide it until the war was over. One problem: the Germans would arrive in the city in a matter of hours, so there wasn't time to ship it overseas and out of the war zone that covered most of Europe, let alone get it outside of town.

Van den Gheyn found an ally in a Belgian federal cabinet minister (whose identity has never been publicly disclosed), who drew up—or rather forged—official government documents to make it look like they'd shipped *Adoration of the Mystic Lamb* to King George V of England. That would give the pair something to show German officials who would notice the painting was gone and inevitably start sniffing around about its whereabouts. Van den Gheyn also lied to Saint Bavo's Cathedral staff, telling them the altarpiece had been safely shipped off to England.

But really, *Adoration of the Mystic Lamb* hadn't gone far. On the day before Germans rolled into Ghent, Van den Gheyn utilized the cathedral's one-hour closing for lunch and gathered four locals (their names unknown) who took the panels out of Saint Bavo's into the adjoining Episcopal Palace. Then they brought in four large wooden cases (disassembled so as not to arouse suspicion), put them together inside the palace, and, that night, wrapped each panel in blankets and loaded them into the wooden cases. On August 31, 1914, with a borrowed junk cart from a traveling merchant, the four accomplices drove the broken-down *Adoration of the Mystic Lamb* through Ghent, undetected. They left some pieces at the bishop's home, and some at other houses.

As of 2020, the U.S. Navy had 11 aircraft carriers, 4 guided missile submarines, 14 ballistic missile submarines, and 50 nuclear attack submarines.

ON THE MOVE

As the war progressed, the occupying German forces persuaded several Ghent residents to serve as spies, to keep an eye on any resistance plans. One such individual heard rumors in 1917 that *Adoration of the Mystic Lamb*—which German leaders were livid to find missing and didn't believe had been shipped away—was still in town. Acting on the tip, a German officer's party tore apart the Episcopal Palace in search of the panels, looking inside walls and ripping up floorboards. But, of course, they didn't find *Adoration* there.

In late 1917 and early 1918, Germans began to commandeer private homes in Ghent to use as barracks for soldiers. With the possibility lurking that one of those houses could be among those where *Adoration of the Mystic Lamb* had been secretly stored, Van den Gheyn and his same four cohorts snuck out the panels in the middle of the night one evening in February 1918 and deposited them at the church of Saint Stephen, which sat on the far north end of Ghent and was of no strategic importance to the Germans. The building was unlikely to be searched, but just in case, Van den Gheyn and company moved the church's confessional booth away from a wall, planted the painting inside the wall, and then moved the booth back into place. World War I would end with an armistice nine months later. Nine days after that, the panels were moved back to display at Saint Bavo's.

WHAT A TREATY

The combatants of World War I agreed to a post-war plan, the Treaty of Versailles, that addressed and ordered the defeated Germans to return art looted not only in the recent conflict but also in the Franco-Prussian war of the 1870s. Although no Prussian or German government or army had technically stolen the portion of *Adoration of the Mystic Lamb* housed in the Berlin gallery—it was stolen and sold to a private collector who then sold it to the king of Prussia—the Treaty of Versailles specifically called for those side panels to go back to Ghent, as a form of reparations.

In 1919, the side panels came down from their perch in the Berlin museum and were loaded onto a train covered in Belgian flags. As it traveled through Belgium, it stopped in every major city, greeted by crowds singing the national anthem, celebrating the return of their greatest national and cultural treasure. At the culmination of a massive public celebration in Ghent, the entire *Adoration of the Mystic Lamb* was reassembled in Saint Bavo's Cathedral for the first time in more than 100 years.

Bob's Burgers fact: Tina Belcher voice actor Dan Mintz has adapted the "Tina groan" into his own life.

SOMETHING'S MISSING

On April 10, 1934, a panicked crowd gathered inside and around Saint Bavo's Cathedral on account of an emergency: two of the lower portions of *Adoration of the Mystic Lamb* had disappeared. Gone were "The Just Judges" (which featured two biblical figures painted to look like the artists, Jan and Hubert van Eyck), and "Saint John the Baptist." Investigating police commissioner Antoine Lysterborghs didn't have the time to gather evidence right away, as a store across the street from Saint Bavo's was robbed of an expensive wheel of cheese at the same time, and the cheese took precedence.

A few days after the paintings disappeared, the anonymous thief sent police a ransom note, demanding one million in Belgian francs for the return of "The Just Judges"; as a demonstration of good will, the thief returned "Saint John the Baptist" along with the demands and instructions. When briefed on the matter, Belgian prime minister Hubert Pierlot refused to pay the ransom. "One does not do business with gangsters," he said. "We're not in America." Thus, "The Just Judges" was never returned, and it's never resurfaced. A decade after the theft of the original, Ghent leaders paid an art forger to paint a replacement.

So, who stole "The Just Judges"? It's very likely a Belgian stockbroker named Arsène Goedertier. In November 1934, Goedertier collapsed at a political rally and, just before dying of a heart attack, told his attorney, Georges de Vos, "I alone know where the *Mystic Lamb* is." He directed Vos to a drawer in his writing table, where Vos discovered unsent ransom notes and a baffling "clue" about the painting's whereabouts that didn't lead to any discoveries: "It rests in a place where neither I, nor anybody else, can take it away without arousing the attention of the public."

NEW WAR, SAME PLAN

With World War II underway in 1940, and with Nazi Germany's Adolf Hitler on a quest to conquer Europe, a German invasion of Belgium was inevitable. Authorities at Saint Bavo's Cathedral in Ghent made plans to get *Adoration of the Mystic Lamb* as far out of town was possible. The Belgian government arranged for the altarpiece to head to Vatican City, the city-state headquarters of the Roman Catholic Church and an enclave surrounded on all sides by Italy.

But while the painting made its way to the Vatican under armed guard, Italy declared war, joining Germany in a military coalition. With the Belgian contingent no longer able to traverse Italy to get to the Vatican, they had to dump the painting in friendly territory, so they deposited it in a museum in the French city of Pau. The

Edward Scissorhands was filmed in a neighborhood in Carpenter's Run, Florida. (Does that make Edward a Florida Man?)

German military was well aware of the location of *Adoration of the Mystic Lamb*, but signed an agreement with Belgium and France that stated all three governments would have to approve any proposed moves of the painting.

DON'T GET SALTY

Nevertheless, in 1942, after Germany completed its takeover of Belgium, the Nazis took *Adoration* anyway. Hitler ordered it sent to Schloss Neuschwanstein, a castle in Bavaria. Nazi officials justified the seizure as a way to protect *Adoration* from getting destroyed in the war. However, not long after it arrived in Bavaria, increased Allied air raids created an undeniably unsafe atmosphere; the painting was moved underground, into the Altaussee salt mines in Austria. *Adoration of the Mystic Lamb* stayed intact there, but the salty air damaged the painting.

Hitler had big plans for *Adoration of the Mystic Lamb*: after he'd taken over Europe, he'd display the painting, and tens of thousands of other looted masterpieces taken as war spoils from across the continent, in his Fuhrer-Museum to be built in Linz, Austria, near his hometown.

In April 1945, with the defeat of the Nazis inevitable and imminent, Hitler committed suicide in his bunker—but not before issuing a decree that all treasures acquired during the war were to be destroyed. The Allies had already created the Monuments, Fine Arts, and Archives program, employing a network of specialized spies who daringly recovered thousands of pieces of art purloined by the Nazis before the Nazis could destroy them, and who coordinated returning the pieces to their rightful owners.

YOU CAN GO HOME AGAIN

Since the end of World War II, *Adoration of the Mystic Lamb* has enjoyed one of the longest periods of uninterrupted peace in its 600-year history. After some minor retouching work in the early 1950s to repair damage incurred from the salt mines, the entire piece underwent an eight-year restoration at the cost of $2.4 million. Upon completion in 2020, the painting was installed in an impenetrable fortress of an enclosure at Saint Bavo's Cathedral in Ghent. The $35 million bulletproof glass case stands 20 feet tall, boasts a climate-controlled interior measuring 1,000 square feet, and hangs from steel supports above the cathedral's altar, which itself is cordoned off by two thick metal security doors. So if anybody wants to steal *Adoration of the Mystic Lamb* again, at least it will be *extremely* difficult to pull off.

The U.S. Army is one year older than the U.S.

FIRST BOOK / WORST BOOK

*Everybody has to start somewhere, even some of the greatest
and most successful writers of all time.*

AUTHOR: DAN BROWN

Notable Works: Brown wrote *The Da Vinci Code* and other best-selling books *(Angels
& Demons, Inferno)* about Robert Langdon, a brilliant art history professor adept at
solving conspiracies.
First Book: In the late 1980s, Brown wrote a humorous book sending up the era's
dating culture (and the many serious books about it) called *187 Men to Avoid: A Survival
Guide for the Romantically Frustrated Woman.* Brown wrote it with his wife, Blythe Newlon,
and under what could just barely be considered a pen name: Danielle Brown.

AUTHOR: STEPHEN KING

Notable Works: King is one of the best-selling authors of all time, known primarily
for his horror and science-fiction works, including *The Stand*, *The Dark Tower*, *The
Tommyknockers*, *Misery*, *The Green Mile*, *Cujo*, and *Christine*. His career took off in 1974
with the publishing of *Carrie*, a novel about a murderous telekinetic teenage girl.
First Book: Before *Carrie*, King wrote a few books under the pseudonym Richard
Bachman, the first being a short early 1970s novel called *Rage*. A horror story
grounded in realism, it was about a troubled teenager who goes to school with a gun
and kills several teachers and students. Published years before the time in which
school shootings became a regular occurrence in the U.S., four real-life shooters in the
1980s and 1990s would claim their actions were influenced by *Rage*. When his early
writings were later repackaged in a collection called *The Bachman Books*, King asked
his publisher for *Rage* to be removed from publication and future reprintings.

AUTHOR: NEIL GAIMAN

Notable Works: One of the most acclaimed authors of science-fiction, fantasy,
and horror books for adults and children, Gaiman won a Newbery Medal for *The
Graveyard Book*, won Hugo Awards for *American Gods* and the comic book *The
Sandman*, and wrote the popular novels *Stardust* and *Good Omens*.
First Book: When he was starting out as a work-for-hire writer in 1984, Gaiman
got a chance to pen a pop-star biography that could be sold to kids and teens. The
publisher gave him a choice between Def Leppard, Barry Manilow, and Duran Duran.
He picked the latter, because the New Wave band had recorded the fewest albums

Oldest U.S. government agency: the Department of Defense,
established in 1789 as the "War Department."

of those options, and *Duran Duran*, a book about the first four years of the fab five, would be the easiest one to write.

AUTHOR: SUZANNE COLLINS

Notable Works: Collins launched a publishing phenomenon in the 2000s with *The Hunger Games*, a dystopian young-adult trilogy about a teenager who goes from fighting to the death in a futuristic reality TV show to starting a revolution against a totalitarian government.

First Book: Before books, Collins wrote for children's television, including the Nickelodeon 1990s detective show *The Mystery Files of Shelby Woo*. That gig led to her first published print work: an entry in a novel series that acted as a tie-in for the show, *Fire Proof: Mystery Files of Shelby Woo No. 11*.

AUTHOR: DR. SEUSS

Notable Works: Dr. Seuss is probably the most famous and beloved children's book author and illustrator of all time, and his prolific career that gave the world *Horton Hears a Who!*, *The Cat in the Hat*, *How the Grinch Stole Christmas*, and *Green Eggs and Ham* began in earnest with the 1937 publication *And to Think That I Saw it on Mulberry Street*.

First Book: The first books to bear the name Dr. Seuss (a pseudonym for Theodor Seuss Geisel) was a series of humor titles for adult readers. In 1931 and 1932, Geisel published four small books about "boners," which was 1930s slang for "errors" or "bloopers." *Boners*, *More Boners*, *Still More Boners*, and *Prize Boners for 1932* featured comical descriptions of real-life silly goofs and mistakes drawn from news accounts. Geisel used the pen name Alexander Abingdon, and his illustrations were credited to Dr. Seuss.

AUTHOR: J. G. BALLARD

Notable Works: English author J. G. Ballard wrote the autobiographical World War II novel *Empire of the Sun*, adapted into a film by Steven Spielberg in 1987, as well as *Crash*, a controversial but acclaimed erotic novel about people who derive pleasure from car accidents. Ballard came to prominence in the 1960s as part of the "new wave of science fiction" with his hit novel *The Drowned World*.

First Book: Before *The Drowned World*, Ballard wrote another book called *The Wind from Nowhere*. In the apocalyptic novel about a natural disaster, the world is reduced to ruins by prolonged, global hurricane-like storms. It was published in 1962, after Ballard threw it together in two weeks. He'd later call it "a piece of hack work" and all official Ballard biographies and bibliographies don't include it, at the author's request.

The long paw of the law: there are approximately 50,000 police dogs in the United States.

WHAT IS GLUTEN?

Good question. Here's another one: should you go gluten free?
Check out this quick breakdown before you talk to your doc.

JUST PASSING THROUGH

Whether or not you should give up gluten depends on your physiology and overall health. But before we get to that, let's look at just what gluten *is*. A clue comes from its etymology: it's from the Vulgar Latin *glutis*, "sticky substance," which also gave us the word *glue*. Gluten isn't any one compound but the general term for various proteins called *prolamins* that are mainly found in grains such as wheat, barley, and rye, and in foods and beverages such as bread, pasta, soups, and beer. In baking, gluten proteins behave like a glue that gives dough its elasticity and helps it rise. In the digestive tract, gluten proteins meet up with powerful *protease* enzymes, whose job is to break down the gluten proteins in the lower intestine, or bowels, and yield a nice, healthy poop. But if those protease enzymes are missing or compromised, the peptides in the gluten escape through the intestinal walls into your body and trigger a response. Here are the main ways gluten can cause harm:

- About 1 percent of Americans have celiac disease, a genetic autoimmune condition that affects the cells in the lining of the small intestine (called enterocytes). Even a small amount of gluten triggers an autoimmune response that causes havoc in not just the GI tract but the entire body: nutrient malabsorption, inflammation, weight loss, and diarrhea.
- People with gluten intolerance, called non-celiac gluten sensitivity, can handle a little bit of gluten, but too much triggers stomach pains, fatigue, and diarrhea.
- Then there are those who are allergic to wheat itself, not gluten. Consumption of wheat can lead to difficulty breathing (anaphylaxis) and be fatal.

TAKING STOCK

So, should *you* jump on the gluten-free bandwagon? Most definitely, if you have celiac or an autoimmune disease such as Hashimoto's thyroiditis or rheumatoid arthritis. Gluten makes those conditions a lot worse. You also might have a gluten intolerance and not even know it. If you're tired a lot, suffer from acute abdominal pain after eating certain foods, and you're not regular, try eliminating gluten and see if it clears up. (Also, see a doctor.) And even though a growing number of health and wellness professionals are urging everyone to give up gluten—which can also worsen irritable bowel syndrome—if it doesn't seem to bother you and you're otherwise healthy, you get to eat all the breadsticks. But keep in mind that a gluten intolerance can make other underlying conditions worse. The good news is, there are more gluten-free options than ever before in grocery stores and at restaurants. (Just make sure to remind your server to keep the croutons off the salad.)

Manhattan comes from *Manhatta* ("Land of Many Hills").
That's what the Lenape people called the island when the Dutch landed there in 1625.

BEHIND THE SCENES

Now for some true stories of movie magic!
(Disclaimer: not all of these are magic.)

THE SOUND OF MUSIC (1965)

While filming the nighttime gazebo scene in which Maria (Julie Andrews) and the Captain (Christopher Plummer) profess their love for each other, Andrews couldn't stop laughing. Why? Because the buzz coming from the lights sounded like farts. Andrews recalled, "Christopher would be looking into my eyes and saying, 'Oh, Maria, I love you,' and there'd be this awful raspberry coming from the lights above us." Solution: they shot the scene in the dark, so the two lovebirds barely show up as silhouettes.

CRAZY RICH ASIANS (2018)

The production had a problem. They needed a very large taxidermied tiger—standing on its hind legs in an "I'm about to kill you" position—for the mansion where Nick's (Henry Golding) grandmother lives. (Backstory: Nick's grandfather had shot the tiger while it was hiding under their pool table.) The mansion was in Malaysia, but the stuffed tiger they wanted was in London. The international shipping was turning into such a logistical nightmare that the filmmakers decided to have their art team in Thailand make a replica stuffed tiger out of foam. The artists got right to work and delivered—well, *tried* to deliver—a perfect re-creation, but it was *so* perfect that Thai customs agents didn't believe the tiger was made of foam. It barely got there in time to film the scene.

IT (1990)

Tim Curry played Pennywise the Clown in the first on-screen adaptation of Stephen King's horror novel. But no one was more scared than Curry himself, who suffered from coulrophobia, or fear of clowns. His case was so severe that he had it written into his contract that all the mirrors had to be removed from the set when he was in his clown makeup. At one point a makeup assistant broke that rule...and Curry got a glimpse of Pennywise. The assistant was nearly fired. (It took almost 20 years for Curry to finally acknowledge he was even in *It*.)

IT (2017)

Bill Skarsgård took over the Pennywise role and was terrified that he'd terrified child actor Jack Dylan Grazer, who was playing Eddie, during a scene in which Pennywise puts his face right up to the trembling boy's face, yells maniacally at him, and even

The first woman in the U.S. military: a spy known only as Agent 355, who reported to General George Washington. Her true identity is unknown.

chokes him. Afterward, Skarsgård approached Grazer and asked if he was OK. The boy's reply, "That was fun! I love what you're doing with the character."

THE DARK CRYSTAL (1982)

Brian and Wendy Froud met while working on this puppet fantasy from the Jim Henson Company. He was the conceptual designer, and she designed the elf-like Gelflings. They fell in love, got married, and started a family. A few years later, the Frouds were both working on Jim Henson's follow-up, *Labyrinth*, which features David Bowie stealing a baby. When the original baby actor wouldn't stop crying at the sight of the scary puppets, Brian and Wendy offered up their eight-month-old son, Toby. Baby Toby had no issues with the puppets and nailed the part.

Fast forward to 2017: the Jim Henson Company, now led by the founder's daughter Lisa Henson, was developing a prequel series called *The Dark Crystal: Age of Resistance*. Henson heard that the former baby actor Toby Froud was a sculptor at another studio. "We loved his work, we asked him to come to L.A. and work... on the initial build of characters for the show...As weeks went by, we realized he was providing an invaluable role helping to translate his parents' designs into the concrete build of the puppets and the costumes. Toby was really in charge of translating all of the designs into the actual build and the look of the puppets."

THE LORD OF THE RINGS: THE TWO TOWERS (2002)

The Riders of Rohan consist of hundreds of skilled Middle-earth horsemen. However, it wasn't easy to find that many skilled horsemen in New Zealand, where the movie's filming took place. Solution: half of the Riders of Rohan are played by women riders wearing fake beards.

THE MUMMY (1999)

Early in the film, Rick (Brendan Fraser) survives a hanging. The wide shot in which he first falls from the gallows utilized a stuntman wearing a harness, but for the close-up shots, they put a noose around Fraser's neck, and he had to act like he was choking while his feet were firmly planted on a platform...until they weren't. When director Stephen Sommers asked for a second take, he had the prop master tighten the noose around Fraser's neck. That extra tension raised the rope a bit, and Frazer was on the balls of his feet. They tightened it a bit more, and then he was on tiptoe. "I'm not a ballerina," Frazer recalled. "I remember seeing the camera start to pan around, and then it was like a black iris at the end of a silent film. It was like turning down the volume switch on your home stereo, like the Death Star powering down. I regained consciousness and one of the EMTs was saying my name. The

Only 7 percent of the U.S.A.'s history has been free of war.

stunt coordinator came over, and he said, 'Hi! Welcome to the club, bro! Ha-ha-ha!' And I was like, 'Ha-ha, funny? Ha-ha?' Like, What the hell? I want to go home!"

SPLASH (1985)

John Candy, who played the womanizing Freddy in the romantic mermaid comedy, was a consummate professional. So when he was late for his call time one morning, director Ron Howard started to get worried. Right before they sent out a search party, Candy arrived, somewhat disheveled, repeating how sorry he was and that he'd never let it happen again. Candy's excuse: He was at a bar the night before, when Jack Nicholson approached him and said he was a fan. (Nicholson was as big a star as there was in 1984.) Jack bought John a drink, and then another, and then another. Candy kept saying, "I've got to go shoot!"

Nicholson kept saying, "You're going to be all right, kid. Don't worry about it."

After the all-nighter, Candy shot the day's scene with zero sleep and a blistering hangover. The scene: Freddy, while he's smoking and drinking a beer, is playing racquetball against his much-more-in-shape brother, Allen (Tom Hanks). The scene ends when Freddy hits the ball against the wall and it comes back and smacks him in the head. Candy did it one take. What a pro!

PREY (2022)

This *Predator* prequel (and the best reviewed film in the franchise) features an epic battle between an alien Predator (Dane DiLiegro) who hunts a young Comanche woman named Naru (Amber Midthunder). But the "actor" that steals the show is Naru's dog, Sarii. The filmmakers adopted a shelter dog named Coco specifically to play the part. In their attention to historical detail (the movie takes place in 1719), they chose a Carolina dog—a breed that hasn't changed for centuries.

But Coco ended up getting a lot more screen time than originally scripted. Why? Because she had zero acting experience and was having so much fun running around in the woods and playing with everyone. "We were trying to get Coco out of scenes," said director Dan Trachtenberg, "but the opposite ended up being true, and we ended up including her more—even in some of the action set-pieces because I just thought it'd be so fun." Not everyone was amused by the dog's antics: Midthunder called Coco "a bit of a hot mess."

NOMADLAND (2020)

To prepare for this Oscar-winning drama about a woman named Fern who lives "off the grid," star Frances McDormand lived off the grid herself, learning the nomadic lifestyle and even working the same odd jobs as other nomads. Suffice it to say,

What do giraffes and ocean-bound cargo ships have in common? A lifespan of 25 to 30 years.

she learned how to blend in—so well, in fact, that other nomads who were cast as themselves in the movie, and who were unaware of McDormand's body of work (she won an Oscar for *Fargo*), assumed she was "one of them."

After shooting an emotional scene where Fern tells real-life nomad Bob Wells about the death of her fictional husband, he approached McDormand to console her. As she recalls, "He said to me privately that it meant a lot for me to tell him that story and that everything was going to be OK. And I said, 'Bob, I just want you to know that my husband's name is Joel, he's alive and well, he makes movies [*Fargo*], and I'm going home to him after this.' Bob was like, 'Oh. How did you do that? I really believed you.' And I said, 'That's my job, Bob! That's what I do for a living! Isn't that weird?'"

STAR WARS: EPISODE VI—RETURN OF THE JEDI (1983)

The throne in the Emperor's throne room had a built-in mechanism that made it swivel on command. But while filming the pivotal scene where Luke confronts Darth Vader and the Emperor, the mechanism didn't work. So, in order to swivel the throne, Emperor actor Ian McDiarmid had to subtly shuffle his feet. Try not to let that distract you next time you watch the movie.

* * *

BEYOND THE VOLCANO

It's a well-known fact that the coolest thing to do with baking soda at home (other than keeping an open box in the fridge) is to make a tabletop volcano. But baking soda can do so much more!

- Add half a cup of baking soda to the wash during the rinse cycle, and you'll have softer, fresher-smelling clothes.

- Upset tummy? A teaspoon of baking soda dissolved in a tall glass of water makes an effective antacid.

- After brushing your teeth, gargle a baking-soda solution to make your teeth even whiter (and your breath even fresher).

- Sprinkle some baking soda into your socks to keep your feet from stinking.

- Bee stings and bug bites can be treated with a paste of baking soda and water.

- Remove cooking oil stains from your deck, or motor oil stains from your driveway, by coating the surface with baking soda and scrubbing it off with a wet brush. (Baking soda is so adept at absorbing oils, you can clean sweat stains and even remove excess oil from your hair.)

- Sprinkle some baking soda in your cat's litter box to neutralize the odors.

- If your dog gets sprayed by a skunk, baking soda—along with some water, hydrogen peroxide, and a bit of soap—will neutralize the stink.

First country music video played on MTV (five years after its 1981 launch): "Honky Tonk Man" by Dwight Yoakam.

CLEAN IT RIGHT

So, you finally found the time and energy to clean your home—
to really get down in there and scrub everything to a perfect shine
with all manner of products and concoctions.
We've got some bad news: you may have done some of it wrong.

MYTH: Running a heavy vacuum, and using suction to dislodge dirt and dust, wears down carpets.

TRUTH: Vacuuming every day, or at least on a regular basis, actually helps prolong the life of a carpet: not only does frequent vacuuming keep everything cleaner, it doesn't give dust a chance to accumulate deep within. That deep dust slowly and steadily eats at the carpet material.

MYTH: Handwashing dishes is better than using a dishwasher in every way.

TRUTH: Over the course of a year, a modern dishwasher uses 5,000 fewer gallons of water to clean dishes than it would take to wash those same dishes by hand. Additionally, dishwashers make for cleaner dishes. They heat the water to 140°F, enough to kill germs and provide sanitation; that simply doesn't happen with the lukewarm or barely hot water used to hand-wash a sink full of dirty dishes.

MYTH: The best way to remove ink stains from clothing is with hairspray.

TRUTH: Decades ago, hairsprays were primarily made of alcohol, which could (and still can) remove ink stains. But hairsprays are mostly alcohol free now, so using that as a cleaning agent won't just fail to remove the ink, but other chemical ingredients could introduce more stains to a soiled garment.

MYTH: Washing windows with newspaper, as opposed to a rag or paper towels, gets them the cleanest, and leaves them free from streaks.

TRUTH: This way may have been true once, but newspaper publishers have switched to new formulations of both paper and ink. The paper is thinner and will break down mid-job. The ink can leave residue on the windows, making them dirtier than before you started, with smeared ink and streaks left behind. Newsprint, if used often, can also slowly degrade the glass surface of the window.

Hannah Adams's (1755–1831) claim to fame: the historian was
the first American woman to earn a living as a writer.

MYTH: When dusting furniture and wooden surfaces, always use furniture polish or dust spray.

TRUTH: It's fine to use occasionally, but not all the time, because it actually encourages dust particles to settle and accumulate due to a thin layer of sticky, attractive chemicals that remain even after wiping. Experts say the best day-to-day method for dusting is with a clean, dry, lint-free microfiber cloth—it picks up the dust and leaves almost nothing behind.

MYTH: Feather dusters quickly pick up dust.

TRUTH: If "duster" means "something that spreads dust around," then a feather duster is aptly named. It disperses and moves the dust around while picking up almost none of it. And even then, unless that feather duster is specifically made from ostrich feathers (and not those of another bird, or of a synthetic material), it's picking up very little.

MYTH: Disinfectants work instantly, killing germs and bacteria the second they're sprayed or squirted onto a surface.

TRUTH: It can take as long as five minutes for the germ-killing product to kill the 99 percent of germs its packaging promises. That means that even with a disinfectant wipe, it's best to leave the surface (soaking) wet and untouched for a while before it's safe to touch again.

MYTH: "Cleaning" and "disinfecting" are interchangeable words—they mean the same thing.

TRUTH: The Centers for Disease Control has defined both terms, and they're very different. Per the CDC, "cleaning" involves removing the dirt and dust from a surface, which kills some germs in the process. "Disinfecting" is about killing all those germs, using chemicals to destroy them.

MYTH: Got a stinky garbage disposal? Throw some fresh lemon peels in there and turn it on.

TRUTH: The odors released by the oil in the lemon peel smell pleasant and clean, but they're only temporarily masking the scent of rotting garbage lining the disposal's walls. Peels may also clog the machinery and wear down the blades. A better solution is a 2:1 mixture of white vinegar and baking soda, followed by boiling water. That kills germs *and* their smells.

The word *butterfly* goes back to the Old English *buttorfleoge*: "butter" and "fly."
Its actual origin is unknown.

MYTH: If your clothes are extra dirty, use additional detergent when you send them through the washing machine.

TRUTH: Only so much soap is required to launder clothes; anything else is just excess. Put too much soap in the washing machine, and it just goes down the drain or stays behind as soapy residue on clothes.

MYTH: Bleach is an ideal all-purpose cleaning solution.

TRUTH: Bleach effectively kills lingering bacteria, so it's more properly defined as a sanitizer or disinfectant. But it doesn't "clean," because it doesn't remove or disintegrate dirt. It may work to lighten stains and give the *appearance* of cleanliness, but it's not effective at many household tasks, such as grease removal. (And always remember that bleach should be used with care, because the liquid and its fumes are toxic.)

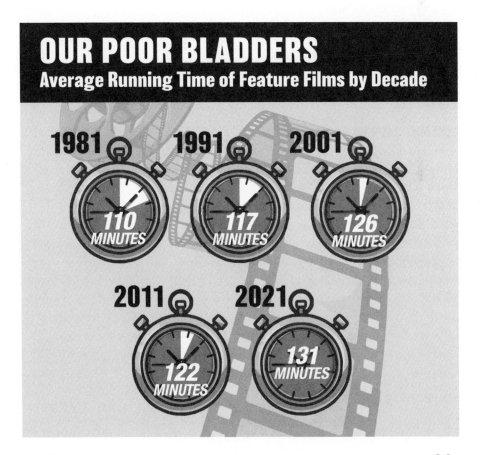

OUR POOR BLADDERS
Average Running Time of Feature Films by Decade

1981 — 110 MINUTES
1991 — 117 MINUTES
2001 — 126 MINUTES
2011 — 122 MINUTES
2021 — 131 MINUTES

What is Oak? The original name for the programming language Java.

UBER CRIMES (AND MISDEMEANORS)

*App-based services such as Uber, Lyft, and DoorDash, in which regular folks earn
a living or some extra money by working as drivers or delivery people for hire, are
a regular part of life now. So are weird news stories involving those apps.*

YOU MAY GET SOMETHING EXTRA DELIVERED

In November 2021, a resident of an upscale apartment building in the tony
Los Angeles suburb of Brentwood, reported to the manager that there appeared to
be human feces in the lobby. Sure enough, there was, and when the manager, Lisa
Stanley, reviewed security footage to identify the rogue pooper, she was startled to
see that a DoorDash delivery driver, in the building to drop off a food order for
Stanley, had tried to use a lobby trash can to defecate (and apparently missed). "You
know what they say, 'when you gotta go, you gotta go,' and boy did she ever," said
Stanley. "You're four steps away from outside where there's a bush or your car, or I
don't know." Stanley filed a complaint with DoorDash, who gave her a $20 credit
and refunded the cost of her order (plus the driver's tip).

YOU MAY HAVE TO APOLOGIZE

Australian man Mark Polchleb placed a DoorDash order in July 2022. When his
driver approached the home and got near the door, Polchleb's dog started barking
loudly and uncontrollably. As Polchleb attempted to open his front door to grab his
food off the porch without letting the dog out, he yelled, "Get away from the door,
mate!" Doorbell camera footage shows the driver's face drop, and shows him leave the
food behind and inch away from the house in distress. He clearly thought Polchleb's
stern warning was directed at *him*. Later that night, when he was reviewing his security
footage, Polchleb realized that he'd accidentally screamed at his DoorDash driver and
felt *really* bad about it. His account of the encounter on TikTok went viral and was
covered by Australian media, and he was quickly put in touch with the driver, Sami,
who was DoorDashing to earn money to visit his son who lives in another country.
Sami's daughter created a GoFundMe, which raised $7,000 in travel funds, and
DoorDash granted Sami Top Dasher status for life.

YOUR ORDER MIGHT BE FREE

DoorDash operates through a smartphone app. Customers pick a local restaurant
from the interface and place an order through DoorDash, which sends a driver

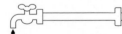

to the eatery to pick it up. On July 7, 2022, the app suffered a major glitch when users suddenly and temporarily weren't required to verify payment. In other words, they didn't have to enter a method of payment *at all*, meaning for one glorious evening, DoorDash covered the price of the meals for thousands of customers who noticed the flaw. The glitch went viral on Twitter, and the company got wise after a few hours. "We immediately corrected the issue. We're actively canceling fraudulent orders and are in touch with merchants impacted to ensure they are compensated for any unauthorized orders they may have received," a DoorDash spokesperson said.

YOU MAY HAVE LEFT YOUR SLIME IN THE VEHICLE

A lot of people ascribe to the astrological belief that when the planet Mercury is "in retrograde," humanity goes a little kooky. According to rideshare service Uber, forgetfulness goes up during this time; when mercury entered retrograde in June 2022, the company decided to release a list of strange items left behind in its drivers' vehicles. The most abandoned (and reported lost) items: cell phones, wallets, keys, and vaping devices. Uber also noted the 50 strangest things customers had called to see if anyone had found. Among those items: an urn containing the ashes of a loved one, a tortoise, a 40-piece order of chicken nuggets, a fanny pack bearing the image of Bernie Sanders, a large quantity of caviar, a bucket of slime, and some Tater Tots. A whopping 40 passengers forgot their CPAP machines in an Uber, and 20 left behind their jewel-encrusted dental adornments, or "grills."

YOUR DRIVER MAY BE A WAR CRIMINAL

In 2018, Uber revamped its driver screening process after reporters discovered that a murderer had successfully applied to work for the ride-share service. Under the new, more rigorous background check process, drivers convicted of felonies and those charged with (but acquitted of) serious offenses could not work for Uber. But because he hadn't been charged with a crime in the United States, Yusuf Abdi Ali passed the background check and was approved to drive for Uber (as well as Lyft) in the suburban Washington, D.C., area. Also known as Colonel Tukeh, Ali is an accused war criminal linked to a wide variety of atrocities in Somalia's civil war in the 1980s. Numerous witnesses attest to watching him burn people alive or drag them behind vehicles, while he's also connected to mass executions. In May 2019, undercover CNN reporters called for an Uber with Ali as their driver and filmed their encounter. Ali had a near-perfect driver rating, but he was fired when his alleged crimes, which didn't come up in the standard background check, came to light.

CUNNING CROWS, PART II

*In Part I, you learned that crows and ravens pack a lot of neurons into
their tiny brains, allowing them to communicate on a higher level than most
animals, to remember our faces...and to stay mad at us when we run afoul
of them. Here are more amazing things that these corvids can do.*

CROWS MAKE TOOLS

In 1960, British naturalist Jane Goodall observed a chimpanzee stripping the leaves
from a twig to make it fit into a termite hole. That discovery changed the very
definition of humankind; we were no longer the animal kingdom's only tool maker.
It turns out that other animals manipulate objects in their environment: Bottlenose
dolphins use sea sponges to forage for food, and elephants tear off tree bark and
chew it into a ball to plug the opening to a water source. Like chimpanzees, New
Caledonian crows (native to the South Pacific) also manipulate and use sticks to
forage for bugs. Crows in Japan are known to place hard-to-crack acorns in crosswalks,
then let the cars do the work for them.

    When crows get into a lab setting, they really show off how smart they are.
In a 2018 Oxford University study, four New Caledonian crows named Tumulte,
Tabou, Mango, and Jungle were presented with a transparent box that contained a
food pellet, along with a long tool with which to retrieve the food. The birds used
the tool almost immediately. In the next phase, the tool was replaced by random
objects that could be put together—such as a syringe plunger and its barrel. It took
about five minutes for the crows to figure out the tools. In the following phases,
the crows were able to craft three, four, and five individual components into tools.
"They figured it out by themselves," boasted lead researcher Auguste von Bayern.
"It involved both combining hollow elements with sticks and the other way around,
as well as turning the tool to insert the solid end in another hollow element." The
experiment shows just how adept crows are at abstract thinking—yet another sign of
high intelligence.

CROWS ARE COMPLEX PROBLEM SOLVERS

A 2014 study tasked New Caledonian crows with the problem in the Aesop fable
"The Pitcher and the Crow." The crows had to figure out which of the variously
sized rocks would fit into which of the variously sized beakers to raise the water level
enough to get to a floating treat. Incredibly, the crows didn't rely on trial and error.

They performed the task in their heads—determining which rocks went in which beaker—and placed all of them in before retrieving their treat (as opposed to checking the level after each rock). The researchers gave the same test to human kids. The crows performed on par with the 7- to 10-year-olds...and they blew the 4- to 5-year-olds out of the water.

In a 2020 study conducted at the University of Tübingen in Germany, two American crows named Ozzie and Glenn had their brain activity tracked as they were given a complex cognitive test that revolved around waiting for a light to flash and then pecking either a red or a blue target. The researchers randomly changed a rule key so they could observe the birds' neurons firing as they "worked the problem" by recalling past experiences and then cycling through different combinations before arriving at a solution. This level of bird intelligence surpasses most mammal species.

CROWS "DOMESTICATE" OTHER ANIMALS

Lots of animal species form mutually beneficial relationships with other species, but *Homo sapiens* is the only one to actually domesticate them. We're not saying that ravens (slightly larger but genetically similar to crows) have domesticated wolves, but they certainly know how to get these canines to do their bidding. That's why many Indigenous people refer to ravens as "wolf birds."

Brad Bulin, senior naturalist at Yellowstone National Park, has been observing this unique relationship for decades. Whenever ravens find a dead animal with too tough a hide for their beaks to penetrate, they land on the carcass and make a series of loud calls that the wolves recognize. The wolves arrive and start to...do their thing, allowing the ravens to get straight to the good stuff. This behavior goes beyond the birds simply using the wolves as "tools," says Bulin. The birds spend much of their time interacting with the wolf pack. "These intriguing birds have been known to grab sticks and play tug-of-war with wolf puppies, to fly over young wolves with sticks and tease the small canines into jumping up to grab the sticks, and even to boldly pull the tails of wolves to initiate a reaction."

CROWS GOOF OFF

With the exception of humans and domesticated animals, play is an activity reserved for the young. For other animals, once you're an adult, it's all business until you die. But adult crows are so adept at finding food and staying safe that they tend to have a lot of free time. To find out what they do with that free time, do an

A Russian superstition says that a bird pooping on your head will bring good fortune.

online search for "crows playing" videos. You can watch them sliding down a snowy rooftop and then flying back up, just to slide down again. Then there's the video of the crow that amuses itself on a teeter-totter, flying back and forth from seat to seat as the board goes up and down.

Crows and ravens also seem to have fun at our expense, as described in this 2021 tweet from a Colorado writer named Krista Langlois:

> Heard a report that some ravens were perched above a downtown building purposefully and gleefully pushing snow onto the heads of people passing by. Happy New Year to the ravens, to the tricksters and survivors, which is to say, to all of us finding glimmers of joy in the darkness

Another way that crows have found glimmers of joy: imitating the voices of dog owners, with the sole intention of getting the dogs to do naughty things. A famous example of this behavior occurred in 1964 when a crow—along with several dogs from a nearby neighborhood—showed up on the University of Montana campus. Here's an account from John Marzluff's book, *Gifts of the Crow*:

> Perched on a low branch of an oak tree, the crow called to its pupils—dogs of every breed, size, shape, and color. A pack of mutts focused their attention on the crow from the base of the bird's lectern. The crow had likely rallied them... from the nearby neighborhoods and lured them to this learned spot. But why? The answer was suggested when the school bell chimed and the students spilled into the Oval...The crow took off low, only a few feet off the ground, with its devoted crowd of canines in noisy pursuit. In and out, the black corvine Pied Piper threaded a mayhem of canines through the students, creating confusion, wonder, and collision.

What other reason would a crow have to do such a thing, other than it being really amusing?

CROWS HAVE CULTURE

One definition of human culture is "all the ways of life including arts, beliefs, and institutions of a population that are passed down from generation to generation." While it's a stretch to say that crows have institutions (though who knows?), they display much of the criteria to be considered cultural—not the least of which is their tool-making prowess. According to a Cambridge University study—in which crows "paid" for snacks from a vending machine with objects that they made, in order to match the tokens they were no longer receiving—this kind of brainpower can be tapped into only via *cumulative cultural evolution*. This "occurs when social traditions accumulate improvements over time." That's one reason why scarecrows often

Best-selling fiction writer of all time: Agatha Christie.
Her 70 crime novels have sold over 2 billion copies.

cease to be effective: once a crow population figures out the ruse, that knowledge is passed down.

According to Kaeli Swift, whose "dead bird" study determined that crows recognize faces and hold grudges, both of our species "live in a so-called fission-fusion society. There are groups that come together, we interact, we go our separate ways for a little while then we come back. We're constantly seeing people, saying goodbye, and then seeing them again, and there's a lot to track there cognitively." This fission-fusion theory explains how crows—which mate for life—can form lasting bonds with people and other animals, how they can learn our schedules, how they can communicate with us, and even how they investigate the deaths of their friends. (Was it...murder?) So take heart: we humans aren't the only animals that have to go to meetings.

CROWS MIGHT KNOW US BETTER THAN WE KNOW THEM

Crows aren't just smart; they're getting smarter. A 2020 Keio University study in Tokyo observed eight wild large-billed crows, each of which had been exposed to Japanese speakers for much of their lives, as they listened to voice recordings. When the voice spoke Japanese, the crows didn't react too much. But when it started speaking Dutch, the birds got excited. One possible reason, say the researchers: the crows know that tourists—who speak other languages—are a much better food source than stingy locals. So, not only can crows understand the difference between our languages, they utilize that knowledge to increase their chances of finding tasty treats.

Will we ever learn to speak "crow"? Ornithologists have been able to isolate broad patterns and intentions—such as whether a call is in response to something (called contextual) or if it's responding to nothing in particular (non-contextual). It's more likely that crows will learn to speak "person." Some laboratory crows have learned more than 100 words and can put together 50 sentences. One crow even learned to count to seven—that might not seem like a lot, but counting requires more brainpower than the lion's share of this planet's animals possesses. So, if you ever do become the subject of a calamitous crow conversation, yell up at them, "I'd like to assist you, but I don't understand what you're saying. Any of you happen to speak English?" What's the worst that could happen?

*   *   *

*"If men had wings and bore black feathers, few of them would be
clever enough to be crows."*

—Henry Ward Beecher

Lip prints are as unique as fingerprints.

WHAT'S THE DIFFERENCE BETWEEN...

Uncle John knows pretty much everything—even the subtle nuances that separate common, similar, and frequently confused things.

...A MEMOIR AND AN AUTOBIOGRAPHY? Both are nonfictional accounts of a person's life, written or cowritten by the subject themselves. A memoir is about a specific time in the individual's life, such as their childhood or career, while an autobiography covers the person's entire existence—their life story.

...STRAW AND HAY? They come in piles and bushels of dry, long blades of plant material, but hay seeds are planted specifically to grow into hay, a food used as animal feed. It's cut in such a way that it resembles straw, but straw itself is excess, unusable waste material left over from the production of grains and seeds.

...RAW SUGAR AND BROWN SUGAR? After it's harvested from beets or sugarcane, sugar is processed into fine white pellets known as table sugar. Early in the manufacturing process, it takes the form of gold-colored crystals. That's raw sugar. Then, as the raw sugar is processed into white sugar, the extracted liquid is collected and becomes the basis of molasses. Brown sugar is simply finished white sugar with about 3.5 to 7 percent molasses added to it.

...AN APARTMENT AND A CONDOMINIUM? An apartment is a smaller living space inside of a complex or building owned by an individual or company. Condos are physically much like apartments—living spaces within a larger community—but they can be individually owned by tenants and collectively managed by a condo association, an organization comprised of the individual owners.

...RABBITS AND HARES? Rabbits and hares are both members of the *Lagomorpha* order of mammals, and they look like one another, but these bunny-like hoppers are quite different animals with pronounced singular features. Hares have longer ears, longer and stronger hind legs, and larger feet than rabbits, as well as black markings on their fur. As for rabbits, both their overall bodies and their individual body parts are smaller, and they're the slower of the two creatures. Another big difference is what they do when threatened: a hare will outrun a predator, a rabbit burrows into its warren.

...A CATHEDRAL AND A BASILICA? In Latin, the traditional language of the Roman Catholic Church, a bishop who oversees all activities in a certain region, or diocese,

MTV's highest-rated show of all time: *Jersey Shore.*

sits on a big chair called a *cathedra*. His home church, and thus the headquarter church of his diocese, is a cathedral. It doesn't necessarily have to be a big, grand, ornately decorated church, but it usually is. A church of that type—with or without the bishop in residence—may also be called a basilica, a special designation offered by the pope to denote a historically or architecturally important house of worship.

...ETIQUETTE AND MANNERS? Etiquette refers to the system of rules that a society or community has ruled to be the proper way to behave. Manners are the attitudes and reasons that inform etiquette and the principles for adhering to them.

...A COAT AND A JACKET? A coat is intended to be the outermost article of clothing worn on cold days and extending down to the hips (possibly longer). A jacket cuts off at the waist and is made of lightweight materials; it's supposed to be worn for mild weather, or simply for fashion, and offers a tighter fit.

...A HURRICANE AND A TYPHOON? The two words are often used interchangeably to describe a very windy tropical storm that starts at sea, runs onto land, and causes devastating destruction. The distinction lies in where and when the storm originates. Hurricanes start out in the western Atlantic Ocean in the fall. Typhoons develop in the northern Pacific Ocean in the summer.

...A TERRACE AND A BALCONY? By and large, a terrace is a spacious outdoor flat space. It can be on the ground, on the side of a building, or on the roof. A balcony is a kind of terrace, but one elevated above ground on account of how it's attached to the side of a building and accessible only via a door or window from a room inside.

...MAGMA AND LAVA? They're the same thing—it just depends on where they're encountered. According to volcanic scientists, molten rock that stays underground (usually underneath or inside a volcano) is called magma. If it finds an opening (such as a crack or the top of a volcano) to head up to the earth's surface and get exposed to oxygen, the magma becomes lava.

...A BASEMENT AND A CELLAR? Both are underground, but only one is *completely* underground. Under the strictest definition, a basement is half a level below street level and may even have windows to prove that fact. A cellar, however, is all the way below ground level.

...LEFT AND RIGHT TWIX? The two-pieces-to-a-pack candy bar employs a long-running ad campaign suggesting no difference between a "right Twix" and a "left Twix," but they do differ very slightly. There's a bit less caramel in the right Twix, along with a denser cookie.

The U.S. Department of Defense works out of 4,800 sites in more than 160 countries.

AUDIO TREASURES: LOCKDOWN

Without the ability to tour during the COVID-19 pandemic, these music artists retreated into the studio and created masterpieces.

Album: Paul McCartney, *McCartney III* (2020)
Genre: Rock
Review: Recorded in isolation during the pandemic, 78-year-old McCartney played every instrument and sang every vocal part. "A big commercial album it is not, and yet its outstanding and subjective quality as DIY music puts it ahead of the more obvious attempts to score hits. While it is certainly visionary and experimental in places, it's still perfectly accessible material that never feels difficult or a major challenge to get through." (XS Noize)

Album: Charli XCX, *How I'm Feeling Now* (2020)
Genre: Electro-pop
Review: "Recorded in just six weeks while she self-isolated in her Californian mansion...she crafted a pandemic-snapshot that bristles with anxiety and fizzing hooks. In the initial days of this pandemic, it felt like there was a pressure to concoct your own era-defining *King Lear*. While the pages to your novel languish in the bottom drawer, Charli actually did it." (NME)

Album: Brothers Osborne, *Skeletons* (2020)
Genre: Country
Review: "In more ways than one...*Skeletons* was the perfect album for 2020. It includes lead single 'All Night,' a feel-good earworm meant to take fans' minds off of their

troubles, as well as 'Hatin' Somebody,' a pointed message to keep things civil during a politically divisive time. But perhaps most magnificently, *Skeletons* encapsulates the feel of a live show during a time when country concerts...have become distant memories." (Country Now)

Album: Matt Berry, *The Blue Elephant* (2021)
Genre: Progressive Rock
Review: "[Taking] a trip back into the heyday of late-'60s psychedelic pop... diving in headfirst and bringing back armloads of paisley-clad treasures, Berry uses every trick in the book on the record, sending songs through the flange cycle, dumping the vocals into giant vats of reverb, coating guitars in crispy fuzztones, and generally sounding like he's having a blast using every piece of gear in his collection." (AllMusic)

Album: Nick Cave and Warren Ellis, *Carnage* (2021)
Genre: Pop Rock
Review: "*Carnage* is infused with profound and almost inescapable grief. But as this particularly audacious singer-songwriter grapples with isolation, loneliness, loss and the hard emotional graft of endurance, all set against a backdrop of apocalyptic threat, the personal becomes universal. *Carnage* may just be the greatest lockdown album yet." (*The Telegraph*)

A fever temperature in the armpit: 99°F; in the mouth: 100°F; in the rectum: 100.4°F.

THE SUPREMELY CHEESY HISTORY OF MACARONI AND CHEESE

The ultimate story of the ultimate comfort food.

AD 500: The Talmud—one of the foundational holy texts of Judaism—is first transcribed around this year, combining elements of the newer, more complete Babylonian Talmud with the older Jerusalem Talmud. Compiled in what was then called Palestine, it includes a reference to *itrium*, a simple pasta-type food made from ground wheat and cooked by boiling.

827: The Muslim conquest of Sicily, the island that's now part of Italy, begins. The final outpost of the Byzantine Empire falls in 965, and the area will remain under Islamic rule until conquered by the Normans about a century later. During this time, many hallmarks of what's now considered Italian food are introduced by Muslims and Arabs. Eggplant and spinach are grown throughout the Italian region for the first time, and pasta is introduced and popularized.

1300s: Sometime early this century, the *Liber de Coquina* (literally "the book of cooking") is published. One of the oldest surviving medieval cookbooks, it's written by two anonymous authors, one French and one from the Italian region of Naples. The Italian cook's portion includes a recipe for *de lesanis*, the first printed instructions for a dish combining pasta and cheese. It calls for a flat sheet of pasta—lasagna noodles—to be cut into small squares, boiled in water, and then tossed with grated Parmesan cheese.

1390: The master cooks serving the court of King Richard II in England publish *The Forme of Cury*, the oldest extant cookbook in the English language. Used as a household reference by wealthy, literate families for hundreds of years, the book includes a recipe for *makerouns*, inspired by *de lesanis* and other Italian dishes. The name is derived from an Italian word that means "to make food from barley," which describes the idea of wheat-based pasta, and also the first step to the adoption of the word *macaroni*. Before long, *macaroni* would be a generic term used to

Between 1500 and 1660, an estimated 80,000 Europeans were executed for being "witches."

describe all pastas and noodles; it wouldn't be a specific, elbow-shaped tube pasta for centuries. The recipe for *makerouns* found in *The Forme of Cury*—which is almost the same as those found in Italian-language cookbooks of the era—calls for a thin piece of pastry dough to be cut into small chunks, boiled in water, cooked again, then arranged in layers with grated Parmesan cheese and melted butter.

1600s: Gourmet cooking, or *haute cuisine*, begins in France with chef Marie-Antoine Carême, who classifies all of French cooking's many sauces into four "mother sauces." The oldest, most basic, and most used of those is the *béchamel*, named after the fact for its creator, Louis de Béchamel, stewart of King Louis XIV in the 1600s. The sauce recipe begins with a *roux*, flour and butter combined over low heat until it forms a paste; it's then mixed with milk, with butter and flour added. Béchamel is the basis of most cheese sauces, including that which would be associated with all forms of macaroni and cheese.

1700s: Because it's made with a gourmet sauce associated with high-end French cooking, and out of Parmesan cheese and pasta made from durum wheat flour—both virtually impossible to find outside of Italy or without paying a small fortune to import—mac and cheese is a dish reserved for the wealthy and elite of western Europe.

1769: A recipe for saucy, cheesy macaroni and cheese appears in the cookbook *The Experienced English Housekeeper*. It consists of béchamel mixed with macaroni, sprinkled with Parmesan, then baked until bubbling and browned over.

1780s: Mac and cheese comes to the formerly English colonies in the New World, not through England, but via France. In 1784, Founding Father and Declaration of Independence author Thomas Jefferson is appointed the brand-new United States' minister to the Court of Versailles in France, where he goes wild for macaroni and cheese after eating it at a royal dinner. (It's a decadent and expensive dish, indicative of the kind of royal excess that would lead to the French Revolution, and King Louis XVI losing his head in the guillotine.) When Jefferson heads back to the U.S. in 1789, leaving France as the French Revolution heats up, he brings with him a hand-cranked macaroni press that he'd ordered from Naples. Once back to his Virginia plantation, Monticello, his French-kitchen-trained personal cook (and slave) James Hemmings learns to make macaroni and cheese and prepares it regularly, particularly for Jefferson's wealthy, powerful, and influential guests.

The smallest known dinosaur, the Microraptor, was the size of a crow and had four wings.

1790:   Cheddar cheese, made since the 12th century in the English village of Somerset, is being exported to British expats living in the newly formed United States, where cheese makers start making it fresh. Cheddar becomes the de facto cheese in American macaroni and cheese because it's cheaper, easier, and faster to get than Parmesan.

1802:   Now president of the United States, Thomas Jefferson serves macaroni and cheese, or "macaroni pie," as the baked casserole–style dish is called at the time. (It's alternately called "macaroni pudding"). The Reverend Manasseh Cutler, a guest who had the dish at a state dinner, wrote in his diary that he found it "not agreeable," and confused the baked noodles on the bottom for a pastry dough crust, and the soft noodles for onions.

1824:   Virginia aristocrat (and Thomas Jefferson's cousin) Mary Randolph loses her fortune and publishes *The Virginia Housewife: Or, Methodical Cook*, a collection of her slaves' recipes. It's the first published cookbook of Southern cuisine and includes the first American recipe for macaroni and cheese. It involves boiling macaroni (meaning any kind of unspecified noodle) in milk and water, layering it in a dish with butter and cheese (also unspecified as to type), then baking it all.

1848:   French émigré Antoine Zerega opens the first American pasta factory in Brooklyn, with machinery powered by a horse in the basement, and the pasta dried on the roof.

1851:   The first cheese factory is built in the U.S., mass-producing cheese for the first time, making it less expensive and more readily available. It's also around this time that English cheese makers figure out how to mass-produce cheddar cheese, and England and the U.S. become the two largest exporters of cheddar in the world.

1886:   A macaroni and cheese recipe in *Mrs. Rorer's Philadelphia Cook Book: A Manual of Home Economies* promotes macaroni and cheese as a middle-class food, arguing that the glutinous noodles used are healthier than bread because they contain more protein.

1911:   The methods to make processed cheese are perfected by Kraft. Cheese, particularly cheddar cheese, is emulsified and cooked, removing most of the liquid and making it a nonperishable, shelf-stable item. This will eventually lead to the creation of Velveeta and processed cheese slices, but the first thing Kraft makes is powdered cheese. Safe and perfectly good

McDonald's tested bubble-gum-flavored broccoli as a healthy side for kids. They didn't like it.

but otherwise imperfect fresh cheese, or excess production, can thus be converted into something useful and sold to distributors.

1914: A lot of pasta was being made and sold inexpensively in the U.S., but domestic production takes over when World War I cuts off all imports from Italy. By the time the Great War ends in 1919, the number of American pasta companies has exploded from 370 to 560.

1930s: Kraft starts selling processed American cheese—dried and so finely grated that it resembles a powder—in two-ounce envelopes, marketing the product as an ingredient for use in casseroles, soups, and sauces. Cooking in such a way is seen as an extravagance and an unnecessary extra expense in Depression-era America, and the product flops. Then a St. Louis area salesman for the Tenderoni macaroni company gets the idea to combine the cheese powder with his macaroni. He ties powder envelopes to boxes of his noodles—bite-size, tubular, elbow macaroni— and hands them out as free samples to customers and to store managers. That sales rep (his name is lost to history) inadvertently invents modern-day packaged macaroni and cheese. When Kraft notices that sales of cheese powder are so strong in St. Louis, it finds out why and offers that rep a job.

1937: Kraft Macaroni & Cheese Dinner debuts in stores. Marketed as "a meal for four in nine minutes" and sold for 19 cents per box, Kraft moves 19 million packages in just one year. Many of these find their way into homes via Depression-era "relief societies," or church-run food banks.

1940s: During World War II, Kraft sells more than 50 million boxes of its Macaroni & Cheese Dinner. It's at this time that it becomes firmly entrenched in the American culinary landscape, because it's both comfort food and inexpensive, even during wartime rationing. One food ration stamp—intended to cover one meal for a family—can be used for two boxes, making a two-for-one deal.

1950s AND 1960s: After President Harry Truman establishes a federally subsidized school lunch program, macaroni and cheese—in the style made by Kraft or its competitors—becomes a kid cuisine staple because it's a cheap, crowd-pleasing meal.

2022: Kraft officially changes its flagship boxed dinner's name from Kraft Macaroni & Cheese to Kraft Mac & Cheese. (That's what everybody calls it anyway.)

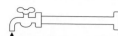

One bale of cotton, which weighs nearly 500 pounds, will make about 215 pairs of blue jeans.

🗣 MOUTHING OFF 🗣

SAY SOMETHING BORING

We've pored through thousands of quotation lists over the years to deliver the most provocative/funny utterances ever uttered. But for every great one, there are dozens of clunkers. Our apologies if these don't entertain you; just know that finding the least-interesting, most painfully obvious A-lister quotations sure was cathartic for us.

"I love making new friends and I respect people for a lot of different reasons."
—Taylor Swift

"I guess we'd be living in a boring, perfect world if everybody wished everybody else well."
—Jennifer Aniston

"I like simple things. I like to sneak in the theater and watch movies. I'm a movie buff."
—Justin Timberlake

"I've done several commercials and I've done voice-overs for documentaries."
—Jeff Bridges

"I DON'T READ BOOKS MUCH."
—LeBron James

"FAMILIES IN REAL LIFE DON'T TEND TO RESOLVE THINGS NEATLY."
—Drew Barrymore

"I got into stand-up because I love stand-up. Specifically, in stand-up, I love jokes. I love short, structured ideas and a punch line."
—Demetri Martin

"Wrestling seemed like something I might be good at, so I stuck with it and gave it a shot. I ended up in a pretty good place. I was very fortunate."
—Seth Rollins

"The great marriages are partnerships. It can't be a great marriage without being a partnership."
—Helen Mirren

WHAT HAPPENS IN CAHOKIA

*On the Illinois side of the Mississippi River—just across from St. Louis, Missouri—lies
a grassy landscape dotted with dozens of mounds, the largest of which is 10 stories high.
These mounds are not natural. A thousand years ago,
they were home to "America's first city."*

BACKGROUND

The Native Americans who populated North America—whose numbers peaked at
60 million in the 15th century—prior to the arrival of the first Europeans weren't
the primitive nomads we sometimes think of them as: they had culture, technology,
politics, and other attributes of modern civilization. Nowhere was that more apparent
than in the ancient American megacity of Cahokia, the cultural center of the
Midwest.

Constructed circa AD 900, Cahokia hit its peak in the 11th century, when as
many as 30,000 people inhabited this six-square-mile city—that's twice the population
of London at the time. Just as with modern municipalities, city planners divided
Cahokia into precincts, and thousands of dwellings were laid out in a large grid.
But Cahokia isn't like any modern American city. You might describe it as a sort of
"spiritual Las Vegas."

By the time French explorers reached what is now Missouri in the 1600s,
most of the city's architecture was gone. The region at the time was populated by
the Cahokia tribe, so the city was named after them. It's uncertain if they were
descendants of the original inhabitants, which anthropologists refer to as the
Mississippians. The city's real name is unknown because, other than markings on
pottery, these people didn't leave behind any written records—but that doesn't mean
they weren't advanced.

MOUND OVER MATTER

Mounds used to be a big thing in pre-Columbian America, not unlike pyramids in
other parts of the world. Cahokia originally had about 120 mounds of varying sizes,
80 of which survive today. Towering above them all is Monks Mound. The largest
man-made prehistoric structure in North America, it was (and still is) 100 feet high

Give it a try: it's impossible to hum while plugging your nose.

and has a base as large as the Great Pyramid of Giza. Using large wicker baskets, workers moved 55 million cubic tons of soil and clay to build it, one basketful at a time. A large building once stood on top of Monks Mound; based on its foundation, it was 100 feet long and up to five stories high.

Adjacent to Monks Mound is the 50-acre Grand Plaza. Another marvel of engineering, this once-hilly terrain was leveled in some spots and filled in in others to create a flat plain 1,600 feet long. The smaller mounds were built among swamps, creeks, and ponds accessed by elevated walkways that linked Cahokia's numerous neighborhoods.

SPIRITUAL CROSSROADS

Until recently, scientists had assumed that Cahokia functioned similarly to other ancient megacities that were built around trade and commerce. Timothy Pauketat is an archaeologist at the University of Illinois who's been studying this city for decades. He told the BBC that—with only a few thousand permanent residents—Cahokia instead served as a spiritual gathering place. And just as Rome wasn't built in a day, Cahokia, along with Monks Mound, started out much smaller and was gradually built up over the centuries. (The addition of maize crops led to a huge boost in construction.)

The building site was most likely chosen because it's close to the river and has an abundance of creeks, ponds, and tree stands. This was important, explains Pauketat, because "water is this barrier between the world of the living and the world of the dead." Adding further credence to this assessment, much of the city was laid out in its relation to celestial events. Buildings were aligned in cardinal directions, and there were wooden structures similar to Stonehenge (now fittingly referred to as Woodhenge): located near Monks Mound, they were large circles of equally distanced wooden posts that aligned with the equinox and solstice.

LET'S GET READY TO CHUNKEY!

Cahokia was the setting that played host to huge celebrations, some lasting for weeks at a time. Based on the wide array of artifacts left behind, these events drew in people from up to 1,000 miles away—as far west as the Rockies and as far south as the Gulf of Mexico. If you made the trek to Cahokia, you'd find yourself among thousands of people in a bustling city filled with the aromas of grilled meats and the sounds of loud music and cheering crowds.

What the hex? According to a 2018 study, the U.S.A. had 1.5 million practicing witches, up from 8,000 in 1990.

- Rows of vending booths offered wares and services such as body-painting, hot food, and yaupon tea—made from a species of holly, it's the only caffeinated plant that grows in North America, and Cahokian baristas brewed it into strong drinks.

- The entertainment included "flying bird" dance performances similar to those still performed by Mayans. Long flags tied to the tops of tall cypress poles allowed the dancers to perform impressive aerial feats.

- The main sporting event took place on the Grand Plaza, a sprawling field surrounded by packed-clay pyramids, where 10,000 sports fans would bet on a game called chunkey. An official would roll a stone disc across the flat terrain, and then one player—or several at a time—would throw a spear toward the spot they predicted the disc would come to a rest.

"It's hard to capture the intensity, the grandeur, the multi-dimensionality of an event like that," said Pauketat.

THE FALCON WARRIOR

Cahokia wasn't all fun and games. This "land between earth and water"—reminiscent of the Aztecs' territory to the south—was a center for ritual human sacrifice. Buried beneath Mound 72 in the main urban precinct is a man of some importance. After dying in his mid-40s, he was laid to rest over a bed of 20,000 shells forming the shape of a falcon and surrounded by many styles of arrowheads, possibly indicating that hunters from near and far paid their respects (or perhaps the arrowheads were war trophies). More than 250 skeletons were buried along with the Falcon Warrior—though not all at the same time, indicating the burials took place over centuries. About 50 of the skeletons were women in their early 20s, laid in pairs, side by side. Many of the young males had been brutally murdered. Most disturbing: based on "the vertical position of some of the fingers, which appear to have been digging in the sand," dozens of these people were buried alive.

And then something happened in the 1400s that led to a mass exodus from Cahokia. The remains of spiked fences and watchtowers suggest invaders might have been the reason. Other evidence points to a change in the climate resulting in long droughts interspersed with major flooding. Whatever caused the exodus, most structures were dismantled or destroyed. An American city wouldn't surpass Cahokia's population for another three centuries, when Philadelphia reached 30,000 people in the 1780s.

Deadliest 20th-century tornado in the U.S.A.:
the 1925 "Great Tri-state" (Missouri, Illinois, Indiana) tornado killed 695 people.

SECRETS IN SECRETIONS

How can scientists know so much about the Mississippians if they didn't leave written records? Because they left something else behind (other than the thousands of artifacts): fecal stanols. These are molecules that were produced in Native people's guts when they ate meat; they then were pooped out and eventually became part of the topsoil in the region. Researchers look for fecal stanols because they take thousands of years to break down—so their presence in soil samples provides vital clues to human population numbers.

In 2020, UC Berkeley anthropologist A. J. White (after diving to the bottom of nearby Horseshoe Lake and retrieving core samples from ten feet below the lakebed) published a paper in the journal *American Antiquity* with new fecal stanol findings that show Cahokia was quickly repopulated after the mass exodus of the 1400s. Analysis of the core samples for charcoal deposits and pollen adds further evidence that this era of Cahokia consisted of smaller farming communities; residents hunted bison, grew maize, and even used controlled burning to keep their fields fertile. But the city remained a shadow of its former self. White says that, while there is still much to be learned, "The story of Cahokia was a lot more complex than, 'Goodbye, Native Americans. Hello, Europeans.'"

WALKING THROUGH PREHISTORY

Cahokia was the largest of many such sites in the Americas. Not far away, a smaller city of mounds was leveled to develop St. Louis. But it doesn't look like that will be Cahokia's fate: Cahokia Mounds State Historic Site is open to the public and protected as a UNESCO World Heritage Site. While the site is not as large as the original city, you can explore 2,200 acres of grassland, swamps, woodlands, and 70 mounds, including a staircase to the top of Monks Mound (it's 154 steps). Looking below, you can glimpse the past in the re-creations of Woodhenge and other structures. Looking across the river, you can view the present in the St. Louis Gateway Arch.

There's been a push in recent years to make Cahokia a national park. Assistant site manager Bill Iseminger, who has worked at the site for nearly 50 years, says "America's first city" is every bit as impressive as the remaining sites of ancient Egypt: "I always tell people if we'd had a stone pyramid, people would know about us. But we've got earthen mounds and earthen pyramids. For some reason, that is not as impressive to people as a stone structure would be." Whether it becomes a national park or not, Cahokia would be a much-welcomed addition to the American history curriculum. Meanwhile, if you want a taste of the good old days, chunkey is still played on some Native American reservations, and yaupon tea is making a comeback.

Deadliest 20th-century tornado:
the 1989 Daulatpur–Saturia tornado in Bangladesh killed 1,300 people.

OOPS! AGAIN

Everyone makes outrageous blunders from time to time.
So go ahead and feel superior for a few minutes.

WHAT A DOLL

Governments on many levels will issue an AMBER Alert in the event that a child or teenager goes missing and there's a possible threat to their safety. In January 2021, the Texas Department of Public Safety sent out an AMBER Alert—which appeared as a text message on the smartphone of every Texas resident—to make the public aware of two missing children named Glen and Chucky. Glen was reported to be dressed in a blue shirt with a black collar, while Chucky was last seen in blue overalls with a striped shirt underneath and "wielding a huge kitchen knife." Glen and Chucky are actually evil, homicidal dolls from the *Child's Play* series of horror movies (hence the knife). No children fitting that description were missing, nor had the dolls entered the real world for a crime spree. According to DPS officials, the IT department had written up a faux AMBER Alert for a system test, and accidentally sent it.

A LOTTO MISTAKES

One Tuesday in May 2022, TV host John Crow read out the Mega Millions lottery numbers in a televised segment that aired in 45 states, as he'd done hundreds of times before. He called out the five numbers from the ping-pong balls spit out by the picking machine: 15, 19, 20, 61, and 70. But when the golden "Mega Ball" emerged, Crow called it as a 6…even though it was a 9, with a line drawn underneath it, something done to prevent such misreading errors. There was no winner for the $86 million jackpot prize, but several players in New York state matched all six numbers, including the technically incorrect 6. Mega Millions went ahead and paid them their winnings anyway, a total of just over $5,500. "The 9 ball was drawn in the chamber and is the official result," Mega Millions said in a statement. "We apologize for the confusion."

ORDER ON THE COURT

Early one morning in February 2022, the Tuscaloosa, Alabama, police department's Hazard—the bomb squad—rolled up to the local federal courthouse to investigate a report of several suspicious and presumed dangerous objects left on the government building's front steps. Other officers set up a perimeter in the area and blocked nearby streets to prevent anyone from getting in or out. Once the bomb squad could get a closer look, crisis was averted and life went back to normal less than half an hour

Star Wars trivia: The "TIE" in TIE fighter stands for Twin Ion Engine…

after the lockdown. According to police, the packages contained "an assortment of regular and Doritos Locos Tacos, along with four Beefy Five-Layer Burritos." The questionable items were then destroyed, via being left in a trash bin behind the city's police department headquarters.

I DO BUT I DON'T
In the summer of 2022, Nikita and Karishma Rameshlal, two sisters from the Indian city of Ujjain, held a lavish double wedding, including nearly identical dresses and veils. During the middle of the ceremony, the power went out, plunging the wedding party and guests into complete darkness. But the wedding continued on, and was completed before power could be restored, at which point the sisters realized they'd each married the other's groom-to-be by mistake. After some heated arguments, the officiant nullified the previous vows and performed the ceremonies again (and correctly).

JUST PLANE WRONG
Michael Lowe was hanging out at a friend's Fourth of July party in New Mexico in 2021 when he was arrested and booked into jail in the Quay County Detention Center. Police were fulfilling a warrant for Lowe's arrest, issued by Tarrant County, Texas. Lowe, who is not a resident of Tarrant County—and who didn't even know where Tarrant County is (it's close to Dallas)—didn't understand why he was being arrested or detained. For 17 days and nights, he claims, he sat in his jail cell without anybody telling him what crime he'd allegedly committed. Finally, after he was released, he figured out what had happened: he'd been in Dallas Fort Worth International Airport on a layover during a flight from Arizona to Reno in 2020...and the airport is in Tarrant County. While he was there, as surveillance photos indicate, a man robbed a duty-free shop and boarded the same flight as Lowe. American Airlines fingered Lowe as the culprit, despite his not matching a physical description of the actual suspect. Lowe sued American Airlines, seeking a financial sum for emotional distress and lost wages.

DATA ERROR
As of June 2022, the western Japanese city of Amagasaki no longer exists—technically, or digitally, that is. The only records that city officials had of the city's 460,000 or so residents weren't stored on some main computer terminal or in a data storage cloud, but on a palm-sized, portable USB flash drive. The name, address, date of birth, bank account numbers for residents on government assistance, and more bits of information covering every person in Amagasaki existed only on that flash drive, which was lost by an employee of a company the city hired

...but George Lucas originally called it TIE because it resembled a bow tie.

to help execute COVID-19 relief measures. He had placed it in a bag, and after going out drinking, he lost it.

NATURE CALLED (AND ANSWERED)

A resident (name was withheld from news reports) of Allen Park, Michigan, was driving directly along the banks of the Rouge River (not a road) one night in February 2022, so late and so far from town that when he felt the need to urinate, he had little other choice but to pull over and do his business right there outside. The individual successfully stopped his SUV as he was relieving himself, but the vehicle, which hadn't been properly parked, started to slide...and then picked up steam, and then rolled all the way into the Rouge River. The SUV was completely submerged in the water, and the driver had to call the Allen Park and Dearborn fire departments for help. "Don't drive on the banks of the Rouge River," police said. "Thanks."

NO SON OF MINE

After more than 80 years of operating as a small family business in Cardiff, Wales, the civil engineering company Taylor & Sons Ltd. officially incorporated in 1875, and operated for well over a century, closing up shop in 2009. At that point, it was placed in administration, or endgame, by Companies House, a U.K. government organization that dutifully shutters bankrupt businesses, dispersing their assets and settling debts. However, Taylor & Sons wasn't bankrupt and Companies House didn't mean to shut down the business—it had intended to close up Taylor & Son (not Taylor & *Sons*), but still set the paperwork in motion to the point where the just-fine Taylor & Sons *did* close down. More than 250 people lost their jobs, and owner Philip Davison-Sebry successfully sued the U.K. government for £8.8m ($10.8 million) in damages.

NOT DEAD YET

In May 2020, Omkar Lal Gadulia checked himself into a hospital in Rajsamand, in western India, but didn't tell his family he was going to have his liver issues looked at. On the same day, another patient, Goverdhan Prajapat, was admitted to the same hospital in advance of an operation, but he died during the procedure. Hospital staff then forgot to properly label Prajapat's remains, listing him as unidentified and triggering local police to put out a call to identify the body. Gadulia's family saw the circulated photos and thought it was their relative, so they identified the remains (both men had a similar scar on their hand) and took the body away for a funeral. About a week after the burial of who they thought was Gadulia, the family was stunned when the man returned home from his hospital stay. "Appropriate action will be taken in the matter" on mortuary workers and nurses, a hospital administrator told reporters.

Lobsters taste with their feet and have three stomachs, one of which contains their teeth.

BIG WORDS

Time to spruce up that vocab. (Just try not to come off as circumlocutory.)

ASSONANCE (n.): Like a rhyme, but instead of the ends of the words sounding the same, the vowels do within the words. Poets, orators, and rappers use this literary device to add a musical, rhythmic feel to language.
"The assistant haphazardly answered, 'assonance.'"

BIBBLE (v.): Not to be confused with Bibble, Elina's pet puffball in the *Barbie: Fairytopia* movie series, this word (mainly used in the U.K.) means to make a lot of noise while eating or drinking.
"He bibbled his popcorn so loudly that I couldn't hear the *Barbie: Fairytopia* movie."

BIBLIOBIBULI (n., plural): In the mid-1950s, American satirist H. L. Mencken combined the Greek *biblio* ("books") and *bibulous* ("drinks a lot") to come up with this collective noun, which he defines thusly: "There are people who read too much: bibliobibuli. I know some who are constantly drunk on books, as other men are drunk on whiskey or religion. They wander through this most diverting and stimulating of worlds in a haze, seeing nothing and hearing nothing." (Mencken would have loved smart phones.)

CIRCUMLOCUTORY (adj.): Using unnecessary, long-winded jargon in order to be vague or evasive.
"After an hour and a half, the defense attorney's circumlocutory opening statement had put the opposing counsel, the judge, the gallery, and the jurors to sleep. (Then he and the defendant ran away.)"

DIDACTIC (adj.): Intending to teach or instruct—often in an overly moralistic manner.
"There was this didactic minister / Who told me of sinister things." —Michael Nesmith, "Roll with the Flow"

EFFULGENT (adj.): Shining brightly; radiant.
"Can you put a dimmer on that effulgent mood until I've had my morning coffee?"

ERF (n): A plot of land, usually about half an acre in size.
"The *Independence Day* filming location—where Will Smith punched that alien and said, 'Welcome to Earf!'—was about an erf in size."

What do chimpanzees, gorillas, giraffes, and tortoises have in common? They can't swim.

HALLUX (n): The big toe; or the innermost digit on any animal's lower limbs or hind section. The plural is *halluces*.
"For the last time, it's called a *hallux*, not a 'widdle piggy that went to market'!"

HEBETUDE (n.): Mental lethargy.
"The Dude pulled down the shades, turned off his brain, and fell into a blissful state of hebetude."

MERETRICIOUS (adj.): Falsely alluring; seemingly attractive but has no real value.
"Now go away then, and leave me alone. I don't want any more of your meretricious persiflage." —D. H. Lawrence

PERSIFLAGE (n.): Similar to *banter* in that it's small talk, but engaged in mockingly.
"Now go away then, and leave me alone. I don't want any more of your meretricious persiflage." —D. H. Lawrence

QUERULOUS (adj.): Constantly whiny, complaining about everything.
"After one too many complaints from his querulous stowaway—'There's trash everywhere,' 'There are maggots on me'—the driver said, 'For the last time, this is my garbage truck, not your Uber!'"

RABELAISIAN (adj.): Coarse, raunchy humor—it makes you laugh...and then feel a bit guilty for doing so. This *eponym* (a word derived from a person's name) comes from French novelist François Rabelais (1490–1553), who was known for such humor.
"The sleepy meeting became a Rabelaisian fart fest after Brian let one rip and everyone else stopped holding back."

SACCADES (n.): Rapid, usually involuntary movements of the eyeballs made when reading text or quickly assessing a room, as opposed to the more intentional *smooth pursuit movements* of the eyeballs.
"They gazed into each other's eyes; well, *he* gazed—her eyes were jumping around in saccades trying not to notice his one-inch-thick unibrow."

ZOANTHROPY (n.): A medical term referring to a *monomania* (an all-encompassing obsession with one specific thing) in which the delusional sufferer believes they are a small animal.
"No, Uncle John, you are not a little bunny rabbit, nor are you suffering from zoanthropy—now give that little girl her ears back."

CALLING WALTER SHAW

Here's the story of the man who revolutionized how phones are used by inventing various gadgets and technologies...but who wound up working for the Mafia. Why? That's just the nature of the business.

ON THE LINE

Walter L. Shaw dropped out of school in the ninth grade and worked a series of low-paying jobs in and around Miami. In 1935, he landed a position as a lineman with Southern Bell, a branch of AT&T, the originator of telephone service and which would enjoy a complete and total government-authorized monopoly on telephony in the United States. Shaw was a "pole climber," installing lines for a base salary plus bonuses for how many feet he could set up in a day. Shaw also had a natural aptitude for electronics and telephony, and at home he'd tinker with existing gadgets, invent his own small gadgets, and draw elaborate schematics for complicated inventions he couldn't afford to build, usually things related to improving or expanding on telephony.

Shaw eventually applied for and gained entry to AT&T's in-house engineering school, a feeder program for Bell Labs, its research-and-development division where the company devised new gadgets both for its telephone network—which stretched across the country on account of how AT&T had swallowed up smaller, independent carriers—and other clients. Throughout the 1940s and 1950s, while working days as a low-level engineer at Bell Labs, assigned to help out on projects devised and led by others, Shaw would go home to his garage workshop and draw detailed illustrations or make crude prototypes of his telephony-improving devices. Among the technologies Shaw came up with on his own, at home:

- The speakerphone
- A burglar alarm that automatically calls police
- Conference calling
- Call forwarding
- Touch-tone dialing

HOLD, PLEASE

Shaw worked up the nerve to bring his inventions and ideas into work, to show them to his bosses. They were impressed, and they saw a lot of promise (and profits) in what he created. They also had him in a bind: As AT&T was the only phone company in the country, Shaw couldn't exactly take his inventions to a competitor. If he wanted his gadgets to enter mass production and widespread use, he'd have to take whatever deal AT&T offered him. In 1952, Bell Labs executives offered to make Shaw a department head and provide a huge salary boost. In return, he'd have to sign the rights to all his inventions over to the company, meaning they'd get any and all profits and royalties generated. Shaw refused the deal, and he resigned from his position at Bell Labs.

Shaw thought he had some leverage, thinking the opportunity to move to another competitor, or to start his own electronics company, was just around the corner. His exit from Bell Labs coincided with U.S. Attorney General J. Howard McGrath filing an antitrust lawsuit against AT&T, accusing the company of operating a monopoly and stating that by not allowing for competition, they were impeding progress to the detriment of consumers. But the lawsuit failed—AT&T would continue to be the one and only phone company for another 30-plus years. As a result of making enemies with the only company that would require or be interested in his unique talents, Shaw was essentially blacklisted from working in telephony. AT&T was so powerful that it was actually a federal crime to add attachments to the telephone-line system that they owned and operated in full, meaning Shaw couldn't sell, market, use, or even test out any gadgets he might invent without incurring the wrath of the largest corporation in the world, or of the police.

TRANSFERRING THE CALL

Nevertheless, Shaw, with a wife and two kids to support, continued to trudge ahead in his profession. He figured he'd worry about getting AT&T's approval later on, after he already developed and built successful prototypes for phone equipment so undeniably beneficial that the company would have to take notice. He sought out financing, but the deals fell through owing to a lack of interest from monied inventors, or a lack of money from investors who turned out to be con artists.

With no other options, a humbled and desperate Shaw returned to Bell Labs in 1953, officially requesting permission to legally connect one of his inventions to AT&T's lines. The invention: a fully realized voice-activated speakerphone. He'd built 200 units for a wealthy investor who'd dropped out of the project, so he even had a test shipment all ready to market, ship, and sell. But once more, since AT&T held all the cards, they were able to dictate the terms. They agreed to let Shaw hold the patent in his name, but the company would get all the rights to the project. In exchange for a nominal one-time flat fee, AT&T would get all control over the speakerphone and all revenues it would generate.

AN URGENT CALL

After the botched speakerphone deal, Shaw had exhausted his savings and his family was nearly destitute. Putting his lofty dreams of inventing and distributing expensive, industry-changing phone devices on hold, he took a job as a repairman for Philco Television. The hours were long, the pay was meager, and in his free time, Shaw

The Empire State Building has its own ZIP code: 10118.

continued to tinker with his ideas and find people willing to invest in them, but with no lasting success.

Things seemed to turn around in 1955, however. Bell Labs was one of the chief contractors for the U.S. Armed Forces, providing advanced military technology for both combat operations and for spying on the Soviet Union and its Communist allies. It was under the auspices of the latter that Bell asked Shaw, who was much farther ahead than anyone in-house on emerging technologies, to rejoin the company as a freelance contractor to work on a series of top-secret military projects. Shaw left his family on the East Coast for a year and decamped to Elmendorf Air Force Base in Anchorage, Alaska, where he helped to create the Distant Early Warning Line, a missile-tracking system that would alert the U.S. government the second the Russians launched intercontinental weaponry. And in hopes of preventing the DEW Line from ever needing to be used, Shaw, promoted to the rank of lieutenant, created the legendary "red phone": a direct connection linking the Soviet prime minister in the Kremlin in Moscow to the American president in the White House in Washington, D.C., which worked via switching tech created by Shaw that sent a telex over phone lines.

A BAD CONNECTION

For the first time in his career, Shaw was happy—he was making interesting and important things and he was well-respected and well-paid for it. But then, in 1956, the armed forces discharged Shaw, no longer requiring his services. He returned to his family's home in Florida, once again with no job prospects and little hope of earning a living.

Shaw didn't have much of a choice when he was approached by Ralph Satterfield, a self-described businessman from Miami Beach who claimed affiliation with a group of wealthy industrialists in New York City—his uncle ran a jewelry store that catered to mobsters looking to buy garish and expensive items for their wives and mistresses. Satterfield's uncle connected Shaw with his Mafia clients, particularly Joseph Valachi, a low-level soldier and arranger in Lucky Luciano's crime family, one of the five constituent organized criminal organizations that comprised La Costra Nostra.

Valachi's bosses were so impressed with Shaw's technical know-how, and what he could do for them, that they moved him and his family to New York, installed him in a nice apartment with a hefty salary, paid for his kids to attend private school, and gifted him a Cadillac. They couldn't thank him enough because he'd enabled an illegal gambling ring to earn tens of millions of dollars. Under Mafia supervision, Shaw did what he did best and made a useful, next-level telephone gadget: he called it a black box, which utilized a number rerouting system to make

The world's largest stained-glass window, located at an Illinois cemetery, is over 2,200 square feet and has 2,000 panels.

free and untraceable long distance phone calls. For five years, the Genovese family ran a nationwide bookmaking operation, without detection by the FBI, through Shaw's invention. They manufactured 1,500 black boxes and distributed them around the country.

HANGING UP

The system fell apart in 1961 when Shaw's escort into the Mafia, Ralph Satterfield, got too bold, taking out a classified ad in the *Miami Herald* that read, "Call me if you want to make free phone calls." That aroused suspicion from AT&T's internal security forces, who alerted the FBI. Federal agents tracked down Satterfield through the ad, and it wasn't long before they found Shaw, too. Posing as a criminal goon, an FBI operative went to Shaw's house and pretended to want to purchase a black box. When Shaw presented one, he was handcuffed and arrested, along with Satterfield and some other gangsters involved in the scheme.

Unfortunately for Shaw, the exposure of the phone-hacking scheme and his subsequent arrest coincided with a federal government drive to root out organized crime. The U.S. Senate established a subcommittee on racketeering, and senators John L. McClellan and John F. Kennedy presided over hearings, some of the first ever to be televised. Shaw was called to testify and he did, taking the fall for the phone scheme. In front of the subcommittee, Shaw acknowledged that he was the inventor of the black box, but he refused to call out anyone with whom he'd worked.

Shaw was tried for complicity in illegal gambling operations and for unauthorized attachment to telephone lines, both federal crimes. He was sentenced to a year in prison, but served nine months.

CALLING BACK

After he was paroled, Shaw went back to his old way of life, devising and modeling telephony inventions and attempting to get wealthy backers to finance and market them. He filed and received a few patents in the 1960s, but his benefactors transferred the rights into a shell company to avoid fully paying Shaw what they were worth.

In 1972, while working on a touch-tone phone improvement, Shaw connected the machinery to a phone line for testing to see if it worked. AT&T's security forces detected the unauthorized use of the lines and had Shaw arrested; because that criminal act mirrored some of his past criminal acts, it was a violation of his parole. Despite a defense that he was just testing equipment, and not actually making illegal phone calls, Shaw was sentenced to four years in prison, one year for each of the four "calls" or tests he'd conducted.

Upon his release from his second prison term, Shaw didn't do much work with telephones anymore. He died of prostate cancer in 1996, months after his son found him broke, emaciated, and living in a bus station in Reno. He was 79.

Sleep experts say: the ideal duration for a nap is 20 minutes.
Any longer and you risk feeling groggy.

KILL A KING, BE A KING

The inside story of the remarkable, violent, and quick-moving
succession of power in an ancient Asian kingdom.

- In 437 BC, Pandukabhaya established the kingdom of Anuradhapura on the island of Sri Lanka. Regarded as the first true king of Sri Lanka, he ended conflict among local clans and indigenous groups and united the population, at least on the northern half of the island, while also staking claim over the rest of the land and enduring brief, tribal independence movements over the years.

- Pandukabhaya and his successors of the Sinhalese cultural group kept Anuradhapura an independent kingdom for hundreds of years, though they did suffer occasional invasion and overthrow by aggressors from southern India, which is separated from Sri Lanka by the 34-mile-wide Palk Strait.

- In 237 BC, King Suratissa's ten-year reign ended when two powerful horse dealers, Sena and Guttika, of the Tamil ethnic group indigenous to south India, invaded and overthrew him when they killed him in battle. Sena and Guttika were corulers of Sri Lanka for 22 years, until they were overthrown by Asela, a relation of Suratissa and descendant of previous monarchs. Asela's rule lasted just 10 years, from 215 to 205 BC, whereupon Ellalan, another Tamil invader from the Chola dynasty, killed Asela and assumed the throne.

- Ellalan ruled until 161 BC, and according to records was a just and favorable leader among both the native Sinhalese and Tamil. Nevertheless, a movement sprung up around Dutugamunu, a Sinhalese Anuradhapura-aligned prince from the Sri Lankan kingdom of Mahagama. After beating back a political challenge by his brother, Dutugamunu united the southern part of the island against Ellalan, starting a yearlong war. After a final battle in which both monarchs actively fought from the backs of elephants, legend says a fatal dart shot by Dutugamunu himself struck and killed Ellalan.

- Dutugamunu, called Dutugamunu the Great in Sri Lankan historical texts, died in 137 BC; his son, Saliya, had been disowned and disinherited, allowing Dutugamunu's brother Saddha Tissa to succeed Dutugamunu instead. When Saddha Tissa died in 119 BC, he was succeeded by his son Thulatthana, who was replaced by his brother Lamani Tissa, then his brother Khallata Naga, and then Saddha Tissa's last son, Valagamba of Anuradhapura.

- After nearly a century in Sri Lanka of relative political stability and solid border defense, the Tamil invaders returned. In 103 BC, a mere five months

Cave paintings discovered in India show that people
have been dancing for at least 9,000 years.

after he took the throne of the Anuradhapura Kingdom, Valagamba was overthrown by a consortium of five conquering Tamil chiefs from southern India. Known as the Five Dravidians and representing the Pandyan Dynasty that ruled over a portion of what's now southern India for hundreds of years, they sought to expand their empire by invading Sri Lanka, and the Kingdom of Anuradhapura. When Valagamba's residence at Kolambalaka was raided, the king fled in a chariot (with one of his wives, Queen Somadevi, sacrificing herself for capture to lighten the chariot's load so it could get away faster), and he settled in exile in Malayarata.

• The supreme chief of the five Tamil chiefs was Pulhatta. Because his actions were the most vital in the departure of Valagamba, he was selected as the new king of Anuradhapura. He appointed another of the invading chiefs, Bahita, to be his chief advisor and prime minister. The arrangement didn't last long—Pulhatta reigned as king from 103 to 100 BC, at which point he was killed by Bahita, who took the throne for himself.

• Following the precedent established by Pulhatta, Bahita appointed Panya Mara, another member of the Five Dravidians, to be his Prime Minister. And Panya Mara did what his successor did and murdered the king for his job. Bahita's death at Panya Mara's hand in 98 BC allowed the latter to become the new king of Anuradhapura.

• With only two others of the Five Dravidians remaining alive, King Panya Mara appointed one of them, Pilaya Mara, to the office of Prime Minister. And it's not hard to guess what happened after that: Panya Mara's reign lasted seven years and no longer, because Pilaya Mara murdered him, then appointed himself king of Anuradhapura.

• The shortest reign of all the Five Dravidians, from 91 to 90 BC, was that of Pilaya Mara, because he was murdered by the fifth and final Tamil Chief, Dathika.

• King Dathika ruled over northern Sri Lanka for just two years. In 88 BC—after 15 years in exile, during which time he secretly amassed an army—deposed king Valagamba returned to Anuradhapura and invaded the kingdom that had been invaded and taken away from him. He defeated Dathika's forces, Dathika was killed, and Valagamba resumed the throne of his kingdom.

• Valagamba's descendants in the Dutugamunu dynasty would mostly rule Sri Lanka for the next 500 years...until AD 436, when, once again, a new crop of Tamil and Dravidian invaders would overthrow the king and rule for 16 years. The final three of the six Dravidians in charge would be killed by the forces of deposed Anuradhapura king Dhatusena, who reestablished his rule in 452.

If you're a professional dancer, there's an 80 percent chance
you'll have one major injury during your career.

CAR PARTS

Most of us take our cars for granted. These machines are a collection of systems and scientific marvels that all combine to get us from point A to point B, and all they ask for in return is the occasional oil change. Here are how some of those sophisticated systems and parts came to be included in the modern automobile.

AUTOMATIC TRANSMISSION

The system by which a car changes gears to go faster or slower or handle different terrains is called a transmission, and it can fall into one of two categories. The first, and the one loved most by car enthusiasts, is the manual transmission, also known as "stick shift," because it requires the driver to use a lever to manually switch (or shift) gears (while also using a clutch pedal at the same time). This process can be quite difficult and sometimes annoying to time correctly—otherwise, a driver may "grind gears" or the car may lurch uncomfortably. This is why most cars today have the second kind of transmission, called automatic, in which the car shifts to the proper gear with no driver input. In the 1920s, an inventor from Portland, Oregon, named Earl A. Thompson developed the first automatic gear-shifting mechanism. Using a Cadillac that his brother, a car dealer, loaned him, Thompson installed a system that synchronized, or matched up, the speed of the car with the speed of the changing gears. As the car sped up, for example, the gears were forced to keep up...and switch. Thompson then drove his test car all the way to Detroit, where he pitched it to several car companies. Cadillac hired him on as a consultant, and in 1928, Thompson's "Silent Synchro-Mesh" became a standard feature in Cadillac and LaSalle vehicles.

HYDRAULIC BRAKES

The first type of brakes used in cars were drum-based and mechanical. The driver had to step down *hard* on the brakes to get them to work. Pro: cars definitely stopped when the brakes were applied. Con: drivers had to press down on the brakes with all their might—so much force that it was easy to lose control of a car. This was obviously an area in which early cars needed improvement, and the first person to come up with the much smoother hydraulic brake system was race car manufacturer Fred Duesenberg in 1914. With hydraulic brakes, when the brake pedal is pushed by the driver, a lever in the engine forces a piston into a pipe. That motion then fills cylindrical tubes surrounding the wheels with water. The sudden pressure of heavy water in those adjacent cylinders prevents the wheels from moving. It was a brilliant

Ironic fact: the hippopotamus (Latin for "water horse") can't swim.
(It's big and buoyant enough to "hop" along the river floor.)

idea, but only available in Duesenberg race cars at first, until the company realized they had a good thing going. In 1921, the company hired airplane-parts maker Malcolm Loughead (he'd later change the spelling of his name and start airplane manufacturing company Lockheed-Martin) to improve hydraulic brakes and make them standard in its regular, passenger cars.

AIRBAGS

While driving in rural Pennsylvania one day in 1952, John W. Hetrick hit an errant rock in the road. He lost control and veered into a ditch, all the while instinctively reaching into the back seat to hold back his young daughter from flying through the windshield (seat belts were not in wide use at the time). This gave Hetrick, who happened to be a torpedo engineer for the military, an idea for a safety device that would deploy only in the moment of a crash. He thought an inflatable system would work best and take up little room, and he patented the first airbag in 1953. It consisted of an air accumulator, an inflatable cushion (the "bag" part of the airbag), and a valve to regulate the sudden influx of air into the cushion. His plans called for one to be mounted inside the steering wheel to protect the driver, one in the glove compartment to protect a passenger, and one on the instrument panel to protect people riding in the backseat. Hetrick's idea was a good one, but a bit ahead of its time. The problem lay in mechanical sensors, which would detect impact and set off the inflation of the airbags. The ones available in the 1950s were too slow: in crash tests, the bags couldn't fill up with air fast enough to be of any use. Undeterred, Daimler-Benz acquired the rights to the airbag from Hetrick—he purposely didn't accept any money for the patent because he wanted the potentially life-saving device to be developed more than he wanted to make money off it. It took the company more than two decades and 250 impact tests before it was perfected, but in 1981 the airbag debuted in the Mercedes Benz S-Class. A 1998 law mandated that all new cars sold in the U.S. include front airbags, which have saved an estimated 30,000 lives.

SELF-STARTER

Another imperfect annoyance about early automobiles: to turn them on, you had to turn a heavy crank by hand. This fed gas into a cylinder, which would move a piston. Once enough momentum had been built up by hand-cranking, the piston could start to move on its own, allowing the gas to flow into the engine and make it run. Not only was this a hassle, but it required a great deal of physical strength to do properly. It was also dangerous—the crank had a way of using some of that built-up energy to rear back and

There's a Black Sabbath cover band called Mac Sabbath.
They dress up like McDonald's characters.

knock down the person turning it. In 1910, that happened to a friend of Cadillac founder Henry M. Leland—the crank cracked him in the face and broke his jaw, an infection set in, and he died. Enough was enough with the hand cranks, according to Leland, and he hired electrical engineer and inventor Charles F. Kettering to come up with some way to make cars start that didn't lead to injury. Kettering studied the way a car starts and theorized that the energy provided by a hand crank could also be provided by a jolt of electricity. In Kettering's electric starter, a magnetic field provides an electrical current. That passes through a metal wire. This replaced the energy that came from the crank, and the electricity that passes through the metal wire forces the pistons to move on their own, flowing gas into the engine and starting it. Kettering installed his system in a Cadillac, which was set in motion by a simple push-button mechanism by the steering wheel. A driver pushed the button to activate the first step (the magnetic field generating a current). Leland installed the push-button starter in all 1912 Cadillacs. The development of the car key didn't fundamentally change the self-starter—when a key is inserted into the car and turned, that's what starts the electrical process.

*   *   *

HOLY BOY WONDER, BATMAN!

On the campy 1960s TV show Batman, *sidekick Robin's catchphrase is blurting out "Holy [whatever weird situation we're in], Batman!" Here are some of the strangest.*

Holy sarcophagus, Batman!

Holy hardest metal in the world, Batman!

Holy *Journey to the Center of the Earth*, Batman!

Holy *Hamlet*, Batman!

Holy human pearls, Batman!

Holy remote-control robot, Batman!

Holy uncanny photographic mental processes, Batman!

Holy reverse polarity, Batman!

Holy hieroglyphics, Batman!

Holy shrinkage, Batman!

Holy rocking chair, Batman!

Holy priceless collection of Etruscan snoods, Batman!

Holy armadillos, Batman!

Holy hypodermics, Batman!

Holy Fourth Amendment, Batman!

Holy purple cannibals, Batman!

The Importance of Being Earnest **author Oscar Wilde spent two years in prison for being gay.**

WHAT CAN BROWN DO FOR YOU?

Think poo is gross? You're right—it is. But it can also be very useful.
And so can pee!

Poo Paper. Muskox poop is so fibrous that you can make paper out of it. A Canadian teacher discovered that fact (we're not sure how) and, with the help of a paper maker from Alberta, teaches her grade school students the process. The class collects the scat on literal "field trips."

Pee Mountain. Arizona Snowbowl in Flagstaff, Arizona, doesn't get much snow naturally—but people pee a lot, so they've made that into snow. It's actually more environmentally friendly than chemically derived synthetic snow, or real snow trucked in from far away. To acquire enough material for snow making, the resort teamed up with the city of Flagstaff to buy its wastewater—after it's been treated, of course.

Poo Fuel. Experts say that before long, we may be filling our cars with fuel made from the feces of chickens, pigs, or even humans. Poo fuel will cost about 10 cents per gallon and offer better mileage than gasoline does. Some large poultry and pig farms have already begun to use poop for power. A plant in western Minnesota converts 700,000 tons of turkey droppings per year into electricity. In the Netherlands, another plant recycles enough chicken waste to power 90,000 homes annually. And human waste treatment plants could soon become sources of perpetual poo power.

Pee Gardens. Amsterdam, the Netherlands, is revered for its lush rooftop gardens, and all that greenery requires fertilizing nutrients—nitrogen, potassium, and phosphorus—that could become scarce in coming years. Conveniently, all three are found in a substance plentiful on Earth: urine. So in the 2010s, Amsterdam began harvesting those wasted nutrients from public urinals for use in fertilizing gardens. Officials say that urine from the city's 1 million people can produce 1,000 tons of cheap, natural fertilizer each year.

Eau de Poo. Whale poop, technically called ambergris, is used as the base scent in fine perfumes. It's a fatty deposit that develops when sperm whales eat squids. The squid's indigestible beak gets snagged in the whale's intestines, and the whale's body generates a smooth cholesterol glob that hardens around it. The glob is eventually excreted, and after floating through the ocean for a while, it washes up on a beach. If you find some ambergris, plug your nose and take it home; perfume manufacturers will pay up to $1 million for a large chunk.

The ancient Mayan calendar is more precise than the modern Gregorian calendar.

Double "Pee" Batteries. After drinking a whole bunch of water (we assume), a team of researchers at Singapore's Institute of Bioengineering and Nanotechnology discovered that if you drop a wee bit of wee onto an assembly of copper chloride, magnesium, and copper, it causes a chemical reaction that can power a battery.

Poo Medicine. Researchers from Johns Hopkins Medicine have successfully transplanted fecal matter from healthy donors into the intestines of patients suffering from *Clostridium difficile* infections (persistent diarrhea). They've achieved solid results.

Poo Towers. Throughout history and even today, manure has been used like clay for stuccoing and waterproofing huts, buckets, baskets, and beehives. An Indonesian company recently began making bricks from dung. Bonus: they're stronger and lighter than clay bricks.

ShamPOO. Japanese researchers have successfully extracted vanilla from cow dung that's chemically identical to natural vanilla. It can be used to make candles, cosmetics, and hair care products. (We'll stick with the vanilla that comes from a plant for our ice cream.)

"Tang." The real drink of the astronauts is urine. Sending up fresh supplies of water every few months would cost a fortune, so equipment on the International Space Station recycles every single drop of water possible—including sweat, the moisture the astronauts exhale when they breathe, and urine. More than 90 percent of all water used on the station, including urine, is reclaimed, reused, and repackaged into potable water. Using an artificial gravity system, keg-sized distillers purify the urine immediately after it leaves the astronaut. It might seem disgusting, but the space station's recycled wee is purer than most drinking water on Earth.

Poo Steak. That's not a typo. There is so much sewage being created every day by Japan's 127 million poo-producing citizens that innovative ways are being sought to deal with it. One solution: Researcher Mitsuyuki Ikeda came up with a process that extracts the bacteria-spawned protein from human excrement and then cooks it to kill off the harmful bacteria. The extracted protein is then combined with a chemical-reaction enhancer and put through an extruder to create the new meat product, which is then enhanced with soy protein for flavor and colored with red dye. The resulting "steak," claims Ikeda, is 63 percent protein and reportedly contains fewer calories than conventional meat.

Crappy Art. Lots of "edgy" artists incorporate corporeal leavings into their artwork. Here's one of our favorites: In his show "Why I Am So F***ing Special: It's All About Me," Miami-based artist Robert Wyndam Bucknell displayed four glass jars. The first three contained actual "stool samples" from a Realtor, a pharmacist, and the art gallery owner. The fourth jar contained what Bucknell said was his own poo, but actually contained purple toy dinosaurs. Now *that's* special.

What about saying, "happy almost birthday"?
It's considered bad luck in Russia to prematurely wish someone a happy birthday.

UNAMUSED

Amusement parks are a billion-dollar industry. The success of Disney World or Six Flags makes would-be entrepreneurs drool, but it's not so easy to get a theme park built. Here are some attractions that were never even fully constructed.

Park: Space City U.S.A.
Location: Huntsville, Alabama

What Fun! The 1960s were the golden age of futurism, and space travel and the drive to the moon captured the hope and imagination of millions—including the organizers and investors of Space City U.S.A., a planned interstellar and science-fiction theme park in Alabama. An ambitious expensive endeavor (initially budgeted at $5 million, or $35 million in today's money), it would have rivaled Disneyland in scope and imagination. Set on an 850-acre plot outside of Huntsville along Lady Anne Lake, managers hired Skylim of Alabama, a ride builder that had worked on Disneyland and Six Flags Over Texas, to bring everything to fruition. Guests would enter through a giant "time machine," and then choose which era and locale to travel to—a dinosaur land, the antebellum South, a pirate island, or a futuristic moon colony. They could also gape at an artificial volcano, dine in a lunar-themed restaurant, or take a ride on a monorail or in a glass-bottom boat.

What Happened? Scheduled to open in 1965, budget overruns, weather issues, and financial problems made construction stretch on until 1967, at which point organizers pulled the plug, even though many buildings and rides were nearly built. They never even met that $5 million fundraising goal (even after selling shares in the business to Huntsville locals), ultimately raising only $2 million and spending $500,000 on construction. The rest of the money, about $1.5 million...mysteriously disappeared.

Park: Paris, U.S.A.
Location: Florida

What Fun! In the late 1950s, before transatlantic flights were practical and relatively affordable to middle-class Americans, there was a real market for bringing the delights of Europe a little closer to home. That was the impetus behind Paris, U.S.A., a Parisian theme park and replica of the City of Love on a 150-acre plot of land off

Spiders never sleep.

a highway near the county line separating Dade and Broward counties in southern Florida. Organizers announced that the park's signature attraction would be a near-exact and just-as-tall replica of the Eiffel Tower (which would cost $12 million to build), surrounded by a constructed Parisian street, lined with shops and restaurants, adjacent to a supervised rides area for kids to play on while their parents bought real imported French goods and ate croissants and drank wine.

What Happened? Set to open in 1959, Paris, U.S.A. never finished construction after organizers couldn't raise the necessary funds.

Park: The Marvelous Land of Oz
Location: California

What Fun! Long before the movie *The Wizard of Oz* was released in 1939 and became a well-viewed classic, L. Frank Baum's series of Oz books were mega-best-sellers around the turn of the 20th century. In 1905, Baum set out to build (and build interest in) an Oz theme park. Publicly declaring the area a "fairy paradise for children," Baum promised statues of the Scarecrow, the Tin Man, and other characters, and a majestic Dorothy's Palace. One other big attraction at the Marvelous Land of Oz: Baum himself. He planned to live on-site and greet guests who came to the park on Pedloe Island, off the coast of Southern California.

What Happened? Curiously, Pedloe Island doesn't exist—it's not a real place. Historians say the Marvelous Land of Oz chatter was likely a publicity stunt to promote a big-budget theatrical production of a *Land of Oz* play. That play flopped, and the Marvelous Land of Oz theme park was never spoken of again.

Park: Six Flags Dubai
Location: Dubai, United Arab Emirates

What Fun! Six Flags controls 27 amusement and water parks across the United States and Canada, and, in 2014, announced its 28th attraction, and its first outside of North America: Six Flags Dubai. Oil-rich Dubai is one of the fastest-growing and flush-with-cash cities on earth, home to 54,000 millionaires and the site of a rapid expansion of luxury hotels, resorts, and amusement parks over the last 30 years, all seeking to attract wealthy tourists. Six Flags Dubai was set to feature six different areas, most alluding to North American parks in the company portfolio: Magic Mountain, Fiesta Texas, Great Escape, Great Adventure, Great America, and Thrillseeker Plaza. The latter would

Built like a modern-day ostrich—but much taller—the feathered ornithomimid dinosaur could run 60 miles per hour.

feature six roller-coasters, including what park organizers said would be the world's largest (although they never gave any specifics about it).

What Happened? Just two years later, at a shareholder meeting in 2016, Six Flags's local partner on the project, DXB Entertainments, canceled all construction and plans to ever open the park, telling reporters that it was no longer in the company's "best interests" and choosing instead to add on to and rebuild Dubai parks that were already open.

Park: Beastly Kingdom
Location: Orlando, Florida

What Fun! There are a total of six different theme parks inside the Disney World entertainment complex in Florida, including Animal Kingdom, a combination zoo and animal-themed ride fest. Shortly after opening Animal Kingdom in 1998, Disney planned to expand right away with an immersive area called Beastly Kingdom, a fabricated zoo themed like a medieval fairy tale, featuring highly realistic animatronics of mythical and fictional animals. In a maze called Quest of the Unicorn, visitors would wander around and search for golden idols, entitling them to an encounter with a unicorn, while Dragon Tower would include a fire-breathing dragon.

What Happened? Disney played around with the idea for a decade but found that it would be far too expensive to build Beastly Kingdom—because its engineers would have to invent the technology to make the creatures they wanted to include before they could build those creatures. Nevertheless, Disney was so sure that Beastly Kingdom would be built that the Animal Kingdom logo includes a depiction of a dragon—a vestige of the expansion that never came.

Park: Charlie Daniels Western World and Theme Park
Location: Saddlebrook, Florida

What Fun! In 1986, country music superstar and actress Dolly Parton bought the Silver Dollar City Wild West theme park in Pigeon Forge, Tennessee, and turned it into the massively successful and well-attended Dollywood amusement park, entertainment complex, and tourist destination. Another country music icon, fiddler and singer Charlie Daniels, best known for the 1979 hit "The Devil Went Down to Georgia," probably saw Parton's dollar signs in his eyes when he started plans on Charlie Daniels Western World and Theme Park in 1994. While attending

The average person spends 38 days of their life brushing their teeth. (Not all at once.)

a rodeo with a stockbroker, Daniels figured he should open a rodeo venue in the already tourist-luring state of Florida. Then he decided he should open a theme park built around himself and his songs. Daniels and his partner bought 2,000 acres in Saddlebrook, Florida (outside Tampa), employed a theme-park design firm, and started preproduction on an attraction and proof-of-concept called The Devil Went Down to Georgia: The Live 3-D Spectacular.

What Happened? Charlie Daniels Western World was set to open in 1997, provided that Daniels and company received an investment of several million dollars from a venture capital firm or corporate entity. That monetary influx never came, and all park plans were abandoned.

Park: Blockbuster Park
Location: Miramar, Florida

What Fun! The home video revolution of the 1990s had one big winner in the business of VHS tape rental: Blockbuster Video, a chain of 9,000 locations at its peak. Bad business decisions and the arrival of Netflix's DVD-by-mail and streaming video services would completely kill the company in the 2010s, but in 1993, Blockbuster was raking in a fortune under active owner Wayne Huizenga. His personal net worth stood at more than $1 billion, which he used to buy an NHL team (the Florida Panthers) and a Major League Baseball team (the Florida Marlins). During an investor earnings call in the fall of 1993, Huizenga mentioned that he planned to build a sports and theme-park complex under the Blockbuster name, which would include a new venue for each of his teams, along with a theme park (featuring traditional thrill rides, "simulation theaters," and virtual reality–fueled attractions), a shopping district, hotels, restaurants, live music halls, a marine park, a multiplex movie theater, office space, and 1,000 apartments to house some of the estimated 17,000 people it would take to staff the so-called Blockbuster Park. At 2,500 acres, it would've been the second-largest theme park in the U.S., behind only Disney World. Huizenga and Blockbuster had to jump through a lot of hoops. Because the park would straddle land in two counties and a city, it had to get every decision approved three times, and it also had to convince locals that the negative impact on the environment and water use wouldn't be a big deal, as well as get them to pay $91 million in taxpayer funds to expand roads and rail lines. Within one year, the budgeted cost to open Blockbuster Park doubled from $1 billion to $2 billion, with $35 million spent just on land.

What Happened? While all this was going on, media conglomerate Viacom was attempting to buy Paramount Pictures, and bought Blockbuster as a way to bolster its coffers. By the time the deal was finalized in late 1994, Viacom realized it was $18 billion in debt after the purchase of two companies and didn't want to spend another $2 billion on a theme park complex. They canceled the project; Huizenga left the company within a year.

Park: Park of Culture and Rest
Location: Pripyat, Ukraine

What Fun! To build morale and trust in the Communist government, the government of the Soviet Union built several theme parks in major cities, each labeled a "Park of Culture and Rest." A company called Attraction built the rides for all of them, including the one built in Pripyat, a city in the then-Soviet republic of Ukraine. The park was small and offered exactly five attractions: Circular Overview (a Ferris wheel), Autodrome (bumper cars), a flying/suspension ride (Chamomile), Russian Swing (a swing boat), and a midway with carnival-style shooting games.

What Happened? The grand opening planned for May 1, 1986—May Day, a massive holiday in the Soviet Union—didn't come to pass because five days earlier, on April 26, 1986, an explosion at the nearby Chernobyl Nuclear Power Plant led to one of the worst atomic disasters in history. The city of Pripyat was completely evacuated, and, owing to radiation levels that remain toxically high in the area more than 30 years later, was completely abandoned. The almost completely ready, brand-new Park of Culture and Rest remained unopened and untouched.

* * *

IN SPACE, NO ONE CAN HEAR YOU TRANSLATE

A bootleg DVD of the 1979 horror classic *Alien* contains a synopsis that was written by someone who had a better grasp of the movie than they did the English language:

"Space ship people get up from sleeping coffin and have eat. Computer woman find strange noisings on planet and astronauts go to seeing. Astronauts find big elephant man who dead then find too many egg.

"Astronaut is possess by egg demon and new egg demon is come when eat bad noodle. Seven friends and cat all try to find egg demon before space ship go home but is hard working.

"Who will life to escaping? Who is bad milk blood robot? Scream not working because space make deaf."

Original name for candy corn: Chicken Feed.

TURTLE TALES

Remember that strange kid who went viral for blurting out "I love turtles!"
during a local news interview? That kid is Uncle John's kindred spirit.

WHERE WAS I GOING AGAIN?

"If I didn't let you eat for three days, and then I put you 100 yards from a really nice restaurant...you'd probably make a beeline straight to that restaurant." But not hawksbill sea turtles, says Professor Graeme Hays of Deakin University in Victoria, Australia. Most migrating birds, fish, and mammals tend to know where they're going. But after Hays's research team fit 22 female hawksbills with tracking tags and tracked their migration to feeding grounds in an archipelago in the Indian Ocean, they discovered that these sea turtles either like to mosey, or they don't know where they're going. It's unlikely, says Hays, that they're moseying. Why not? Because these turtles are hungry—most haven't eaten for weeks or even months. They travel in "generally the right direction," but their "crude" navigational skills make them zig and zag. Most of them travel about twice the distance required, and it took a detour of more than 800 miles for one wayward hawksbill to reach her feeding grounds 100 miles away. In their defense, says Graeme, "These hawksbill turtles are going to isolated targets that are submerged banks in the open ocean. The navigational challenge is a lot greater." But thankfully, they all got there in the end.

THE BALLAD OF BRUCE AND BIANCA

Bruce and Bianca never got along. He's a small French bulldog, and she's a 50-pound sulcata tortoise. They cohabitate at the Fortin household in Scottsdale, Arizona. One day in 2021, Bruce went missing. The family of four combed the neighborhood and put up "lost dog" flyers. Later that afternoon, Michelle (the mom) heard muffled barks coming from somewhere in the backyard. She traced it to...Bianca's den. As tortoises do, she'd dug a large burrow to sleep in and to keep her temperature regulated. The entrance was only as wide as Bianca, and it went down a few feet at a 45-degree angle before opening up into a larger hole...which was serving as a dog jail cell. It's unknown if Bianca had lured Bruce in or if he'd wandered on his own, but Bianca was deep in the hole, her head facing the entrance, with her butt blocking Bruce from escaping, despite repeated requests from the family.

The Fortins didn't know what to do. There was no way to reach in and grab the tortoise, and they were uncertain how much air, if any, the dog had. So they called

911. Four firefighters showed up and didn't know what to do, either—digging could cause a cave-in. They called Russ Johnson, president of the Phoenix Herpetological Sanctuary. When Johnson arrived, Bruce had been in the den for at least three hours, and he'd stopped barking. Had he run out of air?

The Fortin kids were taken inside. Johnson told the firefighters to dig around the edges of the entrance to widen it while also maintaining structural integrity. As they were doing that, Bianca decided to poke her head out to see what was happening. Firefighters were able to grab her by the shell and pull her out of there; Bruce ran right out after her. He was a little dehydrated but otherwise OK. The kids brought cookies to the firefighters, and Bruce the Idiot (as Michelle described him) was taken to obedience school.

🐢 SAVING THE PUNK TURTLE

Not your average terrapin, the Mary River turtle, only found in Queensland, Australia, has a punk-rock-esque "green mohawk" on its head made of algae, and two fleshy, fingerlike appendages that hang down from its chin. Also, it can breathe through its butt thanks to gill-like organs that allow it to stay underwater for up to three days. (That's how all the algae grows on it.) But it's more than the mohawk that makes the Mary River turtle special. For one, it's a *monotypic genus*, meaning that the genus has only one species. The other species previously in the genus died out long ago, making this turtle a relic of Australia's prehistoric past.

Until recently, the Mary River turtle was in danger of going extinct. Known as "penny turtles," they were sold into the Australian pet trade in the 1970s, which reduced their numbers in the wild by 95 percent. At the same time, habitat loss led to fewer places for them to lay their eggs, leaving their hatchlings easy prey for wild dogs, foxes, goannas (lizards), and fish. Because the turtles can take 25 years to mature, they required some help to make it to another breeding generation. That help came from the Foundation for Australia's Most Endangered Species (FAME), a conservation group that has been raising hatchlings in replicas of their natural habitat—but protected from predators—until they mature enough to make it on their own. Without FAME's help, the Mary River turtle would be gone forever.

🐢 WATCH FOR FLYING TURTLES

In 2021, a turtle (species not named in press reports) was taking a walk...on Interstate 95 in Daytona Beach, Florida. A vehicle either hit or ran over the turtle, somehow knocking it into the air. It went through the windshield of a speeding car and ricocheted off the forehead of the driver, a 71-year-old woman (also not named in

Average home price in 1980: $47,000; average family income: $21,000. Average home price in 2020: $392,000; average family income: $97,000.

press reports). She managed to pull over to the shoulder, but she was bleeding *a lot*. At first, neither she nor her daughter knew what had happened. The daughter jumped out and flagged down a passing vehicle. The driver ran over to help, looked in the back seat, and proclaimed, "There's a turtle in there!"

"A turtle?" replied the daughter. "An actual turtle?" Yep. Paramedics arrived and treated the woman's head wound, which wasn't as serious as it looked. As for the turtle, it had a bit of a scratch on its shell but seemed none worse for wear. It was let go on the side of the highway and scampered off into the woods.

*　*　*

> "The best we can do is lean toward the light.""
> —Joseph Campbell

Nine out of ten dance teachers became dance teachers
due to a career-ending dancing injury.

ALMOST CAST: SPLASH

Who doesn't love this charming 1984 romantic mermaid comedy that made household names of Tom Hanks and Daryl Hannah? It's tough to picture anyone else playing Allen or Madison, so it might surprise you to know that the actors wouldn't have landed their parts had a bevvy of even more famous actors not passed on them first. Here's the story about...

A MAN AND A FISH

Name a famous leading man and leading lady from the mid-1980s, and chances are they were either considered for, auditioned for, or turned down *Splash*, a sleeper hit about a New York City produce wholesaler named Allen Bauer who falls in love with an exotic woman that's hiding a big secret. (Spoiler alert: she's a mermaid!) Producer Brian Grazer and director Ron Howard wanted big-name stars for the leads, but Howard hadn't really established himself as a director yet. Most people thought of him as that TV actor who played the little boy, Opie, on *The Andy Griffith Show*, and the teenager Richie on *Happy Days*. As a director, Howard had done only two feature films—*Grand Theft Auto* and *Night Shift*—neither of which had made a huge...splash.

But Howard had a grand vision for this movie, which was borne out of an idea that Grazer had had back in 1977: as he was driving on the Pacific Coast Highway, he started wondering what would happen if a modern man met a mermaid. When the project was finally greenlit in 1983 after several studios had rejected it, Howard turned down offers to direct *Mr. Mom* and *Footloose* (which were both hits) to make *Splash*. The rated-PG movie—with its partial nudity and a lot of implied sex—was slated to be the first production from Touchstone Pictures, a new division of the struggling Walt Disney Corporation that they'd launched to produce more grown-up fare, but without sullying the Mouse House's G-rating reputation. There was a lot riding on *Splash*.

FINDING ALLEN

That's one reason why Touchstone executives told the filmmakers to find a big star to play Allen. Bill Murray was offered the part first, but turned it down and did *Ghostbusters* instead. The studio also courted Chevy Chase, Jeff Bridges, John Travolta, Michael Keaton, Dudley Moore, Richard Gere, Burt Reynolds, and Kevin Kline. They all declined. Why? Tom Hanks has a theory: "If you were a big-name guy and got an offer for a movie directed by Mayberry's Opie Taylor for Walt Disney, you weren't going to leap at it."

But Hanks, who had nothing to lose, did leap at it. As a TV actor, he made some memorable appearances on shows like *Diff'rent Strokes* and *Family Ties*. He was best known for the cross-dressing sitcom *Bosom Buddies*, but it was canceled after two seasons in the spring of 1982. According to Hanks, he got to audition for *Splash* only because he was "in the right place at the right time"—that would be when he appeared on a late-season episode of *Happy Days*, after Howard had left the show. Hanks brought big laughs playing a jerk who picked a fight with the Fonz. Among those he impressed were two *Happy Days* staff writers—Lowell Ganz and Babaloo Mandel—who were later hired to rework the *Splash* script. (The story originally took place in an underwater city; they changed the setting to New York so it would be cheaper to film.) According to Hanks, the writers told Howard, "Take a look at that guy who got fired from *Bosom Buddies*."

Hanks originally read for the comic-relief role of Allen's brother, Freddy. But Howard liked Hanks better for Allen—although the director did admit that if Travolta or Keaton had taken the lead, Hanks would have been cast as Freddy. Two others considered for the lead were Robin Williams and Christopher Reeve, but the final decision came down to two little-known actors: Hanks and Steve Guttenberg, who *really* wanted this part...but it went to Hanks. (Not long after, Guttenberg got the lead role in *Police Academy*. And he'd performed so well in his *Splash* audition that Howard cast him as the lead in his next film, *Cocoon*.)

FINDING MADISON

It's cliché to say that someone was born to play a role, but Daryl Hannah had been obsessed with mermaids ever since reading Hans Christian Andersen's "The Little Mermaid" when she was a little girl. When her family was vacationing in the Bahamas, she tied her ankles together in the hotel pool and swam mermaid style. Call it coincidence or call it fate, but the scene in *Splash* where Hannah's character first meets the grown-up Allen was filmed on that very same beach in the Bahamas.

But it was only after Jodie Foster, Rosanna Arquette, Brooke Shields, Diane Lane, Kathleen Turner, Sharon Stone, Michelle Pfeiffer, Julia Louis-Dreyfus, Tatum O'Neal, Melanie Griffith, and a few more big-name actors all turned down the part of Madison that Hannah was even considered. Howard also considered Ally Sheedy (who had done *War Games*) and Shelley Long (from *Cheers* and the first Grazer-Howard film collaboration, *Night Shift*). Debra Winger, fresh off the successes of *An Officer and a Gentleman* and *Terms of Endearment*, auditioned, and she reportedly wanted the part, but Howard didn't think she was right for it.

California has more turkeys than any other state. (The farm animal, that is.)

Coming from a theater background, Hannah's biggest film role to date was in the 1982 sci-fi noir film *Blade Runner*. When she auditioned for *Splash*, she told Howard about her mermaid obsession; he later admitted he thought she was "just saying that to get the part." Either way, when Hannah started reading for Madison—who needed to be sexy, naïve, curious, and secretive all at once—Howard knew she was right. "Daryl has the ability to be a presence and to communicate with just her eyes and use her body and motion to create an image and an emotional reaction in the audience," he said shortly after the movie was released. "We knew she wasn't going to be dull and boring when she wasn't talking" (which is the first full half of the movie).

The filmmakers were also impressed with Hannah's swimming prowess: she really did look like a mermaid. So much so, in fact, that when Howard auditioned Olympic and acrobatic swimmers to find a stunt double, none of them could match the effortless grace of Hannah herself. "She was the only one who didn't look like she was holding her breath," he said. So Hannah filmed most of the underwater scenes herself. (Hanks, being a heavy cigarette smoker, had a much tougher time in the water.)

A FEW OTHER CASTING NOTES

Freddy Bauer and Dr. Walter Kornbluth: John Candy was already a revered comedian from the Canadian sketch series *SCTV*. And he had a memorable turn in the Bill Murray comedy *Stripes*. When Candy was asked to read for *Splash*, he wanted the role of the mad scientist, Dr. Walter Kornbluth, who spends the movie trying to reveal Madison's secret...and gets hurt a lot.

Candy was concerned that because didn't look anything like Hanks, audiences wouldn't buy them as brothers, but Howard loved their chemistry so much that he knew casting Candy as Freddy would work. Two other Freddy candidates: Michael Keaton and a little-known stand-up comic named Tim Allen. It was Candy who suggested another *SCTV* alum, Eugene Levy, to play Kornbluth (it's hard to imagine an actor other than Levy saying, "What a week I'm having!").

The Mermaid's Tail: There had never been a big-budget mermaid movie before (or very many low-budget ones), so audiences were eager to see how Hollywood would handle it. (Today, it would be done by CGI.) Robert Short, the visual-effects designer behind E.T.'s heart light (and, later, the ghouls in *Beetlejuice*) originally proposed "a dolphin-esque mermaid, with a smooth gray skin that would be biologically real and make zoological sense." Howard said he didn't want natural—he wanted mermaid. So they decided to go more tropical. Result: the mermaid's tail has the colors of a goldfish and the anatomy of a koi fish. Short wasn't quite on board with the idea

until he saw the final result, realizing that orange was the key: "You lose a lot of color underwater."

It took a makeup team five hours to put the 35-pound tail on Hannah, and she couldn't even eat while wearing it (there was no way to go to the bathroom). And on land, she was "a beached whale." But in the open water, the fully functioning tale allowed her to outswim the safety team.

FIN

Splash was released the same year as *Ghostbusters*, *Indiana Jones and the Temple of Doom*, *Gremlins*, and *The Karate Kid*. It didn't make as much as any of those blockbusters, but it made a respectable $69.8 million from an $11 million budget, and it outperformed *The Terminator*, *The Natural*, *Red Dawn*, *Purple Rain*, and Hanks's other breakout hit, the raunchy comedy *Bachelor Party*. The gamble certainly paid off for Disney, whose last live-action success had been 1969's *The Love Bug*.

Splash was Grazer and Howard's third movie but their first big hit. The duo launched Imagine Entertainment a year later and have since made some of the most critically acclaimed and successful movies ever—including a few more with Tom Hanks: *Apollo 13* and *The Da Vinci Code*.

Hanks followed up *Splash* with the movie that made him a superstar: *Big*, directed by Penny Marshall (who was also on *Happy Days*). And *Splash*, which was nominated for an Academy Award for screenwriting, has a perpetual place in lists of the best romantic comedies of all-time (and yes, it made the name Madison a thing). In 2022, Howard explained why the movie still holds up: "*Splash* is an example of basically a '30s romantic comedy. It makes all the boy meets girl, boy loses girl, boy gets girl back, all the obstacles—they're right out of the screwball comedies. Which I always adored. Even in the '80s when we made *Splash* it was already too tired to do it in a literal way, yet adding the fantasy element of her being a mermaid, it made all of that okay."

* * *

BEHIND THE LINE

When John Milius was writing the screenplay for 1979's *Apocalypse Now*, he wasn't sure about one of the lines: When Lieutenant Colonel Kilgore and his unit are watching an air raid dropping bombs and napalm (a chemical weapon) across a river, Kilgore declares, "I love the smell of napalm in the morning." Milius almost nixed the line because, as he later recalled, "This is over the top. This will be the first thing they take out." Not only did they not take it out, but the napalm line—as delivered by Robert Duvall—has become as well known as the movie itself and came in at #12 on the American Film Institute's "100 Years...100 Movie Quotes" list.

The rarest color of plants and animals is blue.

TACO TREK

A crunchy corn shell filled with ground beef and shredded cheddar cheese is a purely American version of a signature dish of Mexico. But there's an abundance of authentic varieties. Here's a look at the many regional types of tacos found in (and just outside of) Mexico.

AL PASTOR

When Lebanese immigrants settled in large numbers in Puebla and nearby Mexico City in the 1930s, they adapted the traditional Lebanese dish of shawarma, slow-roasted marinated lamb on a spit, sliced or shaved off and served wrapped in pita bread. Originally called *tacos arabes* ("Arab tacos"), Lebanese transplants substituted much-more-prevalent pork for lamb but prepared it in the same vertically grilled manner and served it on soft tortillas instead of pita. Today, purveyors of tacos *al pastor* (which means "shepherd," a nod to the dish's lamb-based origins) generally prepare the pork *al carbon*, or roasted over coal, then top the tacos with cilantro, onion, and occasionally pineapple.

DE SUADERO

Found most often in Mexico City, this taco is named for the cut of beef that's central to the dish: the smooth-textured meat found between the cow's leg and stomach. It's sliced thin and then prepared as a confit (slow cooked in beef tallow) or fried. The greasy meat is then slathered in spicy salsa and sprinkled with onion, cilantro, and lime juice.

DE CAZO

A *cazo* is a metal bucket, used here as a cooking vessel in the preparation of tacos *de suadero*. It begins with softer beef cuts, scraps and leftovers from butchering or other meal preparations, which are slow-cooked in beef fat in a cazo suspended over an open fire until they're buttery and tender.

BIRRIA

Named for the savory stew of the same name, *birria* tacos originated in the Jalisco city of Guadalajara. In that region, goat is the traditional meat used, but outside of Jalisco, birria tacos are usually made with beef. Regardless, the meat is prepared the same way: slow roasted and served with a cup of *consomé*, a sauce or broth made from the runoff of fat and meat juices and blended with tomatoes and onions.

MIXIOTE

Mixiote translates to "mixed," because it traditionally and often consists of multiple meats—usually beef and pork, or beef and mutton—pit barbecued, cut into cubes, and heavily seasoned with garlic, cloves, cumin, thyme, and guajillo and pasilla chiles, then wrapped inside the opaque leaves of the maguey plant and topped with *nopales*

Robot comes from a Czech word that means "forced labor." (The first robots were peasants.)

(cactus), spicy salsa, and onions. This taco originated in central Mexico, particularly in the Hidalgo and Guerrero areas.

CABEZA

First made in the central Mexican city of Bajío and then the nearby capital of Mexico City, these tacos originated with cows imported by Spanish settlers who, out of practicality, sought to use every part of the animal. *Cabeza* means "head," and that's where the meat in these beef tacos comes from. Several variations exist, their names referring to the specific parts of the cow from whence the beef came, all beginning with a steamed head to make the meat tender and soft. *Maciza* or "solid" meat includes cheeks, lips, mouth, and neck, while *lengua* is made primarily of cow tongue. *Surtido* combines the *maciza* with the *lengua*.

DE CANASTA

Found throughout the larger cities of Mexico—particularly in the south-central state of Tlaxcala, as well as San Vicente and Mexico City—are these fast-food, snack-size tacos usually sold and consumed in multiples. Made early in the morning and sold streetside to people on their way to or on a break from work, *tacos de canasta* means "basket potatoes." They're prepared by placing potato, pork rinds, beans, and a sauce into tortillas, which are then drenched in hot fat. That step keeps them warm for several hours, when they're placed into a plastic-lined basket from which they're vended.

COCHINITA PIBIL

Native to the Yucatán Peninsula of Mexico, *cochinita pibil* translates roughly to "baby pig," because the main ingredient in these tacos is young pork shoulder. It's marinated in a tangy bright citrus sauce that also includes cloves, cinnamon, and achiote paste. Then it's braised and barbecued, shredded, and put into a tortilla along with habanero salsa and pickled red onions.

ARRACHERA

By and large, the northern states of Mexico favor flour tortillas, while corn tortillas are the preference in the southern part of the country. Bigger northern, relatively well-moneyed cities such as Tijuana and Monterrey are the most likely place to encounter *arrachera* tacos. Into flour tortillas are placed thin strips of beef skirt steak; grilled until it's pink in the middle, the meat is the star of the taco and needs little adornment beyond a little salsa and some onions.

CHORIZO AND LONGANIZA

Chorizo is a spicy, paprika-heavy pork sausage that originated in Spain, and Spanish settlers brought the dish (because it's a good way to preserve meat for months) to Mexico. *Longaniza* is the Mexican evolution of chorizo. Comprised of paprika-flavored

The world's most expense pizza, the Louis XIII, takes three days to make and costs $12,000.

pork, longaniza uses minced meat (as opposed to ground pork in chorizo), and, unlike chorizo, isn't cured. They're similar enough to each other that they're used throughout Mexico as a taco filling.

CARNITAS

Carnitas means "little meats," and refers to how the pork that's used to made it is shredded into small pieces. Created and popularized in the far southwestern state of Michoacán, carnitas is one of the oldest slow-roasted pork preparations in the Americas, in which the meat is marinated and then cooked for hours in its own fat until it falls off the bone. Served on corn tortillas, carnitas tacos are hefty, filling, and greasy, and topped with pork fat rinds, onion, cilantro, and lime juice.

DE PESCADO

Pescado is Spanish for "fish," and fish tacos got their start in the far western Mexican coastal peninsula of Baja California. Still found in major surf spots such as Ensenada and Puerto Vallarta and brought back to the U.S. by California-based surfers, tacos *de pescado* were originally made with shark meat. But variations sprung up based on what was available by area and by season, so fish tacos can include smoked marlin, grilled octopus, or battered-and-fried cod.

BARBACOA

Unlike many other taco types, the name of this dish refers to the way the filling is prepared, not the type or cut of meat used. *Barbacoa*, or "barbecue," involves slow-roasting meat in an outdoor pit over an open flame. Meats such as sheep or goat have traditionally been used, but beef cuts are now the predominant option in modern Mexico, where barbacoa is a popular Sunday preparation.

GUISADOS

The name means "stew," and it's used in reference to breakfast or lunch tacos sold in food stands throughout Mexico City or prepared at home. Ingredients generally found in tacos *guisados* include rice, eggs (hard boiled or scrambled in tomato salsa), nopales, onions, and sliced poblano chiles cooked in cream.

DORADOS

Dorados literally translates into English as "gilded," meaning golden, an apt description of a fried corn tortilla. Tacos *dorados* are tortillas filled with meat and then stuck with toothpicks to hold everything inside, and then fried. It's a precursor of flautas as well as an inspiration for the crispy corn taco shells found at Taco Bell or at American grocery stores. Tacos dorados found popularity in the 1940s in Mexican restaurants in the U.S., and Juvencio Maldonado, a Mexican transplant who ran the New York City Mexican restaurant Xochitl, filed a patent for a tortilla-frying process in 1947.

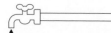

Worth it: a handful of French fries has about 80 calories.

HIGH-TECH UNDERWEAR

*Who says underwear should only be clean and comfortable? Here's
a look at some skivvies with extra built-in features.*

SKIIN BIO-SENSING GARMENTS

What They Are: Sports bras, underwear, and chest bands that track heart health

Details: Skiin's line of undergarments all include a hidden port where users plug in a palm-sized sensor, which tracks and records their heart activity and sends the data to a connected app on their smartphone. That data can be viewed by both the consumer and the consumer's cardiologist to recommend treatments or medications, depending on what kind of data the Skiin sensor records through daily wear. The sensor can run daily electrocardiogram tests to check for strange heartbeat anomalies while also collecting information on the user's activity, steps, posture, and body temperature.

TRAVEL POCKET HIGH-WAISTED BRIEFS

What They Are: Full coverage underwear with a secret compartment

Details: According to manufacturer B2BODY, these panties go all the way up to the hip and over the stomach, and are made from a stretchy nylon blend that's breathable and stays put. The fact that they don't move factors into the product's other selling point: the front of the underwear includes a slim pocket where valuables such as cash, credit cards, ID, or a passport can be stashed. That compartment is accessible to whoever is wearing the underwear (with just a little bit of demure finagling) but is undetectable and impossible for pickpockets to reach.

DISPOSABLE 100 PERCENT COTTON UNDERWEAR

What They Are: Use-once-and-discard underwear

Details: Virtually every product that surrounds or encounters a person's nether regions is explicitly disposable, such as toilet paper and feminine hygiene products. And yet we wear the same pairs of underwear, over and over, for months or even years at a time, washing them between uses (we hope). Underworks thinks underwear can and should be a single-use product. Made of 100 percent cotton, just like many styles of traditional women's underwear, these ladies' briefs look like normal, simple underwear, but are ideal for emergencies, doctor appointments, trips, or regular use,

The 1949 cookbook *A Taste of Texas* contains the first appearance
of the word *nachos* in English.

and they're sold 20 to a pack. And because they're made completely out of cotton (just with less material than regular underthings), they're biodegradable. (Men's styles are also available.)

C-IN2 NO SHOW PROFILE SLING SUPPORT BRIEFS

What They Are: An underwear insert to gives guys an, ahem, boost

Details: C-IN2 markets the product as the male equivalent of appearance-enhancing undergarments long sold to women. Like panties with a padded bottom to simulate a fuller rear-end, or a push-up bra designed to make a bust seem larger, the Sling Support Briefs make a man's, uh, stuff look larger and more prominent. It's essentially a combination of a sling and a pouch, and when a guy puts his business in there, it separates and lifts those parts up off the body, tricking the eye into making it all look bigger.

WARM BIZ BRA

What It Is: A bra that heats up

Details: In an effort to reduce carbon emissions, Japan has enacted many laws and requested that during winter months, when it gets cold, residents think twice about turning up the thermostat and instead wear warmer clothes. A Tokyo-based underwear company called Triumph International recognized that getting the body to a comfortable level means more than just a sweater or some thick socks, and they unveiled the Warm Biz Bra, a women's support garment outfitted with removable pouches. Thick and gelatinous, they're meant to be microwaved to the user's specifications (never for more than a minute), returned to the bra, and then the whole thing goes back on. No more cold days!

MARRIAGE-HUNTING BRA

What It Is: A bra that lets the world know precisely when a woman is ready to be a bride

Details: Over the last two decades, marriage rates, and subsequently birth rates, have fallen drastically in Japan, creating something of a social and public health crisis written about and discussed extensively by the country's leaders. Underwear maker Triumph released a product that's something of a novelty or a joke (we hope) to call attention to the issue. After buying the Marriage-Hunting Bra (*Konkatsu Bra*), women decide at exactly what age they wish to get married. That's programmed into the bra, and a light-up LED display on the undergarment starts counting down the seconds until the wearer hits that benchmark age. The clock can be stopped only if a wedding ring is inserted into a special compartment—at that point, the bra pipes out romantic music and allows access to a pen, used for singing a marriage certificate, hidden in a seam.

Not kidding: nearly 75 percent of the world's population eats goat meat on a regular basis.

FAKERS!

Sometimes, the more outlandish the lie, the more likely people are to believe it.

FAKE STRONGMEN

THE RUSE: For a few months in 2016, two "strongmen" who called themselves Chop & Steele appeared on several local morning-news shows throughout the United States. Wearing tacky track suits, the two young bearded men—neither of whom was very muscular—demonstrated "feats of strength" that included stomping on wicker baskets, karate-chopping VHS tapes, and lifting an entire shopping cart over their heads. To reiterate, they performed these feats of strength with straight faces on numerous shows...and they were taken seriously.

FOUND OUT: About a year later, someone associated with Gray Television—which owns one of the pranked stations, WEAU News in Eau Claire, Wisconsin—came across a YouTube video featuring the Brooklyn, New York, comedy duo of Nick Prueher and Joe Pickett showing highlights of their hijinks as Chop & Steele, two characters they made up. Realizing that their newsroom had been had, Gray Television sued Prueher and Pickett for "copyright violation, fraud, and conspiracy to commit fraud."

Referring to the lawsuit as a "really stupid First Amendment battle," Prueher and Pickett explained that they didn't originally set out to fool morning news teams, but after appearing on a few of these local broadcasts to promote a comedy festival, they realized that newsrooms rarely did any research and got all kinds of details wrong, and that the anchors would react the same way no matter what the duo said or did.

So, they decided to have some fun. First, their "buddy Mark" (Mark Proksch, who would later play "energy vampire" Colin Robinson on *What We Do in the Shadows*) pretended to be "an award-winning and master yo-yo-ist," even though he sucked at yo-yoing. Then Prueher posed as a celebrity chef and made disgusting smoothies that the anchors pretended to like...every time. But it was the Chop & Steele prank that got the pair in hot water.

OUTCOME: A few months after announcing the suit, Gray Television abruptly dropped it. It's unclear why—perhaps they realized whose side people would take if the case were to drag on. The TV company said in a statement that it reached an "amicable settlement" with Prueher and Pickett, who agreed to stop pranking them. Gray TV claimed victory, but the duo sees it another way: "They basically had to admit in their lawsuit that they are bad journalists."

Only one in 2,000 babies is born with a tooth.

FAKE CANCER

THE RUSE: In December 2013, Meaghan Hudson, a 25-year-old nursing student living in Chula Vista, California, shared some terrible news with her friends and family back in her home town of Dayton, Ohio: she'd contracted a rare type of bone marrow cancer and didn't have long to live.

Hudson's friends got right to work setting up a website and launching fundraisers— and the donations started pouring in. When Hudson said her hair was falling out from chemotherapy, three of her friends shaved their heads in solidarity. Then they got matching inspirational tattoos that said "Sing On." When a friend traveled to California to bring Hudson back to Dayton, she pushed her through the airport in a wheelchair.

FOUND OUT: As time passed, Hudson's story started falling apart. For starters, her hair was growing back thick, which doesn't happen after chemo. Her friends were suspicious. About a year after Hudson's announcement, an anonymous tip was sent to the Chula Vista Police Department, accusing her of faking her cancer. When confronted by police, she confessed.

OUTCOME: Hudson was arrested on fraud and theft charges in 2015; after pleading guilty, she received three years of probation.

Hudson's family apologized to everyone who donated and promised to refund all $7,000 raised. Hudson herself later appeared on *Dr. Phil*, and he really read her the riot act. "Now, every time they look at it," Dr. Phil said of the tattoos that her friends got, "they'll just think 'sucker.'" Hudson nodded solemnly, explaining that she didn't do it for the money—she never expected her friends to shave their heads or hold fundraisers. She said she only did it because she really missed them. "If you miss us," remarked one former friend, "you ask us to come visit you. You don't tell us you're dying."

FAKE MONKEE

THE RUSE: In 1979, an American con man named Barry Faulkner noticed that he bore a resemblance to Michael Nesmith, a Texas-born singer-songwriter who'd become famous on the 1966–68 TV show *The Monkees*. But Nesmith wasn't *that* famous in Australia, which is where Faulkner lived. Claiming to be the former Monkee, Faulkner booked himself on radio and TV interviews. The imposter got Nesmith's distinctive folksy drawl down pat and by all accounts was an entertaining interview. Taking full advantage of his stardom, Faulkner attended celebrity parties and checked into fancy hotels as "Mike Nesmith," then skipped out on the bill.

By comparing the topography of both, scientists have determined that Florida is flatter than a pancake.

FOUND OUT: Faulkner got Nesmith booked on a Melbourne TV studio's telethon to help deaf children. He'd told producers that his own daughter was deaf (not true) and went on camera to beg viewers to donate. The hosts asked "Nesmith" to sing a song, and he promised that he would...later that evening.

Faulkner might have been able to *act* like Mike Nesmith, but he sure couldn't sing and play like him. He called the TV station from his hotel room and said he couldn't return because his deaf daughter had been killed in a car crash. A suspicious telethon producer called the real Michael Nesmith in California, who had no clue that any of this was going on. Meanwhile, as the fake news spread that Nesmith's daughter had died, he started receiving condolences from all over. "This fraud has caused Michael a lot of personal grief," said his record company in a statement. "He wants to reassure everyone that all of his family is in perfect health, and that he is terribly upset about this cruel trick."

OUTCOME: Faulkner was arrested in Sydney and never impersonated Nesmith again. But the identify theft was just one of at least 50 cons he had pulled off. He'd also posed as a commercial airline pilot and actually flown jumbo jets. He'd been a doctor, a CIA agent, a U.S. Marine colonel, a photographer, an Olympic official, and who knows what else in his 40-plus years as a con man. And all for what? According to one judge, "Sexual gratification and financial profit."

Dubbed the "Catch Me if You Can" bandit, Faulkner later said that whenever an episode of *Australia's Most Wanted* featured one of his cons, "I would ring them up and tell them I had seen [Faulkner] at the other end of the country." By 2018, after serving a few months for his 80th conviction (for once again pretending to be an airline pilot), Faulkner had spent an estimated total of 44 years in jail. According to the *Daily Mail Australia*, "Faulkner claims to be retired from a life of conning people at the age of 69, but it may be a ploy to stay out of prison."

FAKE FAMILY MEMBER

THE RUSE: David Spargo is what you call a "superfan" of the Australian electronic music duo Peking Duk, consisting of DJs Adam Hyde and Reuben Styles. In 2015, Spargo, a mental-health practitioner from Melbourne, discovered that the duo was going to be playing at a movie release event in his city, so he went to see them. After their set finished, Spargo was near the backstage door and thought it would be fun to meet the band, but he didn't have a backstage pass. "I was about to head home," he said, "then I just had a light-bulb-above-the-head kind of moment and thought, yeah, I'll give it a crack. No harm in trying, is there?" Spargo opened his phone and went to

The first digital camera weighed eight pounds and had a resolution of 0.01 megapixels.

Peking Duk's Wikipedia page. He clicked the "edit" button, and then, under the list of the band's family members, he typed his own name.

Then he told the security guard he was Hyde's stepbrother. The guard was skeptical, so Spargo showed him the Wikipedia page on his phone. The name matched the name on his ID, so the guard brought him backstage and told him to wait. "I stood out there for five minutes and I started to think this isn't going to work. Then Reuben pops his head out and is like, hey bro, come on in."

FOUND OUT: When Spargo walked in to the greenroom, they asked him who he was. He said he's just a fan that really wanted to meet them, so he added his name to their Wikipedia page.

OUTCOME: Peking Duk invited Spargo to stick around and have some beers. "It was probably the most genius, mastermind move that I've ever witnessed," said Hyde. "He wasn't a creep or anything. He was like the most normal dude we've ever met. That's what makes it more hilarious."

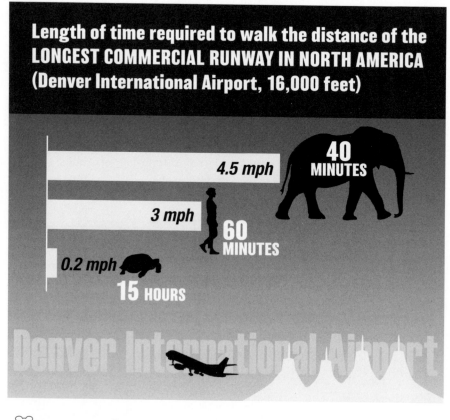

Length of time required to walk the distance of the **LONGEST COMMERCIAL RUNWAY IN NORTH AMERICA (Denver International Airport, 16,000 feet)**

4.5 mph — 40 MINUTES

3 mph — 60 MINUTES

0.2 mph — 15 HOURS

Earlier than you'd think: the first color photograph was taken in 1861.

WHAT THE FRAK?

Looking for some substitute curse words that the censors can't bleep out? Try some of these smegging examples from film and TV, you cotton-headed ninny-muggins.

Bugs Bunny: Eh, what's up, Doc?
Yosemite Sam: I'm no doc, ya flea-bitten varmint! I'm Riff-Raff Sam, the riffiest riff that ever riffed a raff!
—*Looney Tunes*

"This is serious chiz!"
—Freddie, *iCarly*

"Sweet niblets!"
—Miley, *Hannah Montana*

"Mule muffins!"
—Colonel Potter, *M*A*S*H*

Bart: That ain't been popular since aught-six, dag-nab it!
Homer: Bart, what did I tell you?
Bart: No talking like a grizzled 1890s prospector. Consarn it!
—*The Simpsons*

"Sufferin' succotash!"
—Sylvester, *Looney Tunes*

"Road apples!"
—Colonel Potter, *M*A*S*H*

"Dis somanumbatching country was founded so that the liberties of common patriotic citizens like me could not be taken away by a bunch of fargin iceholes like yourselves."
—Roman Moronie, *Johnny Dangerously*

"Why don't you just say it: I'm a cotton-headed ninny-muggins."
—Buddy, *Elf*

"And what in the name of Merlin's most baggy Y-fronts was that about?"
—Ron Weasley, *Harry Potter and the Deathly Hallows*

"You scared the cuss out of us!"
—Mr. Fox, *Fantastic Mr. Fox*

"Great balls of fire!"
—Colonel Potter, *M*A*S*H*

"Blurgh!"
—Liz Lemon, *30 Rock*

"Shazbot!"
—Mork, *Mork & Mindy*

"Why don't you smegging well smeg off, you annoying little smeggy smegging smegger?"
—Rimmer, *Red Dwarf*

Sheldon: Jeepers, that's yucky!
Leonard: Whoa, it's a little early to start dropping J-bombs, don't you think?
—*The Big Bang Theory*

"I had to walk all the way down the mother-fudging stairs!"
—Moss, *The IT Crowd*

"Pluck my life."
—Red, *The Angry Birds Movie*

"Oh, shiitake mushrooms!"
—Carmen, *Spy Kids*

"What the fetch?"
—Grant Wilson, *Ghost Hunters*

"Pigeon pellets!"
—Colonel Potter, *M*A*S*H*

Inventor irony: because his jeans were designed for laborers, Levi Strauss, an aristocrat, never wore them.

BASEBALL BIZARRE

Uncle John loves strange stories, and he loves America's favorite pastime. Here then are the greatest and weirdest things to ever happen in Major League Baseball.

◗◖ SORRY, MOM

In 1939, early in the fourth season of his Hall of Fame career, Cleveland pitcher Bob Feller was selected as the starting pitcher for a Mother's Day game against the visiting Chicago White Sox, and his family attended the game. White Sox batter Marv Owen connected with a Feller pitch but hit it out of play and into the seats where it struck a fan in the face: Feller's mother. Medics treated her for the wound, which required six stitches above the eyebrow. (At least her son registered a win for the game).

◗◖ NO HITS, NO PROBLEM

The Cincinnati Reds began the 2022 season with one of the worst starts in Major League Baseball history, winning three games and losing 19 in their first three weeks of play. The team managed to sink even lower with its May 15 game against the Pittsburgh Pirates. Starting pitcher Hunter Greene and reliever Art Warren teamed up to throw a no-hitter, a rarified baseball achievement. But the Reds actually lost the game—they couldn't convert any of their four hits into runs, while the Pirates loaded the bases after Warren walked three straight batters. Rodolfo Castro, on third base, then crossed home plate during a ground-out. Final score: Pittsburgh 1 (with no hits), Cincinnati 0.

◗◖ WRONG POSITION, CLONINGER

Modern baseball is highly specialized, with hitters focused on hitting and pitchers focused on pitching—pitchers rarely even step up to the plate since the advent of the designated-hitter position. As such, pitchers are historically and notoriously bad batters, and that includes 12-year Major League Baseball veteran Tony Cloninger, who amassed a paltry .192 career batting average. However, on July 3, 1966, he was responsible for one of the most impressive and productive hitting performances of all time. While playing for the Atlanta Braves in a game against the San Francisco Giants, he hit two grand slams—home runs hit when the bases are loaded—resulting in eight runs batted in.

◗◖ HEADS UP!

According to the official Major League Baseball rule book, if a batted ball touches the outfield grass and then bounces out of play and into the grandstands, it's scored a ground-rule double, and the batter takes second base. If the ball hits the outfielder and goes into the stands, it's a home run. And that's what happened in a May 1993 game between Cleveland and the Texas Rangers. Cleveland's Carlos Martínez hit a long fly ball deep into right field. The Rangers' Jose Canseco ran all the way to the back wall in an attempt to catch it, but instead it struck him right on top of the head and out of play. Home run.

🏐 HAVING A BALL

Altering or tampering with a bat is against the rules in Major League Baseball, with numerous players over the years getting caught for hollowing out their instruments of offense, or filling them with lightweight, buoyant materials such as cork or bouncy balls that make bats easier to wield and use for power hitting. The New York Yankees' Graig Nettles wasn't punished for a tampered bat incident in a September 1974 game against the Detroit Tigers, because he was deemed an innocent party to the rule breaking. On his first at bat after a home run, Nettles connected hard with a pitch and easily made it safely to first base. However, he'd hit the ball so hard that it broke his bat, sending its contents scattering onto the field around the batter's box: six small Superballs. Nettles later claimed that he had no idea the bat had been juiced, and that a fan had given it to him as a good luck charm.

🏐 NEVER LOOK BACK

In 2013, the Milwaukee Brewers called up shortstop Jean Segura from its minor league affiliate because of his substantial base-stealing skills. During the eighth inning of an April game against the Chicago Cubs, Segura made it to first base on a single and then easily stole second base. Then teammate Ryan Braun reached first on a walk, prompting the Brewers to attempt a double steal. Had the play worked, Segura would advance to third and Braun to second. Instead, the Cubs pitcher foiled the plot and tried to pick off Segura, who tried to return to second base, but Braun was already there. Thinking quickly and noticing that first base was now unoccupied, Segura headed there. But that's illegal—a runner can't steal first base, especially not from second base.

🏐 INSIDE JOB

In 1989, the Toronto Blue Jays moved into the SkyDome, a state-of-the-art sports facility that was the first in history to have a motorized, retractable roof: it could be opened on sunny days and closed when rain was in the forecast. On one game day that first season in the SkyDome, the weather report suggested a little drizzle, so stadium staff decided to just leave the roof open. Instead, just before game time and with thousands of fans already in their seats, the rain came down in buckets. So why not just close the roof, a process that takes only about 20 minutes? Because the sky also brought unexpectedly high winds, which prevented a safe and effective closure. The Blue Jays decided to wait it out and called a rain delay, starting the game hours later. It's the first and only time in baseball history that there was a rain delay at a domed stadium.

The saddle shape of Pringles chips is known mathematically as a hyperbolic paraboloid.

IT'S A WEIRD, WEIRD WORLD

Here's proof that truth is stranger than fiction.

FILLING THEM IN

While traveling on Interstate 70 outside of Rostraver Township near Pittsburgh one evening in May 2022, the driver of a tractor-trailer lost control of the vehicle when driving too fast and veered into the shoulder. The truck collided with a small grove of trees, and the sudden impact caused the trailer to overturn and its back doors to open, jettisoning the cargo at high velocity back onto the road. The payload in transit: 15,000 pounds of meaty goop, various cow and pig parts ground into a paste that was on its way to a hot-dog manufacturer to be used as filler. It took authorities five hours to clean up all that (technically edible) goop.

GO FISH

Black Lake sturgeon are an ancient species of fish, and there's evidence that they lived in the Great Lakes of the upper Midwest more than 50 million years ago. Today, they're a threatened species, and each fishing season, the Michigan Department of Natural Resources imposes strict catch limits on the creatures, which can weigh as much as 200 pounds apiece. For those reasons and more, lake sturgeon are highly sought after by serious sport fishers, but in early 2022, their chances of catching one were unusually low. Total catch limit (for 565 registered anglers): six sturgeon, and all six had been caught just 36 minutes after the season began.

FLYING FISH

All over the world, bee populations are on a steep and dangerous decline. Without pollinators to help crops grow, the planet's ecosystem and food sources are under threat, ironically because earth-damaging farming practices and widespread pesticide use lead to the death and destruction of bees and bee habitats. The California Fish and Game Commission pinpointed four bee species as possible candidates for endangered- or threatened-species protection, but the state's powerful agricultural trade organizations filed lawsuits to prevent any such status from being enacted into law, because it would make their farming costs rise. The Fish and Game Commission fought back in court—and found an odd legal loophole to avoid the protests of the farming industry and protect the bees. In 2022, a panel of judges approved the Fish and Game Commission's proposal to legally classify bumblebees

In 1862, the King of Siam offered to inhabit the U.S. with elephants, but President Lincoln declined.

as fish, which are much more guarded by the California Endangered Species Act. "We generally give words their usual and ordinary meaning. Where, however, the Legislature has provided a technical definition of a word, we construe the term of art in accordance with the technical meaning," Justice Ronald Robie wrote. "In other words, bees are fish."

CHEESY DOES IT

Parmigiano Reggiano enjoys protected designation of origin (PDO) status by the European Union, which means that only Parmesan cheese produced in five provinces in Northern Italy can officially be called Parmigiano Reggiano. Sales of the true cheese account for about $2.4 billion in annual revenue, but fraudulent, fake Reggiano is a big, threatening business, too, with sales of about $2.1 billion each year. To cut down on cheese fraud, the Consorzio del Formaggio Parmigiano Reggiano, the Parmesan producers' co-op and trade organization, began using alphanumeric tracking codes on its cheese wheels in the early 2000s. In 2022, they introduced food-safe transponders made by the p-Chip Corporation, a scannable tag roughly the size of a grain of salt that is inserted into a Parmigiano Reggiano wheel and allows computers to track and identify the cheese at every step of its journey from dairy to plate. "By integrating p-Chip micro transponders into Casein tags, [the Consortium] can better control its inventory, protect and differentiate its products against look and sound-alike brands and have access to unmatchable track-and-trace technology," said Joe Wagner, CEO of p-Chip.

A STORY ABOUT NOTHING

French artist Yves Klein was at the forefront of both the modern art and the New Realism movements, and between 1959 and 1962, he debuted an audacious and strange offering: he offered six "zones of immaterial and pictorial sensibility" for sale and accepted payment only in the form of gold coins or bars. What is a zone? It was an intangible and invisible object; in other words, nothing, although buyers received a receipt as proof of ownership, which Klein required be burnt. The zones sold and the new owners dutifully allowed Klein to burn their receipts, but not antiques dealer Jaques Kugel, who held onto his proof of purchase until 2022. After going on display at several major European museums, it sold to gallery owner Loïc Malle, who auctioned it off in 2022. Final selling price of the receipt, signed by Klein, to denote ownership of something that doesn't exist: $1.2 million.

BUT DID THEY THROW RICE AT THE END?

Indonesian man Khoirul Anam seemingly had finally found "the one" in 2021 when he married his rice cooker, an extra-large and deluxe model. He wore fancy clothes, dressed the appliance in a white bridal veil, and shared the pictures on Facebook, including one of the couple sharing a kiss and one of them signing a marriage

certificate. In the post, Anam explained that he married his rice cooker because it was "fair, obedient, loving, and good at cooking." Just four days later, however, Anam announced his intention to divorce his rice cooker after he realized that the only thing his rice cooker can cook is rice.

DON'T BOTTLE IT UP

Lokendra Sethiya, of the Indian state of Madhya Pradesh, sent a written complaint to the local home minister, Narottam Mishra, and a letter to the excise department complaining that the alcohol he'd purchased had been watered down or not really alcohol at all. His issue: he'd purchased four 180-milliliter bottles of locally made liquor, drank two of them with a friend, and then didn't feel the least bit drunk. After the liquor store didn't really do much to make him feel better, he hand delivered a complaint, along with the remaining bottles for evidence.

"I want justice for the drinkers. I drink and also earn but what about those who don't earn and only drink. I have been drinking for two decades and I soon realized that the liquor was adulterated," said Sethiya.

WHAT A DOLL

In 2022, researchers at the University of Texas Marine Science Institute's Mission-Aransas Reserve, which studies animal life along the Texas shoreline, announced that for years they've encountered a strange phenomenon in their work. While they often encounter (and study) debris on the beach, they routinely find old, beaten-up dolls washed up on a 40-mile stretch of coastline, usually covered in seaweed or barnacles and missing a limb, hair, or eyes. But why? According to Reserve director Jace Tunnell, the area naturally collects junk. "Texas coastal bend beaches get 10 times the amount of trash," Tunnell said, more "than any other beach in the Gulf of Mexico," because of a loop current that pushes materials. As for why so much of that trash is creepy old dolls...that's a mystery.

DIRTY TALK

Getting persistent litterbugs to change their habits and pick up after themselves is an enduring problem for governments around the world. In 2022, city planners in Malmö, Sweden's third-largest city, adopted a new approach to trash collection, installing two waste bins in a well-traveled area that reward garbage disposers with a lascivious, pre-recorded message. Pedestrians who place their waste into the cans on the Davidshallsbron Bridge hear a playful, suggestive female voice say "Mmm, a bit more to the left next time," "Come back soon and do that again," or "Oh, right there, yes!" Malmö initially bought 18 trash cans with voice-chip technology back in 2017; during the COVID-19 pandemic in 2020, they voiced polite reminders to citizens to respect social distancing guidelines.

Where is your vermilion border? It's where your lips meet your face.

ANSWERS

KILLER OR BROADWAY STAR? *(Answers for page 133.)*

1. Actor. Two-time Tony nominee, who won Best Performance by an Actor in a Leading Role in a Play for *The Lehman Trilogy* (2022).

2. Killer.

3. Actor. Four-time Tony nominee, who won Best Actor in a Musical in 2000 for *Kiss Me, Kate*.

4. Killer.

5. Actor. Two-time Tony nominee, who won Best Featured Actor in a Play for *The Normal Heart* (2011).

6. Killer.

7. Actor. Three-time Tony nominee, who won Best Featured Actor in a Play for *The Invention of Love* (2001).

8. Actor. A 1994 Tony nominee for *Angels in America: Perestroika*.

9. Killer.

10. Killer.

11. Actor. Nominated for Tonys in 1974 and 1975 for *What the Wine-Sellers Buy* and *Black Picture Show*.

12. Killer.

13. Actor. Won the Tony Award for *How to Succeed in Business Without Really Trying* in 1962.

14. Actor. Won the Featured Actor in a Musical Tony in 1996 for *Rent*.

15. Killer.

16. Killer.

17. Killer.

18. Actor. Won Best Actor in a Musical Tonys for *Dirty Rotten Scoundrels* (2005) and *Catch Me if You Can* (2011).

19. Actor. Four-time Tony nominee, including a win in 2020 for *A Soldier's Play*.

20. Killer.

21. Actor. Nominated for a Tony Award in 2017 for *August Wilson's Jitney*.

22. Actor. Nominated for Tony Awards twice, for *The Young Man from Atlanta* (1997) and *Morning's at Seven* (2002).

23. Killer.

24. Actor. Nominated for a Tony in 2010 for *Superior Donuts*.

25. Killer.

26. Actor. Winner of Best Featured Actor in a Play in 1996 for *Seven Guitars*.

27. Killer.

28. Killer.

29. Actor. Nominated for a Tony in 2022 for *A Strange Loop*.

30. Actor. Nominated for Best Featured Actor in a Play in 1989 for *Ghetto*.

31. Killer.

32. Actor. Two-time Tony Award nominee, for *The Color Purple* (2006) and *Shuffle Along* (2016).

33. Killer.

34. Actor. Nominated for Best Featured Actor in a Musical for *Jagged Little Pill* (2020).

35. Killer.

36. Actor. Won a Tony for Best Actor in a Musical in 2006 for *Jersey Boys*.

37. Killer.

38. Actor. Nominated for a Tony Award for Best Actor in a Musical in 2018 for *My Fair Lady*.

39. Killer.

40. Killer.

SYNONYMOUS BAND NAME QUIZ *(Answers for page 316.)*

1. The Rolling Stones
2. Led Zeppelin
3. Yes
4. The Cars
5. Queen
6. The Doobie Brothers
7. Kiss
8. Genesis

9. Rush
10. The Police
11. Heart
12. Chicago
13. The Stooges
14. Journey
15. U2
16. Eagles

17. AC/DC
18. Pixies
19. The Cure
20. The Zombies
21. Black Sabbath
22. Cream
23. Bad Company
24. Wings

25. The Animals
26. Carpenters
27. T. Rex
28. Badfinger
29. Bread
30. War
31. Garbage
32. The Smiths

We are pleased to offer over 150 ebook versions of Portable Press titles—some currently available only in digital format! Visit *www.portablepress.com* to collect them all!

❏ Bathroom Science
❏ The Best of the Best of Uncle John's Bathroom Reader
❏ Best Movies of the 80s
❏ The Best of Uncle John's Bathroom Reader
❏ The Biggest, Funniest, Wackiest, Grossest Joke Book Ever!
❏ Dad Jokes
❏ Dad Jokes Too
❏ Do Geese Get Goose Bumps?
❏ The Funniest & Grossest Joke Book Ever!
❏ The Funniest Joke Book Ever!
❏ The Funniest Knock-Knock Jokes Ever!
❏ Great TED Talks: Creativity
❏ Great TED Talks: Innovation
❏ Great TED Talks: Leadership
❏ The Grossest Joke Book Ever!
❏ History's Weirdest Deaths
❏ How to Fight a Bear...and Win
❏ Instant Engineering
❏ Instant Genius
❏ Instant Genius: Smart Mouths
❏ Instant History
❏ Instant Mathematics
❏ Instant Science
❏ OK, Boomer: And Other Age-(In)appropriate Jokes
❏ Potty Humor: Jokes That Should Stink, But Don't
❏ Mom Jokes: Like Dad Jokes, Only Smarter
❏ See Ya Later Calculator
❏ Show Me History! Abraham Lincoln
❏ Show Me History! Albert Einstein
❏ Show Me History! Alexander Hamilton
❏ Show Me History! Amelia Earhart
❏ Show Me History! Anne Frank
❏ Show Me History! Babe Ruth
❏ Show Me History! Benjamin Franklin

❏ Show Me History! Frida Kahlo
❏ Show Me History! Gandhi
❏ Show Me History! George Washington
❏ Show Me History! Harriet Tubman
❏ Show Me History! Helen Keller
❏ Show Me History! Jesus
❏ Show Me History! Martin Luther King Jr.
❏ Show Me History! Muhammad Ali
❏ Show Me History! Neil Armstrong
❏ Show Me History! Sacagawea
❏ Show Me History! Susan B. Anthony
❏ Show Me History! Walt Disney
❏ The Spookiest Tricks & Treats Joke Book Ever!
❏ Strange Crime
❏ Strange History
❏ Strange Hollywood
❏ Strange Science
❏ Strange USA
❏ Uncle John's Absolutely Absorbing Bathroom Reader
❏ Uncle John's Actual and Factual Bathroom Reader
❏ Uncle John's Ahh-Inspiring Bathroom Reader
❏ Uncle John's All-Purpose Extra Strength Bathroom Reader
❏ Uncle John's Awesome 35th Anniversary Bathroom Reader
❏ Uncle John's Bathroom Reader Attack of the Factoids
❏ Uncle John's Bathroom Reader Book of Love
❏ Uncle John's Bathroom Reader Cat Lover's Companion
❏ Uncle John's Bathroom Reader Christmas Collection
❏ Uncle John's Bathroom Reader Dog Lover's Companion
❏ Uncle John's Bathroom Reader Extraordinary Book of Facts
❏ Uncle John's Bathroom Reader

Fake Facts
❏ Uncle John's Bathroom Reader Flush Fiction
❏ Uncle John's Bathroom Reader For Girls Only!
❏ Uncle John's Bathroom Reader For Kids Only!
❏ Uncle John's Bathroom Reader For Kids Only! Collectible Edition
❏ Uncle John's Bathroom Reader Germophobia
❏ Uncle John's Bathroom Reader Golden Plunger Awards
❏ Uncle John's Bathroom Reader History's Lists
❏ Uncle John's Bathroom Reader Horse Lover's Companion
❏ Uncle John's Bathroom Reader Impossible Questions
❏ Uncle John's Bathroom Reader Jingle Bell Christmas
❏ Uncle John's Bathroom Reader Nature Calls
❏ Uncle John's Bathroom Reader Plunges into California
❏ Uncle John's Bathroom Reader Plunges into Canada, eh
❏ Uncle John's Bathroom Reader Plunges into Great Lives
❏ Uncle John's Bathroom Reader Plunges into History
❏ Uncle John's Bathroom Reader Plunges into History Again
❏ Uncle John's Bathroom Reader Plunges into Hollywood
❏ Uncle John's Bathroom Reader Plunges into Michigan
❏ Uncle John's Bathroom Reader Plunges into Minnesota
❏ Uncle John's Bathroom Reader Plunges into Music
❏ Uncle John's Bathroom Reader Plunges into National Parks
❏ Uncle John's Bathroom Reader Plunges into New Jersey
❏ Uncle John's Bathroom Reader Plunges into New York
❏ Uncle John's Bathroom Reader Plunges into Ohio

- Uncle John's Bathroom Reader Plunges into Pennsylvania
- Uncle John's Bathroom Reader Plunges into Texas
- Uncle John's Bathroom Reader Plunges into Texas Expanded Edition
- Uncle John's Bathroom Reader Plunges into the Presidency
- Uncle John's Bathroom Reader Plunges into the Universe
- Uncle John's Bathroom Reader Quintessential Collection of Notable Quotables
- Uncle John's Bathroom Reader Salutes the Armed Forces
- Uncle John's Bathroom Reader Shoots and Scores
- Uncle John's Bathroom Reader Sports Spectacular
- Uncle John's Bathroom Reader Takes a Swing at Baseball
- Uncle John's Bathroom Reader Tales to Inspire
- Uncle John's Bathroom Reader Tees Off on Golf
- Uncle John's Bathroom Reader The World's Gone Crazy
- Uncle John's Bathroom Reader Tunes into TV
- Uncle John's Bathroom Reader Vroom!
- Uncle John's Bathroom Reader Weird Canada
- Uncle John's Bathroom Reader Weird Inventions
- Uncle John's Bathroom Reader WISE UP!
- Uncle John's Bathroom Reader Wonderful World of Odd
- Uncle John's Bathroom Reader Zipper Accidents
- Uncle John's Book of Fun
- Uncle John's Canoramic Bathroom Reader
- Uncle John's Certified Organic Bathroom Reader
- Uncle John's Colossal Collection of Quotable Quotes
- Uncle John's Creature Feature Bathroom Reader For Kids Only!
- Uncle John's Curiously Compelling Bathroom Reader
- Uncle John's Did You Know...? Bathroom Reader For Kids Only!

- Uncle John's Do-It-Yourself Diary for Infomaniacs Only
- Uncle John's Do-It-Yourself Journal for Infomaniacs Only
- Uncle John's Electrifying Bathroom Reader For Kids Only!
- Uncle John's Electrifying Bathroom Reader For Kids Only! Collectible Edition
- Uncle John's Endlessly Engrossing Bathroom Reader
- Uncle John's Factastic Bathroom Reader
- Uncle John's Facts to Annoy Your Teacher Bathroom Reader For Kids Only!
- Uncle John's Fast-Acting Long-Lasting Bathroom Reader
- Uncle John's Fully Loaded 25th Anniversary Bathroom Reader
- Uncle John's Giant 10th Anniversary Bathroom Reader
- Uncle John's Gigantic Bathroom Reader
- Uncle John's Great Big Bathroom Reader
- Uncle John's Greatest Know on Earth Bathroom Reader
- Uncle John's Haunted Outhouse Bathroom Reader For Kids Only!
- Uncle John's Heavy Duty Bathroom Reader
- Uncle John's Hindsight Is 20/20 Bathroom Reader
- Uncle John's How to Toilet Train Your Cat
- Uncle John's InfoMania Bathroom Reader For Kids Only!
- Uncle John's Legendary Lost Bathroom Reader
- Uncle John's Lists That Make You Go Hmmm...
- Uncle John's New & Improved Briefs
- Uncle John's New & Improved Funniest Ever
- Uncle John's Old Faithful 30th Anniversary Bathroom Reader
- Uncle John's Perpetually Pleasing Bathroom Reader
- Uncle John's Political Briefs
- Uncle John's Presents: Book of the Dumb
- Uncle John's Presents:

- Book of the Dumb 2
- Uncle John's Presents: Mom's Bathtub Reader
- Uncle John's Presents the Ultimate Challenge Trivia Quiz
- Uncle John's Robotica Bathroom Reader
- Uncle John's Slightly Irregular Bathroom Reader
- Uncle John's Smell-O-Scopic Bathroom Reader For Kids Only!
- Uncle John's Supremely Satisfying Bathroom Reader
- Uncle John's The Enchanted Toilet Bathroom Reader For Kids Only!
- Uncle John's Top Secret Bathroom Reader For Kids Only!
- Uncle John's Top Secret Bathroom Reader For Kids Only! Collectible Edition
- Uncle John's Totally Quacked Bathroom Reader For Kids Only!
- Uncle John's Triumphant 20th Anniversary Bathroom Reader
- Uncle John's True Crime
- Uncle John's Truth, Trivia, and the Pursuit of Factiness Bathroom Reader
- Uncle John's 24-Karat Gold Bathroom Reader
- Uncle John's Ultimate Bathroom Reader
- Uncle John's Uncanny Bathroom Reader
- Uncle John's Unsinkable Bathroom Reader
- Uncle John's Unstoppable Bathroom Reader
- Uncle John's Weird Weird World
- Uncle John's Weird Weird World: Epic
- The Wackiest Joke Book Ever!
- The Wackiest Joke Book That'll Knock-Knock You Over!
- Who Knew?
- Who Knew? Human Anatomy
- Who Knew? Physics
- Who Knew? Women in History

THE LAST PAGE

FELLOW BATHROOM READERS:

The fight for good bathroom reading should never be taken loosely—we must do our duty and sit firmly for what we believe in, even while the rest of the world is taking potshots at us.

We'll be brief. Now that we've proven we're not simply a flush-in-the-pan, we invite you to take the plunge: Sit Down and Be Counted! To find out what the BRI is up to, visit us at *www.portablepress.com* and take a peek!

GET CONNECTED

Find us online to sign up for our email list, enter exciting giveaways, hear about new releases, and more!

Website: www.portablepress.com

Facebook: www.facebook.com/portablepress

Pinterest: www.pinterest.com/portablepress

Twitter: @Portablepress

Well, we're out of space, and when you've gotta go, you've gotta go. Tanks for all your support. Hope to hear from you soon.

Meanwhile, remember...

Keep on flushin'!